terra australis 38

Terra Australis reports the results of archaeological and related research within the south and east of Asia, though mainly Australia, New Guinea and island Melanesia — lands that remained terra australis incognita to generations of prehistorians. Its subject is the settlement of the diverse environments in this isolated quarter of the globe by peoples who have maintained their discrete and traditional ways of life into the recent recorded or remembered past and at times into the observable present.

List of volumes in Terra Australis

Volume 1: Burrill Lake and Currarong: Coastal Sites in Southern New South Wales. R.J. Lampert (1971)

Volume 2: Ol Tumbuna: Archaeological Excavations in the Eastern Central Highlands, Papua New Guinea. J.P. White (1972)

Volume 3: New Guinea Stone Age Trade: The Geography and Ecology of Traffic in the Interior. I. Hughes (1977)

Volume 4: Recent Prehistory in Southeast Papua. B. Egloff (1979)

Volume 5: The Great Kartan Mystery. R. Lampert (1981)

Volume 6: Early Man in North Queensland: Art and Archaeology in the Laura Area. A. Rosenfeld, D. Horton and
J. Winter (1981)

Volume 7: The Alligator Rivers: Prehistory and Ecology in Western Arnhem Land. C. Schrire (1982)

Volume 8: Hunter Hill, Hunter Island: Archaeological Investigations of a Prehistoric Tasmanian Site.
S. Bowdler (1984)

Volume 9: Coastal South-West Tasmania: The Prehistory of Louisa Bay and Maatsuyker Island. R. Vanderwal
and D. Horton (1984)

Volume 10: The Emergence of Mailu. G. Irwin (1985)

Volume 11: Archaeology in Eastern Timor, 1966–67. I. Glover (1986)

Volume 12: Early Tongan Prehistory: The Lapita Period on Tongatapu and its Relationships. J. Poulsen (1987)

Volume 13: Coobool Creek. P. Brown (1989)

Volume 14: 30,000 Years of Aboriginal Occupation: Kimberley, North-West Australia. S. O'Connor (1999)

Volume 15: Lapita Interaction. G. Summerhayes (2000)

Volume 16: The Prehistory of Buka: A Stepping Stone Island in the Northern Solomons. S. Wickler (2001)

Volume 17: The Archaeology of Lapita Dispersal in Oceania. G.R. Clark, A.J. Anderson and T. Vunidilo (2001)

Volume 18: An Archaeology of West Polynesian Prehistory. A. Smith (2002)

Volume 19: Phytolith and Starch Research in the Australian-Pacific-Asian Regions: The State of the Art.
D. Hart and L. Wallis (2003)

Volume 20: The Sea People: Late-Holocene Maritime Specialisation in the Whitsunday Islands, Central Queensland.
B. Barker (2004)

Volume 21: What's Changing: Population Size or Land-Use Patterns? The Archaeology of Upper Mangrove Creek,
Sydney Basin. V. Attenbrow (2004)

Volume 22: The Archaeology of the Aru Islands, Eastern Indonesia. S. O'Connor, M. Spriggs and P. Veth (2005)

Volume 23: Pieces of the Vanuatu Puzzle: Archaeology of the North, South and Centre. S. Bedford (2006)

Volume 24: Coastal Themes: An Archaeology of the Southern Curtis Coast, Queensland. S. Ulm (2006)

Volume 25: Lithics in the Land of the Lightning Brothers: The Archaeology of Wardaman Country,
Northern Territory. C. Clarkson (2007)

Volume 26: Oceanic Explorations: Lapita and Western Pacific Settlement. S. Bedford, C. Sand and
S. P. Connaughton (2007)

Volume 27: Dreamtime Superhighway: Sydney Basin Rock Art and Prehistoric Information Exchange.
J. McDonald (2008)

Volume 28: New Directions in Archaeological Science. A. Fairbairn, S. O'Connor and B. Marwick (2008)

Volume 29: Islands of Inquiry: Colonisation, Seafaring and the Archaeology of Maritime Landscapes.
G. Clark, F. Leach and S. O'Connor (2008)

Volume 30: Archaeological Science Under a Microscope: Studies in Residue and Ancient DNA Analysis in
Honour of Thomas H. Loy. M. Haslam, G. Robertson, A. Crowther, S. Nugent and L. Kirkwood (2009)

Volume 31: The Early Prehistory of Fiji. G. Clark and A. Anderson (2009)

Volume 32: Altered Ecologies: Fire, Climate and Human Influence on Terrestrial Landscapes. S. Haberle,
J. Stevenson and M. Prebble (2010)

Volume 33: Man Bac: The Excavation of a Neolithic Site in Northern Vietnam: The Biology. M. Oxenham,
H. Matsumura and N. Kim Dung (2011)

Volume 34: Peopled Landscapes: Archaeological and Biogeographic Approaches to Landscapes. S. Haberle and
B. David.

Volume 35: Pacific Island Heritage: Archaeology, Identity & Community. Jolie Liston, Geoffrey Clark and
Dwight Alexander (2011)

Volume 36: Transcending the Culture–Nature Divide in Cultural Heritage: Views from the Asia-Pacific. Sally Brockwell,
Sue O'Connor and Denis Byrne (2013)

Volume 37: Taking the High Ground: The archaeology of Rapa, a fortified island in remote East Polynesia.
Atholl Anderson and Douglas J. Kennett (2012)

Volume 38: Life on the Margins: An Archaeological Investigation of Late Holocene Economic Variability,
Blue Mud Bay, Northern Australia. Patrick Faulkner (2013)

terra australis 38

Life on the Margins

An Archaeological Investigation of Late Holocene

Economic Variability, Blue Mud Bay,

Northern Australia

Patrick Faulkner

Australian
National
University

E PRESS

ANU
E PRESS

© 2013 ANU E Press

Published by ANU E Press
The Australian National University
Canberra ACT 0200 Australia
Email: anuepress@anu.edu.au
Web: http://epress.anu.edu.au

National Library of Australia Cataloguing-in-Publication entry

Author:	Faulkner, Patrick, author.
Title:	Life on the margins : an archaeological investigation of late Holocene economic variability, Blue Mud Bay, Northern Australia / Patrick Faulkner.
ISBN:	9781925021097 (paperback) 9781925021103 (ebook)
Series:	Terra Australis ; 38.
Subjects:	Archaeological surveying--Northern Territory--Blue Mud Bay.
	Paleoecology--Northern Territory--Blue Mud Bay.
	Prehistoric peoples--Northern Territory--Blue Mud Bay.
	Hunting and gathering societies--Northern Territory--Blue Mud Bay.
	Nature--Effect of human beings on--Northern Territory--Blue Mud Bay.
	Blue Mud Bay (N.T.)--Discovery and exploration.
	Blue Mud Bay (N.T.)--Antiquities.
Dewey Number:	305.89915

Series Editor: Sue O'Connor

Cover image: Storm clouds at Ngandharrkpuy, Myaoola Bay, Point Blane Peninsula, Blue Mud Bay, Northern Australia. Photograph Marcus Barber. Reference: Figure 1A, page 2 In Barber, M. 2005. Where the Clouds Stand: Australian Aboriginal Relationships to Water, Place, and the Marine Environment in Blue Mud Bay, Northern Territory. Unpublished PhD Dissertation, School of Archaeology and Anthropology, The Australian National University.

Back cover map: Hollandia Nova. Thevenot 1663 by courtesy of the National Library of Australia.
Reprinted with permission of the National Library of Australia.

Terra Australis Editorial Board: Sue O'Connor, Jack Golson, Simon Haberle, Sally Brockwell, Geoffrey Clark

Contents

Abstract

This research is primarily concerned with human-environment interactions on the tropical coast of northern Australia during the late Holocene. Based on the suggestion that significant change can occur within short time-frames as a direct result of interactive processes, the archaeological evidence from the Point Blane Peninsula, Blue Mud Bay, is used to address the issue of how much change and variability occurred in hunter-gatherer economic and social structures during the late Holocene in coastal northeastern Arnhem Land. The suggestion proposed here is that processes of environmental and climatic change resulted in changes in resource distribution and abundance, which in turn affected patterns of settlement and resource exploitation strategies, levels of mobility and, potentially, the size of foraging groups on the coast. Whereas a number of previous archaeological models for coastal northern Australia have used ethnographies as interpretive tools, it is demonstrated that using ethnographies to aid interpretations of the archaeological record is a problematic approach for this specific region. In particular, such an approach has most likely underestimated the nature and extent of variability that may have existed in the late Holocene. Therefore, the focus here is on what the archaeological and ecological evidence can tell us about human behaviour in the late Holocene.

The question of human behavioural variability relative to the climatic and ecological parameters of the last 3000 years in Blue Mud Bay has been addressed by examining issues of scale and resolution in archaeological interpretation, specifically the differential chronological and spatial patterning of shell midden and mound sites on the peninsula in conjunction with variability in molluscan resource exploitation. To this end, the biological and ecological characteristics of *Anadara granosa*, the dominant molluscan species for much of the known period of occupation in the region, are considered in detail, in combination with assessing the potential for human impact through predation. In explaining long-term economic change, the focus has been placed on the analysis of relative changes and trends through time in prehistoric resource exploitation, and their relationship to environmental factors. This research therefore contributes to our understanding of pre-contact coastal foragers by viewing the archaeological record as a reflection of the process of the interaction of humans with their environment. In doing so, an opportunity is provided in which change can be recognised in a number of ways. For example, differential focus on resources, variations in group size and levels of mobility can all be identified. It has also been shown that human-environment interactions are non-linear or progressive, and that human behaviour during the late Holocene was both flexible and dynamic.

Acknowledgements

A large number of people contributed to the production of this monograph, all of whom deserve acknowledgement for their assistance over the years.

The material presented here is based on my PhD research, and I would like to thank Annie Clarke and Peter Hiscock for their initial supervision, ongoing collegiality and friendship. Their influence on my work and career cannot be measured, and I am forever grateful.

I was particularly fortunate to have undertaken the research as part of a larger inter-disciplinary project working in the Blue Mud Bay region. Annie Clarke, Frances Morphy, Howard Morphy and Nicolas Peterson provided an enormous amount of support over the years, and I am forever indebted to them for providing me with the opportunity to work with them on the project. I would especially like to thank Marcus Barber, who conducted his own PhD research in Anthropology as part of this project, for his friendship, support and inspiration throughout our candidatures.

In northeast Arnhem Land, the people of the Yilpara, Dhuruputjpi, Yirrkala, Rurrungala, Gangan and Djarrakpi communities not only allowed us to live and conduct research on their traditional lands, but welcomed us into their communities for extended periods of time. I would particularly like to thank Djambawa Marawili, Nuwandjali Marawili, their Mother who passed away in 2003, Ralwurrandji Wanambi, Waka Mununggurr, Craig Moore, Fabian Marika, Julia Marawili (Wirrpanda) and Boliny Wanambi. Leon White from the Yirrkala School and Will Stubbs from the Buku-Larrngay Mulka Arts Centre were also supportive while in Arnhem Land.

The staff of the School of Archaeology and Anthropology, Archaeology and Natural History, and the North Australian Research Unit at the ANU provided an enormous amount of logistical and administrative support, with particular thanks going to Kathy Callen, Sue Fraser, Amanda Kennedy, David McGregor, Marion Robson, Paul Shepherd, Janet Sincock and Liz Walters. In their various roles (at the time) with the Northern Land Council and the Office of Environment and Heritage, Department of Infrastructure, Planning and Environment, gratitude for their support goes to Wendy Asch, Robin Gregory, Mick Reynolds, Ben Scambury, Jeff Stead, Steve Sutton and Daryl Wesley.

In the field Ian Faulkner, Ursula Frederick, Alison Mercieca, Craig Moore, Becky Morphy and Sarah Robertson all gave up their time to work in particularly trying field conditions. For their assistance in the lab, thanks to Frances Crowe, Virginia Esposito, Ian Faulkner, Margaret Parkes, Ian Pritchard, Sarah Robertson for their considerable time, as well as Cameron Atkinson, Laura Farqhuarson, Malcolm Mann, Krissy Moore and Georgia Stannard.

In addition to those already mentioned, I have been fortunate to have had the opportunity to work with and/or discuss various aspects of this (and related) research with a large number of friends and colleagues, and for this (as well as for comments/reviews over the years) I would like to thank Harry Allen, Brit Asmussen, Tony Barham, Trish Bourke, Sally Brockwell, Doreen Bowdery, Greg Campbell, Wolf Dressler, Gary Estcourt, Andy Fairbairn, Ian Farrington, John Healy, Philip Hughes, Antonieta Jerardino, Jenny Kahn, Tom Knight, Alex Mackay, Ben Marwick, Paul McInnes, Ian McNiven, Betty Meehan, Scott Mitchell, Mick Morrison, Sue O'Connor, Colin Pardoe, Bec Parkes, David Pearson, Mike Pickering, Jon Prangnell, Paul Robertson, Annie Ross, Barb Rowland, Helen Selimiotis, Robin Sim, Mike Slack, Tam Smith, Marjorie Sullivan, Robin Torrence, Sean Ulm, Marshall Weisler, J. Peter White and Richard Willan. My thanks to John Healy for providing access to the Queensland Museum Molluscan collections and advice on several aspects of the research.

This research was initially funded by an ARC linkage grant, with the Northern Land Council as the industry partner, and the radiocarbon determinations were awarded by the Centre for Archaeological Research and the Waikato Radiocarbon Dating Laboratory. For employing me during and after my PhD, I thank Pim Allison, Sue O'Connor, Colin Pardoe and Norma Richardson.

For assistance in preparing this manuscript for publication, I acknowledge Sue O'Connor, Sally Brockwell, Mirani Litster for copyediting and Katie Hayne for layout. I also thank the two anonymous reviewers for their comments. Unless otherwise acknowledged, all figures and tables are my own work.

On a more personal note, I am indebted to Ian Faulkner, Rachael Faulkner, Sarah Robertson and Wyn Nguyen, whose support during or at different stages over the last 12 years has been invaluable.

Lastly, and as always, this research is dedicated to the memory of my mother, Lesley Anne Faulkner (03/10/1946 – 15/07/2001).

List of Figures

List of Tables

Preface

This impressive monograph will be welcomed by our discipline for not merely providing salient answers to long-standing questions in Australian archaeology but also for shaping future investigations into how people operated in the changing landscapes of this continent. The specific study Faulkner presents is focussed on the reconstruction of past coastal economies and particularly the behavioural systems underpinning the production of mounds of shell across the tropical coastline. The phenomenon of mounded shells has been a classic challenge to generations of archaeologists, who have sought to explain their uniformity (across vast distances of northern Australia many mounds share common compositional characters), variety (e.g. they are quite varied in dimensions), magnitude (some are astoundingly large in volume or number of molluscs), and anomalous locations (sometimes far from the modern coastline).

Faulkner's analysis is that in response to the challenge of explaining mound building archaeologists must offer historicism and ecology. Historicising the phenomena enables evolutionary mechanisms to be hypothesised and tested, thereby creating frameworks in which the evolution of ethnographic structures can be explained while avoiding the interpretative constraints that can occur when retrodiction is based principally on ethnography. This historicising arises not from the use of particular physical techniques such as radiometric dating, as those give only chronology not historicism. Rather it arises from an approach to archaeological inference in which researchers do not presume the time-depth of ethnographic social and economic processes, thereby making the level of change or continuity merely an empirical question rather than a conceptual predisposition. In his opening chapter Faulkner lays out his historicising agenda while reviewing the diverse hypotheses and perspectives on mound building; sensitively but forcefully reviewing the use of historical observations; thereby creating an image of dynamically transforming social systems which our discipline is challenged to explicate.

What follows is a detailed, more accurately painstaking, examination of mound locations and composition. Faulkner's study operates at multiple scales – sites, levels, individual animals, and preserved elements – to create a layered, potent and ultimately commanding review of the history of foraging that resulted in mound building in one small region of Arnhem Land. This small region is not a proxy for the tropical north, for that would deny geographic variation in past cultural practice; rather Grindall Bay provides an explicit test of previous and Faulkner's own models of palaeo-economy. Faulkner frames such tests with a sophisticated use of diverse ecological information, including reconstructions of the ecological implications of local landscape/geomorphological change as well as novel syntheses of mollusc life-history and population biology. The result is a compelling argument of the physical context of social and economic change. Provision of that physicality does not, as has sometimes been argued by Australian archaeologists, constitute an avoidance of questions of culture change. Instead that understanding of physical and biological surroundings allows a nuanced modelling of the nature of past economic and social strategies by describing the contingent character of those cultural actions. With his ecological framework and his model-testing practices Faulkner brings us a new characterisation of mound-builders: a plausible and empirically robust vision of economic strategies somewhat unlike historical ones, exploiting ecological resources unlike historical ones, in response to dynamically unstable and transmuting landscapes. Both Faulkner's models and his ecologically historicised arguments are foundational texts for palaeo-economic studies of Australian pre-history.

Prof. Peter Hiscock
Tom Austen Brown Professor of Australian Archaeology
University of Sydney

1

The Potential for Change in Late Holocene Economic and Social Systems

It has been suggested that archaeological evidence for significant economic, demographic and technological variation in response to continuing environmental and cultural change implies that recent observations of Aboriginal Australian activities in the contemporary landscape may make poor analogues for the economic strategies that were in place at earlier times (Hiscock 1999:101; Faulkner 2009). Regardless of the explanatory frameworks used by researchers in coastal northern Australia, be they ecological or socio-cultural in orientation, interpretations of the archaeological record have drawn heavily on ethnographic analogies to directly explain economic and social systems of the late Holocene. This vast area has seen several successive phases of social and economic change following culture contact with both Macassans and Europeans during the historic period (Thomson 1957; Schrire 1972; Clarke 1994; Mitchell 1994a, 1994b), making it inappropriate to indiscriminately apply ethnographic models to the interpretation of prehistoric sites.

The use of ethnographic models within such a context has likely resulted in a reduced recognition of the nature and extent of behavioural variability that may well have existed throughout the late Holocene. The suggestion made here, therefore, is that the degree of change and variability in late Holocene Aboriginal societies has been markedly underestimated. Using archaeological evidence, this research addresses the question of how much change and variability occurred in economic and social systems during the late Holocene, focusing on a coastal area of the Blue Mud Bay region of northeastern Arnhem Land (Figure 1.1).

While some researchers have acknowledged that it is inappropriate to use ethnographic analogy in investigating aspects of human behaviour during the Pleistocene in Australia (see for example Cosgrove 1991), this is not the case for the Holocene. The fact that the north Australian Holocene coastal archaeological record has increasingly been characterised by economic and social variability across the broader region appears to be at odds with the direct use of ethnography, thereby accepting a certain level of cultural continuity and unidirectional development, not just through time, but across vast distances. This situation indicates that the direct use of ethnographic data in interpreting the coastal archaeological record for northern Australia may be inappropriate, and that the archaeological record from this period requires reconsideration.

In discussing elements of change and variability in the archaeological record over the long-term, the main aspects considered here involve assessing potential variability in human behaviour relative to climatic and ecological parameters, as well as examining issues of scale and resolution in archaeological interpretation. As has been noted by Bailey (1981a:13), in attempting to explain long-term economic change, emphasis should be placed on the analysis of time trends in prehistoric resource exploitation. In an archaeological study of this type, therefore, the analysis of relative changes and trends over time in patterns of resource utilisation and their relationship to environmental factors are important considerations. When investigating chronological trends in economic and social patterns in the past, before debating the mechanisms driving that change, the initial step should be to rigorously assess the relationship (if any) between environmental and climatic changes and human behaviour.

This is particularly relevant for the archaeological record of coastal northern Australia, dominated by shell deposits, and often referred to as primarily reflecting economic structures positioned within a constantly shifting landscape (Mowat 1995; Bourke 2000). For this reason, and in line with proponents of environmental-ecological approaches, this research seeks to examine the *interaction* of cultural and environmental processes (Veth *et al.* 2000:58). While change in the environment is seen here as a catalyst for economic and technological reorganisation, the particular behavioural strategies that may follow environmental shifts are not necessarily determined by them, and are not considered to automatically flow on as a direct consequence of environmental or climatic change.

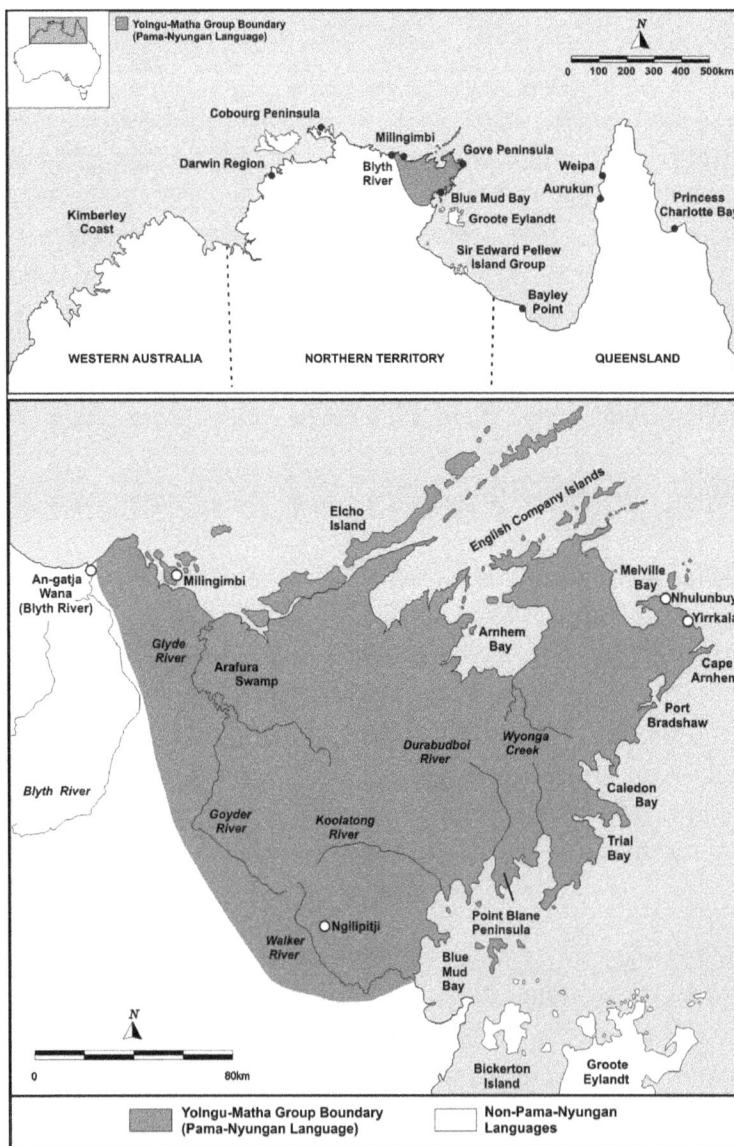

Figure 1.1: North Australian locations mentioned in the text.

Source: Modified from Bourke 2000 and F. Morphy 2004.

A number of researchers have criticised this type of approach as being simplistic and overtly deterministic (see for example Lourandos and Ross 1994; Lourandos 1997; Barker 1999, 2004; McNiven 1999), and some have dismissed late Holocene environmental conditions as a factor contributing to economic and social changes during this period. Instead, these researchers prefer to advocate primacy to socio-cultural processes as causal mechanisms for change. In fact, while these researchers view trends in the archaeological record as indicating that Aboriginal culture has been changing and intensifying over a long period of time, their models tend to be linear, unidirectional and ethnographically based. Rather than being a holistic and integrated model, as has been advocated by Morrison (2003, 2010), this approach is too simplistic, as it removes the structure within which humans, and particularly hunter-gatherers, must operate. For example, Lourandos and Ross (1994:60) have stated that the more recent changes of the historic period are simply a continuation of a tradition that goes back thousands of years. In many respects, this creates interpretations based on social or cultural determinism (e.g. Rowland 1999a:12), a situation as problematic as environmental determinism.

The environment provides the framework that people have to live within, but it is how people structure their economic and social activities within that framework, depending on the configuration and availability of given resources, that promotes change and variability through time. Based on archaeological research carried out since the early to mid 1990s (particularly Clarke 1994 and Mitchell 1994a, 1994b, 1995, 1996), it has been accepted that there have been several phases of change in northern Australia within the historic period, primarily due to processes of culture contact. These include the introduction of new technologies and a shifting resource focus, changes in mobility, group sizes and patterns of settlement, as well as increased ceremonial activity, trade and exchange. It is therefore clear that culture contact introduced external elements acting to stimulate change, as those changes that occurred during this period cannot be described as being driven only via internal processes. While recent research into culture contact and its effects on Aboriginal societies has stressed that the nature of this process was interactive, rather than deterministic, there is potentially no need to separate contact from other environmental or external factors. In effect, the process of contact provided people with opportunities to modify aspects of their social and economic structure. By extension, earlier pre-contact processes of human-environment interaction can be described in a broadly similar way. This suggests that human-environmental interactions are complex, in part because the environment is highly variable rather than static. People were therefore working within a framework that was constantly shifting, but not necessarily unidirectionally. In adopting this approach, possible multidirectional, non-linear changes in Aboriginal economy and society may be recognised.

As the majority of archaeological studies to date from across northern Australia have used ethnographies as their primary interpretive framework (for exceptions see Mowat 1995; Hiscock 1999), it is important to note that the most frequently quoted ethnographic studies are those that were largely conducted in northeastern Arnhem Land between the 1920s and 1970s. These ethnographies are therefore a reflection of groups that had already experienced extensive contact with both the Macassans and Europeans. For this reason, it is necessary to examine how and to what extent these successive processes of contact may have altered the economic and social structures of Aboriginal groups in these areas prior to this recent period of observation. By examining the nature or extent of change and variability throughout the historic period, the use of ethnographic data to interpret the archaeological record and previous models of pre-contact change can be assessed.

Change and variability in the historic period: Culture contact

This overview of change and variability within Aboriginal social and economic systems during the historic period serves two purposes. Firstly, it demonstrates that significant change can occur within short time-frames as a direct result of human-environment interaction; and secondly, it establishes the framework within which to contextualise ethnographic observation. Archaeological and ethnographic data have been used to detail the degree and rate of change in coastal economic and settlement systems following Macassan contact on the Cobourg Peninsula in western Arnhem Land by Mitchell (1994a, 1994b), and in eastern Arnhem Land locations such as Caledon Bay, Port Bradshaw (White 1969, 1970; Schrire 1972) and Groote Eylandt (Clarke 1994). While it is now apparent that Macassan contact occurred prior to 1664 AD, and possibly earlier than 1517 AD, based on the radiocarbon dating of beeswax rock art designs (see Taçon *et al.* 2010), many of these researchers have found evidence from sites that were created after 1720 AD, when contact between Macassans and Aboriginal groups gradually intensified. These studies have demonstrated that there were significant modifications to settlement organisation and subsistence practices during this period. This has important consequences for the applicability of ethnographies relative to archaeological interpretations across much of the north Australian coast.

On the Cobourg Peninsula the size of post-contact middens were often substantially larger than those sites dating to the pre-contact period (Mitchell 1994a:377–98). Additionally, increased midden debris was not only visible near Macassan settlements, as originally predicted by Schrire (1972:664–6), but also in more remote locations. Mitchell (1994a:400) and Clarke (1994:465) have also demonstrated that Aboriginal groups began moving into new areas during the Macassan period, and that these sites contained a greater variety of exotic material and artefacts compared with both the pre-contact period and the subsequent Mission period. This suggests that Macassan contact had both direct, and indirect, effects on Aboriginal economy and society. Broad changes of this kind are therefore best explained as a shift in the entire regional settlement structure, rather than by the suggestion that the only change to hunter-gatherer patterns of settlement and mobility was foreign settlements becoming the main focal points, and landscape use elsewhere remained unchanged (Hiscock 1999:101). Instead, these changes in site location, size and content can be interpreted as representing increased residential group size and decreased residential mobility, with alterations in residential strategies reflecting a number of political, technological and economic changes (Clarke 1994:463; Mitchell 1994a:399).

This process of prolonged contact therefore had a profound influence on Aboriginal settlement. In fact, a series of inter-related economic changes underlie this reorganisation of coastal settlement in the post-contact period, as Macassan contact also led to changes in Aboriginal hunting and gathering practices (Mitchell 1994a, 1996). This evidence includes changes in the faunal composition in Indigenous sites on the Cobourg Peninsula, and ethnographic evidence from places such as Milingimbi, the Gove Peninsula, Groote Eylandt (Tindale 1925–6:93; Thomson 1957; Schrire 1972; Mitchell 1994a, 1996) and the Sir Edward Pellew Island group (Sim 2002; Sim and Wallis 2008). The introduction of dugout canoes and metal-tipped harpoons enabled more effective capture of large marine animals, such as turtle and dugong. New and/or improved technology thus influenced the higher level of exploitation of previously under-utilised resources. The dramatically increased exploitation of turtle and dugong, with the introduction of these new technologies often highlighted as a prime example of this process (Warner 1969:452). The adoption of the dugout canoe also increased the scale and efficiency of marine travel, providing the means to transport more food to a "base camp", as well as increasing the foraging radius of a group. Mitchell (1994a:398) has described the advent of effective water craft as transforming residential patterns from a "forager" form (after Binford 1980) to a structure closer to a logistical pattern.

In addition to these modifications in resource exploitation and settlement patterns, Mitchell (1994b, 1995) has used archaeological evidence to demonstrate that contact with Macassans accelerated the scale and intensity of Indigenous exchange networks across the north. Other researchers have noted similar extensive trade and exchange networks in northern Australia (Davidson 1935; Jones and White 1988:57; Paton 1994; Evans and Jones 1997), all of whom highlight the possibility that many of these stone exchange networks developed relatively recently (Evans and Jones 1997). Several of the early ethnographers in the region, notably Warner (1969:452) and Thomson (1949:91), also make the case that the process of contact facilitated the development and expansion of trade and exchange networks, such as that originating from the Ngilipitji quarry. This quarry is located in the hills close to the upper Walker River on the mainland of eastern Arnhem Land. In the ethnographically recorded past, Ngilipitji was known throughout the whole of eastern Arnhem Land as the only major source of quartzite for the region. Artefacts from this quarry were circulated over a vast area; Thomson (1983:70) records having seen Ngilipitji spearheads in use as far south as the Roper River, and northward to the Goyder, as well as in Caledon Bay. The artefacts were distributed as part of a widespread system of ceremonial exchange (Thomson 1949:87), extending over an area of more than 80,000 km² (Thomson 1949:70; Jones and White 1988:57). Berndt (1951:171) and Thomson (1949:91) have argued that the extensive ceremonial and exchange networks of Arnhem Land intensified largely because of inland people seeking access to the new goods introduced via Macassan contact.

Art was also influenced during this time (Berndt 1965; Clarke 1994, 2000a, 2000b; Sim 2002; May *et al.* 2010; Taçon *et al.* 2010), as shown by stone arrangements depicting ships and processing sites, like those recorded on the Gove Peninsula (Macknight 1970:96; Macknight and Gray 1970). Warner (1969:444) has highlighted the northern diffusion of the "Kunapipi" (Gunabibi) ceremony as evidence for social change within the northeast Arnhem Land region (H. Morphy 2004:3). In addition, many Macassan words were adopted into local vocabularies, with a number of loan words reflecting the phenomenon of contact itself, which relates to processes and items of trade and exchange (Walker and Zorc 1981:111; McConvell 1990:22–3; Evans 1992; F. Morphy 2004:11–2;).

While the targeting of larger, energy-rich animal species and the enhanced trading system substantially reshaped the economy in the post-contact period (Hiscock 1999:101), the implications of contact for Aboriginal society in general were dramatic and far-reaching. While both Clarke (1994:465) and Mitchell (1994a:399) stress the point that the hunter-gatherer economy was not destroyed as a result of foreign contact, this process clearly had major consequences for Indigenous economic and social systems. Changes in settlement and subsistence patterns, ceremonial systems, trade and exchange networks and language are all indicative of a strategic and active response to Macassan contact that substantially reshaped Indigenous social and economic organisation. That Aboriginal people accepted selected features of foreign technology that conferred an advantage within traditional practice (Mitchell 1994a:400) highlights the interactive nature of this process, and emphasises the point that the process of contact provided the opportunity to modify advantageous aspects of their social and economic structure.

Following approximately 200 years of trade and contact with Macassans, the next major phase of change in Aboriginal economic and social systems in northeast Arnhem Land is associated with European contact, primarily the establishment of missions in the early twentieth century. Between the 1920s and early 1970s, the missions had an increasing impact on the settlement and subsistence patterns of Aboriginal people. For example, the Yolngu people of the Blue Mud Bay region left the area for the three relatively widely separated missions of Numbulwar, Groote Eylandt and Yirrkala, and at times during the 1950s and 1960s the bay was almost uninhabited as the majority of the population was concentrated into these mission settlements (Barber 2005:109).

Archaeological research on Groote Eylandt has highlighted a number of implications for Aboriginal economic systems associated with European contact during the Mission period (Clarke 1994; see also Turner 1974). Changes in subsistence practices during the period are seen in terms of a rational and strategic response to the problems posed by prolonged contact with European society. During this time, Aboriginal people acted to incorporate elements of their former subsistence practices into the new social and geographic contexts created by prolonged contact (Clarke 1994:462). As people became more settled within the missions, they had fewer opportunities for extended foraging; therefore, when the opportunities did arise, they targeted accessible and favoured bush foods (Clarke 1994:460). Consequently, midden sites examined on Groote Eylandt relating to this period consist of a limited number of taxa, all of which were available in the immediate environment. As a result of this process, these sites were seen to conform to the criteria outlined by Meehan (1988a) for 'dinner-time' or temporary camps (Clarke 1994:458). People presumably operated within a dual subsistence system: one that had a commodity-based component involving the consumption of European resources, and a hunter-gatherer lifestyle that integrated traditional practice with elements of the new (Clarke 1994:462). As indicated previously, however, many of these traditional practices had arisen during the period of contact with Macassans.

Culture contact within the historic period had profound implications for the nature and extent of change and variability within coastal north Australian social and economic systems. It is abundantly clear that the introduction of new technologies, particularly the dugout canoe and metal harpoons, meant that both new and existing methods of resource procurement could be refined, and that specific resources could be targeted more efficiently. Social aspects, particularly trade and ceremonial exchange networks, and patterns of mobility and settlement, underwent changes during this time. It is particularly interesting to note that these changes were not restricted to those sites in close proximity to the Macassans, but in fact appear to have been integrated into virtually all aspects of life. With the escalation of European contact and the arrival of the missionaries, settlement and economic patterns altered yet again. This time, however, economic intake was restricted to easily available and seasonally abundant resources. Once again, a strategy was adopted for the incorporation of advantageous food resources and technologies with easily maintained features of the established economic and settlement system. The approximate 200 years of contact prior to the recording of detailed ethnographies in many areas of northern Australia undoubtedly had an immense impact upon Aboriginal life.

The ethnographic present as an analogue for the archaeological past?

Much of the detailed ethnographic data used to interpret the nature of coastal occupation in the past from archaeological remains, comes from studies in central and eastern Arnhem Land. In particular, archaeologists within Australia look to the work of Warner (1969), Thomson (1949) and Meehan (1982). These ethnographies have been used as analogues for the interpretation of archaeological sites from northern Western Australia, the Northern Territory and across to north Queensland.

The first ethnographic observations for the northeast Arnhem Land region began in conjunction with European colonisation at the onset of the Mission period, between 1910 and 1920. This comparatively late period of European contact is reflected in the relative absence of any pre-1920s ethnographic information for the region. For example, the focus of anthropological research in the northeast Arnhem Land region began with Warner (1969:ix), who worked in the Milingimbi area between 1926 and 1929, following the establishment of the Methodist Overseas Mission in 1922. The first anthropologist to work in the Blue Mud Bay area was Donald Thomson (1983:7–8), whose influential work started in 1935. In this area, the Church Missionary Society established the Roper River Mission (Ngukurr) in 1908, the Groote Eylandt Mission in 1921, and the Methodist mission at Yirrkala in 1935 (H. Morphy 2004:4, 11). In contrast, Meehan's research with the An-barra people in the Blyth River area of north-central Arnhem Land, which has arguably been the most influential study for coastal and north Australian archaeology, occurred during the homeland movement between 1972 and 1973 following the Mission period (Coombs *et al.* 1980; Meehan 1982, 1983, 1988a, 1988b).

These ethnographers working in northeast Arnhem Land, and across northern Australia, have generally characterised the economic structure as being gender and age differentiated, with a yearly round (or wet and dry seasonal dichotomy) based on the seasonal availability of resources (Thomson 1939, 1949:16; McCarthy and McArthur 1960; Warner 1969:4). Referred to by Warner (1969:127–8) as a fission/fusion type of social organisation, movements and group sizes were regulated by the seasonal cycle. During most wet seasons, large areas of eastern Arnhem Land become inaccessible due to flooding, which clearly would have exerted a major influence on seasonal mobility. Ethnographies record that at that time of year, people traditionally had to base themselves at semi-permanent, well-resourced camping places, often on the coastal margins. Additionally, group size tended to be small due to the dispersal, or fissioning, of the population (Thomson 1949:16; Warner 1969:127; H. Morphy 2004:141). While the ethnographic record indicates that the main food supply, except at restricted seasons of the year, was vegetable rather than animal (Thomson 1949:21, 1983:103–5), during the wet season the estuarine reaches, tidal arms and flood plains yielded large quantities of food, mostly fish, with molluscs collected in quantity from the mangrove zone (Thomson 1949:15, 19–20; 1983:103–5). The dry season appears to have provided two distinct possibilities: people could spread out into small family groups to exploit seasonally available, variably distributed resources; alternatively, large groups could come together for ceremonies, or to exploit a particularly abundant resource. As water levels fell in rivers and billabongs during the early dry season, people tended to move inland. Later in the year, when the swamps and wetlands dried out, water chestnuts and cycads provided an abundant staple vegetable resource (Thomson 1949:19–20; Warner 1969:128, 1983:103–5; H. Morphy 2004:142). Freshwater swamps proved to be focal points, as much as they are at present, as these areas are immensely rich in terms of the density of resources during the mid to late dry season, but for much of the rest of the year they have been viewed as inaccessible and inhospitable (Warner 1969:18; H. Morphy 2004:63).

Based on the ethnographic evidence, it appears that the focus of economic activity in Arnhem Land has commonly been on coastal and freshwater wetland/riverine resources (McArthur 1960:113). It has also been argued more generally that pre-contact population densities were much higher in coastal and well-watered areas than in the drier, inland areas (Birdsell 1953; Keen 2003:125). Explanations for greater population densities in coastal areas have been based on the occurrence of permanent or seasonally semi-permanent water sources, and the density of readily exploitable food resources. Although the coastal zone could support a more permanent population base, seasonal environmental characteristics (such as the availability and distribution of resources, and high water levels) were influential limiting factors. The main point here is that people positioned themselves in the landscape to take advantage of the availability and density of a variety of resources on a seasonal basis. These ethnographic observations also indicate that the structure of the foraging economy within a strong seasonal round meant that there was considerable variation in mobility and the size and density of populations throughout the year. The ethnographically recorded Indigenous economies in northern Australia emphasise the fact that people have always had to operate within distinct resource availability restrictions. It also establishes that on a broad scale, human economic behaviour shows trends towards continuity, but at finer scales there are quite distinct and specific changes relating to external influences, such as the processes of contact, and environmentally induced variation in resource distribution.

The ethnographic record from northeast Arnhem Land also highlights what have been acknowledged as being the basic tenets of human ecology and economy: people will distribute themselves in space and through time relative to the availability of resources (e.g. Foley 1977, 1981a, 1981b; Binford 1980; Isaac 1981; Jochim 1981). This record has provided an overall characterisation of social organisation, but it must be remembered that it only reflects a particular region during a specific period, like a snapshot in time. It has been demonstrated that prior to the initial period of ethnographic observation in the region, extensive changes to settlement, mobility, economy and technology had already occurred as a result of processes of contact. The question remains, therefore, whether these ethnographies are appropriate analogues to assist in the interpretation of the archaeological record. The problem lies not with the nature and value of ethnographies themselves, but in the way in which these observations have been applied by archaeologists to their research. Although several archaeologists have argued that ethnographic analogies derived from contemporary practices should be used to generate models of possible past human behaviour, to be used for comparison against the types of archaeological material present (e.g. David and Lourandos 1997; Bourke 2000; Morrison 2000, 2003, 2010; Barker 2004), in reality they are using the ethnographies to directly interpret the archaeological record. This approach is flawed due to two underlying assumptions. Firstly, it assumes continuity between the behaviour of people in the past with those people observed more recently ethnographically. Secondly, it assumes that relatively little regional change has occurred within the society in question between the time of the ethnographic observations, and the times at which the archaeological record was formed.

A further problem is the use of ethnographic data from distinctly different regions to interpret the archaeological data. Within Australian archaeology, there appears to be a general acceptance that twentieth century ethnographic observations from one area are broadly applicable to other areas that share environmental similarities and have a comparable resource base (Bourke 2000:268). For example, ethnographies from northern Australia have primarily been recorded from groups within the same broad region of northeast Arnhem Land (e.g. Thomson 1949; Warner 1969; Meehan 1982; Davis 1984). The use of ethnographies in this manner is far too simplistic, and potentially limiting. A strict application of this assumption oversimplifies the nature of human-environment interactions, and is likely to conceal or obscure fine-scale variability in the structuring of land-use and settlement patterns in different regions.

Substantial anthropological and linguistic research with the Yolngu people of northeast Arnhem Land within the last century has led to this region being described as a distinct cultural bloc. This interpretation is based on linguistic evidence combined with cultural similarities and high levels of interaction across the region (Keen 1997:271–2, 2003:13; F. Morphy 2004:2–3). Belonging to the Pama-Nyungan language family, Yolngu-matha ('language') is a linguistic enclave, isolated from the rest of its language family by non-Pama-Nyungan languages (F. Morphy 2004:1; H. Morphy 2004:1). For this region, Keen (2003:13) states that:

> Northeast Arnhem Land in the Northern Territory comprises a large triangle of land that forms the northwest corner of the Gulf of Carpentaria. It is the home of the people formerly known as 'Murngin' in the anthropological literature, and now known as 'Yolngu', the word for 'person'. The region has a distinctive culture and group of languages markedly different from their neighbouring ones.

In line with the linguistic evidence, it is reasonable to expect, therefore, that there will also be significant cultural differences. A number of anthropologists have described the Yolngu as being culturally distinct from adjacent groups, based on the kinship system, local organisation, ceremonial structures and trade/exchange networks (Warner 1969:15; Keen 1997:271; H. Morphy 2004). This further strengthens the case that the ethnographies may only be applicable on a regionally specific basis. In fact, there are substantial differences in the ethnographies, even within regional northeast Arnhem Land, particularly in the reported emphasis on molluscan resources. For example, Warner (1969:462–3) indicates that molluscs contributed substantially to the diet, and that people on Milingimbi were still discarding shell on the surface of mounds in the 1920s. This is at odds with Meehan's (1982) work with the An-barra in the 1970s, where molluscs were seen to be a seasonal and minor component of the overall diet. This suggests that it is unwise to assume a strong similarity in social and economic aspects of north Australian coastal groups.

The application of the ethnographic record to archaeology therefore involves issues of scale and time depth. Northeast Arnhem Land is a region of cultural and linguistic distinctiveness, and therefore could be expected to differ in many respects from other parts of northern Australia. Furthermore, it is apparent that there are difficulties not only in using ethnographies recorded from this region in other areas of Australia, but also within this one region. This was an area of great variability and adaptability, which has been amply demonstrated for the contact period. Furthermore, changes in these areas may have occurred at intervals beyond the observational period of the ethnographer (Peterson 1971:241; Beaton 1990:28, 33; Moss and Erlandson 1995:29; Hiscock and Faulkner 2006), and even where there are detailed ethnographic indications of population size relative to the subsistence base (e.g. Meehan 1982), our knowledge of the period of time leading into that ethnographic pattern is inadequate. In effect, the scales of observation simply do not match, and therefore sample points of short duration cannot be used to make inferences about long-term processes, their properties or causes (Erlandson 2001:29; Winterhalder et al. 1988:320–2; contra David and Lourandos 1997; Lourandos and David 1998; Morrison 2003:6, 2010). Yet issues of population size, mobility and ceremonial networks have all been examined archaeologically using ethnographic analogy. Given the changes that occurred in these areas with contact, ethnographic observations of population density and mobility serve as poor indicators for calculating pre-contact demography and understanding the structure of ceremonial activity.

The simple, direct application of ethnographic analogies to hunter-gatherers from different temporal and spatial contexts leads to a simplistic and highly polarised perspective of the variability that exists in those processes structuring settlement and subsistence patterns (Pickering 1997:8). Rather than viewing the ethnographies as an example of the processes of interaction within a broader environmental framework, many researchers have applied the ethnographies in a far stricter sense, essentially as the interpretive framework. These ethnographies are seen to provide accurate models of human behaviour, rather than as examples of aspects of human behaviour within a specific regional context. While change is something that many archaeologists recognise in human behaviour throughout the mid-to-late Holocene record of coastal northern Australia, the degree of variability in the archaeological record has almost certainly been underestimated, in particular the degree of inter- and intra-regional variability in human behaviour. Ironically, the ethnographies suggest that northeast Arnhem Land should be an area with diverse economic and social differences. Instead of a direct interpretive framework, the broad patterning of human interactions with their environment should be extracted from the ethnographies, and used to develop questions to be tested by the archaeological record. There are several issues particularly related to aspects of settlement and resource exploitation, as well as implications for possible changes in population size and levels of mobility, that can be tested with archaeological evidence.

Archaeological characterisations of late Holocene change and variability

Given the dynamic response of Aboriginal society and economy to culture contact, it is interesting to consider whether similar levels of change may have occurred in the past in response to changes in the structure of the physical environment and the nature of the resource base. As chronological and spatial variation in environmental and climatic conditions have the potential to affect the structure of the landscape and the resource base, such changes may correlate with a reorganisation in the foraging economy and settlement structures. Archaeological indicators of this process may include variation in the type of species exploited through time, and/or in the intensity of exploitation. Accordingly, the distribution and structure of settlement patterns may vary. Based on the archaeological and ethnographic evidence for the historic period, this may involve the composition and the morphology of sites, particularly the size, shape and rates of formation.

One issue that has been consistently debated relates to characterising the role of shell deposits in coastal economies, such as the nature of midden variability through time and space. There are a number of factors to consider in identifying and characterising the economic structure of coastal areas. Firstly, there is the role of molluscs in prehistoric economies, and how important they were with respect to other coastal and terrestrial resources within a given area. A recent and relatively prominent interpretation has been that the people occupying coastal areas in northern Australia practised a generalised and flexible subsistence economy, utilising resources on the coastal margins, plains and hinterland (Hiscock 1997:447; Bourke 2000:355; Hiscock and Hughes 2001:44). Following from this, opinions on the contribution of molluscs to the diet vary to a greater degree: molluscs are variously seen as a minor component of a broad-based economy (Bailey 1975a, 1975b; Cribb 1986), as a secondary, fallback resource in times of scarcity, as a seasonal staple (Meehan 1982; Erlandson 1988; Barker 1999, 2004), or as the mainstay of the coastal economy (Beaton 1985). For example, Meehan (1977, 1982:58–80, 141–61, 1988a:498–526, 1991) found in her analysis of contemporary diets that although molluscs were one of the lowest yielding food resources, they were both a supplementary and consistent food source.

Secondly, there is the issue of the extent to which shell deposits may be fully representative of past economic activity (Gaughwin and Fullagar 1995:39; Bailey 1999:107–8). While not being the sole focus, many of the issues considered on the north Australian coastline have been dominated by the consideration of large mounded shell deposits. Those areas that have been a particular focus for research into shell mounds (see Figure 1.1) include the coastal Kimberley and Pilbara regions of Western Australia (O'Connor and Veth 1993; Veitch 1996, 1999a, 1999b; O'Connor 1996, 1999; Clune 2002), Darwin Harbour (Burns 1994, 1999; Hiscock 1997, 2005; Bourke 2000, 2002, 2005; Hiscock and Hughes 2001) and Milingimbi (McCarthy and Setzler 1960: 232–3, 244; Roberts 1991, 1994) on the Northern Territory coast, and Bayley Point (Robins *et al.* 1998), Aurukun (Cribb 1986, 1996), Weipa (Wright 1971; Bailey 1975a, 1977, 1994; Bailey *et al.* 1994; Morrison 2000, 2003, 2010) and Princess Charlotte Bay (Beaton 1985, 1986) in north Queensland. This fascination with what Bailey (1999:105) has referred to as the "mound phenomenon" has arisen partly out of their high visibility and clear dominance in many coastal areas across the north.

There are several implications for the timing and nature of mounding behaviour following the discussion presented above, particularly regarding questions of the role of shell mounds in the economy. While shell mounds are prominent within the Blue Mud Bay study area, they must be viewed as evidence for only one component of the overall economic system. This is important, as, at a fine level, there appears to be significant variation across the north of Australia in the structure of the coastal economy, such as the nature of resources being exploited, and in the size and formation of midden sites. If we are to view these sites as a part of the overall economic structure, then it is imperative that they not be analysed in isolation. O'Connor (1999:48) has stated that shell mounds:

> possibly tell us about changes in logistical versus residential mobility, but this is untestable until we have a better understanding of the role they played in relation to other sites. Where are the other archaeological sites contemporaneous with mounds? How do the latter complement the use of mounds? Are mounds merely dinnertime camps, short-term residential sites, or even ceremonial foci where large numbers of people could be supported over short time periods by a productive and predictable resource? It is time to turn our attention from questions of origin to those which address the role of mounds in the wider system.

There are two main points of view in assessing the importance of shell mounds in the broader economic system. Firstly, mounds are viewed as forming one end of a spectrum, one that included smaller sites and surface scatters of shell and artefacts (Cribb 1996:169; Bailey 1999:105). Many of the interpretations of shell mounds provided by researchers have been primarily economic in nature, relying heavily on environmental and ecological data combined with ethnographic information to explain the mounding phenomenon (for example Bailey 1977, 1983, 1994; Roberts 1991, 1994; Bourke 2000, 2005; Brockwell *et al.* 2005). In this case, mounds are generally not seen as being functionally different, and that difference in the morphology of mound sites relative to middens is a reflection of variations in the intensity of discard at a particular location, but not necessarily with higher levels of intensity in occupation and resource exploitation. Alternatively, several researchers have recently proposed that shell mounds played a ritualistic, or ceremonial, role in Aboriginal coastal economies in Darwin Harbour (Bourke 2000, 2005) and in Weipa in north Queensland (Morrison 2000, 2003, 2010). These researchers have acknowledged the environmental and ecological causes for the proliferation of *Anadara granosa*, the dominant molluscan species in these sites, but have interpreted these mound sites based on ethnographic information relating to ceremonial gatherings in the recent past, i.e. have attributed social reasons as the primary causal factor (see also Clune and Harrison 2009; Harrison 2009). This has been done while still acknowledging that in ethnographic accounts, shell discard resulted in low, horizontally spread out middens, rather than the large shell mounds that accumulated before living memory (Bourke 2005:40). This interpretation suggests that there are quite fundamental functional differences between the low-lying shell midden and the mounded deposits, which may have both temporal and social aspects.

In many areas of northern Australia, such as the Blyth River (Meehan 1982:167), Milingimbi (Peterson 1973:187; Roberts 1991) and the Aurukun Shire and Weipa (Cribb 1996:161), shell mounds are regarded as 'dreaming' or 'story' places. In contrast, discussions with Yolngu relating to the shell mounds on the Point Blane Peninsula in Blue Mud Bay shows that there is no contemporary connection to these sites (Hiscock and Faulkner 2006:214–215). In addition, creation stories relating to the areas in which shell mounds are found on the peninsula relate specifically to the environmental structure of the area as it is now; a freshwater wetland system. Various community interpretations attribute these mound sites to 'Noah time' or to previously distinct occupants of the area. In light of the preceding discussion, and in the absence of a direct ethnographic analogue for mounding behaviour, what do the shell mounds distributed around the north Australian coast actually represent? While there are inherent flaws in the ceremonial argument, based on the misuse of the ethnography, and in some ways a misinterpretation of the ecological parameters characterising *Anadara granosa*, (see for example the discussion in Morrison 2003 and Clune and Harrison 2009), these interpretations are widely cited. As such, these interpretive models will be assessed here relative to the Blue Mud Bay area. In order to do this, it is imperative that mounds not be analysed in isolation, as it is the relative importance of these sites *within* the economy that is crucial for both arguments.

It has been suggested that across northern Australia environmental alteration resulted in changes in resource distribution and abundance, which in turn affected patterns of ecological diversification and settlement, and stimulated social and technological change (Hiscock 1999:96–9). Others have interpreted this type of pattern as a reflection of human interaction with the environment, specifically related to landscape and climatic changes in the Holocene, habitat development, and the availability and distribution of exploitable resources (Jerardino 1997; Wells and Noller 1999; Bourke 2000, 2003; Bailey and Craighead 2003). Variability has been attributed to landscape changes such as erosion, progradation and barrier formation, which have taken place since sea level stabilisation (Head 1983, 1986; Godfrey 1989; Sullivan and O'Connor 1993; O'Connor and Sullivan 1994). In contrast, those working on archaeological material dating to the mid-to-late Holocene who have looked to socio-economic models to explain their material, consider that climatic and environmental oscillations were too insignificant to markedly affect human behaviour (particularly Barker 1999, 2004). As noted by Rowland (1999a:11), however, advocates of purely socio-cultural explanations have tended to underestimate the extent and significance of Holocene environmental change, and to misrepresent the environmental-ecological position. Despite claims to the contrary (see Lourandos and Ross 1994), those environmental-ecological approaches adopted by most Australian coastal researchers have not been deterministic, but have instead acknowledged that people cannot act with no regard to their environment. As Rowland (1999a:12) again states:

> Contrary to some views, space is not just a raw material to be shaped by social process, and landscapes are not merely symbolic constructs. People in the past, as they do today, responded directly to environmental changes, but also indirectly to changes in landscape and resource distribution that were initiated by the changes.

Therefore, given the degree of changes to the north Australian coastline, particularly following sea level rise and stabilisation, can these processes be directly correlated with an ongoing process of economic reorganisation? This can be addressed by examining variation in the type of resources exploited, the locations that people were occupying, and the intensity of economic activity.

During the historic period, there appear to have been changes to population sizes and levels of mobility corresponding with economic reorganisation, particularly between the periods of pre- and post-Macassan contact. Given the potential for changes in resource exploitation and shifting patterns of land-use relative to environmental and climatic change, these may also have been features of the more distant past. For example, the intensive harvesting of shellfish has been regarded by some as a key feature of broad-spectrum early Holocene coastal economies (Bailey 1977), and by others as part of a broadly based response to population pressure (Cohen 1977; Yesner 1980, 1987). The proponents of both of these hypotheses hold that mollusc harvesting may have permitted a more sedentary lifestyle for populations inhabiting coastal or riverine areas. That is, with rising population pressure, more intensive forms of gathering, such as of shellfish and grasses, were used as a buffering mechanism against starvation (Cribb 1996:151). These factors are said to be linked to the broadening of the resource base and an increased emphasis on small organisms (e.g. molluscs). In the view of Lourandos (1983, 1985), this hypothesis is causally related to the process of 'intensification' a widespread socio-cultural phenomenon associated with economic change and increasing population size stimulated by social restructuring (Lourandos 1983:81). Following Hayden (1981), Veitch (1999a, 1999b) has argued, for example, that the large *Anadara granosa* dominated mounds of northern Australia are representative of widespread change in foraging behaviour in the mid-to-late Holocene, characterised by an increased focus on small-bodied organisms. His preferred explanation is socially oriented, linked to increases in population size and the degree of sedentism (see also work by Cohen 1977:76–83; Lourandos 1980, 1983; Stiner *et al.* 1999, 2000; Stiner and Munro 2002). Such an economic shift presumably allowed larger populations to live along the mangrove-lined coasts of the humid and arid zones. This theory suggests that the shell mounds are a reflection of broader behavioural developments, as opposed to a response to environmental changes on the coast (Veitch 1999b:60). Other archaeological studies in these coastal areas of northern Australia have implied that major environmental changes, rather than strictly social changes, preceded growth in human populations, and that the growing productivity of newly created landscapes combined with higher population levels, were causal factors in cultural change, variations in mobility, or increasing land and sea use during the Holocene (Beaton 1985; Jones 1985:291–3; Meehan *et al.* 1985:153; Sullivan 1996:7). In explaining the variability of coastal occupation in the north over the Holocene, a number of researchers have focussed on environmental explanations such as changes in local ecological habitats (Hiscock and Mowat 1993; Mowat 1995; Hiscock 1999; O'Connor 1999), as well as pointing to the links between the appearance of mounds and evidence for increasing aridity and the northward movement of the northern monsoon on the coast (O'Connor and Sullivan 1994; O'Connor 1999). This particular type of ecological perspective does not view human culture as being determined by the environment, nor does it assume perfect adaptation of humans to their environment. Rather, it suggests that the archaeological manifestation of a defined set of human behaviours, such as the structure of economic activity, may be viewed best in terms of the structure of a particular environment (Cribb 1996:150). It follows that the structure and organisation of the economy are often linked to changes in the size of populations and the level of mobility. As such, developing an overall regional chronology in conjunction with assessing the distribution and density of archaeological material, particularly relative to environmental variability over the course of occupation, may go some way toward addressing this question.

Although many archaeologists have emphasised change and variability in the late Holocene, due to the fact that they are placing the archaeological record within a contemporary framework, by adhering strictly to the social and economic patterns described ethnographically for the historic period, there is only so much variability that can be interpreted in terms of these changes. Consequently, such interpretations are to a certain degree linear and unidirectional models of behaviour. Furthermore, when these patterns are projected into the past, particularly given known Holocene environmental and climatic changes, the result is an underestimation of the degree of change and variability within the archaeological record. In assessing the social and economic structures of the past, this methodology creates a circular argument. By interpreting the archaeological record with modern behavioural data, researchers are only able to recognise minor variation within larger scale continuity. Yet while they generally interpret the nature of Aboriginal society and economy as having been dynamic, practising a generalised and flexible subsistence economy, non-linear change or development has not generally been considered. This suggests that further economic and social variability in the late Holocene may yet be demonstrated.

Monograph structure

As the archaeological record within the study area spans the period from the mid-to-late Holocene, to the relatively recent past, the present-day climatic and environmental conditions, and contemporary resource availability are presented in detail in the following chapter. In order to determine the framework that people were operating within at a given period, environmental data from 10,000 BP to present has been compiled broadly from northern Australia and the Indo-Pacific region, covering aspects of sea level change, sedimentation, progradation, climatic changes, salinity, floral and faunal changes. This overview supports the hypothesis that conditions were gradually changing through time, with dramatic effects on the resources available at various periods. As noted above, this has implications for the structure of resource distribution and availability and for the way humans may have interacted with their environment throughout the Holocene.

A discussion of the survey and site recording methodology employed, followed by an analysis of the survey results relating to patterns of settlement, site distribution and resource exploitation follows in Chapter 3. This includes a description of all aspects of the archaeological record documented on the Point Blane Peninsula, such as shell middens, shell mounds and stone artefact scatters. The chronological and spatial patterns identified through the survey of the study area characterise the archaeological evidence for occupation and resource use at a broad level. An interpretation of the survey findings is made, correlating the archaeological pattern with environmental factors, in order to frame the discussion of the sample of sites selected for excavation. The patterns found within this analysis are explored further and at a finer level of detail through analysis of a number of midden and mound sites in Chapters 4 and 5. These results highlight patterns of variability in the economic structure. Six sites were selected for excavation, and Chapter 4 discusses the three mounded deposits excavated on the margins of Grindall Bay, and the three sites excavated at various locations along the open coastal margins of Myaoola Bay. The level of variability in the molluscan assemblages within the six sites is assessed in Chapter 5, relative to previously discussed patterns of environmental change. An investigation of differences in the intensity of occupation and resource use across the peninsula is presented in Chapter 6, drawing in part on the findings from the three previous analytical chapters. In this way, variability and change in the economic structure through space and time is evaluated. Based on these data, a model of occupation, landscape use and the human behavioural-environment interaction is presented and discussed. Chapter 7 considers the relevance of these conclusions for the research questions outlined above, with implications for the broader north Australian context.

In light of the frequently changing nature of the northern Australian coastline, it is necessary to first gain an understanding of how these changes have affected the landscape and economic potential of the region. It is therefore likely that by identifying spatial trends in the distribution of archaeological material, the composition of the middens, and the date at which clusters of middens occur along the coastline, that the nature of the impact of environmental changes on the occurrence of the middens can be explored.

2

The Physical Environment, Landscape Evolution and Resource Availability

It has been widely acknowledged that environmental changes that occurred during the phase of post-glacial amelioration leading into the Holocene were particularly dramatic, and as such affected the long-term structure of the physical environment. Referring to long-term changes within the north Australian landscape, Sullivan (1996:1) has noted:

> The landscape changes at the end of the Pleistocene involved shifts in the position of the coastline over more than a thousand kilometres, and in the nature of coastal landforms. These landform changes were accompanied by massive changes in climate, and hence vegetation.

Due to the significant effect that these environmental and climatic changes would have had leading into the Holocene, a number of researchers continue to state that the nature and degree of environmental and climatic changes that occurred during the mid-to-late Holocene were comparatively insignificant (primarily Barker 1996, 1999, 2004; but see also Lourandos and Ross 1994 and Lourandos 1997). As this assertion is at odds with the position held by most researchers working on the north Australian coastline and elsewhere in the Pacific (e.g. Bailey 1977, 1999; Beaton 1985; Mowat 1995; Hiscock 1997, 1999; Bourke 2000; Allen 2006), it is important to consider Rowland's (1999a:11) position that those adhering to this opinion tend to underestimate the extent and significance of Holocene environmental change. While it is true that climatic and environmental variability from the mid-to-late Holocene may not have been as formidable as those changes that characterised the post-glacial amelioration, the degree and rate of change would still have had significant implications for human economic behaviour. In addition to describing the environmental and climatic conditions of the mid-to-late Holocene for the study area, the data presented here also address the question as to whether environmental and climatic changes of the mid-to-late Holocene would have significantly affected coastal resources, and by extension human behaviour.

The effects of environmental and climatic change on the formation of the landscape and the structure of the resource base will vary considerably both within and between coastal areas, depending on the nature of shorelines (e.g. steep rocky coasts or low lying coastal plains) and the type of processes acting on them. For these reasons the impact the environment may have on human behaviour can vary considerably on a regional basis (as also noted by Barker 1996:32). In order to gain an understanding of past human-environmental interactions through archaeological evidence, therefore, research needs to be placed within an environmental context. The emphasis here is on the difference between the present-day structure of the physical environment and climate and those of the mid-to-late Holocene within the Blue Mud Bay region of eastern Arnhem Land. This facilitates the discussion of changes in the range of resources available to the hunter-gatherer population within the region over time, and the effect that long-term climatic and landscape changes may have had on the resource base structure.

The area selected for the focus of this investigation is the Point Blane Peninsula, situated within the coastal plains of Blue Mud Bay, northeast Arnhem Land (Figure 2.1). The study area is located approximately 200km south of the mining town of Nhulunbuy and the former mission settlement of Yirrkala (both on the Gove Peninsula). The Point Blane Peninsula is the central of three peninsulas on the northern coastal margin of Blue Mud Bay. This area is presently inhabited by the Yolngu people, and as previously noted, the region as a whole is defined as a distinct cultural bloc on the basis of cultural affinities and linguistic boundaries (Keen 1997:271–2). The homelands of the Yolngu people cover the area bounded by the Goyder River to the west, the Gulf of Carpentaria to the east, the Wessel Islands to the north and the Walker River to the south. The Yolngu people from the northern Blue Mud Bay region distinguish themselves further, referring to themselves as Dholupuyngu (translated as 'people of the mud') (H. Morphy 2004:3, 54). The study area (Figure 2.1) encompasses part of the traditional lands of a set of closely related Yolngu clans, The Yithuwa, or saltwater, Madarrpa are a large clan of over 100 people. Madarrpa land is concentrated on the Point Blane Peninsula, and the majority of the Madarrpa live at the Yilpara settlement in this area (Barber 2002:2).

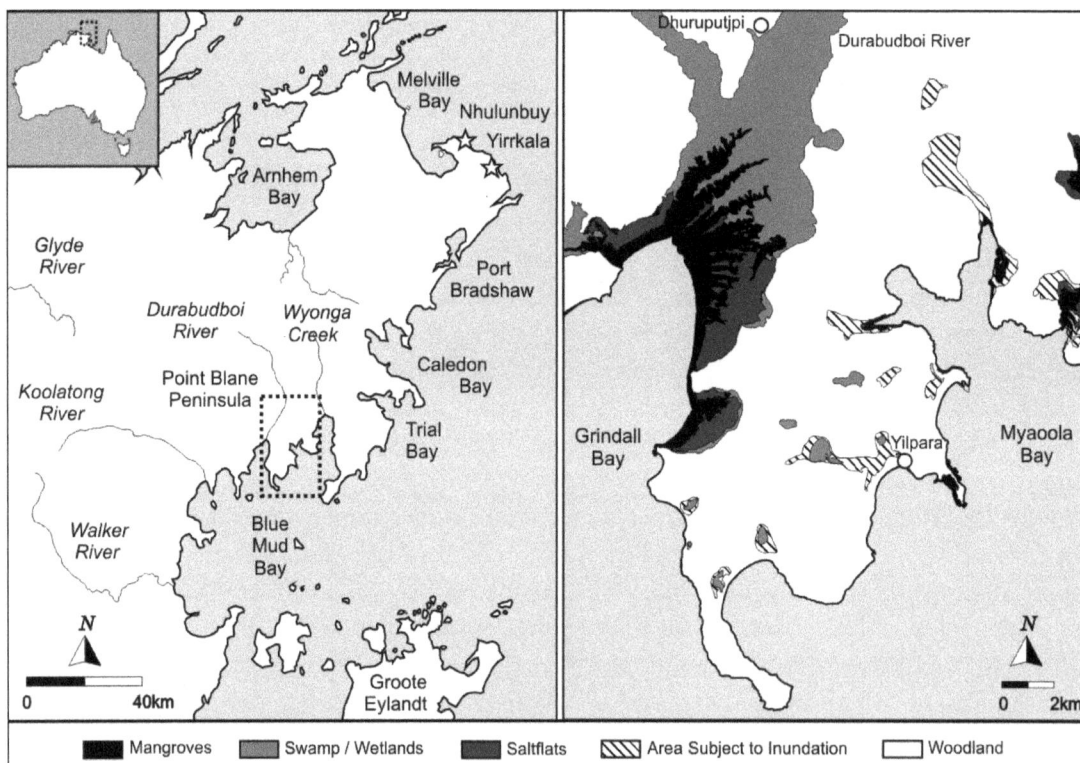

Figure 2.1: Northeast Arnhem Land region and the location of the Point Blane Peninsula study area.

Source: Based on Blue Mud Bay 1:250 000 Base Map and Baniyala 1:50 000 Topographic Map.

Structure of the physical landscape

Present physiography, geology and soils

The Blue Mud Bay region contains three main physiographic subdivisions: the Arafura Fall, the Gulf Fall and the Coastal Plain, the distributions of which are shown in Figure 2.2. The Parsons and Mitchell ranges lie along the major drainage divide separating the Arafura Fall (a region of dissected hilly country with drainage northwards towards the Arafura Sea) from the Gulf Fall (similar terrain with drainage south-eastwards towards the Gulf of Carpentaria). The Coastal Plain is comprised of low relief areas adjacent to the coast, extending up to 90km inland along the southern edge of Blue Mud Bay (Haines *et al.* 1999:1–2). The Point Blane Peninsula forms part of this Arnhem Land coastal plain, with mainly flat or undulating country (up to approximately 200m in elevation), often containing extensive wetlands or coastal swamps. These areas are generally bordered by upland plateaus and ranges along their inland margins. They are often characterised as depositional, low-energy shorelines that are still prograding via seaward and terrestrial sedimentary processes (Bureau of Meteorology 1998:1; Haines *et al.* 1999:91).

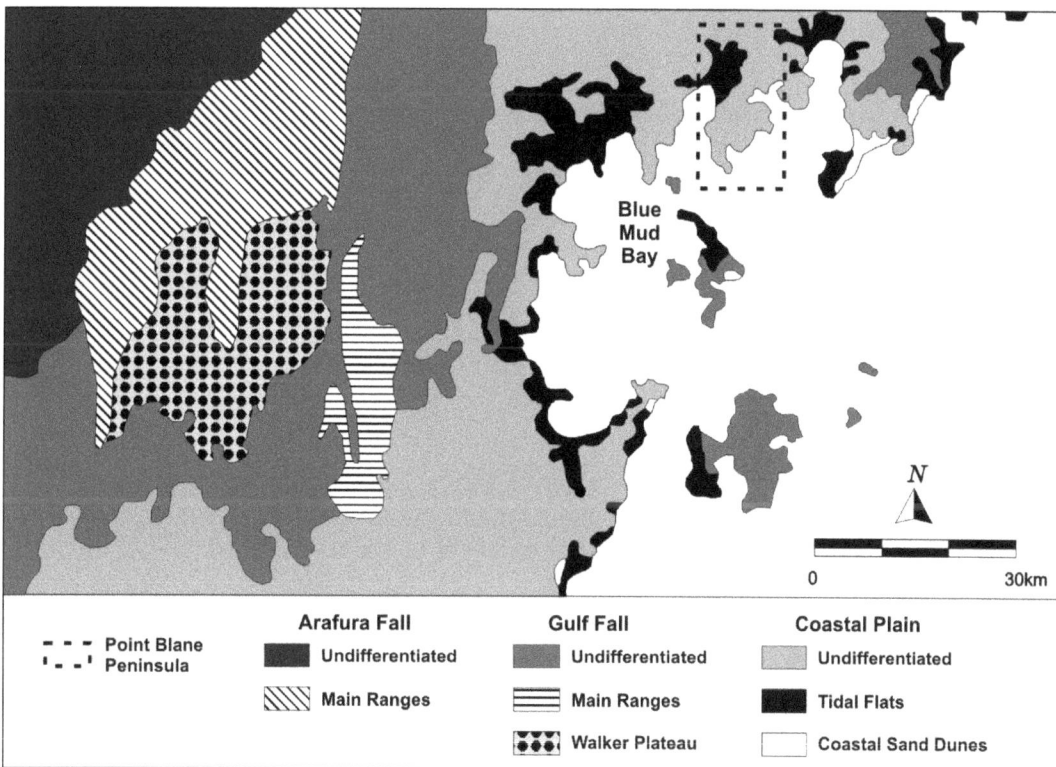

Figure 2.2: Blue Mud Bay physiographic divisions.

Source: After Haines *et al.* 1999:3.

The dominant land surfaces found across the study area are quite thin, as they have only been accumulating in their current configuration since the Holocene period of sea level rise and stabilisation (Haines *et al.* 1999:77). By extension, the archaeological record in this type of coastal landscape is tied spatially and chronologically to this mid-to-late Holocene pattern of landscape formation. The geological provinces located within the study area and neighbouring areas are summarised below in Table 2.1 and their distribution shown in Figure 2.3.

Table 2.1: Main geological/landscape units found within the study area and surrounding region.

Unit	Geological Grouping
*Cz	Shallow and gravelly soils, dominating plateau margins
*Czl	Earthy, gravelly sands, often difficult to differentiate from the above
*Qa	Alluvial gravel, sand, silt and clay, found in active channels, floodplains and outwash areas
*Qb	Grassy black soil and grey clay plains, old coastal deposits stranded by coastline regression
*Qc	Highly saline soils, unconsolidated grey clay, silt and sand with shell debris
*Qd	Aeolian dunefields on exposed coasts, calcareous and siliceous course sands on beach ridges
*Qr	Active/recently active cheniers and beach ridges, comprised of shelly sand
K	Fine- to coarse-grained quartzites with chert granules, part of the Yirrkala and Walker River formations
Pc, Pk, Px, Pew, Pv, Pgk	A composite of sedimentary and metamorphic rocks, shallow granites and undifferentiated volcanics, part of the Arnhem Inlier formation

Note: * indicates those geological units present in the study area.

Source: Haines *et al.* 1999.

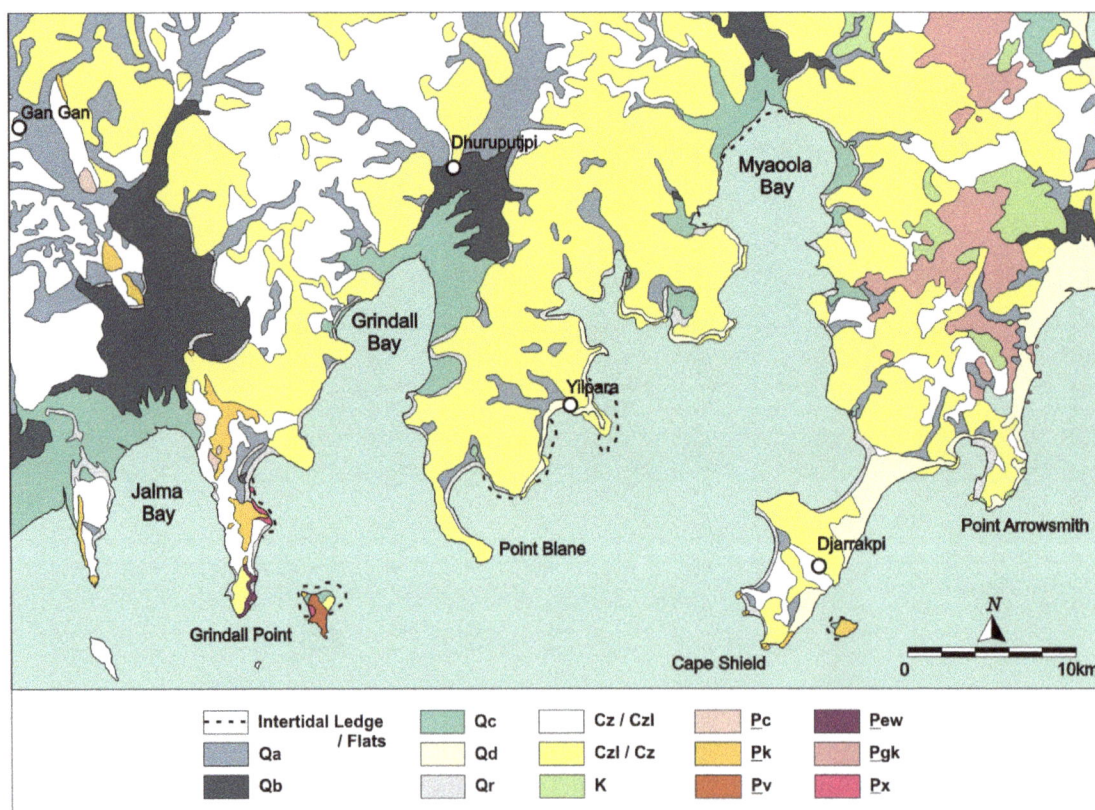

Figure 2.3: Geological divisions for the Point Blane Peninsula and neighbouring areas.

Source: Based on Blue Mud Bay 1:250 000 Geological Map SD 53–7.

Gravelly, earthy sands (Czl) are associated with all soils in the region (Specht 1958:343; Isbell 1983:195; Haines *et al.* 1999:77), with shallow and gravelly soils dominating the plateau margins and dissected areas (Cz). These two geological units are often difficult to differentiate, and have been mapped together in Figure 2.3. Importantly, long-term and intensive weathering and leaching during the formation of lateritic profiles across this region have also resulted in plant deficiencies and severe nutritional impoverishment of the soil profile (Paton and Williams 1972;

Hubble *et al.* 1983:26–7). Figure 2.4 illustrates the dominant geological formations across the study area, with exposed lateritic profiles on the coastal margin presented in Figure 2.5. Alluvial gravel, sand, silt and clay are found in active channels, flood plains and outwash sheets around ranges (Qa), fanning out towards the coastal zone where they merge with coastal sediments (Specht 1958:353–6; Haines *et al.* 1999:77). Highly saline soils are located adjacent to the coast (saltflats), forming on intertidal and supratidal flats and in tidal channels. These are largely unvegetated, apart from stands of mangroves, and consist of unconsolidated grey clay, silt and sand with entrained shell debris (Qc) (see Figure 2.6). The salt content of these soils is very high, with a salty crust present over much of the area (Specht 1958:350; Haines *et al.* 1999:77).

Figure 2.4: Dominant gravelly, earthy sands of the Point Blane Peninsula.

Source: Photo Patrick Faulkner.

Figure 2.5: Exposed lateritic profiles on the coastal margin of Myaoola Bay.

Source: Photo Annie Clarke.

Figure 2.6: Expansive saltflats in the Grindall Bay area.

Source: Photo Annie Clarke.

Figure 2.7: Estuarine meanders and dendritic tidal channels across elevated black soil plains.

Source: Photo Patrick Faulkner.

The saltflat areas are bordered by slightly elevated black soil and grey clay plains (Qb), which are often interpreted as slowly prograded coastline deposits and are traversed by well-developed estuarine meanders and dendritic tidal channels (Figure 2.7). These areas are often inundated by high tides and floodwaters, and some are slowly accreting by the addition of flood plain silts (Specht 1958:349; Isbell 1983:192; Walker and Butler 1983:83–5; Haines *et al.* 1999:77). Aeolian dunefields are located along the exposed coast (Qd), generally characterised as calcareous and siliceous coarse sands on beach ridges (Specht 1958:356; Isbell 1983:191; Haines *et al.* 1999:77). Active and recently active cheniers and sandy beach ridges (Qr) comprised of shelly sand occur as a narrow zone on the coastal fringes of many regions of the Gulf of Carpentaria, and are scattered along much of the coast as narrow ridges a few metres in height (Haines *et al.* 1999:77). Sources of knappable stone occurs in small, localised areas closer to the coast, pink to white quartzites form the bulk of the raw materials recorded in the study area's stone artefact assemblage, and are derived from the underlying Cretaceous and older quartzite, sandstone and granitic deposits. One example of a quartzitic outcropping is shown in Figure 2.8, an area located on the coast approximately 5km north of the Yilpara Community.

Figure 2.8: Example of a coastal quartzite outcropping, Point Blane Peninsula.

Source: Photo Patrick Faulkner.

The present landform characteristics detailed above have largely resulted from two main processes acting on the physical environment throughout the Holocene. The effects of changes in sea levels during the marine transgression, followed by ongoing patterns of progradation and sedimentary infilling initiated during the mid Holocene, strongly indicate that the current landscape is different from that seen in the past.

Changes in sea level

Sea levels have varied significantly from the Pleistocene into Holocene (see Figure 2.9A for sea level curve relating to the past 140,000 years), largely as a response to the cyclic expansion and contraction of the northern continental ice sheets. This process has dramatically altered the land area of Australia over time, affecting localised climatic patterns (Chappell 1983, 1993; Frakes *et al.* 1987).

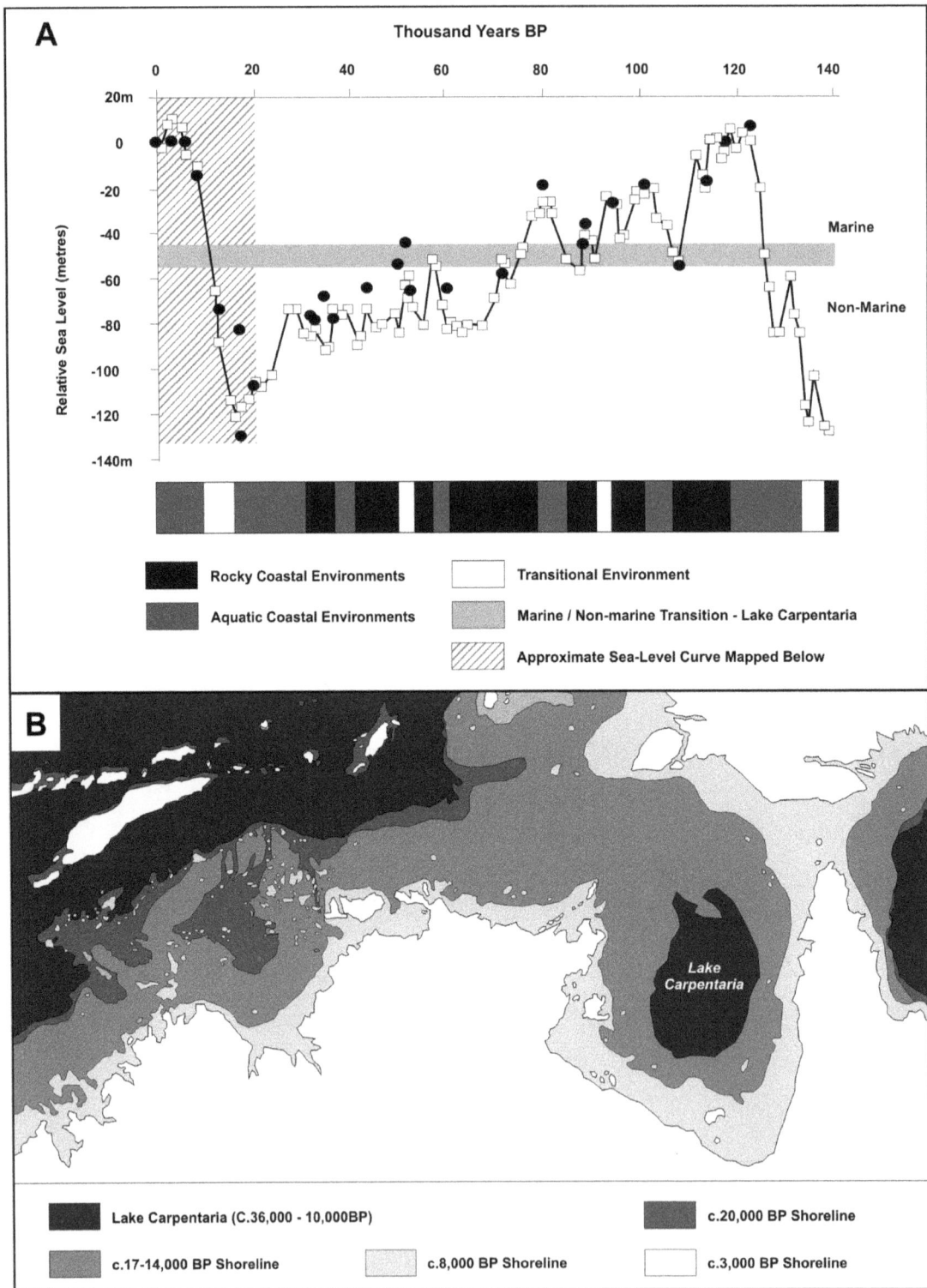

Figure 2.9: (A) Global sea level curve for the past 140 ka; (B) Stages of sea level rise for the past 20 ka for northern Australia and surrounding region.

Source: (A) Chappell *et al*. 1996; Chivas *et al*. 2001:39. (B) After Allen and Barton n.d. 5; Nix and Kalma 1972:88–9; Yokoyama *et al*. 2001:16.

Figure 2.9B illustrates sea level rise from approximately 20,000 BP when sea level was 120 to 130m below current levels (Chappell *et al.* 1996), through the breaching of the Arafura Sill and the marine transgression between 12,000 BP and 9700 BP, and establishment of fully marine conditions by 6000 BP (Chivas *et al.* 2001:24–9) through to the present (Hopley and Thom 1983:13–4; Lambeck and Chappell 2001; Lambeck *et al.* 2002:358–9). Chappell and Thom (1977:283), Torgersen *et al.* (1983) and Schrire (1982:9) have made the point that sea level rise at an approximate rate of 1-3mm per year would have had a dramatic effect on the distribution of fauna and flora in the Carpentaria drainage basin. The consequences of shoreline migration and coastal ecosystem response would have drastically affected human populations retreating from the rising sea levels.

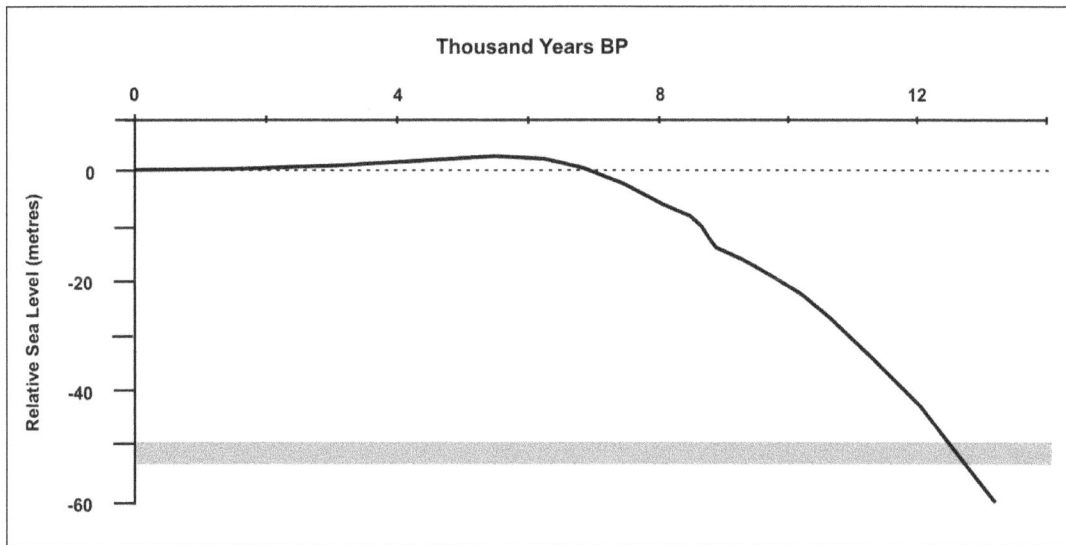

Figure 2.10: Smoothed sea level curve for the Gulf of Carpentaria. Grey band represents the marine/non-marine transition period for Lake Carpentaria.

Source: Nakiboglu *et al.* 1983:349; Yokoyama *et al.* 2001:14; Woodroffe and Horton 2004:3. Grey band following Clarkson, 2004.

Evidence across the north appears to suggest a general pattern, that sea levels stabilised following the last post-glacial marine transgression approximately 1-3m above present levels around 7000 to 6000 BP, with a decline in sea level in response to hydro-isostatic adjustment until approximately 600 BP (Chappell *et al.* 1982; Lambeck and Nakada 1990; Lees 1992b:6; Fleming *et al.* 1998:335; Nunn 1998; Woodroffe *et al.* 1998; Grindrod *et al.* 1999:465; Rowland 1999a:27). Rather than being a smooth decline from sea level highstand, around Australia there is growing evidence for a series of minor oscillations in relative sea level during the late Holocene superimposed over the general sea level trend (e.g. Lambeck 2002; Sloss *et al.* 2007; Woodroffe 2009). There is an absence of such research within the immediate Blue Mud Bay area, and geomorphological research from the Gulf of Carpentaria region as a whole must be evaluated. The smoothed Holocene sea level curve determined for the Gulf of Carpentaria is presented in Figure 2.10, based on data from Nakiboglu *et al.* (1983:349), Woodroffe and Horton (2004:3) and Yokoyama *et al.* (2001:14). This information is derived from slightly emerged beach and chenier ridges from the prograded southeast and east plains along the Gulf, and is indicative of the tidal zone position during the mid-to-late Holocene (Nakiboglu *et al.* 1983:356). In addition, chenier ridge development by 6000 BP along the southern shore of the Gulf of Carpentaria indicates highstands in excess of 2m (Rhodes 1980, 1982), and in the Sir Edward Pellew Island Group a probable highstand of 1.2m has also been reported for this time (Rhodes 1980). At Karumba, chenier ridges indicate a highstand 2.5m above present level, followed by a sea level fall at a uniform rate to its present value (Lambeck and Nakada 1990:159–167). Therefore within the Gulf of Carpentaria, sea levels reached present levels (height at zero metres) at approximately 7000 BP, after a rapid rise from 10,000 BP of approximately 21m in 3000 years. The rate of sea level rise over this period equates to 7mm per year. With continued sea level rise, a maximum highstand of approximately 1.2 to 2.5m was reached between 6000 and 5000 BP, followed by a slow regression over the mid-to-late Holocene.

These changes in sea level are inter-woven with long-term climatic shifts linked to the El Niño/Southern Oscillation (ENSO) cycle, particularly relating to the intensity of the summer monsoon and cycling periods of aridity and increased precipitation. This is due to the fact that the Gulf of Carpentaria is located adjacently to the Western Pacific Warm Pool, which is responsible for the largest transfer of heat from the Pacific Ocean into the Indian Ocean and is implicated in the generation of El Niño/La Niña phases of the southern oscillation (Gagan and Chappell 2000:35; Chivas *et al.* 2001:20).

Landscape alteration: Patterns of coastal progradation and sedimentation

The effect of Holocene sea levels on riverine lowlands can be considered in two episodes, the first from 10,000 to 6500 BP when it was rising at 0.6 to 1.0m for every 100 years, and the second from 6500 to the present when it has been relatively stable. During the rising phase, the sea transgressed upon land and valleys were drowned, an effect offset to some extent by sedimentation (Chappell 1990:70). Following the marine transgression, many of the shallow bays in north Australia were gradually prograded to form freshwater wetlands and salt or mudflat areas. Although few geomorphological studies have been conducted in northeast Arnhem Land, a large amount of research has been carried out in the Alligator Rivers region of western Arnhem Land. The model of estuarine evolution during the Holocene for the Alligator Rivers region indicates that the process of sedimentation continued after the stabilisation of sea level leading to a transition from mangrove to freshwater environments. The diversity of mangrove species and the tidal swamp vegetation increased, creating a variety of environments influenced heavily by rainfall patterns. Channels formed as the surface built upwards and outwards on the tidally inundated flats, to a level where high tide flooding became rare, with brackish and freshwater swamps forming in residual depressions on the landward edge of the coastal plains (Woodroffe *et al.* 1985a, 1985b; Clark and Guppy 1988:679–81). The pattern and timing of the progradation phases for the South Alligator River are as follows:

1. Transgressive phase (8000 to 6000 BP) involving tidal incursion and landward extension of mangroves forests in a prior valley.

2. Big Swamp phase (6000 to 4000 BP) when mangrove forests were established throughout the estuarine plains.

3. Sinuous phase (4000 to 2000 BP) when mangrove forests were eliminated, tidal flows became confined to channels, and freshwater vegetation became established on the plains.

4. Cuspate phase (after 2000 BP) in which the river adopted a meandering form.

With regional variations, the model of estuarine evolution and Holocene deposition demonstrated for the Alligator Rivers region is said to apply broadly to other river systems across north Australia (Woodroffe 1995:80). This general model is shown in Figure 2.11, and it is suggested that the progradational model for the Dhuruputjpi wetlands system in the study area generally follows that of the South Alligator River, although the intensity of sedimentation and the timing of the phases will vary (Chappell 1990:73).

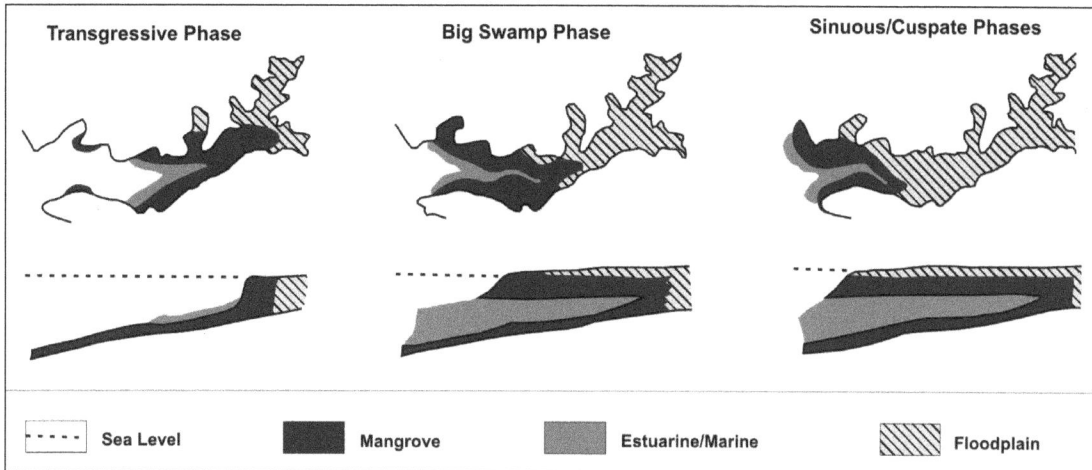

Figure 2.11: Holocene estuarine sedimentation/progradational model.

Source: After Woodroffe et al. 1985b:26.

When sea level rose rapidly (1.3 to 1.5m per 100 years) wave action consistently reworked the nearshore zone, producing a steeper slope, and as a result, little or no mangrove is envisaged on the seaward beach face (Chappell and Thom 1977:287). The rate of late Pleistocene and early Holocene sea level rise, although relatively rapid in the initial stages, had decreased by approximately 8000 BP. Therefore, the spread of mangrove swamps and sedimentation throughout prior valleys virtually kept pace with a rising sea level of 12m (at 0.6m per 100 years) between 8000 and 6000 BP (Woodroffe 1981; Chappell 1990:71; Ellison 1993). It is also thought that during a transgressive period, richer estuarine biota would be expected compared with a regressive phase on a seasonally dry tropical coast, as hypersaline conditions should be absent (Chappell and Thom 1977:287). Stratigraphically, the sequence of infill is composed of intertidal muds and sands, overlain by dark grey muds rich in mangrove fragments, and capped by grey-brown mottled muds. The upper mud is only vegetated adjacent to tidal creeks, estuarine shores and below high spring tide level, seaward of the outmost beach ridge. Vast bare high-tidal flats with hypersaline interstitial waters and localised evaporate deposits lie landward of the outer vegetated fringe (Chappell and Thom 1977:284). The elevation and absence of vegetation on the saline tidal flats are a function of both sediment supply and duration of sea level still-stand. Therefore, in areas of relatively slow input of fine-grained sediment, the transition from sub-tidal, to vegetated intertidal, to bare high-tidal mudflats requires a still-stand of up to several thousand years (Chappell and Thom 1977:284). Therefore, post-glacial processes associated with the marine transgression and sedimentary infill has formed the wetland and saltflat areas of the study area in a broadly similar way to that of the Alligator Rivers region, an example being that of the Dhuruputjpi wetlands area. In line with this pattern of substantial environmental change during the Holocene, there are quite dramatic changes in climatic conditions associated with these processes.

Holocene climatic variability

Current climate

Northeast Arnhem Land, located within Australia's humid zone, is characterised as a tropical monsoon summer rainfall area (see Figure 2.12A). The region experiences two distinct seasons: the wet (October to April) and the dry (May to September), with most rain falling between January and March. Two major atmospheric pressure systems affect the north Australian climate:

a subtropical ridge of high-pressure cells, and the monsoon trough. The subtropical highs move from west to east across southern Australia in winter, providing the driving force behind the southeast trade winds dominating the north Australian weather in the dry season from June to October or November. The monsoon trough runs east-west through the tropics in the summer months, lying for long periods over north Australia, and creating much of the rainfall during this time (Bureau of Meteorology 1998:1). The change between the seasons is usually gradual; the wet season begins during the transition months of October and November (build-up) and culminates during April (McDonald and McAlpine 1991:19–25; Bureau of Meteorology 1998:1).

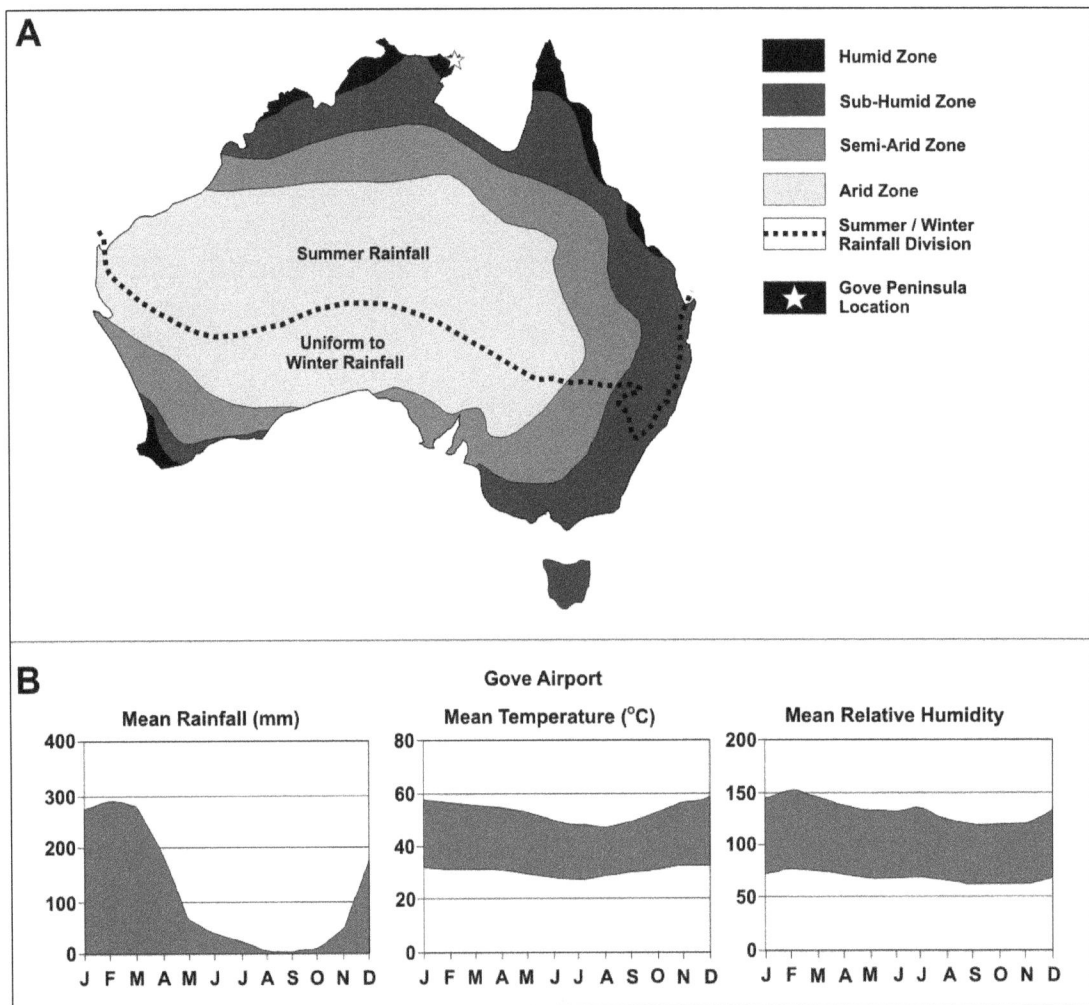

Figure 2.12: (A) Australian climatic regions; (B) Mean rainfall, mean temperature and mean relative humidity at Gove Airport, northern Arnhem Land.

Source: (A) After Pickering 1997 Vol. 2:4. (B) Bureau of Meteorology 1988:101–34; 1998:18–28.

Seasonal differences in rainfall, temperature and relative humidity (minimum and maximum) are shown in Figure 2.12B. These graphs are derived from data obtained at Gove Airport (Bureau of Meteorology 1988:101–34; 1998:18–28), 200km to the north of the study area. From May to September (dry season), the prevailing southwesterly winds bring predominantly fine conditions. In the study area, rainfall is generally low to non-existent with a lessening of humidity during this period (Bureau of Meteorology 1998:2). The periods of highest relative humidity and increases in temperature correspond with the build-up and wet season. During the wet, weather in the north is largely determined by the position of the active and inactive phases of the monsoonal trough. The active phase is usually associated with broad areas of cloud and rain, with sustained moderate to fresh northwesterly winds. Inactive periods, which are characterised by light winds, isolated showers and thunderstorm activity, occur when the monsoon trough weakens or retreats north of Australia (Bureau of Meteorology 1986:4, 1989:45; Zaar *et al.* 1999:9). Tropical cyclones can develop off the coast in the wet season, usually forming within an active monsoon trough. Heavy rains and high winds can be experienced along the coast within several hundred kilometres of a cyclone's centre (Bureau of Meteorology 1998:2–3), causing widespread vegetation and landscape changes.

Climatic change during the Holocene

Many of the longer-term trends in climate change that have occurred during the period spanning the early Holocene to the present day are related to the ENSO cycle (Enfield 1989; Allan *et al.* 1996; Webster and Palmer 1997). During an El Niño episode, rainfall dramatically increases in certain areas of the world, whereas severe droughts occur in other regions (such as the Australian-Indonesian region). The ENSO phenomenon has strongly influenced climatic patterns in Australia for some time (McGlone *et al.* 1992; Shulmeister and Lees 1992; Jones *et al.* 1999), and at present, ENSO represents the principal source of inter-annual climatic variability within the Indo-Pacific region (Glantz 1991; Glantz *et al.* 1991; Diaz and Markgraf 1992; Allan *et al.* 1996; Rowland 1999a). During El Niño events, there is a weakening of sea level pressure in the southeastern tropical Pacific and a decrease in the strength of trade winds. This causes sea-surface temperatures to rise through a weakening of the cool oceanic upwelling along the western coast of South America. Warmer sea surface temperatures create increased heating and evaporation, resulting in intensified convection and rainfall over the western coast of continental America (Diaz and Markgraf 1992; Enfield 1992; Allan *et al.* 1996). Based on a review of long-term palaeoenvironmental climatic indicators, Bush (2001:25), McGlone *et al.* (1992) and Tudhope *et al.* (2001:1516) suggest that the ENSO cycle may have intensified in the last 5000 years. Shulmeister and Lees (1995) and Shulmeister (1999) have also argued that ENSO-scale variability became entrenched in the climatic system after approximately 4000 BP (see also Hughes and Brown 1992; Graumlich 1993; Knox 1993; Rodbell *et al.* 1999; Rowland 1999a, 1999b; Andrus *et al.* 2002; Koutavas *et al.* 2002).

El Niño events have strong ecological and economic consequences. The best-studied effects on ecosystems are in marine environments, where El Niño is correlated with dramatic changes in the abundance and distribution of many organisms (Bourke *et al.* 2007), and the collapse of fisheries (Holmgren *et al.* 2001:89). There are also documented impacts on terrestrial organisms as well, linked to impacts on the vegetation regime. For example, El Niño events have been linked to the almost complete defoliation of mangrove forests (Haberle 2000:66; Holmgren *et al.* 2001:90–1). Therefore, ENSO-related climatic oscillations must have had significant impacts on human populations, primarily affecting the resource base in terms of the long and short-term availability, stability and structuring of these resources (Clarkson 2004:163).

For the reasons outlined above, the Pleistocene to Holocene transition in northern Australia was a time of rapid climatic amelioration, characterised by an increase in lake water levels (Kershaw 1995), and the establishment of vegetation communities in their present position (Nix and Kalma 1972:88–9). This period was one of rapid environmental change, including climatic reversals with the onset of tropical conditions in some areas between 15,000 and 11,500 BP, followed by a swing back to full glacial conditions during the Younger Dryas, between approximately 10,800 and 10,200 years ago (Kershaw 1995). The timing and nature of Holocene climatic changes for northern Australia are presented in Figure 2.13, and the Holocene climatic record and the comparison of wet and arid phases for north Australia are summarised as follows, and expanded on below:

1. Effective precipitation and temperature gradually increase from the beginning of the Holocene until approximately 5000 BP.

2. A period of higher effective precipitation from 5000 BP to approximately 3700 BP.

3. Following this, a sharp falling off in effective precipitation after 3700 BP, with increase in climatic variability from approximately 1000 BP to the present (Shulmeister 1999:82).

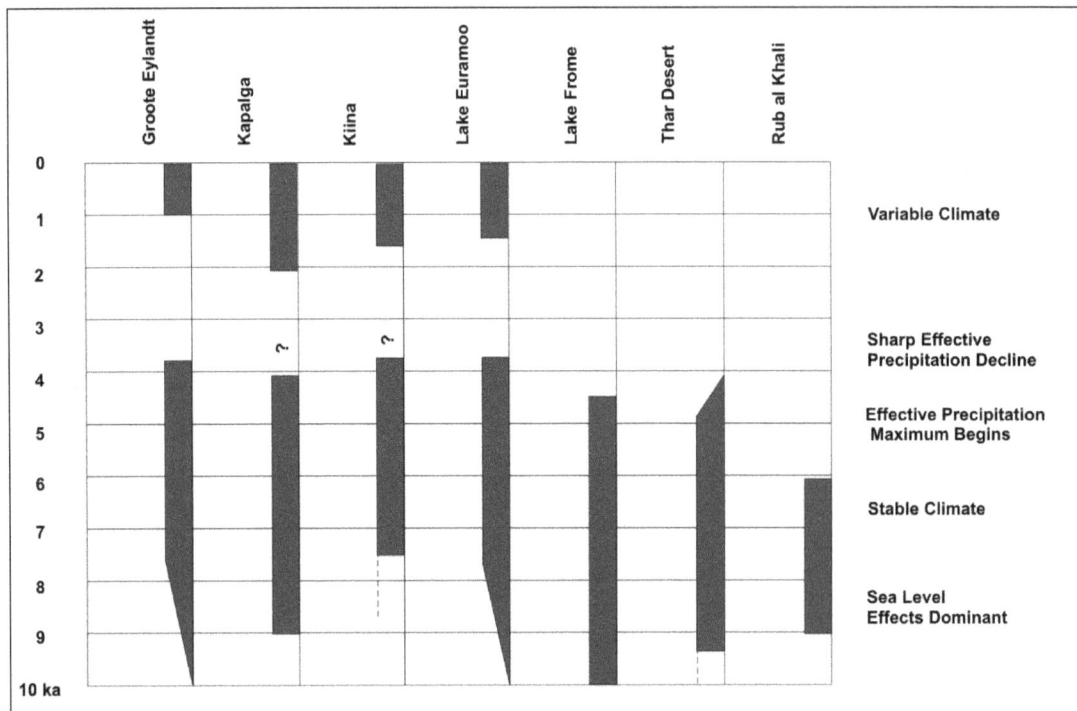

Figure 2.13: The timing and nature of Holocene climatic changes, wet phases indicated by grey shading.

Source: After Shulmeister and Lees 1995:12 and Shulmeister 1999:84.

For the period around 6500 BP, data suggest that the ENSO cycle may have weakened, an interpretation that is in agreement with data suggesting subdued ENSO in the early to mid Holocene from lake sediments in Ecuador, geoarchaeological evidence from Peru, and pollen data from Australia (Tudhope *et al.* 2001:1515). An interpretation of high effective precipitation between 5500 and 3700 BP, with precipitation values between 200 and 1000mm higher and temperatures 1^0 to 2^0C higher, is supported by evidence from Groote Eylandt, correlated with a phase of rapid organic sedimentation (Shulmeister 1992, 1999:82). It appears, therefore, that the north Australian Holocene environmental optimum (in regards to precipitation rather than a temperature maximum) occurred after 5000 BP, significantly at least 1000 years later than in southern Australia (Nix and Kalma 1972; Kershaw 1983, 1995; Kershaw and Nix 1989; McGlone *et al.* 1992; Gagan *et al.* 1994; Shulmeister 1999:83; Gagan and Chappell 2000:44;) alongside a reduction of interannual variability (Chappell 2001:177). Seasonality has continued to increase in the Southern Hemisphere since 5000 BP. It is widely observed that climates, at least in the Australasian region, have been much more variable in the last few thousand years (Wasson 1986; Shulmeister 1999:88), with this increased variability related to the onset of a Southern Oscillation dominated climate. The general trend appears to be a change from low seasonality in the early Holocene to increased seasonality in the late Holocene, a pattern that has been observed in recent reviews of the climate history of the south Pacific region (Markgraf *et al.* 1992; Shulmeister 1999:86). There also appears to be a trend toward increased aridity in the mid-to-late Holocene (after approximately 5000 to 3000 BP) based on coral, foraminifera, varve, lake and sea bottom sediment data from sites in Australian and the circum-Pacific region (McPhail and Hope 1985; Brookfield and Allan 1989; Singh and Luly 1991; McGlone *et al.* 1992; Hope and Golson 1995; Kershaw 1995; Shulmeister and Lees 1995; Nott *et al.* 1999:233; Rodbell *et al.* 1999; McCarthy and Head 2001; Kim *et al.* 2002; Koutavas *et al.* 2002). Geomorphic evidence from cheniers and coastal dunefields (Lees *et al.* 1990, 1992; Lees 1992a, 1992b) indicates that some of the observed changes in these systems are synchronous across north Australia, and may represent coherent, broad-scale climatic signals (Shulmeister 1999:82; Prebble *et al.* 2005:367–9).

While the longer term evidence for climate change is important for contextualising the degree of variability in climate history throughout the Holocene, possibly the most significant period of climatic change for this study relates to the last 1500 years. There is evidence for a warm dry (relative to today) period about 1200 to 700 BP in low latitudes named the Little Climatic Optimum (or Medieval Warm Period). Likewise, there is evidence for the Little Ice Age, a cool dry period following the Little Climatic Optimum, about 600 to 100 BP (Nunn 2000:716). The Little Ice Age appears in most Northern Hemisphere palaeoclimate reconstructions as multiple, century-scale periods of anomalously cold, dry conditions between the 15th and late 19th centuries. Glacial advances in both hemispheres and enhanced polar atmospheric circulation suggest that the Little Ice Age was a global scale event (Hendy *et al.* 2002:1511). The transition between the Little Climatic Optimum and the Little Ice Age appears to be marked by rapid cooling and two stages of sea level fall throughout the Pacific Basin around 650 BP and 500 BP (Nunn 1998, 2000). Recent coral proxy records for sea-surface temperature and sea surface salinity anomalies in the tropical southwest Pacific indicate that a dramatic shift occurred in the tropical ocean-atmosphere system at the end of the Little Ice Age (Hendy *et al.* 2002; Gagan *et al.* 2004:132). Hendy *et al.* (2002) suggest that conditions in the tropical southwest Pacific during the Little Ice Age were also consistently more saline than present, largely between approximately 500 and 200 BP. Sea-surface temperature (SST) and rainfall are closely linked in tropical areas of strong convective rainfall, such as the western equatorial Pacific (Tudhope *et al.* 2001:1511). The lack of significant planktonic foraminiferal faunal change in the western Pacific results in estimated SST differences of only 1.5°C to 2.0°C or less between the present day and around 2000 to 3000 BP in low-latitude regions (Thunell *et al.* 1994:259–60; Shulmeister 1999:86; Tudhope *et al.* 2001:1515). Within the north Australian region, palaeotemperatures indicated by the fossil coral record from the Great Barrier Reef shows that the mean SST approximately 5350 years ago was 27.0°C, which is 1.2°C warmer than the mean SST for the early 1990s. Terrestrial pollen and tree-line elevation records in the tropical southwest Pacific indicate that the climate was generally warmer from 7000 to 4000 BP (Gagan *et al.* 1998:1016). Taken together with the 5°C cooling indicated by palaeotemperatures for late-glacial corals from the southwest Pacific, these results suggest that the full amplitude of the glacial-Holocene temperature change may have been about 6°C (Gagan *et al.* 1998:1017; Wasson and Claussen 2002:823).

While these studies show that there is a degree of regional variation in the timing and nature of cycles of aridity and precipitation, they also demonstrate a generally applicable climatic pattern across a wide area of northern Australia. The combination of substantial environmental and climatic changes throughout the Holocene suggests that the type of resources, their density and distribution, were thus quite different to that observed within the historic period. The current distribution and availability of resources such as water, vegetation and fauna are outlined below, with a brief discussion on the seasonal nature of these resources as they are now, followed by a consideration of the implications of changing environmental and climatic conditions for the availability of resources into the past.

Resource availability

Hydrology

The Point Blane Peninsula contains a number of reliable freshwater sources (Figure 2.14). Smaller creeks and rivers, such as the Durabudboi River and Wyonga Creek, drain the coastal plains (Haines *et al.* 1999:1–2), freshwater wetlands (Figure 2.15), small swamps and billabongs, and sub-surface aquifers make up the remaining components of the hydrological regime. Both the Durabudboi River and Wyonga Creek have large catchment areas, resulting in larger amounts of rainfall runoff and river flow in the wet season. The middle section of the Durabudboi River contains numerous pools and billabongs (Figure 2.16), which contain water even after the poorest wet season rainfall. In contrast, Wyonga Creek will often cease to flow entirely at the end of the dry season. Again, pools and water holes will contain a certain level of water, but are restricted in size and distribution along the course of the creek (Zaar *et al.* 1999:19–20). Both systems rely on groundwater discharge maintained by sandstone aquifers during the dry season. Many of the swamps and billabongs located along drainage lines feeding the main river and creek systems will retain water well into the dry season. In the case of the larger Dhuruputjpi wetlands system, fed by the Durabudboi River, freshwater may be available year round.

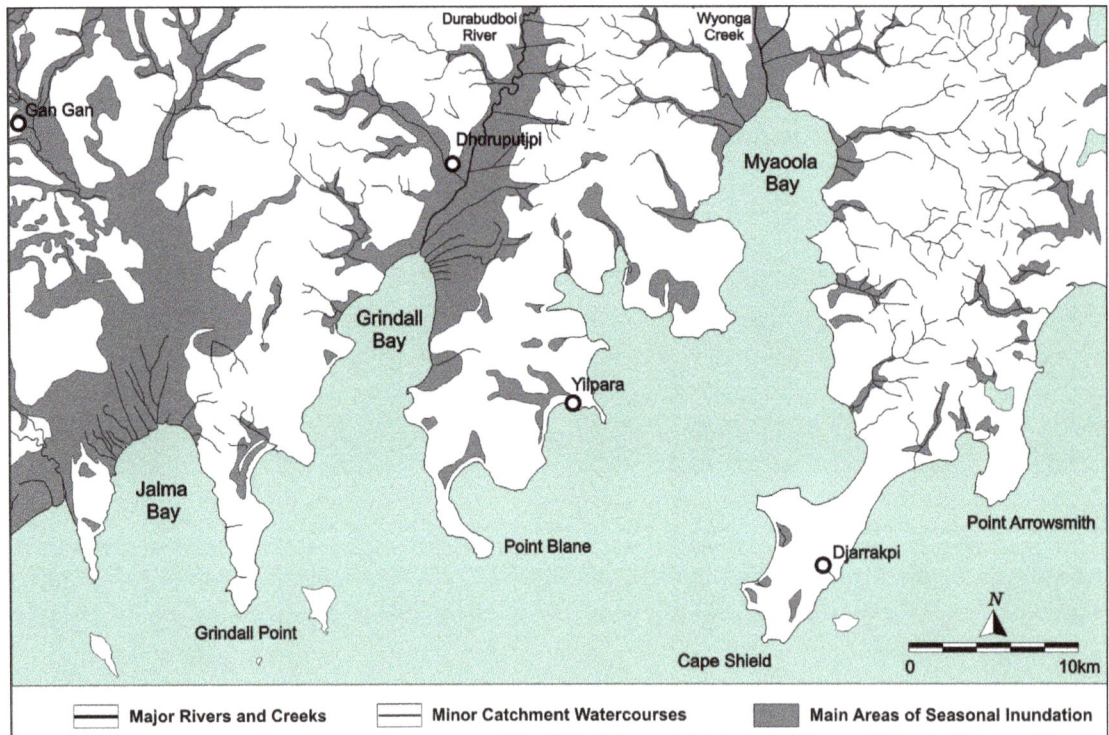

Figure 2.14: The hydrology of the Point Blane Peninsula and neighbouring areas.

Source: Water Resources of North Eastern Arnhem Land Mapsheet.

Figure 2.15: Section of freshwater wetland towards the mouth of the Durabudboi River.

Source: Photo Patrick Faulkner.

Figure 2.16: Durabudboi River billabong.

Source: Photo Annie Clarke.

The study area contains large regional aquifers consisting of poorly consolidated sandstone or limestone. They naturally discharge large volumes of water throughout the year and are responsible for the base flow of many of the large river systems (Zaar *et al.* 1999:9–10). Additionally, high annual wet season rainfall will result in increasing water recharge on the peninsula, resulting in higher water table levels and greater spring flows. In low rainfall years, discharge from the springs will be less and the water table levels will fall (Zaar *et al.* 1999:9–10). The availability of freshwater in the past would have been constrained by very similar factors as those seen at present, but it is likely that the influence of each factor would have fluctuated through time, creating a degree of variability in water availability. A decrease in annual precipitation would have substantially decreased the availability of both surface and sub-surface water, and as already noted, there were several periods of heightened aridity throughout the mid-to-late Holocene. Also, several major sources of surface water in the study area, highlighted as those larger areas of seasonal inundation in Figure 2.14 around the major rivers and creeks, were slowly developing throughout the late Holocene. Therefore, while many of the minor watercourses, seasonal floodplains and lower-lying swamps and billabongs have potentially changed very little throughout the mid-to-late Holocene, there are a number of environmental and climatic factors that may have affected the pattern of water availability through time.

Flora

The dispersal of plant communities is closely associated with the distribution of hydrological and geological zones within the landscape (Dunlop and Webb 1991:50). The distributions of the majority of the vegetation units described below are listed in Table 2.2 and shown in Figure 2.17.

Table 2.2: Main vegetation units found within the study area.

Unit	Vegetation Grouping
04	*Eucalyptus miniata* (Darwin Woolly Butt), *Eucalyptus tetrodonta* (Stringybark) Open-Forest with Sorghum Grassland Understorey
07	*Eucalyptus tetrodonta* (Stringybark), *Callitris intratropica* (Cypress) Woodland with Grassland Understorey
51*	*Melaleuca viridiflora* (Myrtle), *Eucalyptus* Low Open-Woodland with *Chrysopogonfallax* (Golden Beard Grass) Grassland Understorey
54	Mixed Closed-Grassland/Sedgeland (Seasonal Floodplain)
102	Coastal Dune Complex (*Casuarina equisetifolia* woodland, grasslands, Melaleuca swamps/mixed shrublands)
105	Mangal Low Closed-Forest (Mangroves)
106	Saline Tidal Flats with Scattered Chenopod Low Shrubland (Samphire)
01*	Mixed Species Closed-Forest (Monsoon Vine Thicket)
53*	*Melaleuca* Forest (Paperbark Swamp)

Note: * indicates those vegetation units not mapped in Figure 2.11 due to scale.

Source: Specht 1958; Wilson *et al.* 1990; Yunupingu *et al.* 1995; Brock 2001.

Based on changes in the structure of the environment and climatic conditions through time, the organisation and distribution of the majority of the vegetation communities in the area would have been quite different in the past compared with the present. It is possible that there may have been only minor variation in the distribution of the *Eucalypt* dominated woodland communities in the area (Units 4 and 7) through time. Those vegetation units that would have been most affected by processes of landscape alteration and climatic variability include the seasonal floodplain communities (Unit 54), paperbark swamps (Unit 53), the mangrove forests (Unit 105), coastal dune complex (Unit 102) and the samphire dominated saline tidal flats (Unit 106). These areas have been highlighted due to their susceptibility to environmental change, as well as many of these vegetation units being a fairly recent occurrence based on patterns of late Holocene landscape change. The significance of changes in the availability and distribution of these vegetation units relates to their contemporary importance as key seasonal habitats for a number of resources. Changes in the structure of habitat areas through time directly affect the structure of the resource base, a point which is particularly important for a peninsula, where many resources are located within or bordering the margins.

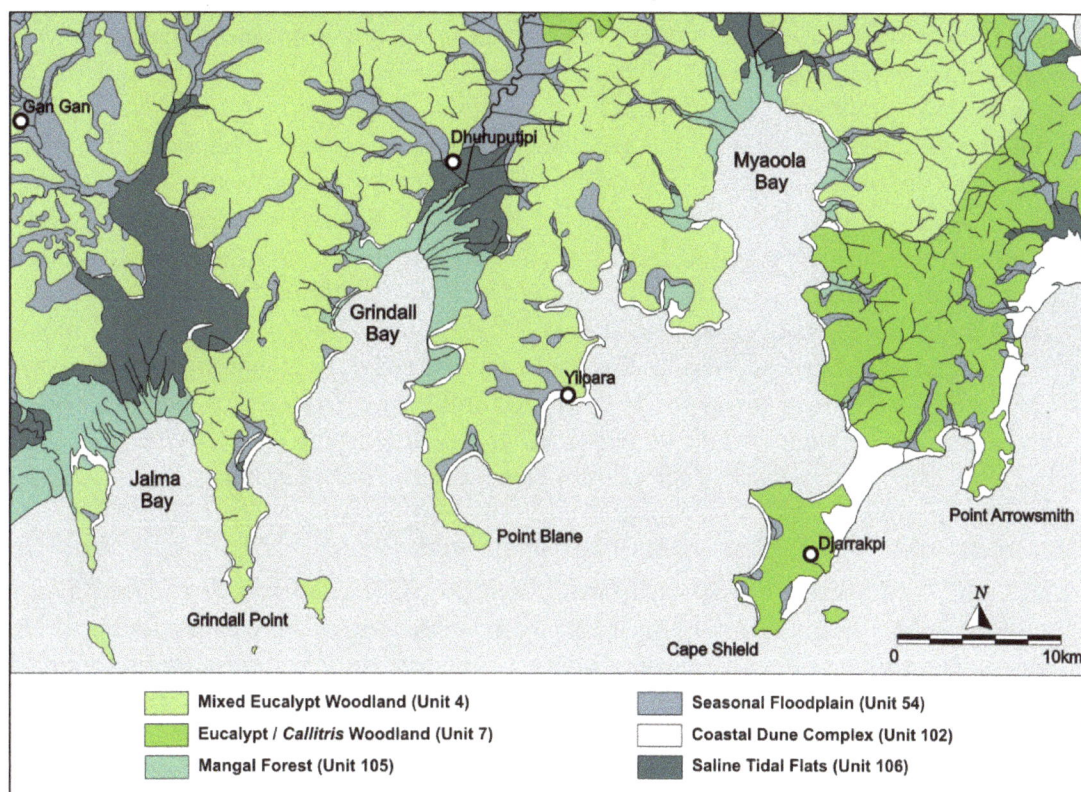

Figure 2.17: The distribution of the main vegetation regimes in the Point Blane Peninsula study area and neighbouring areas.

Source: Based on Wilson *et al*. 1990.

Fauna

A large number of faunal species were observed during the course of the fieldwork. Although little research has been conducted on the fauna in this area, detailed lists of molluscs, fish, reptiles and amphibians, birds, and mammals recorded in Arnhem Land during the 1948 American-Australian Scientific Expedition to Arnhem Land can be found in Specht (1964), with references to the mammals of the area recorded by Donald Thomson between 1935 and 1943 found in Dixon and Huxley (1985:18–174). Recent work by Barber (2002) and personal observation have also contributed to the faunal list. A large number of mammals can be found throughout the sub-coastal lowlands, floodplains and coastal woodlands, including the *Macropus robustus* (Common Wallaroo), *Macropus antilopinus* (Antilopine Wallaroo), *Macropus agilis* (Agile Wallaby), *Petrogale brachyotis* (Short-eared Rock Wallaby), *Petaurus breviceps ariel* (Northern Territory Sugar Glider), *Trichosurus arnhemensis* (Northern Brushtail Possum), *Isoodon macrourus* (Northern Brown Bandicoot) and *Rhinilophus megaphyllus* (the Eastern Horseshoe Bat). Other mammal species which may occur, albeit in low number, include the *Melomys burtoni* (Grassland Melomys), *Pseudomys delicatulus* (Delicate Mouse), *Conilurus penicillatus* (Brush-Tailed Tree-Rat), *Mesembriomys gouldii* (Black-Footed Tree-Rat), *Rattus colletti* (Dusky Rat), *Sminthopsis virginae* (Red-Cheeked Dunnart), *Dasyurus hallucatus* (Northern Quoll), *Antechinus bellus* (Fawn

Antechinus), and *Tachyglossus aculeatus* (Short-Beaked Echidna). Water Buffalo (*Bubalus bubalis*), *Sus scrofa* (Feral Pigs), *Felis catus* (Feral Cats) and *Canis lupus dingo* (Dingoes) are also widespread across the study area, with the two former species building in numbers nearer to permanent and ephemeral water sources, causing a high degree of environmental damage.

Marine and freshwater fauna are extensively exploited within the study area. *Dugong dugon* (Dugong) occurs in limited numbers, grazing on the sea-grass beds. *Scylla serrata* (Mud Crabs) and *Thalassina anomola* (Mud Lobsters) are frequently caught around mangrove stands. Varieties of mollusc species are harvested, including Oysters (*Saccostrea* sp.), mangrove gastropods (*Telescopium telescopium* and *Terebralia* spp.) and the larger near-shore marine bivalves (notably *Anadara antiquata*, *Polymesoda (Geloina) coaxans*, and *Isognomon* species). Fish are an important component of the present-day diet, and species present include *Lates calcarifer* (Barramundi), *Scleropages leichardti* (Saratoga), several *Epinephelius* species (Cod) and a variety of Wrasse spp. Freshwater mussels are also gathered from the billabongs of the major river systems. Reptiles occurring within the study area include the *Crocodylus porosus* (Saltwater Crocodile), *Crocodylus johnstoni* (Freshwater Crocodile), *Varanus* species (Goanna), *Scincidae* species (Skinks), *Varanus indicus* (Mangrove Monitor), and various Marine Turtle species, Freshwater Tortoises, *Acrochordus* species (File Snakes), *Demansia* species (Whip Snakes) and Brown Snakes. Bird species occurring on the coasts and wetlands include *Anseronas semipalmata* (Magpie Geese), *Grus rubicunda* (Brolga), *Ephippiorhychus asiaticus* (Jabiru) and *Dromaius novaehollandiae* (Emu).

The seasonal availability of resources and seasonal mobility

As previously noted, present-day seasonal variations in the climate and structure of the physical environment have an impact on the seasonal range and distribution of resources found within the region. The structure of the economy in the recent past was therefore organised around the current climate and configuration of particular habitats. Based on this, early ethnographers working in northeast Arnhem Land, and across northern Australia, have generally characterised the economic structure as being a yearly round based on the seasonal availability of resources (e.g. Thomson 1939, 1949:16; McCarthy and McArthur 1960; Warner 1969:4). Referred to by Warner (1969:127–8) as a fission/fusion type of social organisation, in addition to differences in the exploitation of resources, group movements and group sizes were also regulated by the seasonal cycle. The ethnographic and historical records indicate that there were significant differences in dry and wet season resource exploitation. For example, as the dry season advanced and the grass dried, systematic burning of the landscape occurred, during which kangaroo, wallaby, goanna and snakes were hunted (McArthur 1960:113). By the time the burning of the grass had been completed, another phase in the cycle was reached, where groups of people followed the drying watercourses, exploiting fish, tortoises and snakes (Thomson 1949:17–9). The main food supply, except at restricted seasons of the year, was vegetable rather than animal, particularly *Cycas media* (Cycad), the Tall Spike Rush corm (particularly in coastal areas), several species of yam, taro and water lilies (Thomson 1949:21, 1983:103–5). Inland groups utilised Cycads (after processing to remove the poison) during the dry season, while in coastal areas the corms of the Tall Spike Rush (*Heliocharis sphacelata*), or rakai, formed the staple food. The rakai was important during the dry season, particularly in those areas subjected to periodic flooding with brackish water (Thomson 1949:15, 19–20, 1983:103–5).

The dry season appears to have provided two distinct possibilities: people could spread out into small family groups to exploit seasonally available, diversely spread resources; alternatively, large groups could come together for ceremonies, or to exploit a particularly abundant resource. As water levels fell in rivers and billabongs during the early dry season, people may have moved inland. Later in the year, when the swamps and wetland dried out, water chestnuts and cycads provided an abundant staple vegetable resource (Thomson 1949:19–20; Warner 1969:128; H. Morphy 1983:103–5, 2004:142). Freshwater swamps proved to be focal points, as they are immensely rich in terms of the density of resources during the mid to late dry season, but for much of the rest of the year they are inaccessible and inhospitable (Warner 1969:18; H. Morphy 2004:63). While the ethnographic record indicates that the main food supply, except at restricted seasons of the year, was vegetable rather than animal (Thomson 1949:21, 1983:103–5), during the wet season the estuarine reaches, tidal arms and flood plains yield large quantities of food, mostly fish, with shellfish collected in quantity from the mangrove zone (Thomson 1949:15, 19–20, 1983:103–5). During most wet seasons, large areas of eastern Arnhem Land become inaccessible due to flooding, and as a result, the wet season exerts a major influence on the seasonal mobility. At that time of year, people traditionally had to base themselves at semi-permanent, well-resourced camping places, often on the coastal margins. In addition to this, group size tended to be small due to the dispersal of the population into geographically restricted areas (Thomson 1949:16; Warner 1969:127; H. Morphy 2004:141).

It has been noted by a number of researchers that shellfish were primarily a wet season resource, as the wet season was a time of limited mobility and limited resource availability, with populations concentrating on the high sand ridges in the coastal zone (Bailey 1977; Cribb 1996:155; Meehan 1983; Peterson 1973). Cribb (1996:169) has characterised coastal wet season occupation, stating that wet season settlement was not continuous in any one campsite but rather moved up and down the coastline from one campsite to the next, with most campsites being unoccupied at any one time. Seasonal movements were therefore made in response to resource depletion, as well as conflict situations and ceremonial obligations. This interpretation of strictly seasonal shellfish use depends on a number of variables, such as the structure of the environment relating to species availability and habitat distribution, and the degree of regional inter- and intra-seasonal population mobility. An example of this is the contemporary pattern of seasonal resource exploitation that has been highlighted by Barber (2002:24–5). The residents of the Yilpara community maintain a stable presence in the coastal areas surrounding their outstation throughout the year, with the main variation in seasonal resource exploitation being the increased use of freshwater fish from billabongs and a reduced use of birds on the floodplains during the dry season (Barber 2002:25). This data is detailed in Table 2.3 and presented graphically in Figure 2.18. Another example is Meehan's (1983:3–5) study on the Blyth River region, related specifically to shellfish exploitation. This research highlighted that there was significant day-to-day, and seasonal, variation in the number of shellfish species collected and in the utilisation of specific habitats. During the late dry season (August to October), the inland shell beds lying in the mangroves and the bivalve species *Batissa violacea* were exploited. During the wet season (January to April), the sandy intertidal zones and the bivalve species *Marcia hiantina* were targeted (Meehan 1983:5). Much of this variation related to issues of specific shellfish species biology and ecology.

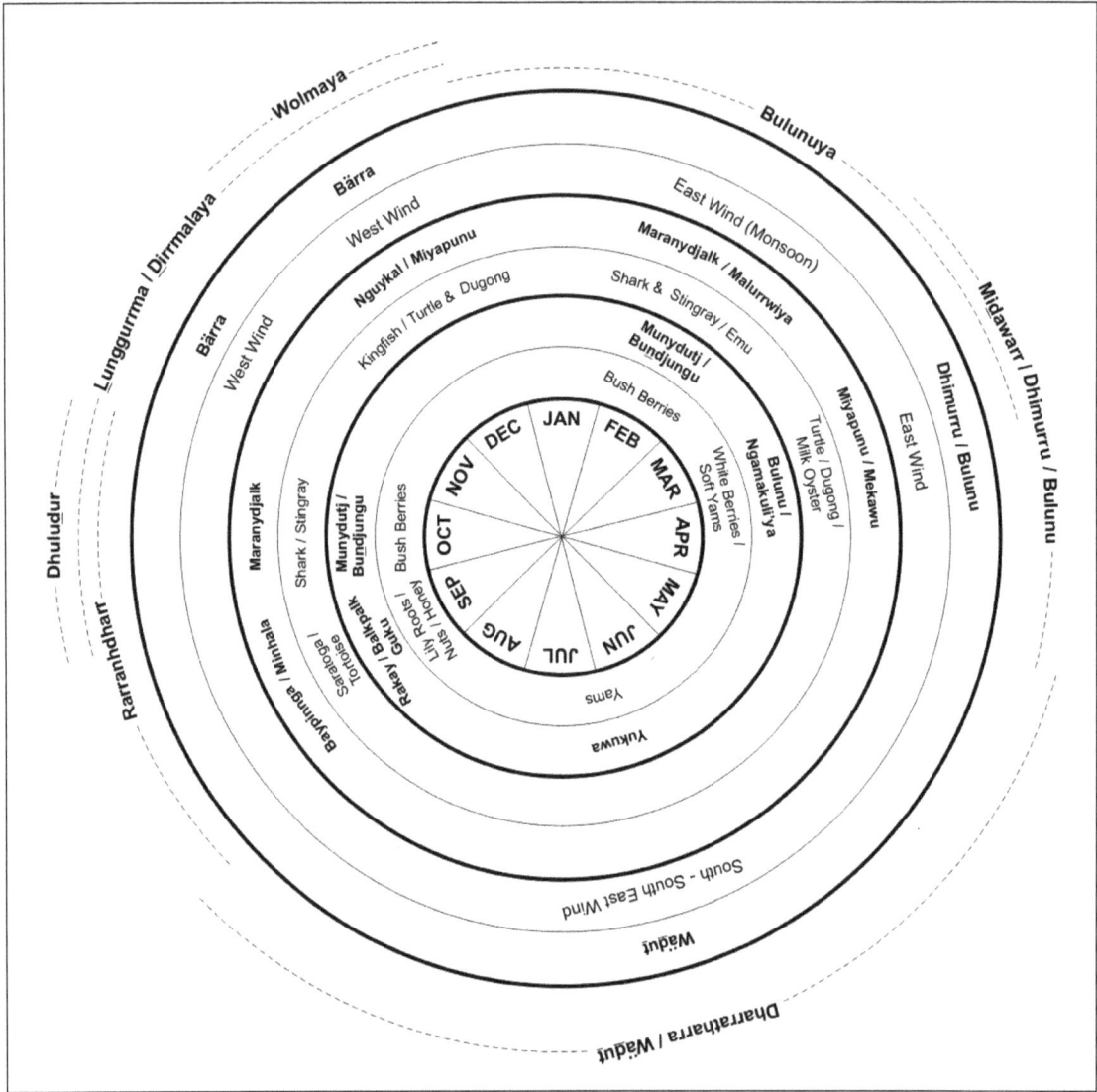

Figure 2.18: Diagrammatic representation of Yolngu seasonal calendar, northeast Arnhem Land from the data gathered by Marcus Barber contained in Table 2.3 (based on a similar diagram by Davis 1984 for a different area of Arnhem Land). The outermost ring represents the Yolngu name of the season, the next ring the name of the predominant wind of that season, and the inner rings are important resources available during that period. Yolngu words in bold are translated in the ring immediately below them.

Source: Barber 2005:90.

Table 2.3: Seasonal calendar from the Yolngu of Blue Mud Bay, northeast Arnhem Land. This table has been collated from information collected by Barber (2002) through direct observation and conversations with Djambawa Marawili and Ngulpurr Marawili.

Season	Wind	Description	Indicators	Food Available
Dhuludur (**October**)		The first rains come, and there is distant thunder and lightning	Bush berries (**munydutj** and *bundjungu*) are ready, indicating that the parrotfish is also becoming fat. Flowering plants signify that the livers of the shark and stingray (**maranydjalk**) are ready. These include the red flowering Kurrajong (**balwurr**), white sand lily (**wärrkarr**), and a creeper (wuluymung).	Bush berries (**munydutj** and **bundjungu**) Parrotfish Shark and stingray (**maranydjalk**)
Lunggurrma / Dirrmalaya (**October – December**)	**Bärra** – west wind (Dhuwa moiety)	The seas are calm and there is some new growth from the first rains, brought by **bärra**, the west wind.		
Wolmaya (**December**)	**Bärra** – west wind (Dhuwa moiety)	Lightning becomes much more prevalent, particularly in the evening after the afternoon clouds have built up. At first the lightning is silent, and the thunder is heard after a few weeks. This is kingfish (**nguykal**) season.	The weather is hot and the mosquitoes come out.	Kingfish (**nguykal**)
Bulunuya (**January – March**)	East wind (monsoon)	High wind season, and high tides during the full moon. There is lush growth from the rains, but the bush foods are not yet ready.	Yellow flowers show that the freshwater saratoga (**baypinnga**) are carrying eggs. Black berries appear on a palm tree at this time, signifying that the emus are fat. White flowers on the paperbark also signify this time. There are still some bush fruit of the early wet (**munydutj**) to be found, as well as other bush fruits such as **bundjungu**.	Saratoga - carrying eggs (**baypinnga**) Emu Bush fruit of the early wet (**munydutj**) Other bush fruits (**bundjungu**)
Midawarr / Dhimurru / Bulunu (**March – April**)	**Dhimurru/Bulunu** – east wind (Dhuwa moiety)	The season just after the wet when bush foods are ripe, animals are fat, seafood is plentiful, and the wind blows more softly from the east (**dhimurru**). It is a good time to hunt turtle and dugong.	The wattle tree flower that grows at this time tells Yolngu that it is the right time for milk oysters (**mekawu**), seagull eggs, and turtle eggs. The wind **dhimurru/bulunu** is associated with white berries called **bulunu** and sometimes the rains come when they are ripe.	Turtle, dugong milk oysters (**mekawu**) seagull eggs and turtle eggs. White berries (**bulunu**) soft yams (**ngamakuli'ya**)

Table 2.3 (continued): Seasonal calendar from the Yolngu of Blue Mud Bay, northeast Arnhem Land. This table has been collated from information collected by Barber (2002) through direct observation and conversations with Djambawa Marawili and Ngulpurr Marawili.

Season	Wind	Description	Indicators	Food Available
Dharratharra / Wädut (May – August)	Wädut - south south-east	Cold weather and rough seas with plenty of yams and bush food. **Wädut** is the name of the strong wind in this season, which flattens the grass, and the morning is sometimes foggy, caused by the bushfires lit in the dry grass. It is the time when all of the animals go into their holes, and Yolngu set bushfires (**worrk**) to burn off the undergrowth, making the holes easier to locate		Yams and bush food
Rarranhdharr (September – October)		The late dry season when it is hot, freshwater is becoming scarce, and some bush animals are getting thin. In the past, coastal Yolngu tended to head inland during this season, and built fish traps (**buyku'**) across the narrow creeks, taking advantage of the low water flow.	The stringybark blossoms signal wild honey, geese, **balkpalk** nuts, and an orange-red flowered bush with a nut inside (**dharranggulk**) are ready.	Freshwater fish and tortoises. Lily roots (**räkay**) and freshwater tortoises (**minhala**) can be found in the drying up mud. Magpie geese Wild honey, **balkpalk** nuts, and the orange-red flowered bush with a nut inside (**dharranggulk**) are ready.

Source: Barber 2002.

These patterns of seasonal resource availability and exploitation are a product of the contemporary climate, environmental structure and distribution of habitats. Based on the level of climatic and environmental variability noted within the region, there are a number of implications for the structure of the economy through time, particularly the structure of seasonal resource availability and exploitation. In fact, based on the data presented above, the patterns of resource availability and associated economic activity observed ethnographically may, at the most, relate only to the last 500 years. This hypothesis is particularly supported by the seasonal emphasis on those faunal and floral resources exploited from the freshwater wetlands. In effect, this knowledge system may only have emerged within the last 500 years with the disappearance of extensive sand and mud flats and the further development of the present extensive wetland systems via progradation. The implication of this is that the contemporary or historically recorded patterns of seasonal resource exploitation should not be automatically used to interpret the archaeological record from earlier time periods.

Implications of climatic/environmental change for human economic behaviour

Outlining the scale of environmental and climatic changes during the mid-to-late Holocene indicates that dramatic differences have occurred to the structure of the coastline itself, and in the distribution of the faunal and floral communities that comprised the resource base relative to the pattern detailed for the present. The extent of these changes has a number of temporal and spatial implications for human foraging economies during this time. In particular, it can be seen that analogies for mid-to-late Holocene resource exploitation derived from early ethnographic observations of economic activity during the recent past in northern Australia are problematic. The availability and abundance of key resources in coastal areas were tied to changes in the climate and of shoreline characteristics throughout the Holocene. Although it is possible that the coastal zone could support a permanent population base, seasonal factors, such as the availability and distribution of resources and high water levels, were limiting factors during the recent past (Peterson 1973; Bailey 1977; Cribb 1996:155). The interpretation of strictly seasonal resource use depends on a number of variables, such as the structure of the environment relating to species availability and habitat distribution, and the degree of regional inter- and intra-seasonal population mobility. Within the type of economic structure emphasised via ethnographic research, movements and group sizes were regulated by seasonal variations in the current climate and structure of the physical environment, and in turn, the seasonal range and distribution of resources (McArthur 1960:113; Warner 1969:127–8; Meehan 1983:3–5). When the degree of landscape and climatic changes occurring throughout the Holocene, and, by extension, variability in the distribution and abundance of key resources, are also taken into account, it is clear that it is inappropriate to project the historically observed model of mobility and resource exploitation onto the mid-to-late Holocene. Instead, it suggests that the structure of the economy during the mid-to-late Holocene was probably quite unlike that recorded ethnographically. Potentially, it could have supported a range of different group sizes and exploitation strategies, particularly as the timing and nature of sea level rise and regression, progradation and climatic shifts would ultimately have created differences in foraging behaviour across the study area.

For instance, the differential spatial and temporal distribution of resources relative to these physical aspects could potentially have lead to differences in the exploitation of some areas. This in turn would have affected levels of mobility and the types of activities carried out in different locations. These patterns may be reflected archaeologically in a number of ways. The intensity of use and the differential distribution of activities across the study area may be measured in terms of the number, density and morphology of sites relative to a number of landscape features. These features include possible changes to the coastline itself, as well as faunal resources, freshwater and stone outcrops. Water is generally viewed as one of the most important variables in the use of tropical areas, and occupation could be expected to concentrate around water sources. Tracking changes in faunal and floral communities is more difficult, largely due to the scale of physical landscape changes over time, however, changes in the distribution and abundance of various faunal resources could be established by identifying trends in species richness throughout the sites themselves. The distribution and availability of suitable stone sources should leave distinguishable evidence in the form of stone procurement, artefact manufacture and transportation. There is also the possibility in an area of low stone availability, like the Point Blane Peninsula, that provisioning from other sources may also have occurred. Based on the data provided here, the nature and timing of the climatic and landscape changes of the mid-to-late Holocene may have had a direct impact on the pattern of occupation and resource utilisation within the study area (contra Barker 1996, 2004). The types of resources and their distribution and density within the landscape were all potentially affected by the palaeoenvironmental processes previously discussed. This in turn would have affected how people distributed themselves across the landscape, and the kind of activities carried out in different locations.

3

Spatial and Chronological Patterns of Landscape Use and Resource Exploitation

Based on the broadly known climatic and environmental parameters for northern Australia and the Indo-Pacific region outlined earlier, and the implications these patterns have for variability in human economic behaviour, it is pertinent to examine the distribution, morphology and content of sites from survey data in order to assess human-environmental interactions. Of particular interest is the identification of those environmental factors that can determine the focal points for occupation and use of resources, and how this has been reflected in broad economic patterns across the study area. This analysis is separated into several sections that investigate the chronological and spatial patterning of the shell-dominated midden and mound deposits, and the distribution of stone artefacts across the Point Blane Peninsula. Assessing the distribution, morphology and content of archaeological sites in this way enables the identification of a higher level of behavioural variability than would be possible with one form of evidence alone. Combining these lines of evidence provides a relatively coarse-grained picture of economic activity in the area, and highlights those localities that merited further investigation in greater detail.

Field methodology

Survey design and implementation

Archaeological fieldwork was undertaken in the study area during 2000 (June to November), 2001 (July to October) and 2002 (July to October). The initial fieldwork strategy was one of guidance through the process of negotiation, consultation, and the familiarisation of the Yolngu living in the Yilpara community with the process of archaeological research. In keeping with the community-based nature of the research, a purposefully directed systematic sampling strategy, whereby survey units were selected based on community direction and personal judgement, was deemed most appropriate for investigating the unknown abundance, characteristics and visibility of the archaeological record in this area (Clarke 1994, 2002; Mitchell 1994a:174). Purposeful sampling is an effective step in defining previously unknown archaeological features of a region, is relatively cost-effective in contrast with random sampling strategies, and facilitates the discovery of highly clustered, small or uncommon elements within the landscape (Schiffer *et al.* 1978:5; Rhoads 1980:147; Redman 1987:251; Banning 2002:133). Given the relative environmental homogeneity of the study area, this survey strategy was considered appropriate given the research questions it was designed to address. A purposeful survey in this context provides an adequate sample for the identification of spatial and temporal trends in the distribution of archaeological material for the purposes of investigating the nature and variability of a regional *coastal* economy (e.g. Mitchell 1994a).

Long, thin survey units, or transects, were selected due to the ease of locating these units within the landscape, increasing the chance of site discovery, and enabling an investigation of site variability and density estimates in combination with ecological observations (Judge *et al.* 1975:88; Plog *et al.* 1978:401; Schiffer *et al.* 1978:11–2; Sundstrom 1993:93; Banning 2002:133, 154). Initial surveys were conducted on the margins of the peninsula through the direction of community members, with transects walked along approximately 22km of coastline in Myaoola Bay and 13km along the edges of the freshwater wetlands of the Durabudboi River in the Grindall Bay area. In order to gain an efficient estimation of non-clustered archaeological elements, bush tracks and roads were used to systematically survey across the peninsula, with a further 46km of transects surveyed in these areas (Figure 3.1). Tracks were used as survey transects as they enabled an example of all landscape zones within the study area to be inspected and, although highly variable, afforded higher ground surface visibility than would have normally been expected through more heavily vegetated areas (Schiffer *et al.* 1978:7). No graded or heavily eroded roads were surveyed, with all tracks surveyed having been formed by vehicle movement, with wheel rutting reaching a maximum depth of 5cm. Vegetation on tracks was generally low and sparse, with approximate ground surface visibility of 80 to 100% on the track itself. This level of visibility dropped to around 20 to 40% outside of the tyre tracks. These surveys covered the vehicle tracks themselves, as well as approximately 10m either side of the wheel ruts. Where possible, surveys were also conducted in recently burnt areas to take advantage of the increased visibility.

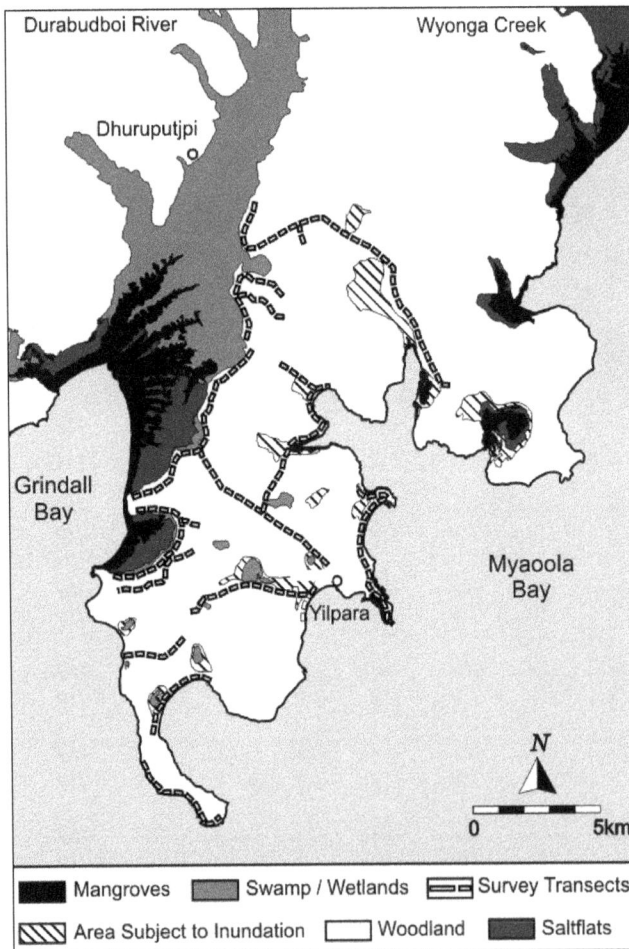

Figure 3.1: Survey transects locations on the Point Blane Peninsula.

Source: Based on Baniyala 1:50 000 Topographic Map.

Site definitions and recording

Sites are defined here by distinguishing those relatively dense, discrete concentrations of archaeological material from the sparsely distributed background or surrounding materials (Plog *et al.* 1978:389; Binford 1982:5). Concentrations of archaeological material that had merged, or where distinct site boundaries could not be identified (such as in large, composite mound sites), were classed as a single site (after Cribb 1996:160). For stone artefacts, it was decided that a single artefact should form the basis for the minimum recording unit (Thomas 1975; Foley 1981a; Dunnell and Dancey 1983:272; Holdaway *et al.* 1998).

Sites are classified following previous archaeological research in northern Australia (e.g. Clarke 1994; Mitchell 1994a; Bourke 2000) as:

- Shell Middens and Mounds: contain more than an estimated 50% weight or more of humanly deposited marine or freshwater molluscs. Middens often take the form of varying layers of shell over, or just below, the land surface. These deposits may also form as unstratified surface scatters, or as a thick mound of shell. In this case, shell deposits are classified as shell mounds if they were estimated to be greater than 30cm deep (Bowdler 1983:135; Sullivan 1989:49; Bourke 2000:60; see also variations proposed by Alexander 2009:74 and Morrison 2010:135).

- Stone Artefact Scatters and Quarries: contain flaked or ground stone artefacts (Hiscock and Mitchell 1993:27). Artefact scatters may occur as primarily surface scatters of material or as stratified deposits. No minimum number or density value of stone artefacts was set as the basis for recording according to the approach described above, with stone artefacts recorded across the study area either as isolated occurrences or in clusters. Following Hiscock and Mitchell (1993:21–22), quarries are defined as the location of a stone source, with or without evidence of procurement activities or extensive stoneworking (see also Ross *et al.* 2003).

- Macassan Site: refers mainly to Macassan Trepang processing sites, often located close to freshwater sources in sheltered bay areas. These sites characteristically contain stone lines for boiling the trepang, evidence of wells and smoke houses, Macassan pottery, glass, metal, shell (*Syrinx aruanus* and *Melo* species) and tamarind trees. Subsets of these features may occur within any given site (Macknight 1976:48–60; also Clarke 1994, 2000b; Mitchell 1994a, 1995, 1996).

The recording process included obtaining grid references with a hand-held Global Positioning System (GPS), taking the maximum and minimum dimensions of the site with a tape measure, noting the surrounding environmental features and landform associations, and characterising the types of cultural material present. An approximate percentage of ground surface visibility for the immediate area and the types of disturbance processes in operation were also noted (Sullivan 1989:51). A photographic record was made where possible, and where appropriate, the sites were mapped using a combination of dumpy level and tape and compass procedures (see Hobbs 1984; Sullivan 1984). All of the mound sites were mapped and cross-section measurements taken at the short (width) and long (length) axes using the dumpy level. Molluscan taxa were noted to identify the level of species richness and habitat selection across the study area, allowing for quantification and description of the variability in the dominant molluscan species exploited by people across time and space within the landscape.

Survey results

A total of 141 archaeological sites were recorded across the study area. The number and rank order of the different site types across the study area are shown in Table 3.1, with the distribution of sites by site type shown in Figure 3.2. Differences in the rank ordering of site types between the Myaoola and Grindall Bay areas suggests differences in the way in which these localities were occupied and variability in the intensity of resource exploitation. Of particular interest here is the dominance of larger shell mounds on Grindall Bay as opposed to the prevalence of lower lying-surface middens on Myaoola Bay. Chi-square results indicate that the Myaoola and Grindall Bay areas are significantly different in terms of the distribution of site types between the two bay areas ($\chi^2 = 55.44$, $d.f. = 4$, $p < 0.001$), suggesting that this is not a random pattern. Cramer's V, which indicates the strength of the association between the two variables, is 0.632.

Table 3.1: Number and rank order of site types within the study area.

Site Type	Total		Myaoola Bay		Grindall Bay	
	No.	Rank Order	No.	Rank Order	No.	Rank Order
Shell Mound	60	1	1	4	59	1
Shell Midden	56	2	31	1	25	2
Isolated Artefacts	14	3	1	4	13	3
Artefact Scatter	6	4	3	2	3	4
Shell Midden/Artefact Scatter	3	5	2	3	1	5
Macassan Site / Well	2	6	2	3	--	--
Total	141		40		101	

Very little archaeological material was recorded across the interior of the peninsula, and as such, the types of sites recorded are evidence of a pattern of landscape utilisation predominantly orientated towards the use of coastal resources. As the study area is a peninsula, the dominant resources, particularly in the past before the formation of the wetland areas, were located within the coastal zone. Shell mounds and middens are generally located in the landscape in areas where there are abundant and varied resources available along the coastline (Meehan 1982; Bailey 1993). Therefore, in the past, people would have primarily focussed on coastal and marine resources, a pattern similar to those found in other north Australian localities, like the Darwin region (Burns 1994, 1999; Bourke 2000:77). In these locations the dominant coastal site types are shell deposits, followed by smaller numbers of surface stone artefact scatters or isolated occurrences of artefacts. In fact, 85.6% of the sites recorded on the Point Blane Peninsula are deposits of marine shell, followed by artefact scatters and isolated artefacts, which make up 14.4%. Of the 139 sites presented above (excluding the Macassan site and the historic well), 38 are situated on the present-day coastline (27.3%), and 101 are located on the edges of the Dhuruputjpi freshwater wetland (an infilled former embayment) or significant seasonal swamps (72.7%).

The information presented in Table 3.1 also emphasises that, while shell deposits are the dominant archaeological site type regardless of location, variation does occur with the differential distribution of shell mounds and middens. When the middens and mounds are combined, they make up 84.2% of the Myaoola Bay and 83.2% of the Grindall Bay sites. With differentiation between shell mounds and middens, however, the mound sites dominate the margin of Grindall Bay at 58.4%, and only make up 2.6% of the sites located on the Myaoola Bay coastline. In comparison, the lower lying shell middens make up 24.8% of the Grindall Bay sites and 81.6% of the sites on Myaoola Bay respectively. This possibly reflects behavioural factors related to resource density within these different locations, the intensity of resource use and patterns of refuse discard. These apparent differences are drawn out to a greater extent in viewing the relationship between the chronological patterns, site distributions and the environmental features of the study area.

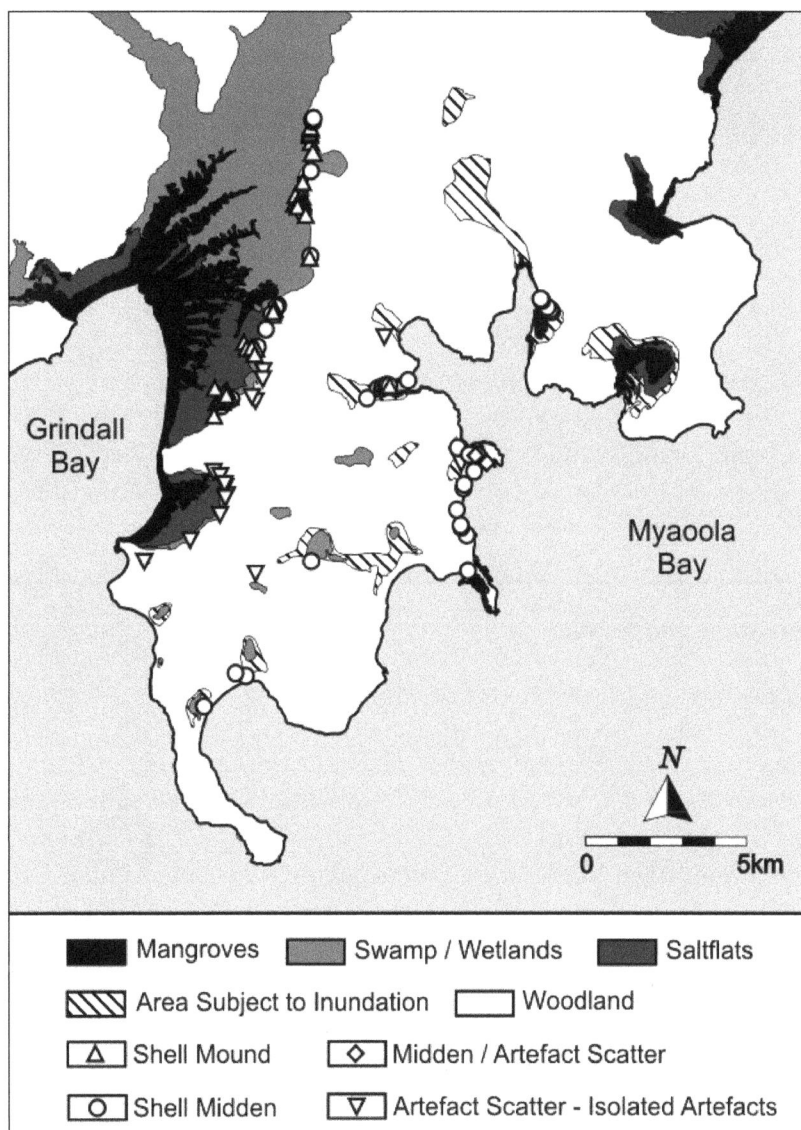

Figure 3.2: The distribution of sites on the Point Blane Peninsula by site type.

Source: Based on Baniyala 1:50 000 Topographic Map.

Chronology and changes in sea level

All of the radiocarbon dates from the midden and mounds sites in the study area were obtained from marine shell samples. All conventional radiocarbon ages were converted to calendar years using the CALIB (v6.1.1) calibration program (Stuiver and Reimer 1993). Those samples greater than 448 BP were calibrated using the marine04.14c calibration curve dataset (Hughen *et al.* 2004) with a ΔR correction value of 55±98 recommended for the Gulf of Carpentaria (Ulm 2006b). Following Telford *et al.* (2004) and Ulm *et al.* (2010b), median calibrated ages are presented here as they represent a central best-point estimate of the probability distribution for each calibrated date. Fifteen radiocarbon dates obtained from the surface of sites in the study area are listed in chronological order in Table 3.2.

Table 3.2: Surface radiocarbon age estimate ranges for sites across the Point Blane Peninsula.

Site Code	Site Type	Square	Excavation Unit	Depth (cm)	Lab Code	Sample	δ¹³C (*estimate)	¹⁴C Age (years BP)	1σ cal Age BP (68.3% probability)	2σ cal Age BP (95.4% probability)	Cal Age BP Median
BMB/084	Midden	Test Pit 1	1	0 - 1	ANU-11911	*M. hiantina*	0.0 ± 2.0*	122.3% ± 1.0%	Modern	Modern	--
BMB/116	Midden	Test Pit 1	1	0 - 1	ANU-12019	*A. antiquata*	0.0 ± 2.0*	650 ± 60	77–333	1#–426	225
BMB/003	Midden	Test Pit 1	1	0 - 5	ANU-11501	*M. hiantina*	0.2 ± 0.1	900 ± 50	336–549	274–640	461
BMB/036	Mound	N/A	--	Surface	ANU-12018	*A. granosa*	0.0 ± 2.0*	980 ± 130	389–667	239–847	526
BMB/045	Mound	Test Pit 1	1	0 - 2	ANU-11717	*A. granosa*	3.5 ± 0.2	990 ± 60	461–637	314–708	539
BMB/067b	Midden	Test Pit 1	1	0 - 2	Wk-17745	*A. granosa*	2.2 ± 0.2	1063 ± 35	511–661	433–773	592
BMB/061	Midden	Test Pit 1	1	0 - 4	ANU-11720	*A. granosa*	4.6 ± 0.2	1510 ± 50	900–1137	776–1243	1009
BMB/067a	Midden	Test Pit 1	1	1 - 5	ANU-11715	*A. granosa*	3.0 ± 0.2	1620 ± 80	992–1247	856–1367	1115
BMB/071	Mound	Test Pit 1	1	0 - 3	ANU-11722	*A. granosa*	2.9 ± 0.2	1700 ± 60	1067–1299	936–1412	1192
BMB/052	Mound	N/A	--	Surface	Wk-17744	*A. granosa*	-3.3 ± 0.2	1763 ± 37	1152–1367	1039–1496	1258
BMB/101	Mound	N/A	--	Surface	ANU-11894	*A. granosa*	0.0 ± 2.0*	2010 ± 80	1369–1657	1269–1809	1518
BMB/093	Mound	N/A	--	Surface	ANU-11893	*A. granosa*	0.0 ± 2.0*	2240 ± 80	1617–1924	1485–2101	1779
BMB/082	Mound	N/A	--	Surface	ANU-11892	*A. granosa*	0.0 ± 2.0*	2340 ± 70	1747–2047	1591–2210	1900
BMB/029	Mound	Test Pit 1	1	0 - 3	ANU-11496	*A. granosa*	-3.4 ± 0.1	2410 ± 50	1850–2120	1728–2279	1985
BMB/033	Mound	N/A	--	Surface	ANU-12017	*A. granosa*	0.0 ± 2.0*	2540 ± 60	2010–2290	1853–2420	2140

Note: # are suspect due to impingement on the end of the calibration data set.

Source: Calibration data from CALIB 6.1.1, marine04.14c (Hughen *et al.* 2004), ΔR = 55±98 (Ulm 2006b).

The distribution of the 15 sites from which these radiocarbon determinations have been obtained from surface samples is shown in Figure 3.3, and the one and two sigma calibrated radiocarbon ages graphed in Figure 3.4. These dates demonstrate a late Holocene sequence of occupation within the study area, ranging from 2140 cal BP to the present for the surface samples. This range of dates conforms well to the patterning of radiocarbon dates established from other coastal areas of northern Australia (for example Beaton 1985; Roberts 1991; Mitchell 1993, 1994a; Bourke 2000), where the occupation of open sites rarely extends beyond approximately 3000 BP. This chronological pattern also relates strongly to discussions regarding the potential for a time lag between sea level rise and stabilisation and the appearance of open coastal sites (for example Beaton 1985; Bourke 2000, 2003). The sea level data for the Gulf of Carpentaria region presented in Figure 2.10 indicates that sea level rise was relatively rapid throughout the early to mid Holocene. The reconstruction of past shorelines, although speculative in nature and associated with a degree of error, has proved to be a useful tool in assessing the use of coastal areas relative to sea levels and associated changes in the physical landscape (e.g. Shackleton and van Andel 1986; Shackleton 1988; Bailey and Craighead 2003). While such studies have focussed on long occupation sequences in caves or rockshelters relative to late-Pleistocene sea level patterns, the same approach may be applied here.

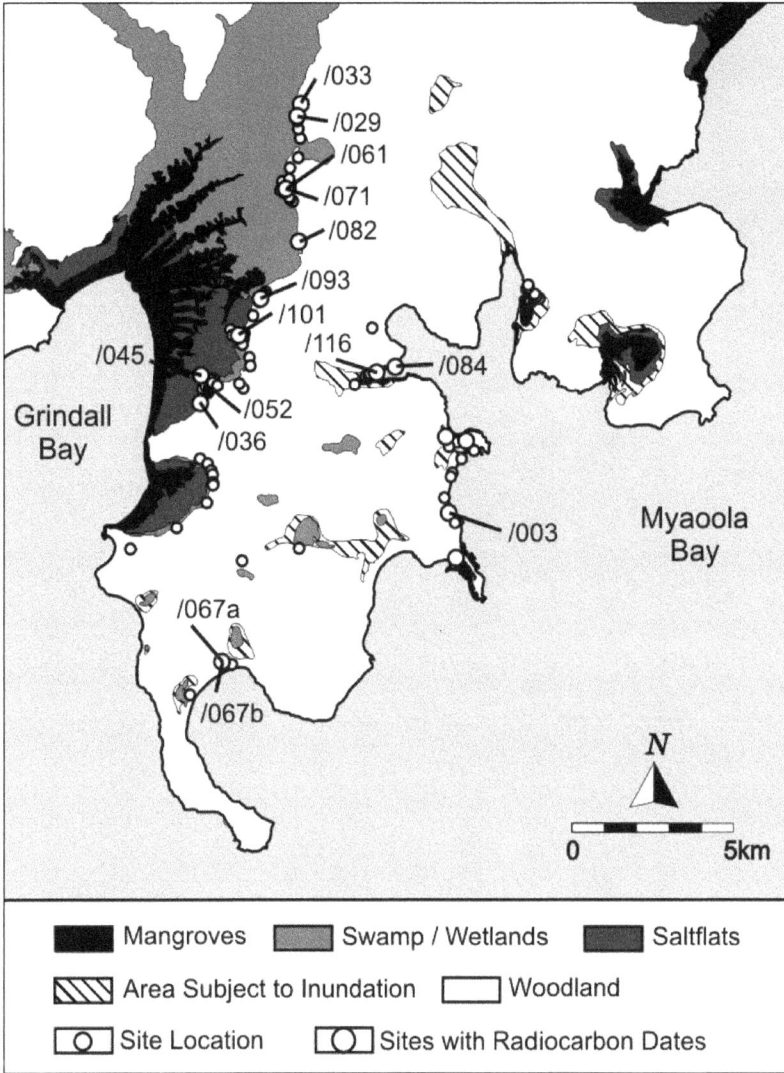

Figure 3.3: Location of sites on the Point Blane Peninsula with radiocarbon determinations obtained from surface samples.

Source: Based on Baniyala 1:50 000 Topographic Map.

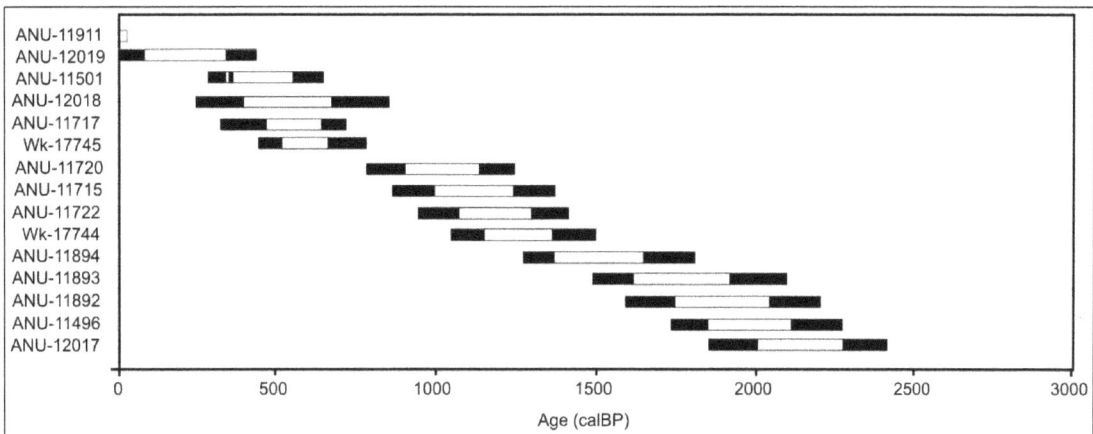

Figure 3.4: Calibrated radiocarbon age estimates (1 and 2σ) from surface samples across the Point Blane Peninsula.

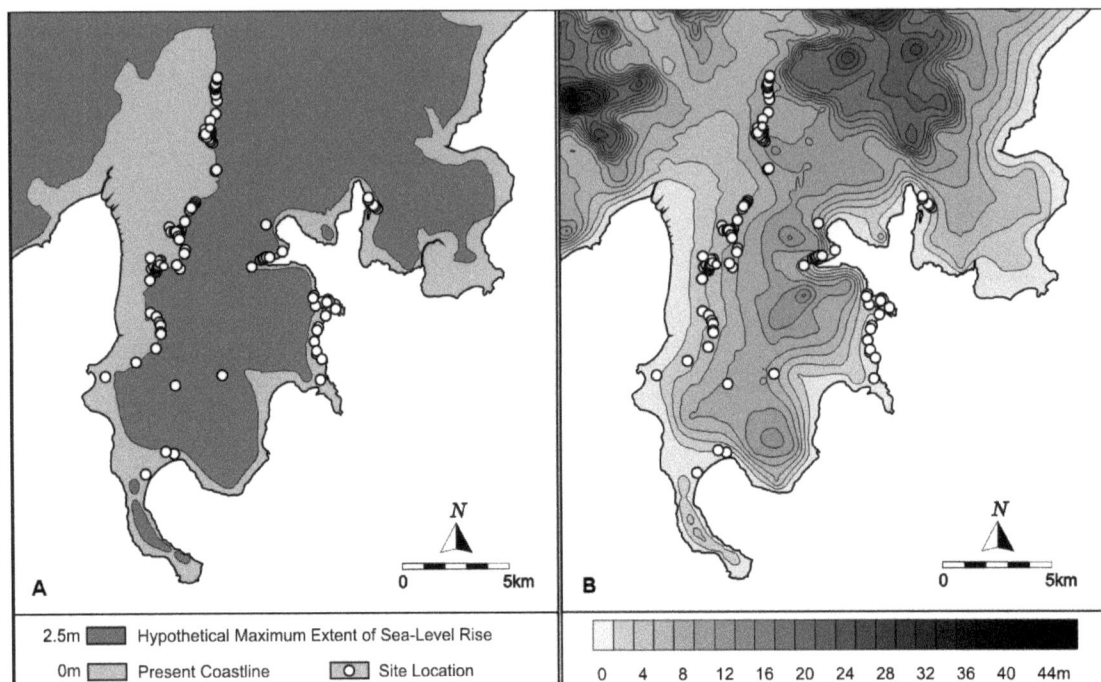

Figure 3.5: (A) Site location relative to the present and hypothetical maximum extent of sea levels; (B) Site location plotted against height above present sea level (2m contour interval) and present coastline (0m).

Source: Based on Baniyala 1:50 000 Topographic Map.

The hypothetical maximum extent of sea level for the Point Blane Peninsula at 2.5m above present, although theoretical in nature, has been calculated based on the sea level curve for the Gulf of Carpentaria, relative to contour height data across the study area and the distribution of older and/or more stable land surfaces. This highlights the distribution of sites relative to the position of the coastline over time, as well as associated landscape alterations. It is apparent that sea level rise would have dramatically affected the physical characteristics of the coastline. An example of this is the prograded Dhuruputjpi wetlands system, which approximately 5000 years ago was a sheltered, shallow embayment. Figure 3.5A presents the distribution of sites relative to present sea level and an approximate maximum sea level height above present. This demonstrates that, with the exception of two sites located within the southern-central area of the peninsula, all of the sites in the study area fall along or below the hypothetical shoreline at the maximum sea level highstand of 2.5m above present. This distribution, combined with the calibrated radiocarbon age range across the peninsula, suggests that the open sites recorded in the area began to be deposited as sea levels were probably receding in conjunction with changes to the landscape via progradation and beach ridge formation, some 2000 years after maximum sea levels were reached (Cotter 1996:200).

To evaluate general processes associated with late Holocene coastal landscape alteration relative to the chronological pattern discussed above, height above sea level and distance to present coastline are used to assess the total distribution of sites by Myaoola or Grindall Bay locality. Height above sea level has been measured according to the nearest 0.5m contour, and the sites grouped within 2m contour intervals for comparison. Distance to coastline has been measured as the shortest straight-line distance between the site and the shoreline. In this case, the sites have been grouped according to 2km distance intervals. The distribution of sites plotted against the 2m contour intervals and relative to present shoreline is mapped in Figure 3.5B. The number and percentage of sites by the 2km distance to present coastline units is presented in Table 3.3. The data are ordered by the total number of sites across the peninsula, as well as being separated by site location into the Grindall and Myaoola Bay areas. In these two areas, the frequency of sites by distance unit is expressed as a percentage of the total number of sites across the peninsula.

Table 3.3: The number and percentage of sites by distance to present coastline relative to all sites.

Distance to	Total		Myaoola Bay		Grindall Bay	
Present Coastline	No. Sites	%	No. Sites	%	No. Sites	%
0 to 2 kilometres	68	48.92	38	27.34	30	21.58
2 to 4 kilometres	32	23.02	0	0.00	32	23.02
4 to 6 kilometres	28	20.14	0	0.00	28	20.14
6 to 8 kilometres	11	7.91	0	0.00	11	7.91
Total	**139**		**38**		**101**	

The site to coastline distance for all sites ranges from 0 to 8km, with 48.9% of sites falling within 2km of the present shoreline, and 71.9 and 92.1% within 4km and 6km respectively. Although a pattern of sites clustering closer to the present coastline would be expected of an archaeological record dominated by shell deposits, the pattern varies dramatically when separated by broad locality. All of the Myaoola Bay sites are situated within 2km of the present shoreline. This contrasts sharply with the Grindall Bay sites, with little difference in percentages between the 2km, 4km and 6km distance intervals. The frequency of sites only tails off between 6 and 8km from the coast. Again, this reflects differential landscape processes between the two peninsula localities. This is also reflected in a comparison of site location relative to height above sea level, with this data presented in Table 3.4. The data are ordered in a similar fashion, by the total number of sites across the peninsula, and by the sites situated in Myaoola and Grindall Bays. In this case, 2m height intervals are used to group the sites.

Table 3.4: The number and percentage of sites by height above sea level interval relative to all sites.

Relative Height	Total		Myaoola Bay		Grindall Bay	
Above Sea level	No. Sites	%	No. Sites	%	No. Sites	%
0 to 2 metres	29	20.86	28	20.14	1	0.72
2 to 4 metres	26	18.71	8	5.76	18	12.95
4 to 6 metres	38	27.34	1	0.72	37	26.62
6 to 10 metres	46	33.09	1	0.72	45	32.37
Totals	**139**		**38**		**101**	

All of the sites fall within a height of 10m above present sea level. Unlike the distance to shoreline data, there is no clear patterning in the frequency of total sites within these height intervals. These data only begin to make sense when comparing the frequency of sites within these height intervals between the Myaoola and Grindall Bay. To investigate whether the Myaoola and Grindall Bay areas differ in the number of sites by height above sea level interval, a chi-square statistic was used. The results indicate that these areas are significantly different in terms of the distribution of sites by height above sea level (χ^2 = 97.74, *d.f.* = 3, *p* < 0.001), suggesting that this is not a random pattern. Cramer's V (0.839) indicates a very strong association between the two variables. The Myaoola Bay sites follow the type of pattern that would be expected in this area given the sea level data and chronological patterns. That is, sites are densely clustered within 2m height above sea level (approximately 75%), then decrease rapidly in number with increasing height. No sites in this area occur beyond 8m above sea level. In contrast, there appears to be little patterning in the frequency of sites per height above sea level interval along Grindall Bay, although the majority of sites in this area are more densely clustered within the 4 to 6m and 8 to 10m height intervals. These contrasting patterns in site location relative to the present coastline and topography across the peninsula suggest differential processes of landscape changes acting within each broad locality. In order to draw this pattern out more fully, however, the strength of the relationship between distance to coastline and height above sea level within these two areas must also be investigated. This enables the relationship between the general topography of the area to be evaluated relative to changes in sea level.

Figure 3.6A presents a scatterplot of the distance to present coastline (km) by height above sea level for all sites located on Myaoola Bay. This suggests that in this area the overall trend is for distance to coast to increase with height above sea level, with the relationship between these variables being moderately strong (Pearson's $r = 0.634$, $r^2 = 0.402$, $p < 0.01$, $n = 38$). It is expected for these site and environmental variables to relate reasonably strongly in this context, as sea levels dropped and physical changes occurred to the coastline with time, older sites would be located higher and further from the present day coastline. The significance of this relationship is, however, only moderate, as evidenced by the r^2 value of 0.402, which indicates a high degree of data dispersion. This pattern may relate to the physical characteristics of this part of the coast, as topographically this area shows significant changes within short distances from the shoreline. The vast majority of Myaoola Bay sites fall within 500m of the shoreline, and within this distance, height above sea level varies between 0.5m and 4m for all but two of the sites. While height above sea level may not correspond significantly with the age of sites in this area, largely due to processes of beach ridge development relative to the variable topography of the coastline, distance from shore is a significant factor relative to the chronological patterns. As a comparison, the scatterplot presented in Figure 3.6B shows distance to coastline plotted against height above sea level for the Grindall Bay sites. In this case the trend for distance to coast to increase with height above sea level stronger. The correlation coefficients (Pearson's $r = 0.920$, $r^2 = 0.846$, $p < 0.001$, $n = 101$) suggest that the relationship between these variables is both strong and significant.

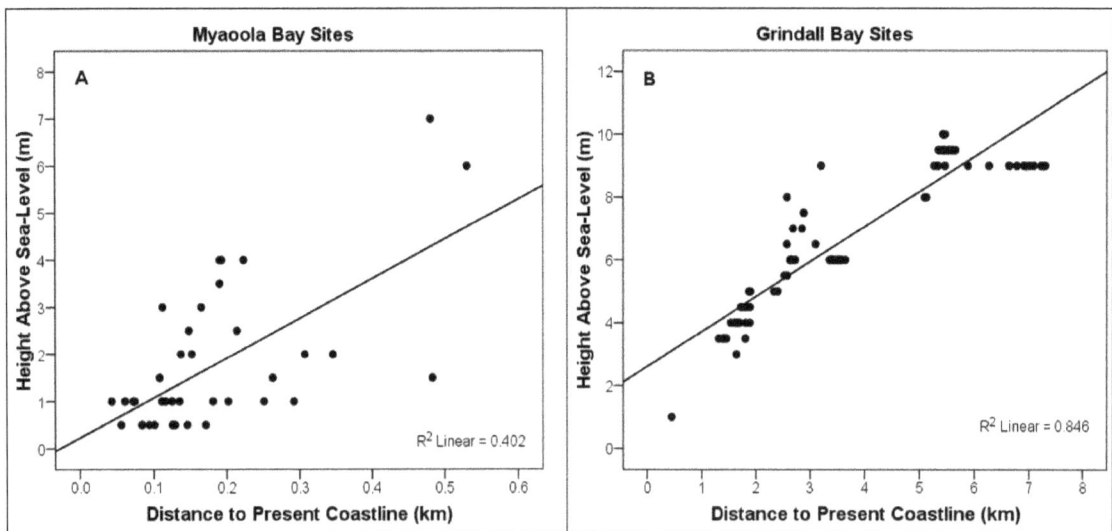

Figure 3.6: Distance to present coastline plotted against height above present sea level for (A) Myaoola Bay and (B) Grindall Bay.

This pattern again relates to the topography of this particular area relative to sea level rise and the stability of the dominant land-surfaces. With increasing distance from the coastline, the landscape rises quickly as it moves away from the relatively low-lying coastal plain. The fact that this relationship is stronger in Grindall Bay compared with Myaoola Bay suggests that different processes have affected site location relative to these variables. This pattern again relates to the physical characteristics of this area, with the majority of the Grindall Bay sites being situated along the laterite ridge that forms the rough extent of maximum sea level rise in this area. The height of this ridge above the wetlands or saltflats varies with distance away from the modern coastline, but in general terms, height above sea level increases as the ridge extends northwards away from the coast (see Figure 3.5A). Over time, as sea levels gradually retreated and sedimentation increased in this embayment, the general trend was for occupation to follow the retreating resource base corresponding to progradation in the bay. The main differences in the location of sites in the study area lie between the eastern and western bays. This is primarily a function of slow sea level regression and differential landscape changes in these areas. This is most likely related to processes of successive beach-ridge development and seaward sedimentation on the largely unprotected coast of Myaoola Bay in the east, and the gradual progradation and wetland formation within the large sheltered embayment on the western margin.

Resource exploitation

Distance to sources of freshwater

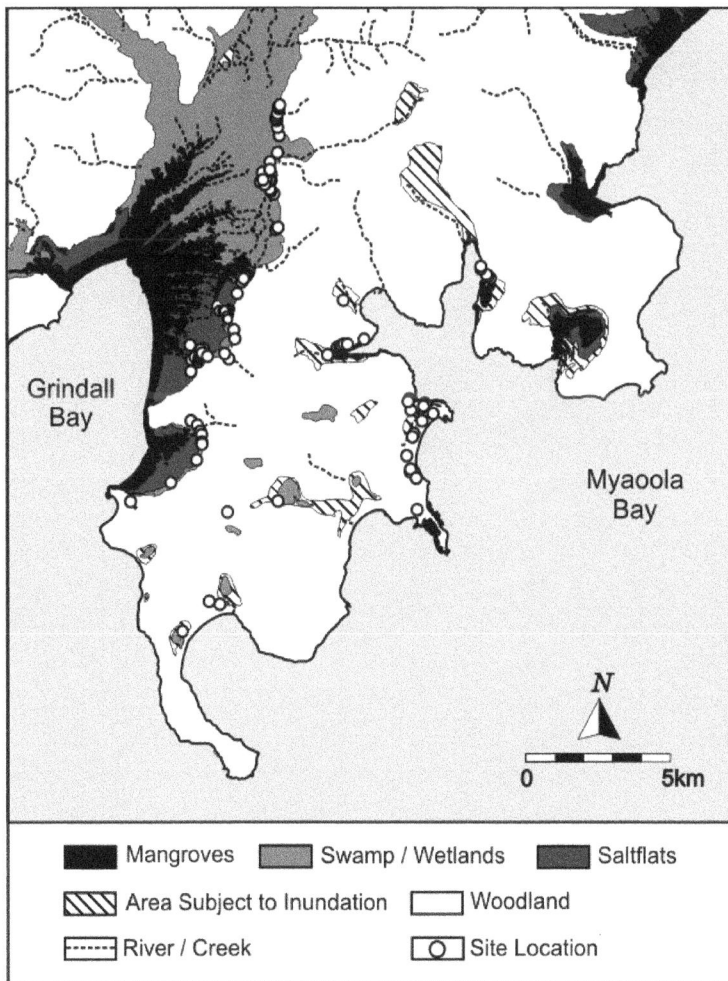

Figure 3.7: The distribution of all sites relative to sources of freshwater.

Source: Based on Baniyala 1:50 000 Topographic Map and Water Resources of North Eastern Arnhem Land Mapsheet.

Sources of reliable, seasonal freshwater are well distributed across the Point Blane Peninsula. Rivers and creeks, such as the Durabudboi River and Wyonga Creek, feed into the many freshwater wetlands, smaller swamps and billabongs in the area. Both watercourses have large catchment areas, resulting in larger amounts of rainfall runoff and river flow over the wet season (Haines *et al.* 1999:1–2, Zaar *et al.* 1999:19–20), with a correlation between the amount of annual wet season rainfall and the availability of both surface and sub-surface water sources throughout the year. Higher rainfall results in higher water table levels and greater spring flows. Even taking into account annual wet season variation in rainfall, this area is a seasonally well-watered landscape. This is apparent in Figure 3.7, which shows the distribution of sites in relation to sources of freshwater.

While the large freshwater wetlands serve as a relatively reliable source of seasonal freshwater at present, this would not have always been the case as they formed subsequent to sea level rise, coastline stabilisation and ongoing processes of progradation. To gain an idea of the location of sites relative to freshwater sources, those creek-lines draining the interior of the peninsula and the lower-lying areas subject to higher levels of inundation have been used. The shortest distance in kilometres from these areas to each site has been taken as the minimum distance to freshwater. The sites have then been grouped according to 200m distance intervals as an indication of occupation density relative to these water sources. The number and percentage of sites within these distance intervals is shown in Table 3.5, and the percentages graphed in Figure 3.8.

Table 3.5: The number and percentage of sites by minimum distance to water interval.

Minimum Distance to Water	No. of Sites	% of Sites
0.0 to 0.2 kilometres	111	79.86
0.2 to 0.4 kilometres	20	14.39
0.4 to 0.6 kilometres	3	2.16
0.6 to 0.8 kilometres	0	0.00
0.8 to 1.0 kilometres	1	0.72
1.0 to 1.2 kilometres	1	0.72
1.2 to 1.4 kilometres	2	1.44
1.4 to 1.6 kilometres	1	0.72
Total Sites	**139**	

While this pattern would at first appear to be significant, with approximately 80% of sites located within 200m of freshwater, all sites on the peninsula are located within 2km of a water source. These site density estimates, combined with Figure 3.7, suggests that water may not be an overriding factor in site location. Although undoubtedly an important and necessary resource in this environment, on the margins of the peninsula freshwater was relatively easily accessible from every location surveyed. As the distribution of sites in the area suggests a higher concentration of activity within embayments (Figure 3.7), in economic terms the distribution of sites may relate more to other factors, such as shoreline changes from maximum sea levels to the present, and the effect of this process on the dispersal of suitable habitats containing exploitable food resources.

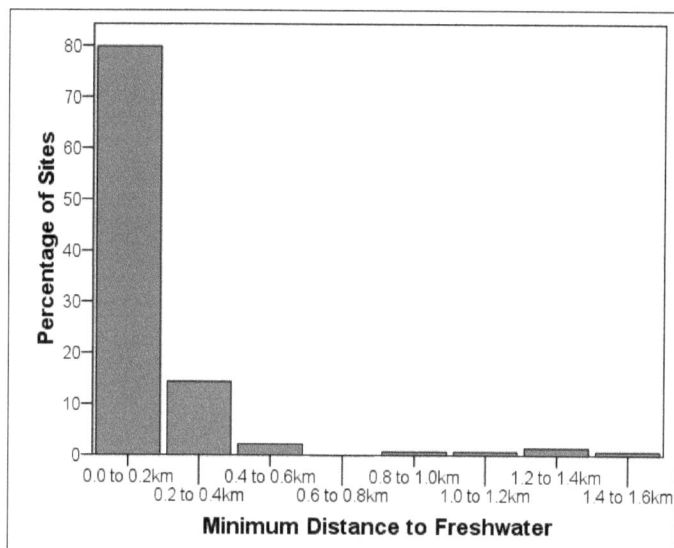

Figure 3.8: The percentage of sites by minimum distance to water interval.

Molluscan species and habitat exploitation

As noted by Bailey and Craighead (2003:176), sea level rise to maximum and subsequent slow regression to present would have had an effect on the nature of the available near-shore habitats, and therefore the differential availability and abundance of molluscan taxa. As a result, the range of taxa and habitats exploited across the peninsula should vary relative to the sea level rise and landscape alteration processes described above. Table 3.6 lists the 30 molluscan species identified on the surface of all sites across the peninsula by family, taxon and their respective habitats. In terms of the available species and habitats exploited within the study area, this list should be viewed as the minimum range, as this relies on the identification of macro remains under trying field conditions. Those species currently exploited (as listed in Chapter 2), albeit in very low numbers at present, are also indicated. Contemporary patterns of molluscan exploitation indicate a limited focus on this resource, where the harvesting of molluscs is limited to only six taxa (Barber 2002, 2005). In comparison, the range of molluscan taxa identified from the archaeological sites in the area suggests that the intensity and diversity of molluscan exploitation was much greater in the past. The number and percentage of sites containing the relevant molluscan species detailed in Table 3.6 is presented in Table 3.7. The taxa have been rank ordered according to the percentages of the total number of sites. This allows for an easy comparison with the percentages of sites in the Myaoola and Grindall Bay locations.

Table 3.6: Molluscan species identified on the surface of the sites and their habitat.

Family	Taxon	Habitat
Arcidae	*Barbatia* sp.	Rock/Debris in Littoral Area, Coral Reefs
	Anadara granosa	Littoral Sand and Mud (Intertidal/marginally subtidal)
	Anadara antiquata*	Littoral Sand and Mud (Intertidal/marginally subtidal)
Chamidae	*Chama* sp.	Coral, Rock, or Shell Debris
Chitonidae	Chitonidae f.	Upper Intertidal to Shallow Sub-tidal
Corbiculidae	*Polymesoda (Geloina) coaxans**	Coastal Rivers, Streams and Estuaries
Ellobiidea	*Cassidula angulata*	Mangroves (*Rhizophora, Bruguiera*) / Mud
Isognomonidae	*Isognomon isognomon**	Mangroves to Under rocks in Shallow Water
Mactridae	*Mactra abbreviata*	Littoral Sand
Melongenidae	*Syrinx aruanus*	Sand and Mud in Shallow Water
	Volema cochlidium	Sand and Mud in Shallow Water
Mytilidae	*Modiolus* sp.	Sand and Mud in Shallow Water – Estuaries
	Septifer bilocularis	Attached to Rocks or Debris
Neritidae	*Nerita* sp.	Mangrove Roots / Rocks
Ostreidae	Ostreidae f.*	Mangrove Roots / Rock / Debris in Sub-tidal Areas
Pinnidae	*Pinna bicolor*	Littoral Sand / Seagrass Beds
Placunidae	*Placuna placenta*	Surface of Mud / Mangroves
Potamididae	*Cerithidea* sp.	Shallow Mud / Mangroves Roots (*Avicennia, Bruguiera*)
	Terebralia sp.*	Mangroves (*Avicennia, Bruguiera*, Ceriops)
	Telescopium telescopium*	Mangroves (*Rhizophora*)
Pteriidae	*Pinctada* sp.	Attached to Substrate in Intertidal / Sub-tidal Areas
Tellinidae	*Tellina* sp.	Littoral Sand and Muds
Trochidae	*Monodonta labio*	Shallow Water
	Tectus pyramis	Shallow Water
Turbinidae	*Turbo cinereus*	Shallow Water
Veneridae	*Gafrarium tumidum*	Littoral Muddy Sand
	Marcia hiantina	Littoral Sand
	Dosinia mira	Littoral Sand
	Placamen calophyllum	Littoral Sand
Volutidae	*Melo amphora*	Lower Intertidal and Sub-tidal Sand / Mud

Note: * indicates those species currently exploited in the study area.

Source: After Meehan 1982; Short and Potter 1987; Wells and Bryce 1988; Lamprell and Whitehead 1992; Lamprell and Healy 1998.

Table 3.7: The number and percentage of sites containing molluscan species by broad locality.

Molluscan Taxa	Total		Myaoola Bay		Grindall Bay	
	# Sites	%	# Sites	%	# Sites	%
Anadara granosa	96	80.67	15	44.12	81	95.29
Polymesoda (Geloina) coaxans	61	51.26	20	58.82	41	48.24
Marcia hiantina	61	51.26	31	91.18	30	35.29
Mactra abbreviata	56	47.06	0	0.00	56	65.88
Telescopium telescopium	51	42.86	9	26.47	42	49.41
Ostreidae f.	47	39.50	17	50.00	30	35.29
Placuna placenta	44	36.97	0	0.00	44	51.76
Terebralia sp.	33	27.73	25	73.53	8	9.41
Isognomon isognomon	27	22.69	23	67.65	4	4.71
Nerita sp.	22	18.49	14	41.18	8	9.41
Cerithidea sp.	21	17.65	10	29.41	11	12.94
Anadara antiquata	21	17.65	15	44.12	6	7.06
Septifer bilocularis	21	17.65	20	58.82	1	1.18
Gafrarium tumidum	19	15.97	17	50.00	2	2.35
Cassidula angulata	15	12.61	0	0.00	15	17.65
Dosinia mira	10	8.40	6	17.65	4	4.71
Pinctada sp.	10	8.40	8	23.53	2	2.35
Syrinx aruanus	9	7.56	7	20.59	2	2.35
Modiolus sp.	6	5.04	4	11.76	2	2.35
Volema cochlidium	5	4.20	3	8.82	2	2.35
Melo amphora	4	3.36	1	2.94	3	3.53
Monodonta labio	4	3.36	2	5.88	2	2.35
Tellina sp.	4	3.36	3	8.82	1	1.18
Barbatia sp.	3	2.52	3	8.82	0	0.00
Pinna bicolor	3	2.52	3	8.82	0	0.00
Tectus pyramis	3	2.52	3	8.82	0	0.00
Turbo cinereus	3	2.52	3	8.82	0	0.00
Chitonidae f.	2	1.68	2	5.88	0	0.00
Placamen calophyllum	1	0.84	0	0.00	1	1.18
Chama sp.	1	0.84	1	2.94	0	0.00

These data show that molluscan species distribution is quite variable between these landscape categories. As this table is reasonably complex to interpret, site percentages for the three categories have been graphed in Figure 3.9. This shows that, depending on the species, the observed differences in the frequency of sites containing various species relates to the distribution of the resource base across the study area. The differential availability of resources across the study area reflects the diversity of environmental conditions and the differential distribution of molluscan habitats, as well as the processes of climatic and landscape alteration of the mid-to-late Holocene. Therefore, some species may have been more abundant, and by extension more heavily exploited, on Myaoola Bay, such as *Anadara antiquata*, *Gafrarium tumidum*, *Marcia hiantina*, *Polymesoda (Geloina) coaxans*, *Septifer bilocularis*, *Isognomon isognomon*, Ostreidae species and *Terebralia palustris*. Other species, such as *Anadara granosa*, *Mactra abbreviata*, *Placuna placenta* and *Telescopium telescopium*, by contrast, are more abundant in those sites concentrated on the margins of Grindall Bay.

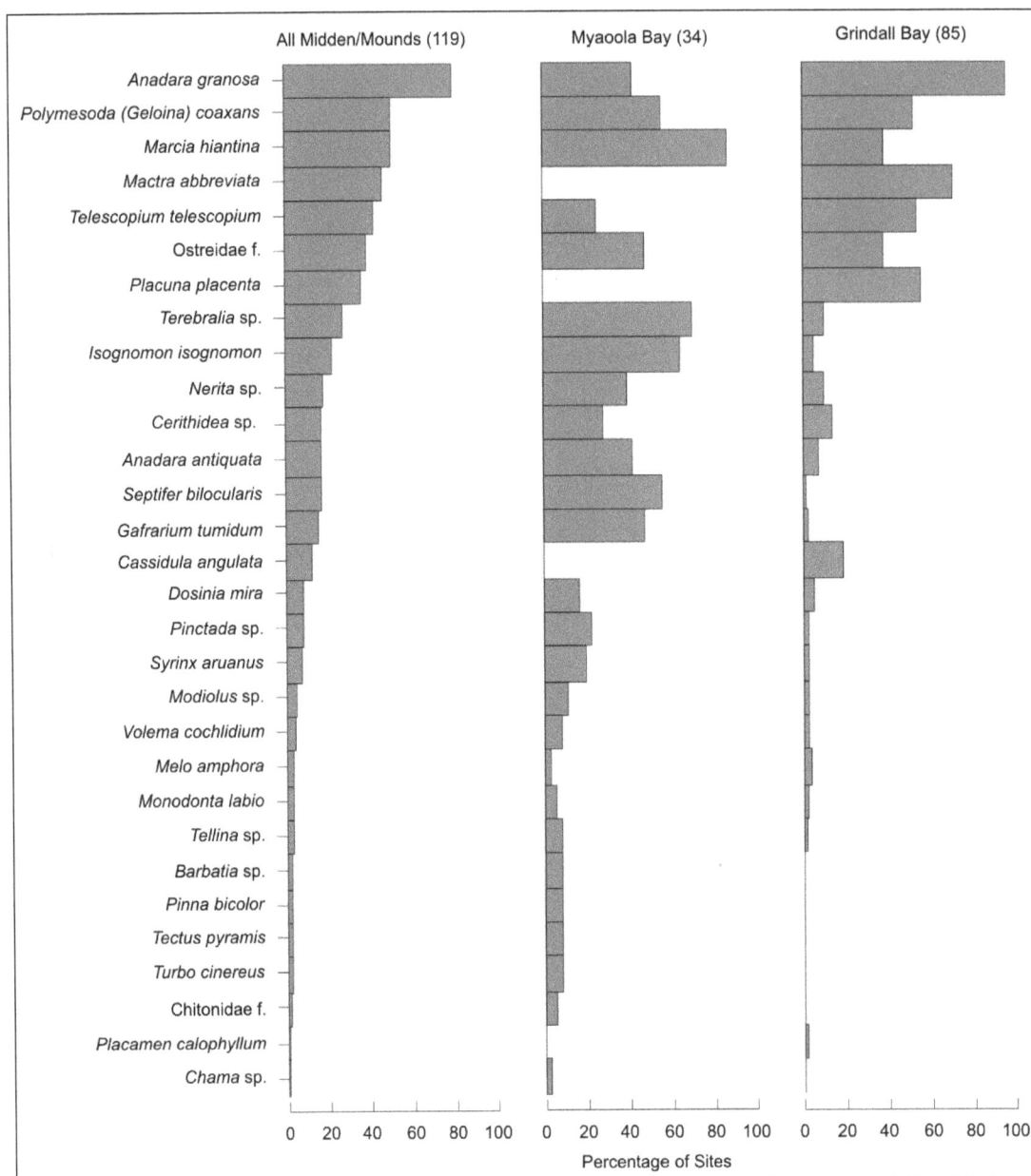

Figure 3.9: The percentage of sites containing molluscan species by the total number of sites and broad locality.

These data also suggest that the Myaoola Bay sites reflect a higher level of species richness compared to the Grindall Bay sites. This is investigated further by comparing the number of molluscan taxa as an indicator of species richness within each site across the peninsula (e.g. Magurran 1988; Broughton and Grayson 1993). Figure 3.10 maps the number of taxa per site across the Point Blane Peninsula, with an extrapolated contour interval of two molluscan species. This provides a general indication of the way that species richness varies between the sites on the margins of the peninsula. It further emphasises the earlier point that embayments, or currently infilled former embayments, were focal points for economic activity in the study area, possibly related to the density of molluscan resources. While it is difficult to draw out specific patterning in species richness from this figure, it does show that the number of species contained within the sites on the western margin is reasonably consistent. The Myaoola Bay sites show quite a different pattern, one where species richness appears to be generally greater and where there are concentrated patches of higher species richness in particular areas. This contrasting pattern of species richness is further investigated below, with descriptive statistics presented in Table 3.8 for the Myaoola and Grindall Bay sites.

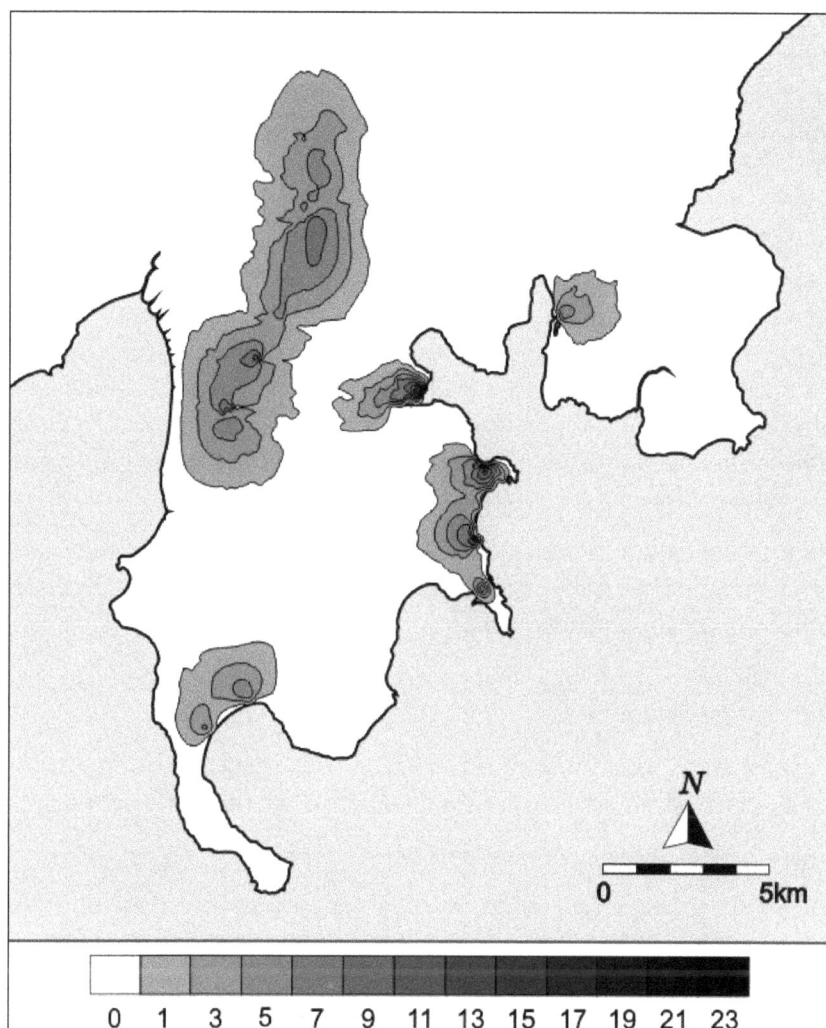

Figure 3.10: Density map of the number of molluscan taxa per site across the study area (contour interval = two species exploited).

Table 3.8: Descriptive statistics for the number of molluscan taxa by broad peninsula locality.

No. of Molluscan Taxa by Peninsula Locality	Myaoola Bay	Grindall Bay
Mean	7.25	5.06
Standard Deviation	4.17	3.01
Minimum	1	1
Maximum	23	23
Range	22	22
Number of Sites	34	85

The Myaoola Bay sites show a mean species richness of 7.25, compared with a mean of 5.06 for the Grindall Bay sites. This pattern suggests that there was a broader range of molluscan species exploited on the eastern margin of the peninsula compared with a limited range of species utilised, and possibly available, in the west. A Mann-Whitney U test revealed a significant difference in species richness between these two areas ($U = 899.5$, $z = -3.463$, $p = 0.001$, $r = 0.32$). In this case, species richness is a useful indicator of the diversity in resource exploitation within the area. Regardless of whether the number of taxa recorded during the surveys represents the average or the maximum diet breadth over a given length of time (Madsen 1993; Nagaoka 2000; Lyman 2003), it is apparent that different exploitation patterns were in operation relative to the broad area in which sites were located. This may be a reflection of the availability of particular resources, as well as choice in the exploitation of available resources. One way of teasing out differences in behavioural versus environmental reasons for the differences in the exploitation of various species may be to look at the number of habitats represented by the species identified in the area. Four broad habitat areas have been defined for the 30 taxa listed in Table 3.6. While it is acknowledged that there is a large degree of overlap within and between molluscan taxa in terms of their habitats, the following divisions provide a basis for analysing broad ecological trends. Following Kress (2000:301–4) and Morton (1983:101), these habitat areas are:

1. Shallow Water: this category contains species that inhabit the rocky, clear water areas in or just below the tidal zone, including parts of the reef and sandy/rocky areas close to the shore. Littoral and tide pool species are also included here;

2. Sand/Mud Flats: the brackish water habitat that encompasses the mud and sand flats that fringe the edge of most mangrove forests;

3. Mangroves: the mangal zone, situated within the mangroves proper, including those species found specifically in mangrove mud, as well as attached to the trees themselves;

4. Estuarine: encompassing coastal rivers, streams and estuaries.

The number and percentage of sites containing molluscan taxa representative of these different habitats is presented in Table 3.9. The species have been rank ordered according to the percentages of sites containing taxa from these four habitat divisions.

Table 3.9: The number and percentage of sites by molluscan habitat and broad locality.

Molluscan Habitat	Total			Myaoola Bay			Grindall Bay		
	# Sites	%	Rank Order	# Sites	%	Rank Order	# Sites	%	Rank Order
Shallow Water	64	53.78	3	30	88.24	3	34	40.00	4
Sand/Mud Flats	116	97.48	1	35	97.06	1	81	97.65	1
Mangroves	99	83.19	2	33	94.12	2	66	78.82	2
Estuarine	62	52.10	4	22	64.71	4	40	47.06	3
Total No. Sites	119			34			85		

Chi-square results indicate that Myaoola Bay and Grindall Bay are not significantly different in terms of the distribution of sites by habitat representation ($\chi^2 = 5.26$, $d.f. = 3$, $p > 0.1$). In terms of the number of sites in which species from different habitats occur, taxa from the mangrove-associated sand/mud flats areas dominate the study area as a whole, followed by taxa from the mangal zone proper. Hard substrate species (those that attach themselves to mangrove roots, rocks and shell debris), and taxa located in shallow waters appear to have been exploited to a greater extent on the exposed coastal margin in comparison with the Grindall Bay sites. Between 50 and 60% of sites in both areas contained taxa obtained from coastal rivers, streams or estuaries. The slight variation in the rank ordering of habitats between the Myaoola and Grindall Bay areas therefore possibly relates to the distribution of resources within each given locality. In order to assess this pattern further, the level of species richness from each habitat is used as a measure of the intensity or focus of exploitation. A comparison of the mean number of taxa exploited per habitat is presented in Table 3.10. In many respects, the number of species exploited from each habitat reflects the previous pattern, with more species exploited from the mangrove-associated sand/mud flat areas relative to other habitat areas. There are, however, differences in the mean number of species exploited by habitat between the Myaoola and Grindall Bay sites, particularly within the shallow water and mangal zone proper habitats.

Table 3.10: Descriptive statistics for the number of molluscan species from the defined habitats by broad peninsula locality.

| | Myaoola Bay | | | |
Habitats	Shallow Water	Sand/Mud Flats	Mangroves	Estuarine
Mean	1.70	2.70	2.19	0.68
Median	1	3	2	1
Standard Deviation	1.58	1.53	1.47	0.63
Minimum	0	0	0	0
Maximum	8	7	6	2
Range	8	7	6	2
Total No. Sites	34	34	34	34
	Grindall Bay			
Habitats	Shallow Water	Sand/Mud Flats	Mangroves	Estuarine
Mean	0.43	2.26	1.61	0.51
Median	0	2	1	0
Standard Deviation	0.52	0.89	1.34	0.55
Minimum	0	0	0	0
Maximum	2	6	6	2
Range	2	6	6	2
Total No. Sites	85	85	85	85

Table 3.11: t-test results for the relationship between the mean number of molluscan taxa by habitat for the Myaoola and Grindall Bay sites.

Molluscan Habitats	Myaoola Bay No. Taxa	Grindall Bay No. Taxa	t	d.f.	p
Shallow Water	1.7027	0.4268	-4.799	40	< 0.001
Sand/Mud Flats	2.7027	2.2561	-1.659	47	> 0.1
Mangroves	2.1892	1.6098	-2.046	64	< 0.05
Estuarine	0.5122	0.6757	-1.368	62	> 0.1

Table 3.11 details the results of t-tests performed to determine the significance of the differences between the mean number of taxa exploited per habitat between the eastern and western margins of the peninsula. These results suggest that, whereas there is a certain level of consistency in the number of species exploited within sand/mud flat areas and estuarine environments between these two areas, the differences observed between shallow water and mangrove habitats are significant. If the level of species richness for these habitats accurately reflects the level of exploitation intensity, then species gathered from hard-substrate areas in the shallow water zone and from the mangrove forests were exploited to a greater degree on the exposed coastal margin of Myaoola Bay. This result combined with that of species richness indicates that the differences observed between the two areas are a product of resource availability linked to long-term changes in the

coastline. This strongly suggests that, although there is always a certain level of choice involved in the exploitation of resources, decisions are ultimately constrained by what is available in the immediate area.

Stone artefacts on the Point Blane Peninsula

Stone artefact recording

All stone artefacts were recorded in the field, and the methods used for the identification and recording of artefacts in the field follows that of Hiscock (1984, 1989), Hiscock and Hughes (1983) and Andrefsky (1998) (see also Clarkson 2004; Holdaway *et al.* 2004; Shiner 2004; Faulkner and Clarke 2009). The five features detailed below were selected as being appropriate for this research:

1. Stone artefact raw material type: predominantly five types of stone were noted. These were chert, quartz, quartzite, silcrete and volcanic. This feature was recorded to gain an understanding of raw material movement across the landscape and use in artefact production.

2. Artefact types (following Hiscock 1989:25–6) were recorded as Flaked pieces: an artefact that cannot be classified as a flake, core, retouched flake or implement (e.g. broken piece); Unretouched flakes: any primary piece of stone detached from a core or another flake, generally characterised by the presence of initiations and terminations and containing a bulb of force, ringcrack and eraillure scar; Retouched flakes: a flake which has subsequently been re-flaked, and where secondary flake scars extend onto either surface after the removal of the flake from the core; and Cores: a piece of flaked stone with one or more negative flake scars and no positive flake scars.

3. Breakage: for flakes it was noted whether the broken piece represented a proximal, medial or distal piece, or whether the piece had snapped laterally or longitudinally. The breakage position was recorded so that a minimum number of artefacts could be calculated for the overall assemblage. Following Hiscock (2002:254), the minimum number of artefacts (MNF) is calculated by MNF=C+T+L, where C is the number of complete flakes, T is the largest category of transverse fragments (excluding medial fragments) and L is the count of longitudinal fragments.

4. Cortex: measured in terms of Primary decortication: dorsal surface 100% covered; Secondary decortication: 1-99% of the dorsal surface covered; and Tertiary decortication: with no cortex present (0%). On non-bifacial cores, cortex is measured as Type one (primary): cortical platform and cortex on the flaking surface; Type two (secondary): cortex on the flaking surface but none on the platform; and Type three (tertiary): no cortex on the flaking face or the platform.

5. Artefact measurements: on flakes, the percussion length, or the distance along the ventral surface from the ringcrack to the flake termination (Hiscock 1988), was measured with width and thickness taken at the midpoint of the percussion length, and platform width and thickness were taken relative to the point of force on the platform. On cores, the length was taken as the percussion length and width of the largest negative scar, as well as the maximum platform thickness. The number of platforms and the number of negative scars were also recorded on cores as an indicator of core rotation and core use. Weight was recorded for all artefacts as another comparative size measure (Roth and Dibble 1998; Marks *et al.* 2001:24–26; Clarkson 2004:109–110; Holdaway *et al.* 2004:57; Braun *et al.* 2005).

Assemblage characteristics and raw material variation

Given the lack of stratigraphic context and the inability to assign a chronological framework to these sites (e.g. Holdaway *et al.* 2004:34), the study area is considered to be a single catchment area (see Vita-Finzi and Higgs 1970), and the artefacts analysed as a single assemblage. As surface stone artefact scatters are generally time-averaged deposits, and result from repeated activities rather than a single event (Holdaway and Wandsnider 2006:192–3), spatial patterning of artefactual material does not necessarily provide a strong temporal context. While the study area is analysed as a single catchment, the aim here is to understand the sum of those activities, and the variability that entails, at particular locations (e.g. Holdaway *et al.* 2004; Shiner 2004; Holdaway and Wandsnider 2006) rather than assume chronological similarity. This approach enables general trends in stone raw material use, artefact manufacture and spatial distribution to be analysed. A total of 250 stone artefacts were recorded during the course of the survey, and as with the distribution of the other sites in the study area, these sites are largely concentrated on the margins of the peninsula (Figure 3.11). In order to identify diversity within this assemblage, the frequency of the major artefact and raw material components of the assemblage are shown in Table 3.12.

Table 3.12: Number and type of stone artefacts per raw material.

Artefact Type	Raw Material						
	Chert	Quartz	Quartzite	Silcrete	Volcanic	Total	%
Core	--	1	11	--	--	12	4.84
Flaked Piece	--	--	40	4	--	44	17.74
Retouched Flake	--	--	6	4	--	10	4.03
Unretouched Flake	1	--	162	18	1	182	73.39
Total (MNF)	**1**	**1**	**219**	**26**	**1**	**248**	**100**
Percentage	0.40	0.40	88.31	10.48	0.40	100	

As noted by Hiscock (2001) and Grayson and Cole (1998:928), assemblage richness or diversity is largely dependent upon sample size. While this may hold true for the Point Blane Peninsula with small numbers of artefacts recorded across the study area, a number of useful points can still be addressed. The data presented in Table 3.12 suggests a very low level of assemblage diversity in both artefact type and raw materials utilised. Unretouched or unmodified flakes dominate the area at 73.4%, followed by flaked pieces at 17.7%. The latter may represent the by-products of manufacture and/or use of stone artefacts. Cores and retouched flakes represent minor components of the assemblage at 4.8% and 4.0% respectively, though they still provide information on the way in which stone was used within the area. Although an unmodified flake will provide a sharp, functional edge, retouched flakes can potentially serve as an indicator of stone raw material conservation, as this process enables a flake to remain in operation for a longer period of time. There are 10 retouched flakes (4 silcrete and 6 quartzite), comprising 4.0% of the assemblage. The unretouched flakes dominate the composition of the assemblage, with a 16:1 ratio of flakes to cores, and an 18.2:1 ratio of unretouched to retouched flakes (Faulkner and Clarke 2009:23). The following analysis will focus on raw material variability and distribution across the landscape, as differences in stone raw material abundance and quality may place constraints on the variability of the archaeological record (Dibble 1985:391–392; Bamforth 1986; Kuhn 1991:76–7; Andrefsky 1994a, 1994b; Hiscock 1996; Brantingham *et al.* 2000:256; Clarkson 2004:9; Orton 2008).

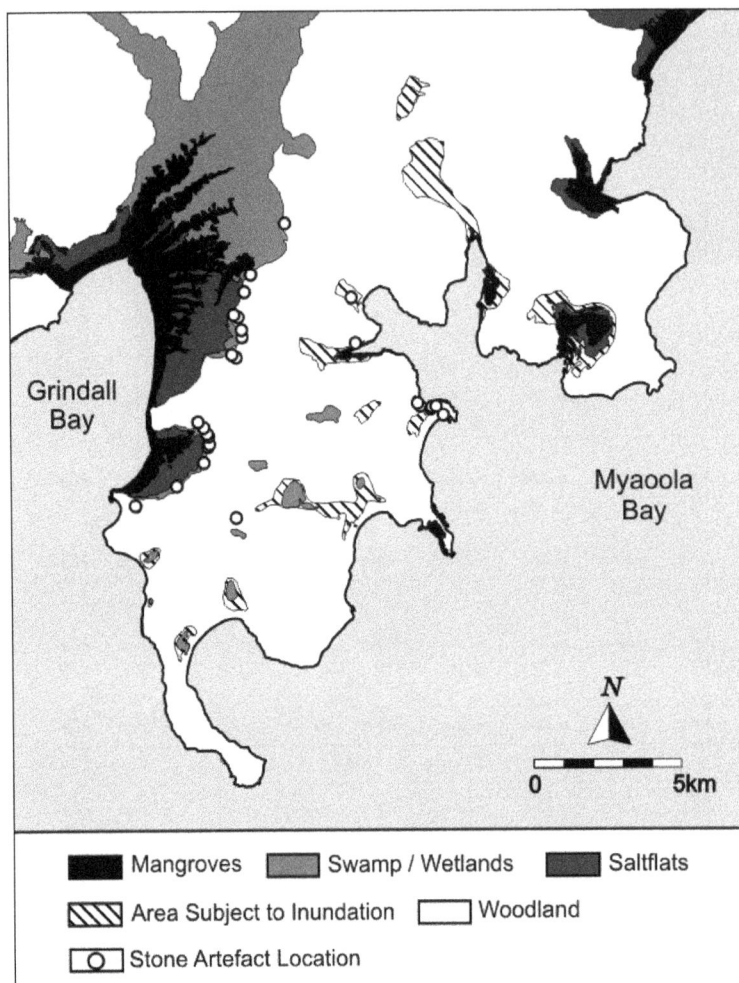

Figure 3.11: The distribution of sites containing stone artefacts on the Point Blane Peninsula.

Source: Based on Baniyala 1:50 000 Topographic Map.

Concentrating on the raw materials present in the study area, this shows that quartzite is the dominant stone raw material (88.4%), followed by silcrete occurring at a considerably lower frequency (10.4%). Given the dominance of quartzite and silcrete artefacts across the peninsula, and the fact that chert, quartz and volcanic artefacts form such a minor component of the assemblage at one artefact each, and a combined 0.4% of the raw materials represented, they are not included in this analysis due to sample size limitations. It is also important to understand the differences between the two main raw material types, as they can appear morphologically very similar, and these are described below (Haines et al. 1999:71–6):

1. Quartzite: a metamorphic rock, which is hard due to the fact that it is primarily made from interlocked quartz particles set in a cementing solution, or matrix, creating a sugary appearance.

2. Silcrete: is a silicified sediment, the quartz grains are usually set further apart within the cementing matrix, creating a peppery surface appearance.

The quartzite in this area varies considerably from relatively coarse-grained to fine-grained, and the silcrete generally occurs at the finer-grained end of the spectrum. This material typically fractures across the individual grains conchoidally, enabling a higher degree of control and predictability in knapping procedures (Andrefsky 1998:55–6).

In conjunction with the morphological characteristics of the various raw materials used in artefact production, the size and shape of the core are important considerations. These factors are directly related to the level of the force required for flake removal and the morphology of the flakes produced (Cotterell and Kamminga 1987:677–8; Kuhn 1995:32; Clarkson 2004:114; Webb and Domanski 2007; Orton 2008). There are 11 cores in the assemblage, comprising 4.8% of the artefactual material recorded. All of the cores on the Point Blane Peninsula are quartzite, the dominant raw material within the area. Table 3.13 presents the descriptive statistics for several variables recorded for the cores to assess the relative level of reduction. A mean weight of 15.91g, in conjunction with the low mean dimension values for cores, indicates a relatively small size for these artefacts. This is supported by the low range of core dimensions, at 10mm and 18mm difference between minimum and maximum measurements for length, width and thickness. Comparing the length and width measurements in Table 3.13 establishes the basic shape of the artefact. In this instance, length is divided by width to provide an elongation ratio. A mean elongation value of 1.11 indicates that, on average, the cores are relatively square. These dimension and shape attributes suggest a reasonable intensity of reduction for the cores from the assemblage, as the level of reduction should correlate with the low elongation value combined with the small, consistent length, width and thickness measurements.

Table 3.13: Descriptive statistics for quartzite core measurements.

	Descriptive Statistics	Weight (g)	Length (mm)	Width (mm)	Thickness (mm)
	Mean	15.91	21.36	22.42	18.12
	Median	13	19.35	21.82	15.14
	S.D.	7.78	3.74	9.64	7.77
Quartzite Cores	Min	7	18.02	10.14	10.1
	Max	31	28.2	45.62	29.35
	Range	24	10.18	35.48	19.25
	No.	11	11	11	11

Examining the number of core platforms and negative flake scarring also enables the intensity of use of this raw material to be examined. For example, once a platform angle becomes too high, or there are too many step-terminated flake scars, continued use of the artefact may only be possible with the creation of a new platform (Hiscock 1988; Clarkson 2004). The data presented in Table 3.14 indicate that variation in core rotation is minimal, ranging from no rotations (single platform) up to two rotations (three platforms), with the mean number of core platforms recorded at 2.18. Combined with the mean number of negative scars per core at 7.18, and the mean number of negative scars per platform at 3.55, these values indicate that these artefacts were worked consistently to a point where the removal of flakes no longer became viable, possibly due to the relatively small core size at the point of discard. This is supported by the percentage of remaining cortex on these cores. The amount of cortex on an artefact may be an indication of the level of reduction, where large amounts of cortex may be indicative of an early stage of reduction, and very little cortex may indicate a higher degree of reduction (Hiscock 1988:369; Clarkson 2004:114; Holdaway *et al.* 2004:50). All of the cores in this assemblage contained little to no cortex at all, with Type 2 (secondary) cortex on two cores, and Type 3 (tertiary) cortex on nine cores.

Table 3.14: Descriptive statistics for quartzite core platforms and negative scars.

	Descriptive Statistics	No. of Platforms	No. of Negative Scars	No. of Negative Scars per Platform
Quartzite Cores	Mean	2.18	7.18	3.55
	Median	2	7	3.33
	S.D.	0.6	2.64	1.97
	Min	1	3	1.5
	Max	3	12	9
	Range	2	9	7.5
	No.	11	11	11

Table 3.15: Descriptive statistics for quartzite and silcrete unretouched flakes.

		Weight (g)	Length (mm)	Width (mm)	Thickness (mm)	Elongation	Platform Area (mm²)	Platform Shape
Quartzite Unretouched	Mean	9.60	27.51	23.97	7.59	1.26	137.67	2.79
	Median	6.00	24.92	21.08	6.53	1.18	92.67	2.42
	S.D.	12.99	12.24	10.78	4.24	0.55	162.70	1.27
	Min	0.50	5.16	6.24	1.30	0.15	7.12	0.66
	Max	92.00	63.57	65.68	24.79	3.11	1229.45	7.49
	Range	91.50	58.41	59.44	23.49	2.97	1222.33	6.83
	Number	162	162	162	162	162	162	162
Silcrete Unretouched	Mean	10.22	28.77	25.35	7.19	1.17	120.76	3.83
	Median	7.50	24.36	25.03	5.76	1.04	93.54	3.29
	S.D.	6.89	14.63	7.70	3.98	0.48	108.99	1.80
	Min	2.00	14.95	11.08	2.38	0.63	6.21	1.84
	Max	24.00	78.25	40.92	16.09	2.51	355.84	8.68
	Range	22.00	63.30	29.84	13.71	1.88	349.63	6.84
	Number	18	18	18	18	18	18	18

Following on from the investigation of cores, the flakes in the area have been divided into unretouched and retouched categories. There are 182 unretouched flakes, comprising 73.4% of the assemblage (162 quartzite and 18 silcrete). The main attributes measured on the flakes from the assemblage give an indication of size and shape, with the addition of a platform shape index (platform length/platform width) (Table 3.15). Mean values for all dimensions and indices appear consistent between the two raw materials, enough so to suggest that although the number of quartzite artefacts outweighs the silcrete artefacts considerably, there are negligible differences in the intensity of reduction and the point of discard. As indicated by the mean dimension values, the size of the unretouched flakes are relatively small and square in shape, with low mean length, width and thickness measurements, and with the elongation and platform shape indices indicating a slightly longer than wide shape with a long and thin platform. As with the amount of cortex on cores, the majority of unretouched flakes contain very little to no cortex, with 99.4% of the assemblage containing either secondary or tertiary cortex. This pattern is consistent with that noted in the analysis of core reduction and rotation (Faulkner and Clarke 2009:23–4).

Regardless of the potential differences in the use of raw materials, the characterisation of the assemblage, the analysis and comparison of artefact sizes and raw materials suggests that while there was not a heavy reliance on stone artefacts, it does appear that the stone artefacts were reduced relatively intensively. In this area, where and when stone artefacts were required, the most important strategy appears to have involved keeping a supply of fresh edges where needed, while at the same time extending the life of the raw material (Faulkner and Clarke 2009). This is a potentially important strategy as sources of reasonable quality stone are only available to a limited degree within the coastal plains of Blue Mud Bay.

Stone artefact distribution

The way that stone artefacts were distributed across the study area becomes important in terms of investigating past economic activity. This may indicate any differences in the focal point of raw material procurement relative to areas of artefact discard (for example Byrne 1980; Foley 1981a:11, 1981b; Isaac 1981; Hiscock 1984, 1994) as material can generally be expected to accumulate in those places that were used more often than locations used infrequently. Figure 3.12 shows the density of artefactual material across the study area with a contour interval of 10 artefacts, as well as the density of stone artefacts between two points across the Point Blane Peninsula (indicated as A and B) also graphed as another relative density measure. Disturbance or visibility factors aside, the higher artefact density on the eastern side of the Point Blane Peninsula is due to the central location of a quartzitic outcrop in this area. The density of material closer to the quartzite outcrop, therefore, illustrates the strong relationship between environmental features and the location of activities within the landscape (Hiscock 1989:22; Fanning and Holdaway 2001:669–70). Although there was no obvious stone working noted within the outcropping, combined with the fact that quartzite artefacts are dominant, this area is significant as it is the only source of flakeable stone located in the study area (Faulkner and Clarke 2009:24). As such, the fact that this exact location does not specifically contain evidence that it was used as a quarry may not be important (see for example Hiscock and Mitchell 1993:27; Ross *et al.* 2003). The distribution of artefacts within the study area is further analysed by testing the proposition that this outcrop was the central raw material procurement point for quartzite in the immediate area.

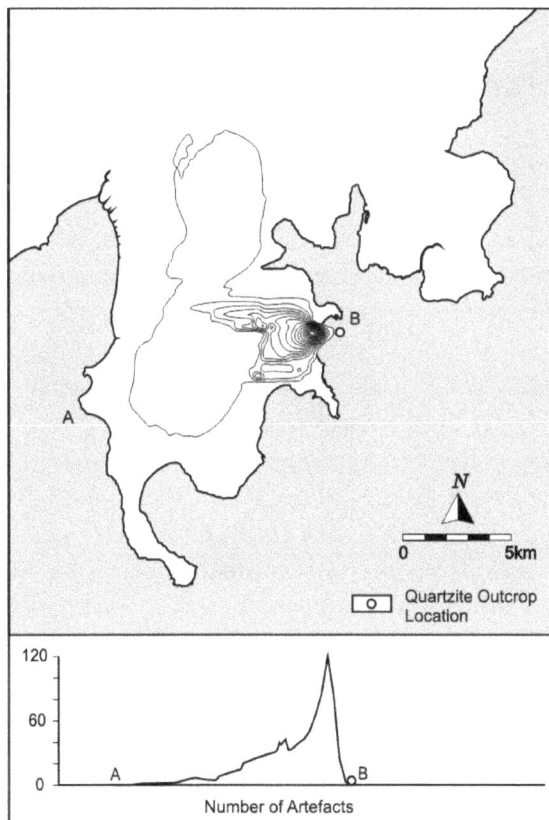

Figure 3.12: Stone artefact densities across the Point Blane Peninsula.

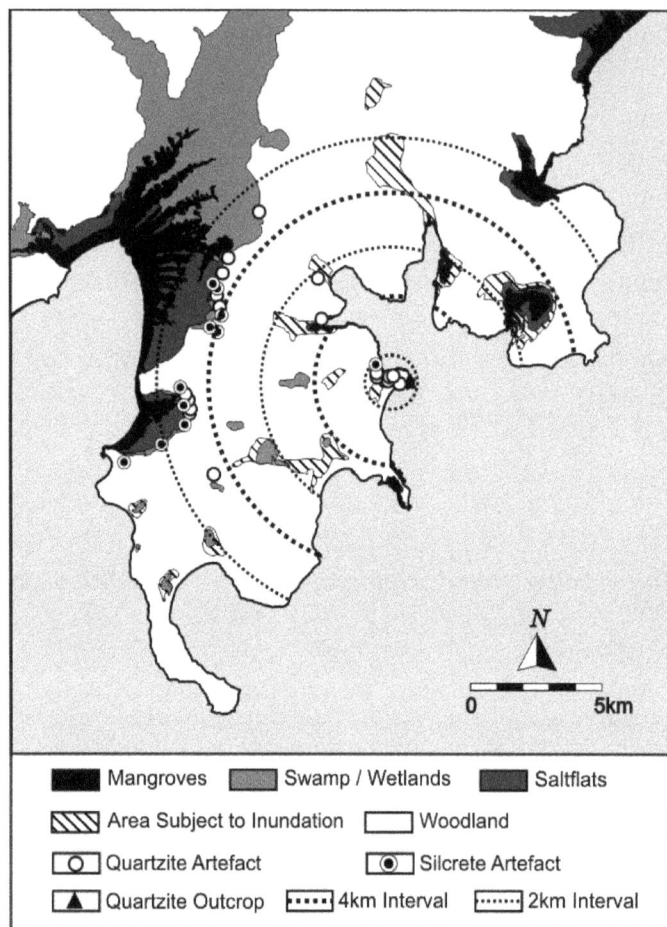

Figure 3.13: Location of quartzite and silcrete artefacts across the Point Blane Peninsula, with 2km (thin line) and 4km (thick line) intervals from quartzitic outcrop.

Source: Based on Baniyala 1:50 000 Topographic Map.

Figure 3.13 shows the location of quartzite and silcrete artefacts within 2 and 4km intervals from the quartzite outcrop, with Tables 3.16 and 3.17 detailing several site and artefact variables within these intervals for the quartzite and silcrete artefacts respectively. The number of quartzite artefacts per 2km interval shows a concentration of stone artefacts on the margins of the peninsula, particularly on the eastern side within the first 4km of the quartzite outcrop. All quartzite cores and retouched flakes occur within this area, with the only artefact classes occurring within all intervals being unretouched flakes and flaked pieces. This concentration of material within 4km of the outcrop does suggest that this area may have been a focal point for quartzite artefact manufacture and use. The dominance of unretouched flakes may indicate use of this raw material primarily at, or near to, the source as it was needed. This material was then transported across the study area away from the source location to much less of a degree (Faulkner and Clarke 2009:24–5).

Table 3.16: Quartzite artefact data at 4km intervals from quartzite outcrop.

Criteria	0 - 4km	4 - 8km	8 - 12km
No. of sites containing quartzite artefacts	6	2	10
No. of quartzite artefacts	197	2	20
No. of quartzite cores	11	--	--
No. of quartzite flaked pieces	37	--	3
No. of quartzite unretouched flakes	143	2	17
No. of quartzite retouched flakes	6	--	--

Table 3.17: Silcrete artefact data at 4km intervals from quartzite outcrop.

Criteria	0 - 4km	4 - 8km	8 - 12km
No. of sites containing silcrete artefacts	1	--	14
No. of silcrete artefacts	12	--	17
No. of silcrete cores	--	--	--
No. of silcrete flaked pieces	2	--	2
No. of silcrete unretouched flakes	9	--	9
No. of silcrete retouched flakes	1	--	3

Although occurring in considerably lower numbers, the silcrete artefacts present a similar distribution pattern to the quartzite unretouched flakes, with the material concentrated exclusively on the margins of the peninsula. In this case, silcrete artefacts occur only within 4km of the quartzite outcrop and at distances of 8km or greater. The same number of cores and unretouched flakes occur at both distances, with a single retouched flake within a 2km radius and three retouched flakes at 8km or greater. With similar numbers of silcrete artefacts occurring within the two areas, there does not appear to be preferential use of this material within any one area. To determine the significance of these distributional patterns, however, the size variables used previously per raw material for the unretouched flakes are assessed by distance from the outcropping. In this case, for comparative reasons the sites are grouped into 0 to 6km and 6 to 12km distance intervals. Due to the small sample size of silcrete unretouched flakes, only quartzite unretouched flakes have been included in this analysis. Descriptive statistics for size variables by raw material and 6km distance interval are listed in Table 3.18. Using length as an indication of artefact size, there is very little difference in mean dimensions between distance intervals, and as evidenced by the elongation ratios, little difference in the shape of the artefacts. Even though it has been shown that there are differences in the density of artefacts, it appears from the size and shape data that there is very little difference in the way the stone material was worked (Faulkner and Clarke 2009:25). That is, regardless of the distance from the source of the dominant raw material, the stone was worked intensively prior to discard.

Table 3.18: Descriptive statistics for quartzite unretouched flakes at 6km intervals from quartzite outcrop.

	Quartzite	Weight (g)	Length (mm)	Width (mm)	Thickness (mm)	Elongation	Platform Area (mm²)	Platform Shape
0 - 6km	Mean	9.13	27.58	23.93	7.52	1.27	141.46	2.82
	Median	6.00	24.97	20.91	6.52	1.18	98.06	2.42
	S.D.	13.05	12.48	10.94	4.24	0.57	168.46	1.30
	Min	0.50	5.16	6.24	1.30	0.15	7.12	0.66
	Max	92.00	63.57	65.68	24.79	3.11	1229.45	7.49
	Range	91.50	58.41	59.44	23.49	2.97	1222.33	6.83
	No.	145	145	145	145	145	145	145
6 - 12km	Mean	11.41	26.65	22.62	7.50	1.21	95.05	2.52
	Median	7.00	22.33	20.84	6.08	1.12	66.02	2.21
	S.D.	11.51	10.97	8.77	4.05	0.30	87.54	1.03
	Min	1.00	13.45	10.78	2.74	0.74	10.24	1.32
	Max	42.00	49.75	36.98	15.39	1.83	352.94	5.38
	Range	41.00	36.30	26.20	12.65	1.09	342.70	4.06
	No.	17	17	17	17	17	17	17

The artefact assemblage in the study area is dominated by locally available raw materials, again indicating a focussed use of resources available within the immediate area. In addition, the size and shape of the artefacts, combined with little cortex being evident, suggests that people in this area were maximising or extending the use-life of stone due to its relative scarcity in the landscape (Dibble 1985; Bleed 1986; Kuhn 1992, 1995; Odell 1996; Brantingham et al. 2000:256–7; Bousman 2005:209; Faulkner and Clarke 2009:24–6). The interpretation of the artefactual assemblage in the study area only becomes significant when viewed as a part of the wider economic and settlement system (Binford 1980; Ugan et al. 2003:1325), particularly given the difficulty of deriving behavioural inferences from surface artefact scatters (Fanning and Holdaway 2001:669). With very little flakeable stone outcropping in this region of the coastal plain, the appropriate raw materials were intensively worked. This may be seen as an aspect of the 'maximising' strategy proposed above, with stone being worked in close proximity to the main source, and then distributed sparingly across the study area as required. Although a small sample, something that potentially reflects less of a need for stone artefacts in these kinds of coastal landscapes, this analysis provides an additional line of evidence for investigating past economic activity in this area. The area surrounding the quartzite outcrop north of the Yilpara community appears to have been the central procurement point for quartzite in the study area. Rather than the exposed outcrop being the specific source, it is this general locality that is of importance. It is possible that other outcrop locations have been exposed in the past, with the dynamic and changing nature of the coastline masking these locations. That is, other outcrops may have been worked in the past and covered with sand and sediment. The paucity of artefactual evidence within this region may also reflect a coastally oriented economy, particularly when viewed in conjunction with the distribution of shell material presented in the site section. The exploitation of near-shore resources such as shellfish and fish may not have required the intensive use of stone artefacts. This type of pattern has been noted in the past by Meehan (1982) and Bailey (1993:9), where relatively few or a limited range of stone artefacts may be discarded in localities where a limited range of economic activities may have been carried out, such as with shell-processing sites.

Conclusion

The nature of the north Australian coastline is fluid and dynamic, with elements of the archaeological record demonstrating that human behaviour was structured relative to these conditions. For example, maximum sea level is hypothesised to have occurred approximately 5000 years ago, following from which it has gradually subsided (with some variability through time), with stands of mangroves following in the wake of falling sea level, creating still, rich nearshore habitats that were suitable for colonisation by a range of molluscan taxa. The absence of archaeological evidence prior to 3000 BP in this area makes it difficult to accurately assess reasons for a possible time lag in occupation following sea level rise. There are, however, a number of possibilities for this pattern, including a lack of preservation of older sites in the area and/or a reorganisation of forager economies relative to changing marine environments during and after changes in sea level. Regardless of the reasons for the apparent lag in the visibility of archaeological evidence for occupation, the distribution and timing of shell mounds and middens in the study area virtually mirrors the process of the receding sea level and establishment of mangroves and shellbeds. At a broad level, they indicate a relatively long-term sequence of occupation and shellfish exploitation from 3000 years ago up to the present day. In combination with the midden sites, the stone artefact evidence suggests that resources were targeted and exploited in a highly localised and discrete pattern within the study area, across both time and space. Given these patterns, it is pertinent to investigate spatial and chronological patterns of resource exploitation in finer detail.

4

The Excavated Shell Midden and Mound Sites on the Point Blane Peninsula

The six sites described here were excavated in order to examine previously identified patterns of resource exploitation at a finer level of detail and chronological resolution. These site descriptions provide initial information on the diverse nature of the archaeological record on the Point Blane Peninsula by outlining site location and environmental context, excavation, stratigraphy, chronology and by presenting an overview and comparison of the recovered cultural material. This analysis is also focussed on examining the issue of possible different site functions between shell middens and mounds, ultimately providing the basis for a more detailed economic analysis.

Excavation and laboratory methods

For the purposes of the broader Blue Mud Bay project, 13 excavations were carried out on shell mound and midden sites situated at various points in Myaoola and Grindall Bays. Radiocarbon age estimates obtained from these 13 shell deposits again demonstrate a late Holocene sequence of occupation within the study area, ranging from approximately 3000 years BP to the present, with the majority of the radiocarbon dates clustered between 2500 years BP and the present (Faulkner 2008:84). Of these 13, six sites detailed here were selected for analysis according to differences in location, environmental context, site morphology and, based on the distribution of radiocarbon dates obtained from surface samples, possible variations in site chronology. The aim therefore was to investigate possible changes through time relative to ongoing processes of landscape alteration and associated changes in resource distribution. The midden sites selected on Myaoola Bay were BMB/018, BMB/067b and BMB/084, and the shell mound sites on Grindall Bay were BMB/029, BMB/071 and BMB/045. These sites are highlighted in Figure 4.1, and provide a comparative sample of locations around the present and former coastline throughout the approximate 3000 year period of occupation identified within the study area.

Field methods followed guidelines provided by Johnson (1980). Excavation areas were marked out using string and an arbitrary 5cm depth was excavated for each unit, keeping to any natural strata observed within the site where appropriate. Levels were checked by recording depths with a dumpy level at the corners and centre of each square. Bucket weights from each excavation unit were recorded with a hand-held spring balance and all excavated material was sieved through a nest of 6mm and 3mm mesh sieves and bagged for laboratory analysis. Bulk (un-sieved) sediment samples from the last bucket of each unit were bagged separately. The excavation method employed differed slightly depending on the type of shell deposit being excavated. The shell mounds were excavated in 1m x 0.5m or 1m² test pits. These excavation squares were further divided into smaller 0.5m² squares or quadrats to enable sampling of the sieve residue following excavation. This level of sampling was required in the examination of the larger mounded deposits due to the time-consuming nature of laboratory sorting and analysis of the large volume of material recovered from each site (Ambrose 1967; Casteel 1970; Barz 1977; Claassen 1991; O'Neil 1993). The lower-lying shell middens were excavated in either 0.5m² or 1m² test-pits. Smaller test pits were used where several areas within the one site or complex were excavated for comparative purposes.

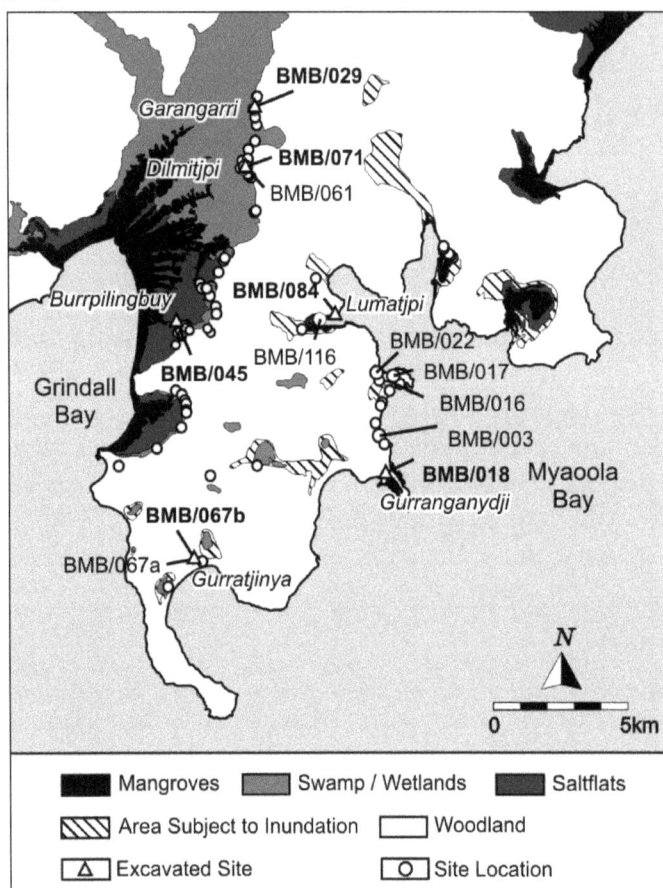

Figure 4.1: Distribution of excavated sites used in this analysis (in bold) and their Yolngu locality name (also indicated are the other excavated sites on the peninsula).

Source: Based on Baniyala 1:50 000 Topographic Map.

In the laboratory all excavated material was weighed and then wet-sieved through a 3mm mesh sieve. The material was then dried, weighed and re-bagged. With the exception of sites BMB/018 and BMB/084, the analysis of the excavated material was limited to the 6mm sieve residue from every second excavation unit due to time constraints and the sheer bulk of material excavated. While not subjected to quantification, visual inspection of selected 3mm samples from the upper, middle and lower portions of the deposits confirmed a lack of any differences in the presence/abundance of the excavated components in comparison with the 6mm residues (e.g. bone). In addition, given the density of material recovered from the midden and mound deposits in combination with the available radiocarbon dates, the analysis of every second excavation unit enables the determination of any trends through time in taxonomic composition, relative abundance and size variability. Components from the 6mm sieve were sorted by hand into major categories of mollusc taxa, bone, crab, fish otoliths, charcoal, ochre, stone artefacts, vegetation and non-artefactual stone. Shell taxa were identified by Dr Richard Willan, Curator of Molluscs at the Museum and Art Gallery of the Northern Territory (MAGNT), and in comparison with photographs from Blackburn (1980), Hinton (1978, 1979), Lamprell and Healy (1998), Lamprell and Whitehead (1992), Meehan (1982), Short and Potter (1987) and Wells and Bryce (1988). Dr Helen Larson, Curator of Fishes at the Museum and Art Gallery of the Northern Territory, identified the fish bone and otoliths. Dr Sally Brockwell at The Australian National University provided further assistance in the identification of this material. Due to their low occurrence within all deposits, the identifiable non-molluscan elements including charcoal, vegetation, bone, ochre and non-artefactual stone were measured by weight alone. Stone artefacts recovered from the excavations were recorded according to the field survey procedures and cross-referenced to retain consistency and a comparative basis for analysis. Each shell taxon was weighed and minimum number of individuals (MNI) and the number of identifiable specimens (NISP) counted. Although relatively time consuming, this methodology was employed based on faunal studies conducted in Australia and internationally, and the implications for faunal quantification that have arisen as a result. As discussed in the following chapter, the combination of weight, MNI and NISP methods provides a more accurate description of the proportion of mollusc taxa, the degree of fragmentation per taxa through the site, and allows for comparison with the non-shell components (Bowdler 1983:140; Grayson 1984; Marshall and Pilgram 1993; Mowat 1995:81–82; Mason *et al.* 1998; Giovas 2009).

The Gurranganydji area

The area known as Gurranganydji is situated to the east of the Yilpara Community, leading onto a sandy headland jutting into Myaoola Bay. This headland is bordered by large stands of mangroves and extensive tidal mud flats. A series of sand ridges extends into this location, with grasslands interspersed by dense stands of monsoon vine thicket, separating the dune areas from the lower lying *Eucalypt* woodland and mixed grassland. The site located in this area, BMB/18, is situated on the upper western margin of a series of sand ridges, approximately 200m behind the mangroves (Figure 4.2).

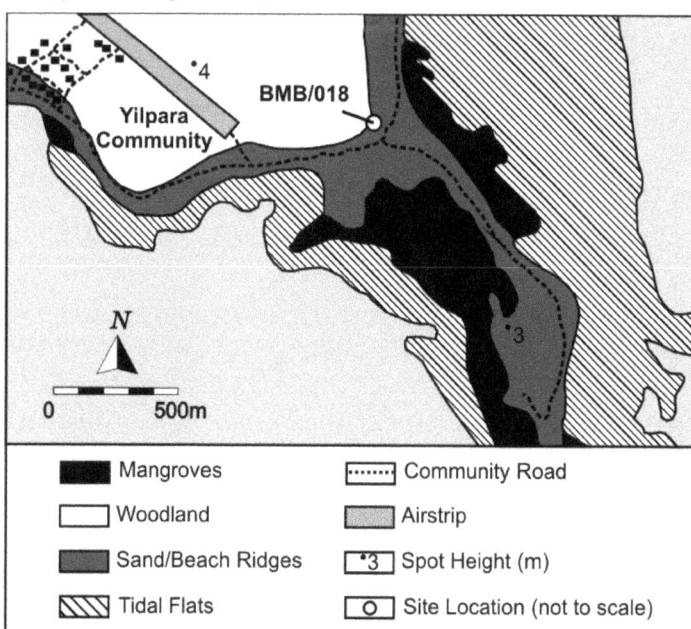

Figure 4.2: Location of the Yilpara community and the site of BMB/018 at Gurranganydji.

Source: Based on Baniyala 1:50 000 Topographic Map.

BMB/018 site description: Stratigraphy, chronology and excavated components

BMB/018 is a highly disturbed site, measuring 10m by 5m. A community vehicle track runs virtually through its centre, and patches of shell are eroding from the centre of the track and along its western edge (Figure 4.3). This track has been formed by vehicle movement, with wheel rutting reaching depths of between 5 and 10cm. The species composition and the condition of the eroding shell were suggestive of a cultural origin for this material, particularly given its environmental context. The dominant species present on the surface was *Septifer bilocularis* and a species of *Pinctada*. This site was excavated as its location suggested that it might have been of greater antiquity than many of the other sites situated within Myaoola Bay. A 1m² test-pit was excavated approximately 2m off the side of the vehicle track into the site (a metre beyond the area circled in Figure 4.3), attempting to avoid areas of higher disturbance.

Figure 4.3: Site of BMB/018 at Gurranganydji, location of vehicle track relative to shell deposits, with shell eroding from the edge of the track (arrow) and the density of shell deposited on ground surface (circled).

Source: Photo Annie Clarke.

The midden deposit was exposed below windblown sand and beach debris comprised of small, non-economic bivalve and gastropod species at a depth of approximately 7cm, with the cultural deposit extending for a further 10cm. Roughly 85cm in area, the lens of midden material reached a depth of between 11 and 17cm, phasing out onto the orange beach sand deposit at the base of the site (Figure 4.4). This lower stratigraphic unit was devoid of cultural material, composed largely of sand, coral and small, non-economic bivalve and gastropod species. Based on the stratigraphic profile and the composition of the four excavation units, this site is interpreted as a thin midden layer deposited onto an existing beach ridge. The midden layer was then subsequently covered by naturally deposited shell and sand, possibly via storm surges, wave action and wind-blown material. It was also apparent during the course of excavation that there might have been a degree of reworking within the deposit evidenced by coral, pumice and shell grit. As shown in Table 4.1, this site returned the oldest date for the study area. An age estimate of 3200±70 obtained from marine shell excavated from the base of the cultural midden layer (excavation unit 3), which calibrates to 2953 cal BP.

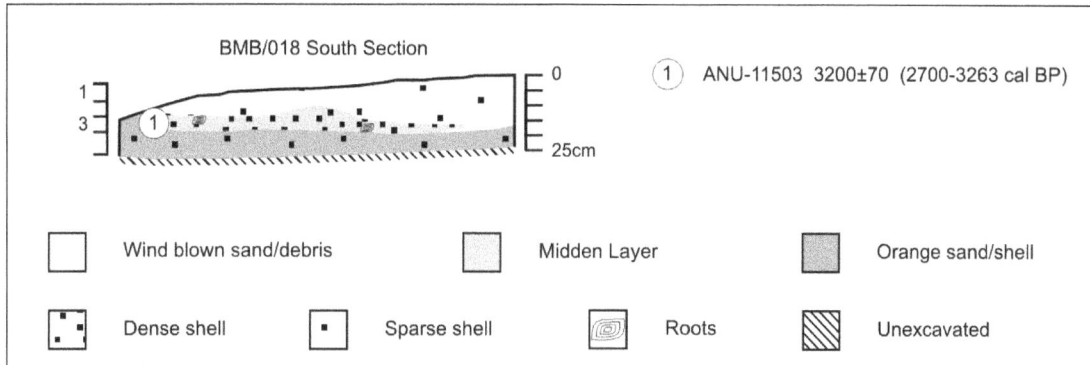

Figure 4.4: BMB/018 stratigraphic diagram, south section, showing conventional radiocarbon age and 2σ calibrated age range.

Table 4.1: Conventional and calibrated radiocarbon age obtained for site BMB/018.

Site Code /XU	Depth (cm)	Lab Code	Sample	δ¹³C	¹⁴C Age	1σ cal Age BP (68.3% probability)	2σ cal Age BP (95.4% probability)	Cal Age BP Median
BMB/018/3	11-17	ANU-11503	*Septifer bilocularis*	0.0 ± 0.0	3200 ± 70	2779–3080	2700–3263	2953

Source: Calibration data from CALIB 6.1.1, marine04.14c (Hughen *et al*. 2004), ΔR = 55±98 (Ulm 2006b).

Table 4.2 presents the quantitative data by weight in grams for the components recovered from the 6mm sieve during excavation, with density estimates of shell, bone, coral/pumice and laterite/rock by excavation unit graphed in Figure 4.5. The increased density of charcoal in the upper unit of the excavation probably relates to seasonal burning of this area, and has little significance in relation to past economic activity within the site, as the density of charcoal within the deposit is very low. Higher densities of bone occur above the identified cultural midden layer, although this represents a minor change, and the presence of this material may relate to natural deposition of faunal material within the windblown sand and beach debris. The presence of coral and pumice throughout the excavation support to some degree the notion of minor reworking of the deposit, with a similar density pattern to that of laterite/rock. These data demonstrate that molluscan material dominates the assemblage by weight at 71.6%, followed by lateritic/rock deposits at 23.2%. The overwhelming majority of shell was recovered from those units identified as cultural (excavation units two and three). As noted above, the dominant molluscan taxa within the site are *Septifer bilocularis* (48.7%) and *Pinctada* sp. (34.8%), with *Gafrarium* sp. (7.7%) as a minor species. Vegetation remains (1.7%), crab carapace (1.1%), unidentifiable fragments of bone (0.1%) and charcoal (0.03%) form minor components of the assemblage. As there is only one radiocarbon date available for this site accurate determinations of variability in site formation are not possible, such as rates of accumulation or deposition of cultural material. That said, additional radiocarbon dates may not provide further clarification due to the inherent error margins involved, and the thin lens of cultural midden material. In many ways, this suggests molluscan refuse discard and a reflection of short-term occupation.

Table 4.2: Quantitative data for the excavated components from BMB/018, 6mm sieve fraction.

Excavation Unit	Depth (cm)	Volume cm³	Laterite/ Rock (g)	Vegetation (g)	Coral/Pumice (g)	Charcoal (g)	Shell (g)	Bone (g)	Crustacean (g)
1	0.0 to 7.5	75000	121.0	49.3	4.5	0.9	234.5	1.1	4.2
2	7.5 to 10.7	32000	253.6	14.6	27.2	0.3	1384.4	---	25.4
3	10.7 to 16.9	62000	539.8	9.8	71.6	---	1453.9	0.5	18.0
4	16.9 to 21.5	46000	129.4	4.1	4.9	0.1	154.0	0.7	0.3
Totals			1043.8	77.8	108.2	1.3	3226.8	2.3	47.9
% of Total Wt. (4508.1)			23.15	1.73	2.40	0.03	71.58	0.05	1.06

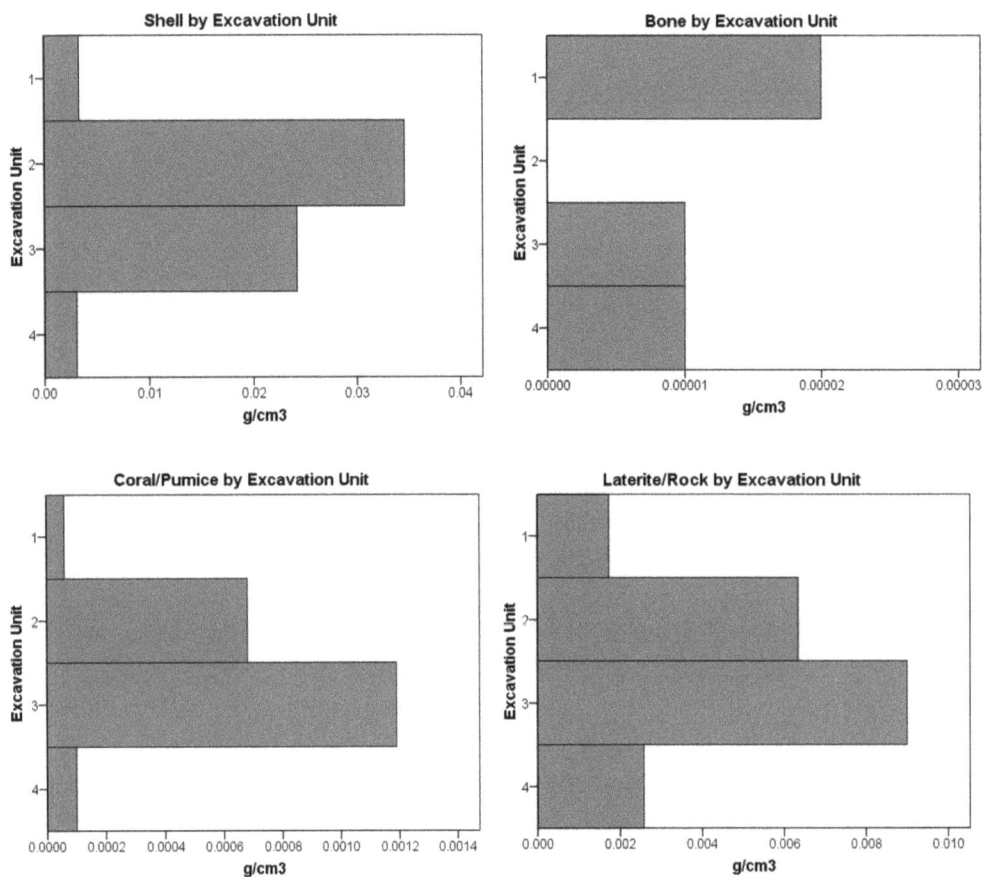

Figure 4.5: Density (g/cm³) of excavated components (shell, bone, coral/pumice and laterite/rock) by excavation unit, BMB/018, 6mm sieve fraction.

The Gurratjinya area

The Gurratjinya area is located to the south-west of Myaoola Bay, at the end of a track that runs through the centre of the peninsula (Figure 4.6). A high series of sand dunes extend from the beach, covered with extensive patches of monsoon vine thicket vegetation and mixed grasslands. From the high third dune the area plateaus for approximately 100m, and then gradually descends into a large, seasonal paperbark swamp that drains into the small bay to the east. Two sites were located within this area, one amongst the dunes and one bordering the edge of the swamp (BMB/067b).

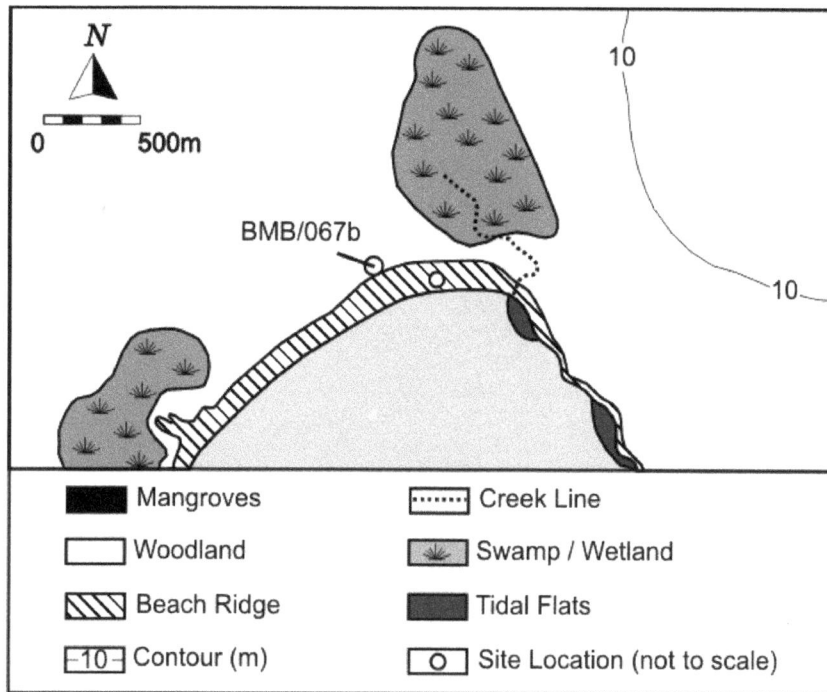

Figure 4.6: Location of site of BMB/067b at Gurratjinya.

Source: Based on Baniyala 1:50 000 Topographic Map.

BMB/067b site description: Stratigraphy, chronology and excavated components

BMB/067b extends down the third beach ridge, which is relatively wide and descends gradually, onto the flatter area bordering the seasonal swamp. It is a dispersed midden, measuring 30 by 400m, with some more concentrated patches across the general low-level surface scatter of shell (Figure 4.7). The surface of the site is dominated by *Anadara granosa, Marcia hiantina, Gafrarium tumidum, Telescopium telescopium, Pinctada* sp., *Septifer bilocularis, Melo amphora, Syrinx aruanus, Saccostrea* sp. and *Polymesoda (Geloina) coaxans*. Several stone artefacts were also located on the surface of this site. Two adjacent test pits (designated as test-pits 1 and 2), each 1m², were excavated into one of the more concentrated sections of the site, with the analysis of the material restricted here to test-pit 1. The area chosen for excavation is located approximately 300m off the edge of the lower-lying mixed grassland and swamp, and was covered with a dense stand of vine thicket vegetation and naturally accumulated sand, sediment and decomposing vegetation. As indicated by the stratigraphic profile (Figure 4.8), there was no clear change in stratigraphy throughout the midden deposit other than a slight decrease in shell in the basal layers. This excavation reached a maximum depth of approximately 35cm, with the base of the excavation indicated by stratigraphic change to beach debris and shelly sand. This deposit contained a large amount of shell material, small amounts of fish remains (possibly a species of Wrasse) and several stone artefacts in a dark humic matrix extending throughout the deposit.

Figure 4.7: Location of site of BMB/067b Test-pit 1 at the base of a large beach-ridge, bordering a small seasonal swamp at Gurratjinya (location of excavation indicated by position of ranging pole).

Source: Photo Patrick Faulkner.

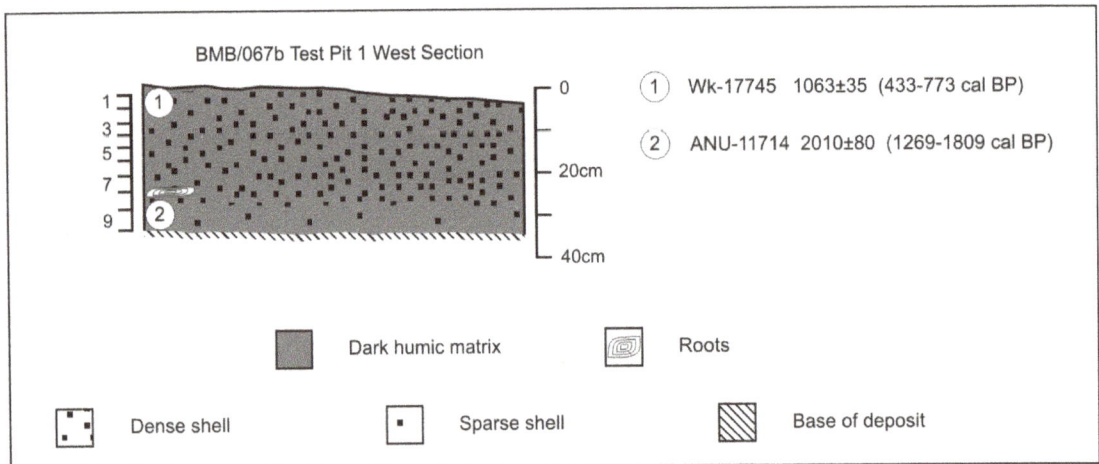

Figure 4.8: BMB/067b Test-pit 1 stratigraphic diagram, west section, showing conventional radiocarbon ages and 2σ calibrated age ranges.

Two radiocarbon age estimates have been obtained from marine shell from the surface and basal excavation units (Table 4.3, and indicated in Figure 4.8). The sample from excavation unit 1 returned a date of 1063±35, calibrating to 592 cal BP, and the sample from excavation unit 9 returned a date of 2010±80, calibrating to 1518 cal BP. These age estimates provide a minimum occupation period of approximately 930 years for this locality, as well as suggesting that this site represents multiple low-level occupation events over a relatively long period.

Table 4.3: Conventional and calibrated radiocarbon ages obtained for site BMB/067b Test-pit 1.

Site Code/XU	Depth (cm)	Lab Code	Sample	δ¹³C	¹⁴C Age	1σ cal Age BP (68.3% probability)	2σ cal Age BP (95.4% probability)	Cal Age BP Median
BMB/067b/1	0 - 2	Wk-17745	*Anadara granosa*	2.2 ± 0.2	1063 ± 35	511–661	433–773	592
/9	27 - 31	ANU-11714	*Anadara granosa*	2.0 ± 0.2	2010 ± 80	1369–1657	1269–1809	1518

Source: Calibration data from CALIB 6.1.1, marine04.14c (Hughen *et al*. 2004), ΔR = 55±98 (Ulm 2006b).

Fragmentation ratios (NISP:MNI) have been calculated for *Anadara granosa* and *Marcia hiantina* by excavation unit (Figure 4.9). The NISP:MNI ratio calculates the approximate number of fragments per individual based on relative abundance counts within individual excavation units. The level of shell fragmentation throughout the site should correspond with phases of increased or decreased occupation. Based on experimental research, it has been suggested that variations in the degree of shell fragmentation may relate more to post-depositional processes rather than those activities occurring at the time of discard, reflecting the intensity of human activity at a site (Muckle 1985:68, 75–78; Claassen 1998:58; Faulkner 2010). For example, when the rate of site deposition is low, cultural material like stone artefacts, shell and bone are exposed on the surface for longer periods, and thus subjected to higher degrees of weathering and fragmentation. Conversely, when deposition is rapid, the length of exposure time and the degree of weathering and fragmentation is lessened (Hiscock 1985:89–90; Bourke 2000:119). Even though the species chosen are representative of robust (*Anadara granosa*) and fragile (*Marcia hiantina*) bivalves, the patterning of fragmentation for both is relatively similar throughout the deposit. These patterns demonstrate that the level of fragmentation increases from a relatively low level at the base of the site and peaks within the central excavation units, then decreases again closer to the surface of the site. The lower levels of fragmentation for both species within the upper layer of the site may be indicative of rapid deposition through natural sedimentation processes occurring after abandonment of the site, therefore protecting the site to a certain degree from weathering and trampling.

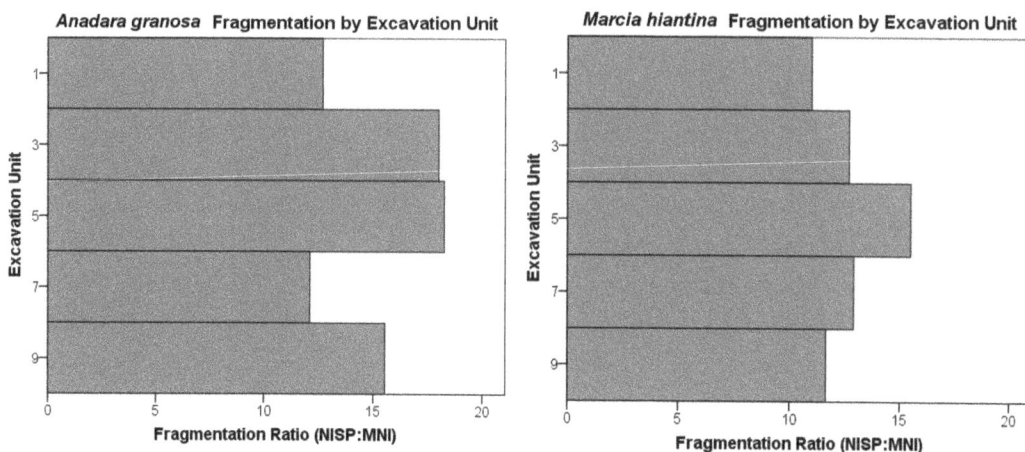

Figure 4.9: BMB/067b Test-pit 1 NISP:MNI fragmentation ratios for *Anadara granosa* and *Marcia hiantina* per excavation unit, 6mm sieve fraction.

Table 4.4 details the quantitative data by weight in grams for the excavated components recovered from the 6mm sieve during excavation, with Figure 4.10 graphing the density estimates of shell, bone and otoliths, charcoal, laterite and rock deposits by excavation unit. Molluscan remains dominate the assemblage by weight at 62.3%, followed by lateritic and rock deposits at 34.4%. Vegetation (0.9%), charcoal (0.01%), bone (0.3%), coral and pumice (1.8%), fragments of crab carapace (0.01%) and stone artefacts (0.4%) form minor components of the excavated assemblage by weight. The significantly increasing density of laterite and rock throughout the deposit (Spearman's r_s = -0.900, $p < 0.05$, $n = 5$) relates primarily to processes of site formation. As this material is the dominant ground surface on the inland margin of the series of beach ridges within the area, the higher density of material in the upper excavation unit relates to the post-depositional covering of the site. Due to the possible slow rate of site deposition, some reworking of the deposit combined with surface exposure would account for this pattern.

Table 4.4: Quantitative data for the excavated components from BMB/067b Test-pit 1, 6mm sieve fraction.

Excavation Unit	Depth (cm)	Volume (cm³)	Laterite/ Rock (g)	Vegetation (g)	Charcoal (g)	Shell (g)	Bone (g)	Coral/ Pumice (g)	Crustacean (g)	Stone Artefacts No./g
1	0.0 to 1.3	13000	700.5	44.6	---	1281.4	1.1	38.2	2.0	4/64.4
3	3.5 to 6.6	31000	1176.0	24.8	---	1941.5	2.1	43.1	---	---
5	10.3 to 13.7	34000	1439.7	46.2	---	2474.0	8.8	48.7	---	---
7	18.9 to 22.0	31000	1154.9	25.3	1.5	2703.5	25.4	60.7	---	---
9	26.7 to 31.3	46000	1388.0	4.5	0.8	2223.6	8.7	118.5	---	---
Totals			5859.1	145.4	2.3	10624	46.1	309.2	2	4/64.4
% of Total Wt. (17052.5)			34.36	0.85	0.01	62.30	0.27	1.81	0.01	0.38

Three main species, *Anadara granosa* (31.9%), *Marcia hiantina* (21.1%) and *Septifer bilocularis* (17.0%), dominate the assemblage. While there are peaks in the density of shell in excavation units 1 and 7, there is not a significant relationship between the density of this material and excavation unit (Spearman's r_s = -0.600, $p > 0.01$, $n = 5$). By extension, the discard of molluscan remains throughout the history of site deposition or occupation was consistent. Relative to the density of the other components recovered during excavation of this site, the dominance and consistent discard of this material suggests that molluscs were the primary focus of resource exploitation within this area. The condition of bone recovered from the site was poor, even given the better preservational environment compared with other shell deposits in the sample. Due to high levels of fragmentation the identification of the bone was limited, with identifiable elements only recovered from excavation units 1, 7 and 9. All of the identifiable bone elements within the site are a species of Wrasse, which inhabits near-shore coral and rocky reefs. The identifiable elements of the bone sample includes two grinding plate fragments and one vertebrae from excavation unit 1, two grinding plate fragments, three mandible fragments and one vertebrae from excavation unit 7, and three grinding plate fragments and one vertebrae from excavation unit 9. The presence of bone within this site is most likely due to the humic nature of the deposit, combined with the possible rapid burial of the site's surface following abandonment. Although there is a peak in the density of bone within excavation unit 7, it is a minor increase, and there is not a significant relationship between the density of bone and excavation unit (Spearman's r_s = 0.600, $p > 0.01$, $n = 5$). This suggests that the use of faunal resources other than molluscs was at a consistently low-level of exploitation, particularly given that the non-molluscan faunal component of the site only comprises 0.3% of the assemblage at an overall weight of 46.1g.

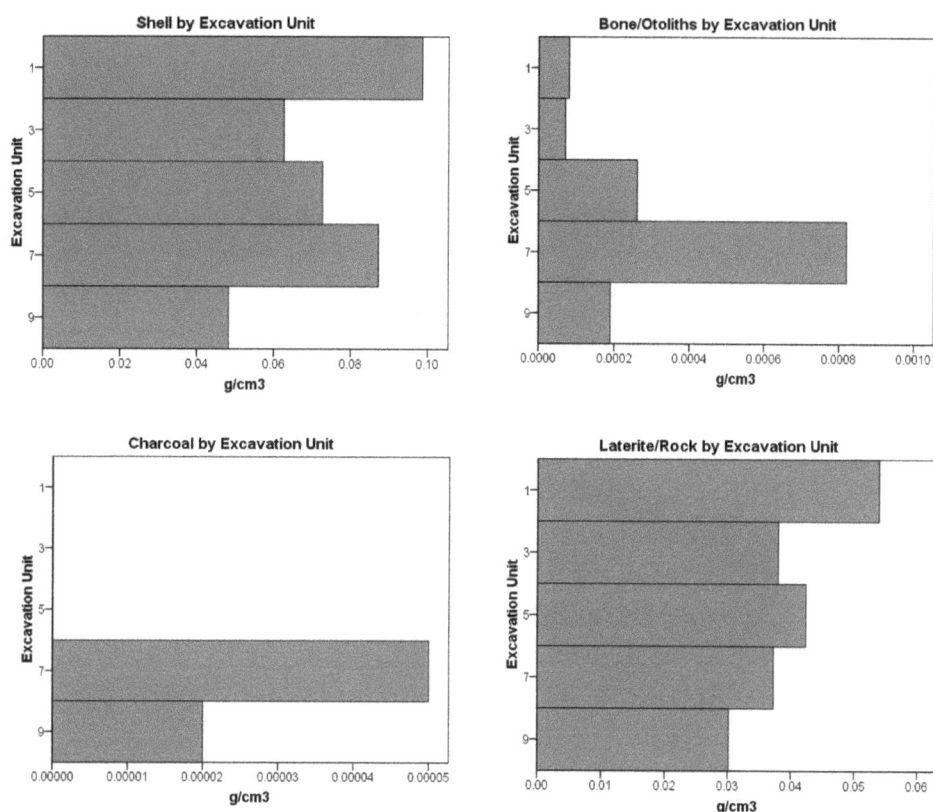

Figure 4.10: Density (g/cm³) of shell, bone/otoliths, charcoal and laterite/rock by excavation unit, BMB/067b Test-pit 1, 6mm sieve fraction.

Four stone artefacts were recovered from the surface and within excavation unit 1 of this site. It is difficult to ascertain whether these artefacts relate to the period of midden deposition, or whether they were discarded within this area after a phase of natural, rapid sediment deposition occurring following abandonment of the site. The artefacts recovered from the surface of the site prior to excavation consist of one silcrete unretouched flake (weighing 19.4g and measuring 32.57mm by 45.72mm), and one quartzite unretouched flake (weighing 10.9g and measuring 27.79mm by 30.46mm). In terms of raw material and artefact size and shape, the silcrete and quartzite artefacts conform reasonably well to those previously analysed. The other two artefacts recovered from just below the ground surface are of a previously unrecorded volcanic raw material within the area. It is unknown where this stone may have been sourced from, although Aboriginal informants indicated that this material comes from one of the small, offshore islands. It is possible that this material could have been sourced reasonably locally, as based on the geological maps there are undifferentiated volcanics (part of the Arnhem Inlier formation) distributed along the neighbouring peninsulas and small islands. These two artefacts are an unretouched flake (weighing 11.0g and measuring 40.46mm by 22.26mm), and a flaked piece (weighing 23.1g and measuring 49.09mm by 16.50mm). The most notable feature on both volcanic artefacts is the presence of use-wear in the form of marginal smoothing/abrasion.

Interpreting the depositional history of this site is difficult, with only surface and basal radiocarbon dates available. Considering this, the dominance of shell throughout the deposits combined with what appears to be a consistent level of discard in molluscan remains suggests a focus on mollusc exploitation and discard.

The Lumatjpi area

The area known as Lumatjpi is located to the north of the Yilpara community on the Myaoola Bay coastline (Figure 4.11). There are nine sites located in this area, and with two exceptions described below, the majority consist of very small, localised patches of thinly spread surface midden material. Mixed *Eucalypt* woodland covers most of the area leading up to a low, mounded laterite ridge that runs parallel to the coastline. Large swampy areas and paperbark swamps on cracking grey clays are situated in this area, drained by several small, seasonal creeks. Dense mangrove stands occur alongside sandy chenier ridges, dissected by extensive laterite platforms.

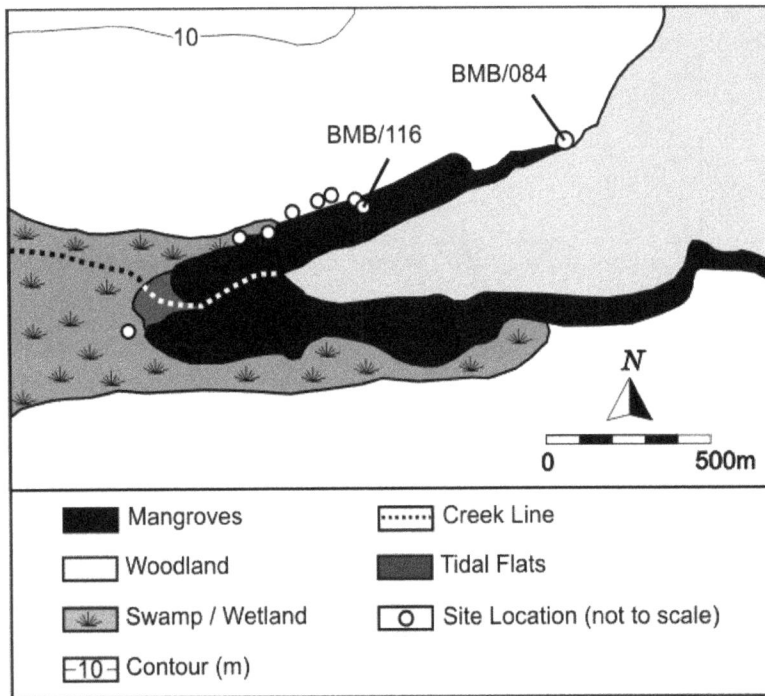

Figure 4.11: Lumatjpi cluster and location of site BMB/084 (excavated and radiocarbon dated site BMB/116 also shown).

Source: Based on Baniyala 1:50 000 Topographic Map.

BMB/084 site description: Stratigraphy, chronology and excavated components

The large midden complex BMB/084 measures approximately 75 by 320m, extending along a low sandy ridge positioned behind mangrove stands. Mangroves and paperbark border the site, except at the eastern end where a laterite gravel ridge forms the boundary. There are variations in the content of midden patches within the site from east to west, with evidence of more recent mollusc exploitation evident along the western edge. One informant (August 2000) stated that her family camped at Lumatjpi to collect freshwater, and to fish and collect shellfish in the 1970s during the early days of the establishment of the Yilpara outstation. This would account for the modern radiocarbon dates obtained from the surface of the site. Four 50cm² test pits were located in different midden concentrations across the site as a whole (Figure 4.12). This was due to the high degree of species diversity and abundance occurring across the site, with these different areas possibly reflecting chronological variability in the use of the area. In all test pits the base of the excavation was indicated by clean, orange sand mixed with shell grit, reflecting the natural sand ridge deposit. Test-pit 1 is the focus for this investigation, with this 50cm² test-pit excavated into a patch of densely concentrated shell within an area of monsoon vine thicket.

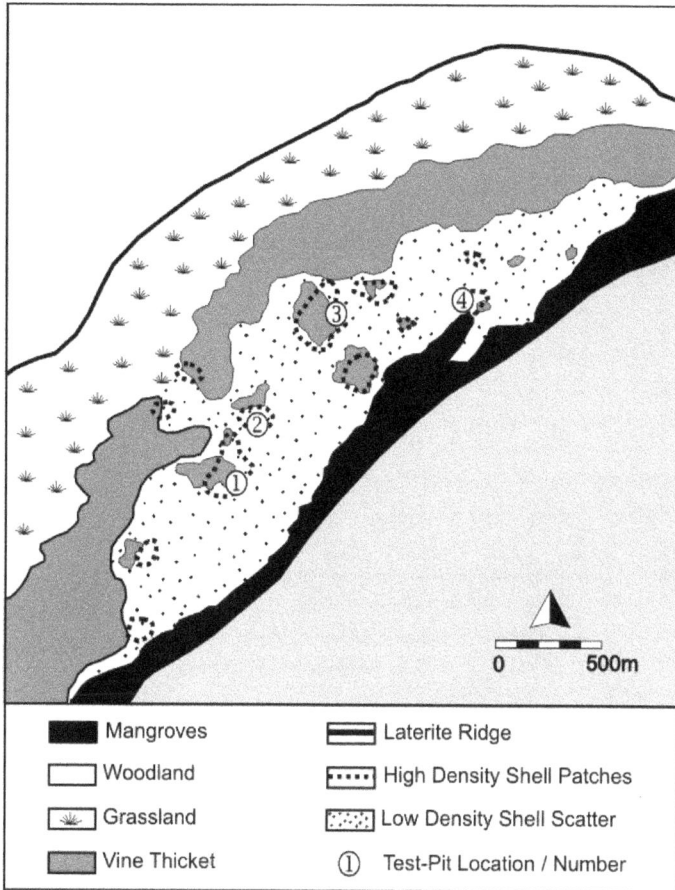

Figure 4.12: BMB/084 site plan at Lumatjpi, showing concentrations of midden material and the location of Test-pits.

The surface of test-pit 1 was covered by loose, whole shell and sand, with two stratigraphic layers recognised in the profile (Figure 4.13). The upper 10cm layer consists of a dark, humic matrix dominated by a species of *Isognomon*. The lower layer, consisting largely of *Marcia hiantina* in a lighter matrix, extends around 20cm down onto the clean, orange sand. Four samples of marine shell were submitted for radiocarbon dating from test-pit 1 to determine if there was a chronological difference between these two stratigraphic units. The approximate locations of these samples, at the surface and base of the site and above and below the stratigraphic break, are shown in the stratigraphic section (Figure 4.13) and detailed in Table 4.5. The surface sample returned a modern conventional radiocarbon age of 122.3%±1.0%, and the sample from the bottom of the initial stratigraphic layer returned a date of 360±60, calibrating to modern. The sample from the top of the lower stratigraphic unit returned an age of 460±70, again calibrating to modern, and a sample from the base of the site returned an age estimate of 860±70, calibrated to 424 cal BP. These age estimates indicate that occupation in this site spans the period from approximately 424 years before present and the present day. This suggests that there may have been at least two phases of occupation within this particular excavated area, one initial phase of intermittent occupation followed by a phase of more rapid deposition in the recent past.

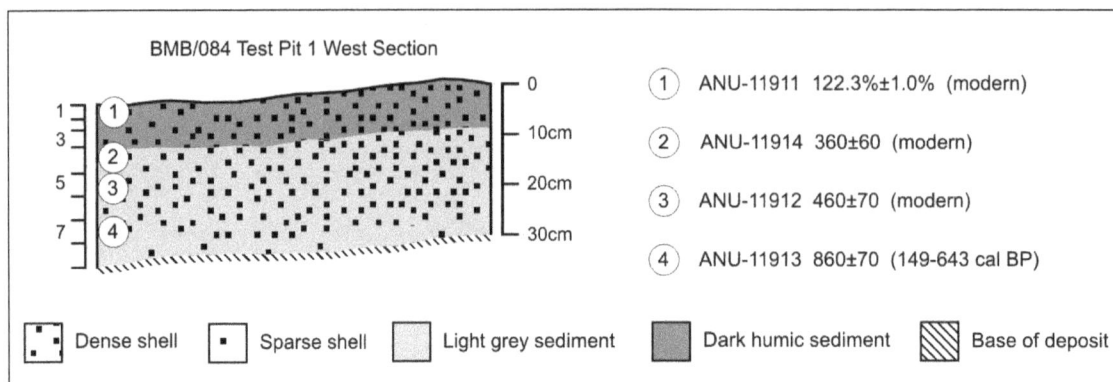

Figure 4.13: BMB/084 Test-pit 1 stratigraphic diagram, west section, showing conventional radiocarbon ages and 2σ calibrated age ranges.

Table 4.5: Conventional and calibrated radiocarbon ages obtained for site BMB/084, Test-pit 1.

Site Code /XU	Depth (cm)	Lab Code	Sample	δ¹³C (*estimate)	¹⁴C Age	1σ cal Age BP (68.3% probability)	2σ cal Age BP (95.4% probability)	Cal Age BP Median
BMB/084/1	0 - 1	ANU-11911	*Marcia hiantina*	0.0 ± 2.0*	$122.3\% \pm 1.0\%$	Modern	Modern	--
/4	4 - 7	ANU-11914	*Marcia hiantina*	0.0 ± 2.0*	360 ± 60	Modern	Modern	--
/5	7 - 11	ANU-11912	*Marcia hiantina*	0.0 ± 2.0*	460 ± 70	Modern	Modern	--
/7	14 - 17	ANU-11913	*Marcia hiantina*	0.0 ± 2.0*	860 ± 70	309–516	149–643	424

Source: Calibration data from CALIB 6.1.1, marine04.14c (Hughen *et al.* 2004), ΔR = 55±98 (Ulm 2006b).

Based on assessment of the proportion of juveniles per taxon, the proportion of shell greater than 15mm in size, shell breakage patterns and the presence and quantity of charcoal, Esposito (2005:68–9) interprets the depositional history of test-pit 1 as reflecting a likely cultural midden deposit occurring over the top of an existing beach ridge. While it was also determined that there was a degree of reworking within the deposit by natural processes (e.g. storm surges), this site is more consistent with an anthropogenic origin than a natural shell deposit. Regardless of the level of reworking or mixing of the deposit, it is still possible to extract information on economic activity within this site, especially when tied to patterns of site deposition and the phase of more modern intensive occupation. This is illustrated by investigating fragmentation ratios by excavation unit for *Marcia hiantina*, a relatively fragile and abundant species within this site (Figure 4.14). The level of fragmentation decreases closer to the surface of the site, with higher rates of fragmentation in excavation units 6, 7 and 8 possibly relating to the initial, intermittent phase of occupation for this site indicated by the analysis of the radiocarbon determinations. The lower levels of fragmentation within the upper five layers of the site correspond with the more rapid rate of deposition identified for the relatively recent past.

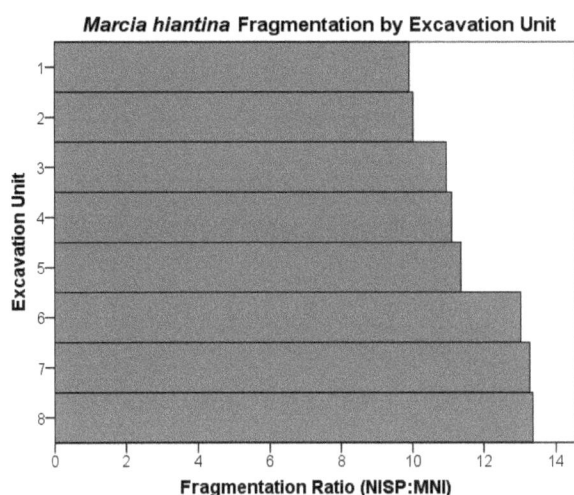

Figure 4.14: BMB/084, Test-pit 1, NISP:MNI fragmentation ratios for *Marcia hiantina* per excavation unit, 6mm sieve fraction.

Table 4.6 details the quantitative data by weight in grams for the excavated components recovered from the 6mm sieve during excavation of test-pit 1, with the density (g/cm³) of shell, charcoal, calcareous worm shell and laterite/rock by excavation unit graphed in Figure 4.15. These data show that there is considerable variation in the distribution within and between these components by excavation unit. Vegetation remains (0.8%) and charcoal (0.4%) form minor components of the assemblage. Variations in the density of charcoal within the site possibly relates to both processes of vertical decay within the deposit and the depositional history of the site. However, there is not a statistically significant relationship between the density of charcoal and excavation unit (Spearman's r_s = 0.252, p > 0.2, n = 8). The low amounts of calcareous worm shell and coral present in the lower levels of the excavation support to some degree the notion of minor reworking of the deposit, as noted by Esposito (2005:68–9).

Table 4.6: Quantitative data for the excavated components from Test-pit 1, BMB/084, 6mm sieve fraction.

Excavation Unit	Depth (cm)	Volume cm³	Laterite/Rock (g)	Vegetation (g)	Worm Shell (g)	Coral/Pumice (g)	Charcoal (g)	Shell (g)	Crustacean (g)
1	0.0 to 1.2	3000	348.6	13.7	---	---	0.1	482.1	---
2	1.2 to 1.9	1750	0.9	9.7	---	---	1.9	1026.4	---
3	1.9 to 4.1	5500	138.2	6.3	---	---	0.2	326.3	---
4	4.1 to 7.4	8250	9.1	3.0	1.5	0.1	0.3	527.1	0.5
5	7.4 to 10.8	8500	180.5	8.3	1.1	---	3.1	830.8	---
6	10.8 to 13.7	7250	41.9	1.9	0.2	---	0.1	573.2	---
7	13.7 to 16.9	8000	433.8	4.3	---	---	15.5	660.2	0.2
8	16.9 to 20.2	8250	51.5	1.5	0.1	0.6	0.8	144.9	0.1
Totals			**1204.5**	**48.7**	**2.9**	**0.7**	**22**	**4571**	**0.8**
% of Total Wt. (5850.6)			**20.59**	**0.83**	**0.05**	**0.01**	**0.38**	**78.13**	**0.01**

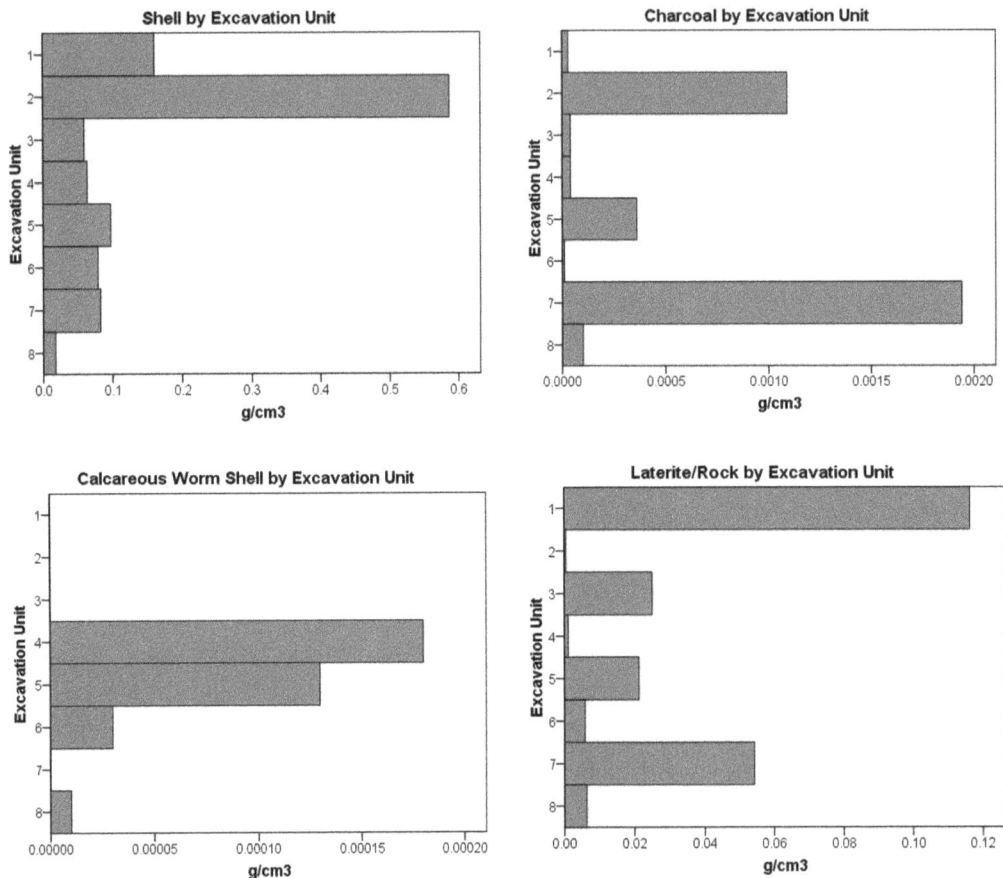

Figure 4.15: Density (g/cm³) of shell, charcoal, calcareous worm shell and laterite/rock by excavation unit, BMB/084 Test-pit 1, 6mm sieve fraction.

The dominant molluscan taxa represented within the site are *Marcia hiantina* (29.0%), *Isognomon isognomon* (27.8%) and a species from the *Mytilidae* family (14.4%). Molluscan material dominates the assemblage by weight at 78.1 %, followed by lateritic and rock deposits at 20.6%. As with charcoal, the relationship between the density of shell and excavation unit is not statistically significant (Spearman's r_s = -0.571, p > 0.05, n = 8) or between laterite/rock by excavation unit (Spearman's r_s = -0.048, p > 0.5, n = 8). This suggests that the variation noted for these components, particularly relative to the various peaks in the density of material throughout the excavation, is only minor. No artefactual material or bone was recovered from this excavation. Even given the potential for at least two phases with marked differences in the rates of deposition, one that appears quite slow and ephemeral followed by a more rapid and possibly intensive phase, there does not appear to be any differences in the distribution of material between these phases. Therefore, while there is variability in the formation history of the site, given the dominance of shell throughout the deposits, site function appears to have been similar throughout the history of occupation.

The Garangarri cluster

The Garangarri area is located approximately 8km inland from the present coastline near the northern extent of the Dhuruputjpi wetlands system in Grindall Bay. The Durabudboi River feeds into this wetland system approximately 1 to 1.5km north of this locality. Mixed *Eucalypt* woodland forms the dominant vegetation component leading up to the edge of the lateritic ridge, the lower lying areas at the base of the ridge in this area are dominantly paperbark swamps, mixed grasslands and seasonal wetlands vegetation. The gradient and height of the laterite ridge in this area varies considerably, with height of the ridge ranging between approximately 1 and 3m. The ridgeline is at its highest and most steep in the middle sections of the area, tailing out on either end. This area is dominated by a cluster of 10 shell mounds and midden sites of various sizes. The sites range from low, surface scatters of shell to mounded deposits of approximately 2.6m in height, and in area range from 35m^2 and 1141m^2. The sites are distributed linearly along the edge of the laterite ridge (Figure 4.16); the largest of the 10 sites is located centrally within this cluster, with site size decreasing northwards and southwards from this location. BMB/029, the excavated mound site within the Garangarri cluster, is situated relatively centrally, adjacent to the largest of the mounds in this cluster.

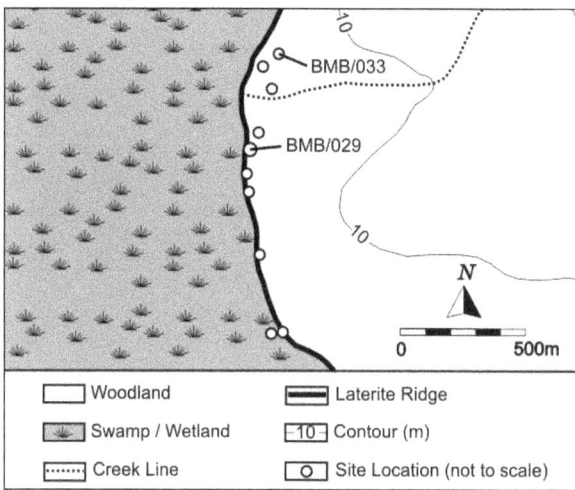

Figure 4.16: Garangarri cluster and location of excavated site BMB/029 (radiocarbon dated site BMB/033 also shown).

Source: Based on Baniyala 1:50 000 Topographic Map.

BMB/029 site description: Stratigraphy, chronology and excavated components

BMB/029 is a low, regularly shaped shell mound, measuring 23.6m by 21m and up to 1m in height, set back approximately 10 to 15m from the edge of the laterite ridge. The site is shown in Figure 4.17, and a contour plan of the site and a cross-section of this mound site are shown in Figure 4.18. This site extends down the ridge slope, and the spilling of the shell deposit down the side of the laterite ridge possibly relates to slumping of the basal laterite surface closer to the edge of the ridgeline. This site was chosen for excavation as it is located centrally within the site cluster and, based on surface inspection, is representative in size and content of sites in this location. Shellfish species dominating the surface of the site include *Anadara granosa*, *Telescopium telescopium*, *Terebralia palustris*, *Marcia hiantina*, *Placuna placenta* and *Polymesoda (Geloina) coaxans*. The shell on the surface of the site exhibits a high degree of weathering and fragmentation, relating to high levels of exposure and trampling.

Figure 4.17: Site BMB/029, view west towards edge of laterite ridge and wetlands.

Source: Photo Patrick Faulkner.

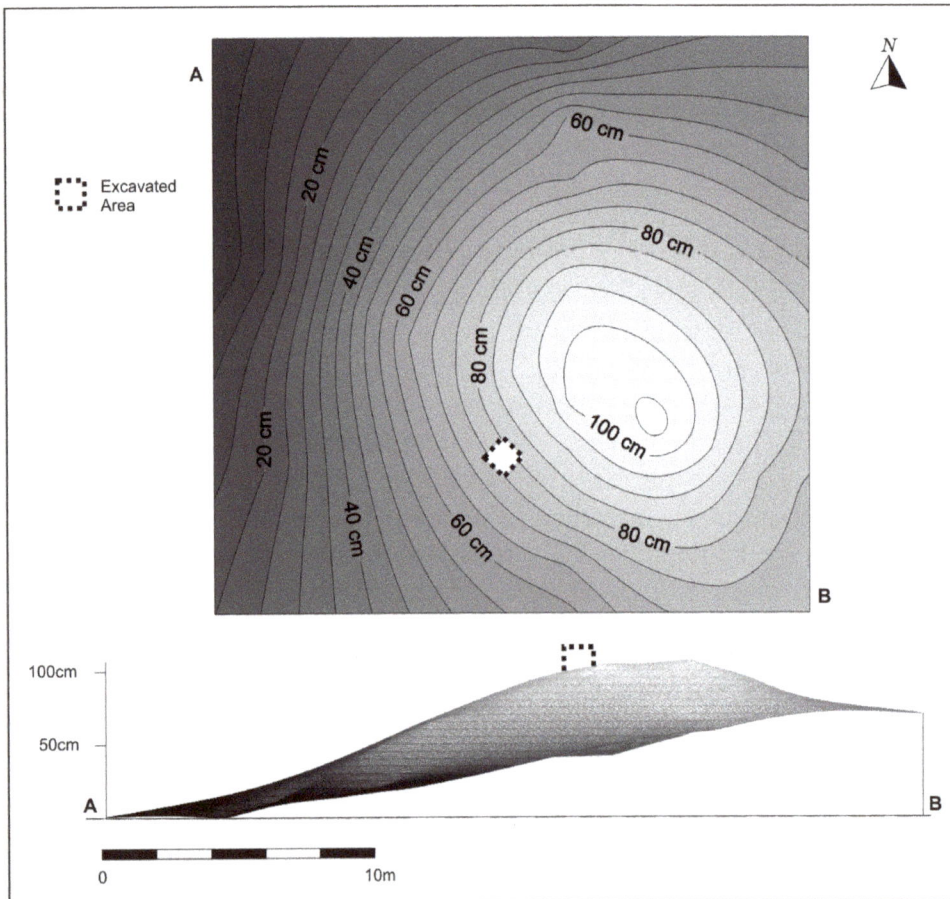

Figure 4.18: Contour plan of site BMB/029 showing location of the excavation square.

A 1m² test-pit was positioned relatively centrally at the higher end of the mound, with the excavation reaching a depth of approximately 90cm. The mound itself is composed of densely-packed shell material, with very little in the way of sedimentary matrix. Several stratigraphic layers were identified (Figure 4.19), although dominantly composed of *Anadara granosa*, mixed with fine grey and white ash material, there are horizontal lenses of *Placuna placenta* occurring throughout the deposit. The surface of the site was heavily fragmented and fine rootlets extended to a depth of approximately 20cm. The lower 20cm to 30cm of deposit consisted of a matrix of yellow brown clay and lateritic pebbles with low numbers of highly fragmented shell material. Excavation ceased on reaching the hard-packed clay and laterite representative of the surrounding ground surface.

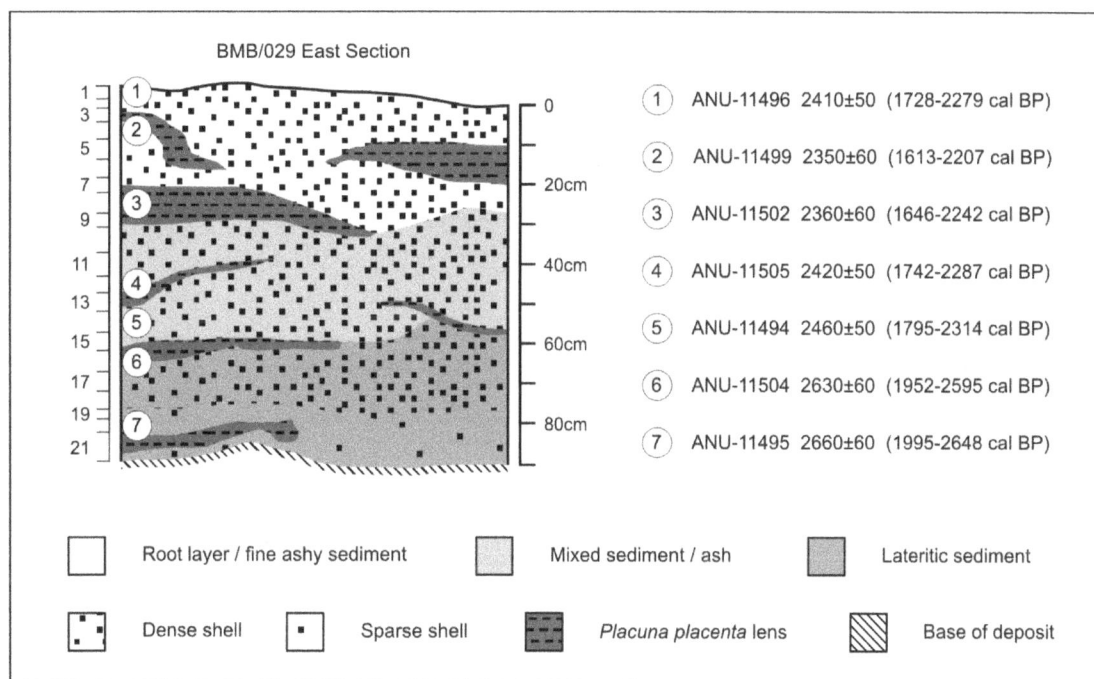

Figure 4.19: BMB/029 stratigraphic diagram, east section, showing conventional radiocarbon ages and 2σ calibrated age ranges.

Seven *Anadara granosa* samples were submitted for radiocarbon dating; the calibrated radiocarbon ages are detailed in Table 4.7 and graphed in Figure 4.20. The surface sample returned a date of 2410±50, which calibrated to 1985 cal BP, and a sample from the base of the site returned a date of 2660±60, which calibrated to 2287 cal BP. The 'test sample significance' function of the CALIB v6.1.1 program indicates that the 2σ calibrated ages for all samples are statistically indistinguishable at the 95% confidence level ($t = 7.19$, *d.f.* = 6). Two phases of deposition were originally identified for this site based on significant differences in the calibrated radiocarbon ages (e.g. Faulkner 2009, 2011), however calibration of these ages using the revised ΔR correction value of 55±98 recommended for the Gulf of Carpentaria (Ulm 2006b) effectively removes the gaps in the calibrated ages. Therefore, while the data suggests an overall age range for this site of approximately 302 years, formation of this deposit was rapid, and cannot be broken down into further depositional phases based on the radiocarbon determinations.

Table 4.7: Conventional and calibrated radiocarbon ages obtained for site BMB/029.

Site Code /XU	Depth (cm)	Lab Code	Sample	δ¹³C (*estimate)	¹⁴C Age	1σ cal Age BP (68.3% probability)	2σ cal Age BP (95.4% probability)	Cal Age BP Median
BMB/029 /1	0 - 3	ANU-11496	Anadara granosa	-3.4 ± 0.1	2410 ± 50	1850–2120	1728–2279	1985
/4	8 - 11	ANU-11499	Anadara granosa	-4.0 ± 0.1	2350 ± 60	1771–2058	1613–2207	1912
/8	23 - 28	ANU-11502	Anadara granosa	0.0 ± 2.0 *	2360 ± 60	1788–2074	1646–2242	1925
/12	41 - 45	ANU-11505	Anadara granosa	-2.8 ± 0.1	2420 ± 50	1858–2129	1742–2287	1997
/14	49 - 53	ANU-11494	Anadara granosa	-2.6 ± 0.1	2460 ± 50	1892–2171	1795–2314	2045
/16	58 - 62	ANU-11504	Anadara granosa	-3.1 ± 0.2	2630 ± 60	2085–2380	1952–2595	2245
/20	75 - 81	ANU-11495	Anadara granosa	0.0 ± 2.0 *	2660 ± 60	2122–2435	1995–2648	2287

Source: Calibration data from CALIB 6.1.1, marine04.14c (Hughen *et al.* 2004), ΔR = 55±98 (Ulm 2006b).

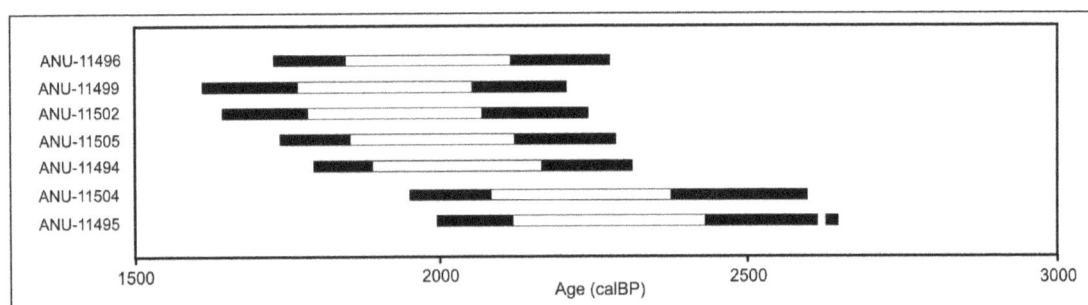

Figure 4.20: Calibrated radiocarbon ages (1 and 2σ) obtained for BMB/029.

To assess variability in the level of fragmentation throughout the deposit, NISP:MNI ratios have been calculated for two different species per excavation unit (Figure 4.21). Levels of fragmentation within the site have again been assessed here using the two dominant molluscan species, the robust *Anadara granosa* and the comparatively thinner-walled *Marcia hiantina*. Using robust and fragile species as a comparison enables a certain level of control with this type of analysis, relating particularly to possible differential patterns of fragmentation related to the structural integrity of individual species. While there are differences in the rate of fragmentation between these two species, there are similarities in the broad patterning of fragmentation relative to depth. The very high rate of fragmentation shown between excavation units 5 and 1 can be related to postdepositional processes of weathering, fragmentation and compaction since abandonment of the site approximately 2140 years ago.

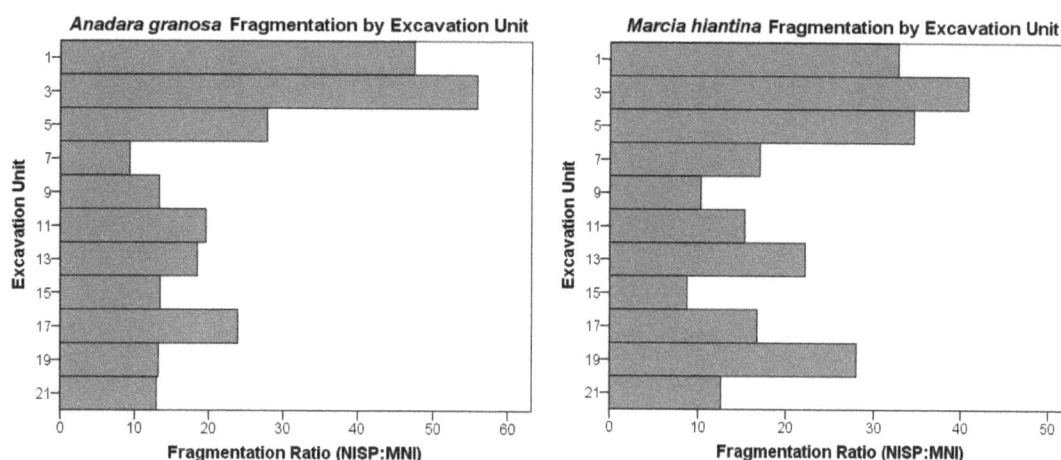

Figure 4.21: BMB/029 NISP:MNI fragmentation ratios for *Anadara granosa* and *Marcia hiantina* per excavation unit, 6mm sieve fraction.

Table 4.8 details the quantitative data by weight in grams for the excavated components recovered from the 6 mm sieve, with Figure 4.22 graphing the density estimates of shell, bone and otoliths, charcoal and laterite and rock by excavation unit. This shows that molluscan remains dominate the assemblage by weight at 75.2%, followed by lateritic and rock deposits at 24.68%. Vegetation (0.1%), charcoal (0.03%), and fragments of crab carapace (0.01%) form minor components of the excavated assemblage by weight. Three species dominate the molluscan remains within this site, these being *Anadara granosa* (68.1%), *Marcia hiantina* (13.5%) and *Placuna placenta* (9.8%). Although molluscan remains dominate this assemblage as a whole, there is a significant relationship between the density of this material and excavation unit (Spearman's r_s = -0.809, p < 0.005, n = 11). The significant increase in the density of shell throughout the deposit possibly relate to the timing and nature of environmental change in the area. The initial use of this location at 2465 cal BP would appear to correspond with the initial establishment of suitable habitats for molluscan taxa with progradation. With further habitat development and possible proliferation of mollusc resources in the area there is a subsequent and rapid phase of occupation highlighted by the greater density of molluscan debris.

Table 4.8: Quantitative data for the excavated components from BMB/029, 6mm sieve fraction.

Excavation Unit	Depth (cm)	Volume (cm³)	Laterite (g)	Vegetation (g)	Charcoal (g)	Shell (g)	Otoliths No./ g	Crustacean (g)	Stone Artefacts No./g
1	0 to 3	7000	35.4	16.8	---	2981.8	2/0.4	1.2	---
3	5 to 8	7500	62.0	8.0	---	3772.0	4/1.6	0.2	---
5	12 to 16	11000	37.7	2.9	0.3	3044.7	1/0.3	0.4	---
7	20 to 23	8250	11.4	1.0	1.2	3496.7	1/0.4	---	---
9	28 to 31	7500	60.8	0.2	0.3	2844.8	---	---	---
11	36 to 41	12750	108.3	0.5	1.2	5091.9	---	0.3	---
13	45 to 49	10000	70.3	0.3	2.1	3522.5	1/0.7	---	1/1.5
15	53 to 58	10250	1391.5	0.2	0.8	1777.3	---	---	---
17	62 to 66	10500	1670.3	0.7	3.1	742.6	---	---	---
19	70 to 72	5250	1091.7	---	1.9	530.3	---	0.9	---
21	75 to 82	15750	4762.8	---	0.3	524.5	---	---	1/4.3
Totals			**9302.2**	**30.6**	**11.2**	**28329.1**	**9/3.4**	**3**	**2/5.8**
% of Total Wt. (37685.3)			**24.68**	**0.08**	**0.03**	**75.17**	**0.01**	**0.01**	**0.02**

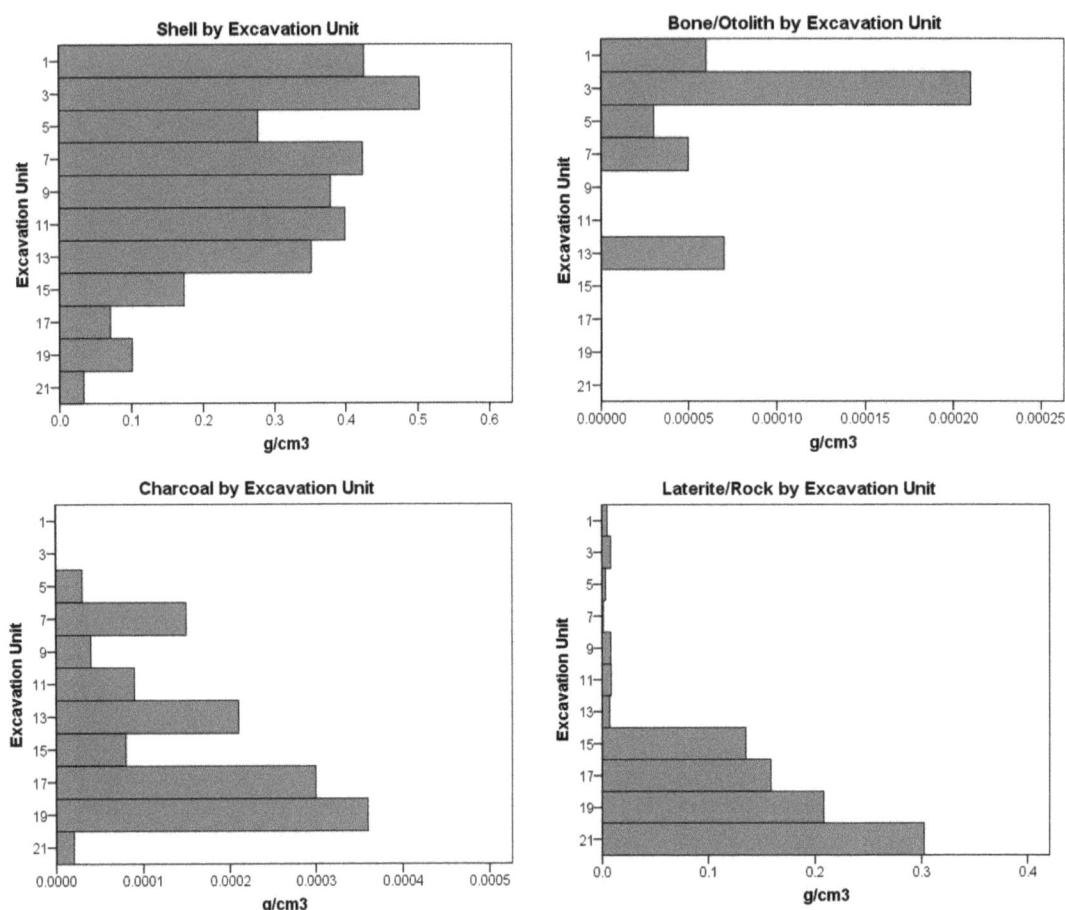

Figure 4.22: Density (g/cm³) of shell, bone/otolith, charcoal and laterite/rock by excavation unit, BMB/029, 6mm sieve fraction.

Eight otoliths were recovered from the upper four excavation units, with one otolith coming from unit 13. All of the otoliths from this site are Catfish (*Arius* sp.), a species that inhabits estuarine to freshwater habitats. That all of the otoliths recovered from this site are concentrated within the upper portions of the deposit suggests that the use of resources other than molluscs may relate to changes to the local environment and the development of appropriate habitats for *Arius* species with landscape alteration. With regard to dietary contribution, this suggests that resources other than molluscs were possibly of minor importance, as the otoliths representing a minimum number of five individuals and comprising 0.01% of the excavated assemblage by weight.

Turning to the non-faunal components of the assemblage, the distribution of charcoal throughout the deposit could relate to either cultural or natural processes. The combination of a relatively dry climate with natural or anthropogenic burning of this environment may account for the density of charcoal, with mixed lenses of ash and charcoal occurring throughout the deposit and charcoal density increasing towards the base. Regardless of its origin or this distributional pattern, there is not a significant difference in the density of charcoal throughout the deposit (Spearman's $r_s = 0.579$, $p > 0.05$, $n = 11$). In contrast, there is a greater density of laterite within the lower excavation units of the site, with a significant decrease in laterite density throughout the deposit (Spearman's $r_s = 0.818$, $p > 0.002$, $n = 11$). With laterite being the dominant ground surface in the area, the higher density of this material towards the bottom of the site would have enabled the movement of laterite into the deposit through natural processes, combined with the lower height of the mound during this phase. Two stone artefacts were also recovered during the course of excavation. One flaked piece (a silcrete medial flake fragment) was recovered from unit 13, weighing 1.5g and measuring 18.93mm by 15.05mm. The second, a complete unretouched flake, was recovered from the base of the deposit in excavation unit 21, weighing 4.3g and measuring 42.45mm by 15.28mm. As noted with the silcrete and quartzite artefacts from site BMB/067b, these two artefacts conform reasonably well to those previously discussed.

Overall, it can be seen that in the apparent rapid formation of this site, as evidenced by the radiocarbon determinations and fragmentation data, combined with differences in the density of molluscan material throughout the deposit, provides evidence for the period of initial occupation and subsequent resource exploitation in the Grindall Bay area.

The Dilmitjpi cluster

The Dilmitjpi area, located to the south of Garangarri and separated by a seasonal water channel and floodway, is in many ways similar environmentally to the previous cluster (Figure 4.23). Mixed *Eucalypt* woodland dominates the landscape leading up to the edge of the laterite ridge, which in this area of the wetlands is quite variable in height, ranging between approximately 1 and 5m. The laterite ridge is at its highest and steepest around the small headland area jutting westwards into the wetlands, with the sites clustering around this area. The structure of the cluster is different to that found at Garangarri, with sites located on the edges of the laterite ridge, as well as on the edges of the wetlands at the foot of the ridge, and several hundred metres into the woodlands moving east away from the wetlands. Twenty-three sites are found in this area, ranging in size from small surface scatters of shell with an area of 26.1m², to a very large mounded shell deposit extending along the upper edge of the laterite ridge, measuring approximately 354m in length, 1.8m in height and covering an area of 10,620m². The sites radiate out from this large composite mound, extending for approximately 300m along the edge of the ridge, with site size decreasing with distance from this point.

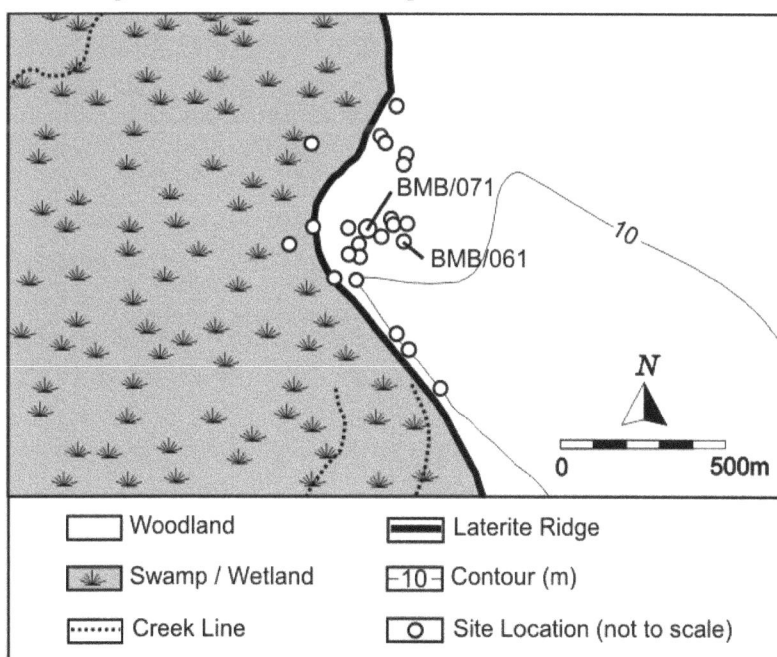

Figure 4.23: Dilmitjpi cluster and location of excavated site BMB/071 (excavated and radiocarbon dated site BMB/061 also shown).

Source: Based on Baniyala 1:50 000 Topographic Map.

BMB/071 site description: Stratigraphy, chronology and excavated components

BMB/071 is a large 1m high shell mound, positioned approximately 100m from the edge of the laterite ridge, measuring 19.8m by 19.4m (Figure 4.24). The mound is surrounded by *Eucalyptus tetrodonta* woodland, with smaller mounds situated between this site and the laterite edge, with much smaller middens leading further into the woodland. This site is situated relatively centrally within this section of the large Dilmitjpi cluster (Figure 4.25). Shellfish species dominating the surface of the site include *Anadara granosa, Marcia hiantina, Mactra abbreviata, Volema* sp. and *Terebralia palustris*. The shell is very heavily weathered and fragmented, with several burnt patches, largely confined to those areas closer to dense vegetation, relating to the annual burning of this area.

A 1m² test-pit was excavated into the side of the site, reaching approximately 50 to 60cm in depth. The mound itself is composed of densely packed *Anadara granosa*, with very little in the way of sedimentary matrix, and fine rootlets extending through the first 30cm of the excavation (Figure 4.26). The base of deposit consisted of a matrix of yellow brown clay and laterite, with highly fragmented shell material. As with BMB/029, excavation ceased on reaching the hard-packed clay and laterite representative of the surrounding ground surface. A small lens of *Placuna placenta* was located at a depth of approximately 40cm, but the quantity of this species is minimal. Rather, it is another bivalve species, *Mactra abbreviata*, which appears to form the sub-dominant component of this site. Three *Anadara granosa* samples were submitted for radiocarbon dating (Table 4.9). The surface sample returned a date of 1700±60 which calibrated to 1192 cal BP, a relatively central sample from excavation unit 6 returned a date of 1810±60 which calibrated to 1310 cal BP, and a sample from the base of the site returned a date of 1980±60 which calibrated to 1483 cal BP. Similar to BMB/029, two phases of deposition were originally identified for this site (Faulkner 2009, 2011), with re-calibration of the radiocarbon dates now suggesting this may not be the case. The age estimates presented here now suggest extremely rapid accumulation of this site, with occupation of approximately 291 years between 1192 and 1483 years BP. As with BMB/029, the 'test sample significance' function of the CALIB v6.1.1 program indicates that the 2σ calibrated ages for all samples are statistically indistinguishable at the 95% confidence level (*t* = 3.01, *d.f.* = 2), indicating rapid formation of this deposit.

Table 4.9: Conventional and calibrated radiocarbon ages obtained for site BMB/071.

Site Code /XU	Depth (cm)	Lab Code	Sample	δ¹³C	¹⁴C Age	1σ cal Age BP (68.3% probability)	2σ cal Age BP (95.4% probability)	Cal Age BP Median
BMB/071 / 1	0 - 3	ANU-11722	*Anadara granosa*	2.9 ± 0.2	1700 ± 60	1067–1299	936–1412	1192
/ 6	19 - 24	ANU-11723	*Anadara granosa*	-2.5 ± 0.2	1810 ± 60	1176–1419	1053–1551	1310
/ 11	42 - 46	ANU-11724	*Anadara granosa*	3.1 ± 0.2	1980 ± 60	1343–1599	1259–1753	1483

Source: Calibration data from CALIB 6.1.1, marine04.14c (Hughen *et al.* 2004), ΔR = 55±98 (Ulm 2006b).

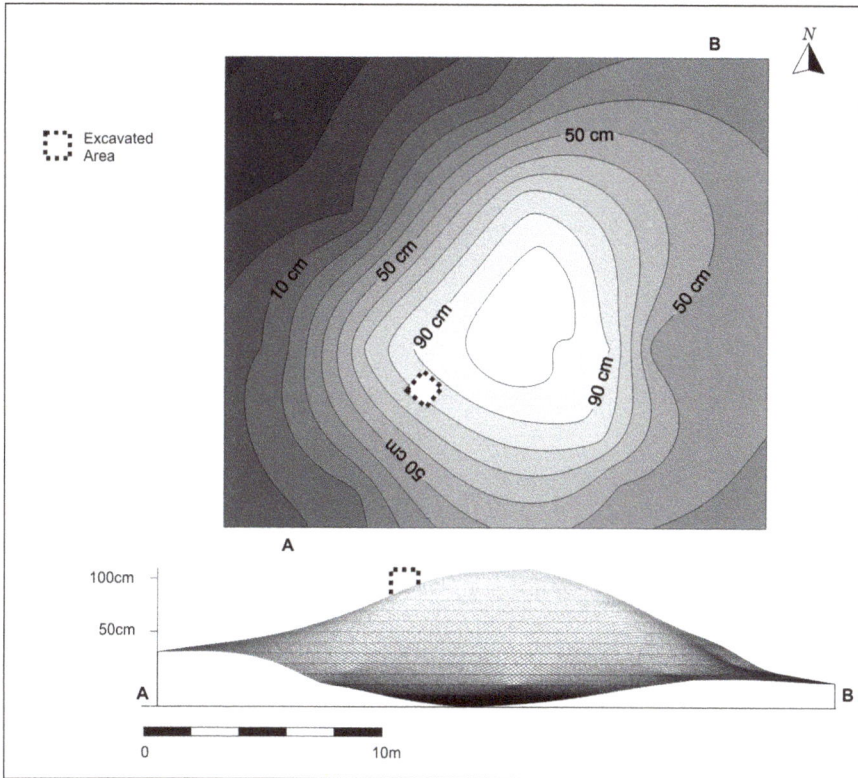

Figure 4.24: Contour plan of site BMB/071 showing location of the excavation square.

Figure 4.25: Site BMB/071, view west towards the edge of the laterite ridge and dense monsoon vine thicket.

Source: Photo Patrick Faulkner.

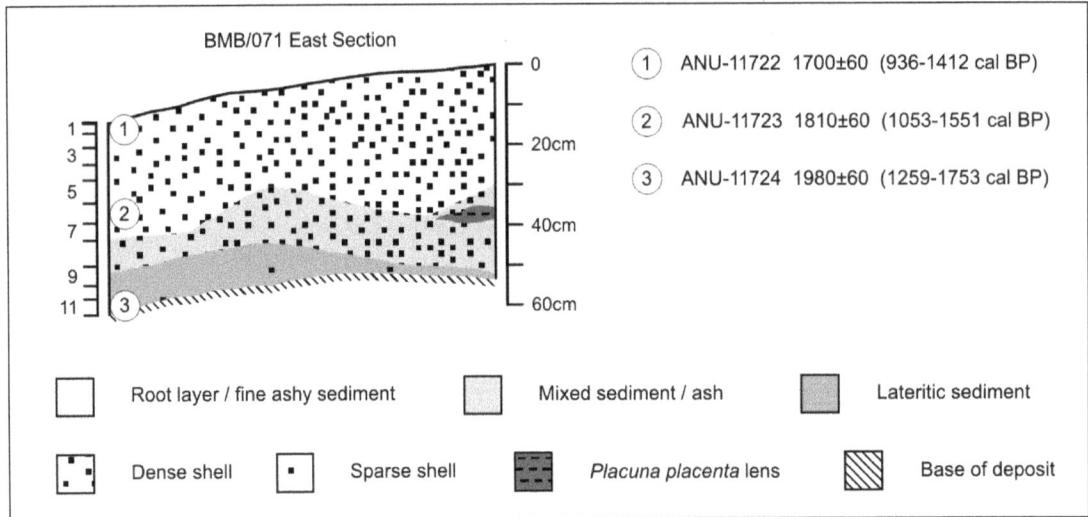

Figure 4.26: BMB/071 stratigraphic diagram, east section, showing conventional radiocarbon ages and 2σ calibrated age ranges.

Levels of fragmentation within the site have been assessed here using the two dominant molluscan species, the robust *Anadara granosa* and the thinner walled and fragile *Mactra abbreviata* (Figure 4.27). While there are differences in the rate of fragmentation between these two species, there are similarities in the broad patterning of fragmentation relative to depth. With the exception of the fragmentation ratio for *Anadara granosa* in excavation unit 11, the rate of fragmentation for both species increases throughout the deposit, possibly relating to post-depositional processes of weathering, fragmentation and compaction since abandonment of the site approximately 1200 years ago. A period of increased exposure may also account for the anomalous pattern in fragmentation in excavation unit 11. The high rate of fragmentation at the base of the site may indicate a hiatus in deposition following the initial period of shell discard in this location.

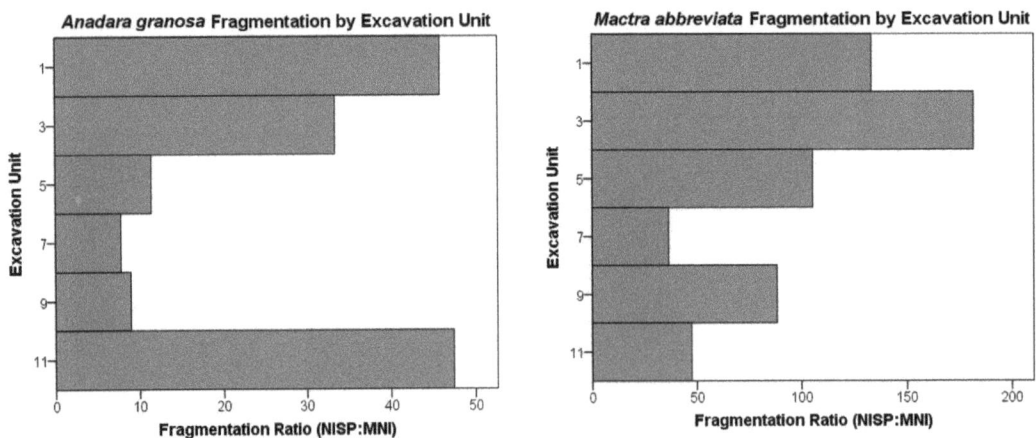

Figure 4.27: BMB/071 NISP:MNI fragmentation ratios for *Anadara granosa* and *Mactra abbreviata* molluscan species per excavation unit, 6mm sieve fraction.

Table 4.10 details the quantitative data by weight in grams for the excavated components recovered from the 6mm, with Figure 4.28 graphing the density estimates of shell, bone and otoliths, charcoal, and laterite and rock by excavation unit. This shows that molluscan remains dominate the assemblage by weight at 99.3%, followed by lateritic and rock deposits at 0.43%. Vegetation

(0.2%), charcoal (0.02%), bone and otoliths (0.01% respectively), fragments of crab carapace (<0.01%) and stone artefacts (<0.01%) form minor components of the excavated assemblage by weight. Molluscan remains, predominantly *Anadara granosa* (87.5%) and *Mactra abbreviata* (7.3%), occur within this site almost to the exclusion of all other excavated components. While the density of shell peaks within the middle excavation units in the site, there is not a significant relationship between the density of shell and excavation unit (Spearman's r_s = 0.257, $p > 0.5$, n = 6). This suggests that the discard of molluscan remains was at a relatively consistent and high level throughout the period of occupation. The non-molluscan faunal components of the site also show no significance in terms of the relationship between the density estimates and excavation unit (Spearman's r_s = 0.029, $p > 0.5$, n = 6). The identifiable elements of the bone and otoliths within the site are all Catfish (*Arius* sp.). One otolith was recovered from each of excavation units 1 and 3, with five otoliths recovered from excavation unit 5. Highly fragmented pieces of mandible were also recovered from both excavation units 5 and 7. Non-molluscan faunal remains occur within the site at a very low density, and even given issues of bone preservation within the tropics, this low density suggests a predominate focus on molluscan resources in the area.

Table 4.10: Quantitative data for the excavated components from BMB/071, 6mm sieve fraction.

Excavation Unit	Depth (cm)	Volume (cm³)	Laterite/ Rock (g)	Vegetation (g)	Charcoal (g)	Shell (g)	Bone (g)	Otolith No/ g	Crustacean (g)	Stone Artefacts No./g
1	0 to 3	7500	0.6	11.7	<0.1	1925.7	0.1	1/0.2	---	---
3	6 to 10	10000	14.5	10.9	0.3	3943.2	<0.1	1/0.1	---	---
5	14 to 19	12500	6.2	14.4	0.4	7140.1	0.5	5/0.9	---	---
7	24 to 28	10000	4.1	4.7	0.2	6672.4	0.9	---	---	---
9	34 to 39	12500	64.0	3.4	5.5	5710.0	0.1	---	---	2/0.9
11	42 to 46	10000	34.4	17.8	---	2981.8	0.4	2/0.4	1.2	---
Totals			123.8	62.9	6.4	28373.2	2	1.6	1.2	0.9
% of Total Wt. (28572)			0.43	0.22	0.02	99.30	0.01	0.01	<0.01	<0.01

Two stone artefacts were recovered, both from excavation unit 9. Both artefacts are quartzite flaked pieces, one is a medial flake fragment (weighing 0.3g and measuring 7.23mm by 14.10mm), and the second artefact is a proximal flake fragment (weighing 0.6g and measuring 12.20mm by 18.02mm). In terms of raw material, these artefacts conform morphologically to the quartzite noted outcropping on the eastern side of the peninsula. While the distribution of charcoal within this site peaks substantially in excavation unit 9 relative to the density estimates for units 3, 5 and 7, correlation coefficients indicate that there is not a significant relationship between the density of charcoal and excavation unit (Spearman's r_s = -0.058, $p > 0.5$, n = 6). This result is mirrored by the distribution of laterite/rock throughout the deposit, where there are peaks in the density of material in excavation units 3 and 9. While the peak in the lower excavation units possibly relates to the relative height of the site as it was being deposited, there is not a significant relationship between the density of laterite/rock and excavation unit (Spearman's r_s = 0.714, $p > 0.1$, n = 6). Therefore, while both of these components show a higher density within the lower portions of the deposit, they occur at such a low level that this variation is relatively insignificant.

Overall, there is very little variation in the formation of this site, as evidenced by the lack of significant differences in the density of material throughout the deposit.

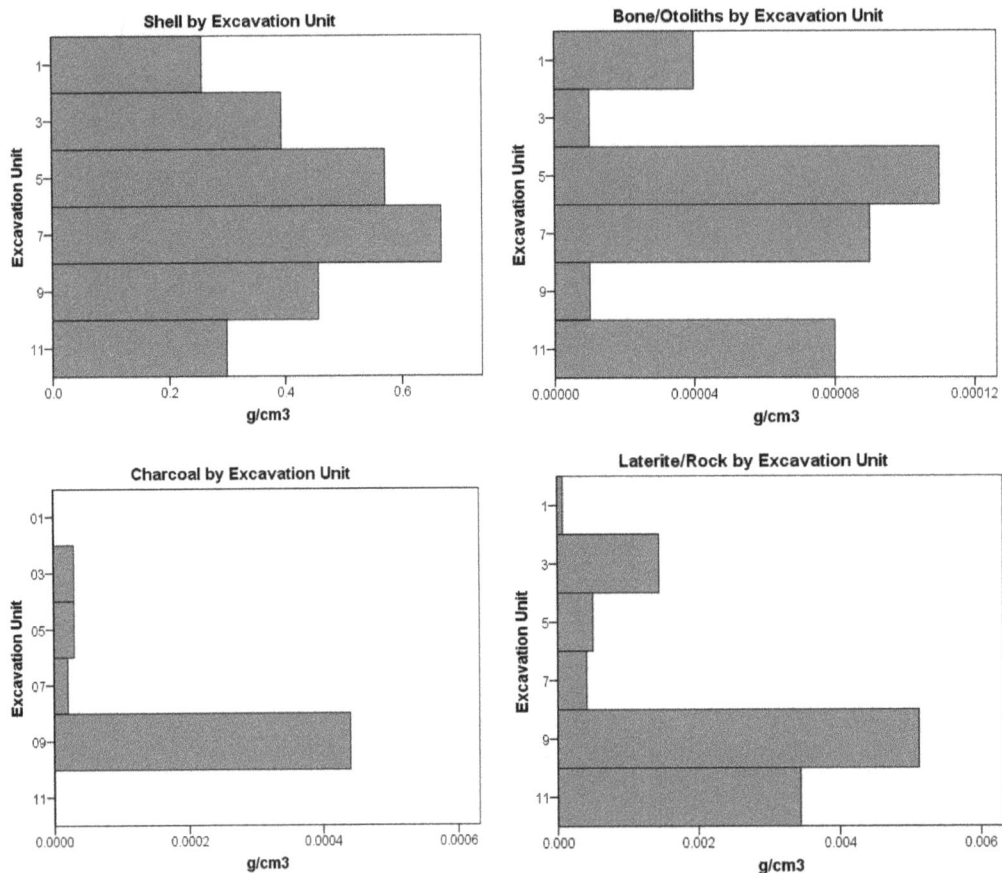

Figure 4.28: Density (g/cm³) of shell, bone/otolith, charcoal and laterite/rock by excavation unit, BMB/071, 6mm sieve fraction.

The Burrpilingbuy cluster

The site cluster located at Burrpilingbuy (Figure 4.29) is similar to Dilmitjpi, with shell deposits clustered around a large site on the laterite ridge, decreasing in size with distance from this point. This area is at the very southern-most end of the wetlands system, with the saltflats merging into an extensive mangrove system. The sites in this area possibly relate to the final phases of occupation within the Grindall Bay area. Mixed *Eucalypt* woodland dominates the landscape leading up to the edge of the laterite ridge, which is approximately 5 to 8m in height in this area. Twenty sites are found in this area, with sizes ranging from low, surface scatters of shell to mounded deposits approximately 3.3m high, with site area varying from 32.76m² to 858.9m². The sites generally decrease in size with distance from the very large composite mound on the edge of the laterite ridge, with several small middens into the woodlands, and a series of mounds located on the saltflats. These sites are generally located close to, or at, the base of the laterite ridge, although one site is situated on the saltflats several hundred metres from the ridge.

BMB/045 site description: Stratigraphy, chronology and excavated components

BMB/045 is a low, elongated mound, measuring 22.7m by 11.4m and 33cm in height above the surface of the saltflats (Figures 4.30 and Figure 4.31). This is the nearest site to the mangroves of all mounds recorded on the salt flats, very close to one of the tributary 'fingers' extending out from the mangroves into the saltflats. It appears that high tides create saltwater intrusions onto the saltflats through these tidal channels. This site becomes covered in sediment when the area floods during the wet season, as indicated by the high cracking clay content on the site surface. The shellfish species dominating the surface of the site include *Anadara granosa*, *Polymesoda (Geloina) coaxans*, *Mactra abbreviata*, *Lucinidae* sp., *Telescopium telescopium*, *Cassidula* sp. and *Cerithidea* sp. The shell exhibits a high degree of weathering and fragmentation on the surface of the site, relating to high levels of exposure and trampling.

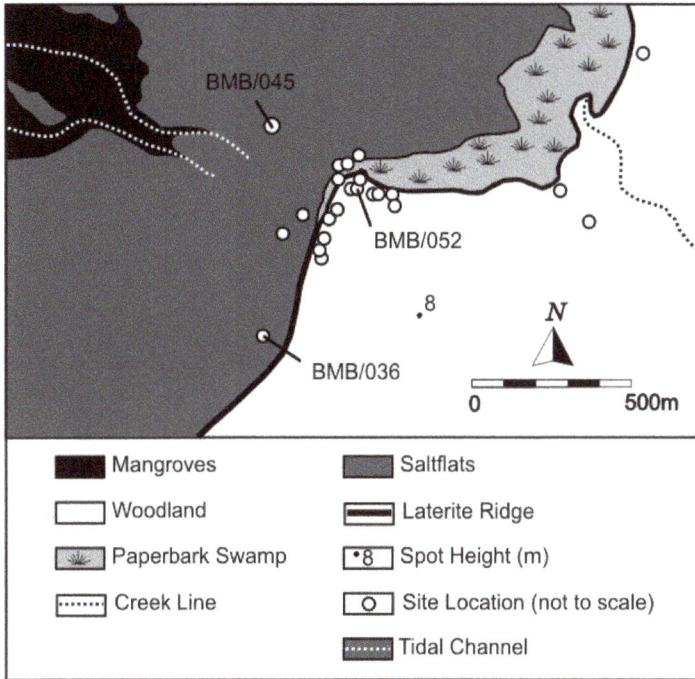

Figure 4.29: Burrpilingbuy cluster and location of excavated site BMB/045 (radiocarbon dated sites BMB/036 and BMB/052 also shown).

Source: Based on Baniyala 1:50 000 Topographic Map.

Figure 4.30: Site BMB/045, view south-west towards the extensive mangrove forest.

Source: Photo Patrick Faulkner.

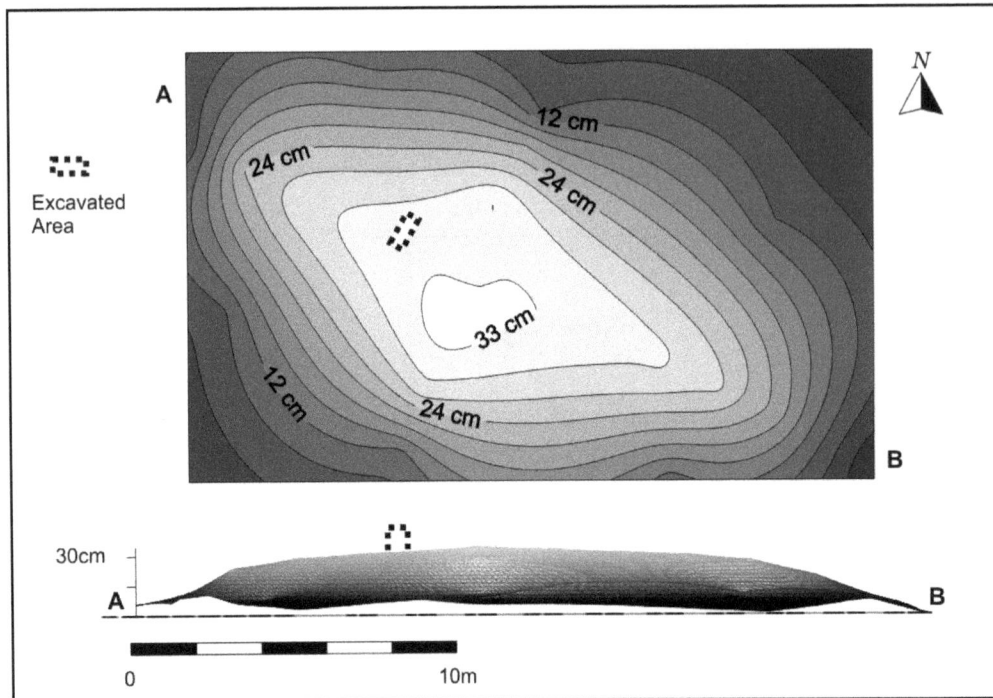

Figure 4.31: Contour plan of site BMB/045 showing location of the excavated area.

A 50cm by one metre square was excavated along the central axis of the site, and although only 33cm above the saltflats, the excavation reached a depth of approximately 1m. Excavation could not continue beyond this depth, having reached waterlogged light grey clay. Only small amounts of shell remained at this point, however, and represents the approximate base of the deposit given the change in the clay and the relative paucity of cultural midden material. The lower half of the deposit appears to have been constantly subjected to these waterlogged conditions due to its close proximity to a tidal channel through the mangroves. This has lead to higher levels of preservation within the deposit, with most of the shells retaining some of their colour and fish bone being noted during excavation. As shown in the stratigraphic profile (Figure 4.32), the surface layers were composed of densely packed *Anadara granosa* cemented in a hard, dried matrix of very fine sediment. The lower half of the deposit was comprised of shell material and charcoal fragments embedded in a matrix of wet clay. Indistinct lenses of more dense charcoal and shell occur throughout the section, as does shell mixed with light grey ash. Three *Anadara granosa* samples were submitted for radiocarbon dating (Table 4.11). The surface sample returned a date of 990±60, which calibrated to 539 cal BP, a central sample from excavation unit 16 returned a date of 1040±60, which calibrated to 577 cal BP, and a sample from the base of the site returned a date of 1050±60, which calibrated to 584 cal BP. The 'test sample significance' function of the CALIB v6.1.1 program indicates that the 2σ calibrated ages for all samples are statistically indistinguishable at the 95% confidence level (t = 0.16, *d.f.* = 2), indicating extremely rapid accumulation of this site, with deposition of a metre of material, potentially within less than approximately 100 years. This suggests a high level of intensity relating to resource use within this locality, with this site the most recent of those dated from the Grindall Bay area.

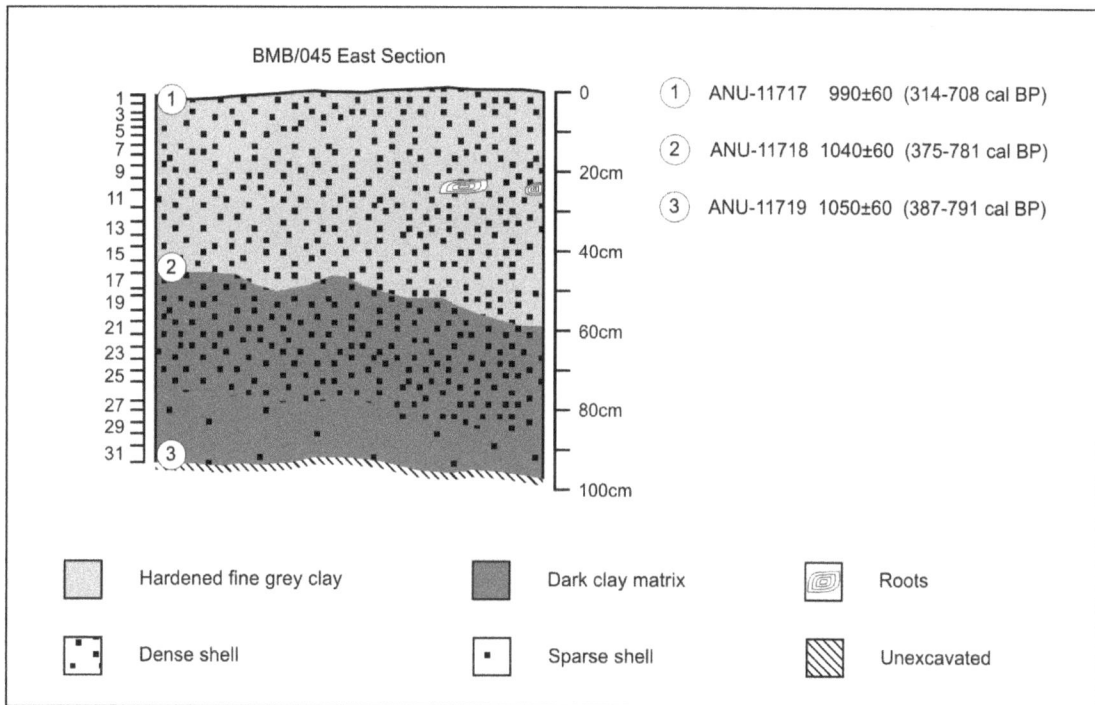

Figure 4.32: BMB/045 stratigraphic diagram, east section, showing conventional radiocarbon ages and 2σ calibrated age ranges.

Table 4.11: Conventional and calibrated radiocarbon ages obtained for site BMB/045.

Site Code /XU	Depth (cm)	Lab Code	Sample	δ¹³C	¹⁴C Age	1σ cal Age BP (68.3% probability)	2σ cal Age BP (95.4% probability)	Cal Age BP Median
BMB/045 / 1	0 - 2	ANU-11717	*Anadara granosa*	3.5 ± 0.2	990 ± 60	461–637	314–708	539
/ 16	43 - 46	ANU-11718	*Anadara granosa*	-3.7 ± 0.2	1040 ± 60	492–659	375–781	577
/ 31	91 - 95	ANU-11719	*Anadara granosa*	3.1 ± 0.2	1050 ± 60	496–664	387–791	584

Source: Calibration data from CALIB 6.1.1, marine04.14c (Hughen *et al.* 2004), ΔR = 55±98 (Ulm 2006b).

Fragmentation levels are again assessed here using *Anadara granosa* and *Mactra abbreviata* (Figure 4.33). The trends in fragmentation presented here can still be described as increasing towards the surface of the site for both species, although the rate of fragmentation varies to a greater degree than that previously seen. Greater depth of deposit combined with a very rapid rate of site deposition may account for this patterning to a certain degree. In addition, the location of this site on the saltflats approximately 250m from the laterite ridge, combined with the high surface clay content caused by seasonal inundation, may have protected this site from the effects of exposure and post-depositional destruction of the shell. Variations in the rate of fragmentation may also relate to phases of more intensive occupation and activity during the formation of the site, as the peaks in fragmentation between the two species roughly correspond. More likely, the patterning in shell fragmentation relates to a combination of these factors.

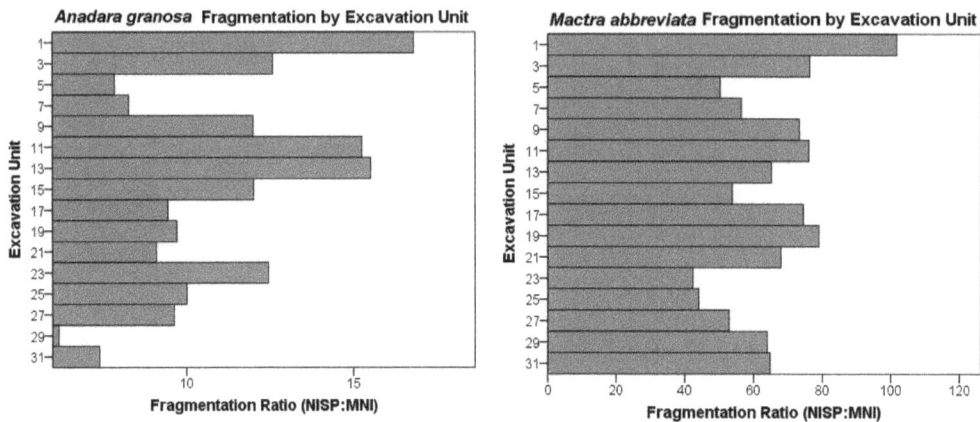

Figure 4.33: BMB/045 NISP:MNI fragmentation ratio for *Anadara granosa* and *Mactra abbreviata* per excavation unit, 6mm sieve fraction.

Table 4.12 details the quantitative data by weight in grams for the excavated components recovered from the 6mm sieve during excavation, with Figure 4.34 graphing the density estimates of shell, bone and otoliths, charcoal and laterite and rock by excavation unit. This data show that molluscan remains dominate the assemblage by weight at 99.8%. This is followed by vegetation at 0.12%, and as the excavation square was positioned close to a relatively dense stand of vegetation, this largely represents present-day root infiltration from the site surface. Laterite and rock (0.1%), charcoal (0.1%), bone and otoliths (0.02% and <0.01% respectively) and fragments of crab carapace (<0.01%) form minor components of the excavated assemblage by weight. *Anadara granosa* (74.2%) and *Mactra abbreviata* (17.2%) dominate the molluscan species recovered from this site. While the density of shell peaks within the middle excavation units in the site, indicating a certain level of variation in molluscan discard, the correlation coefficients indicate that there is not a significant relationship between the density of shell and excavation unit (Spearman's r_s = -0.176, p > 0.5, n = 16). This suggests that the discard of molluscan remains within this site was not only very rapid, but also at a relatively consistent and high level throughout the period of occupation.

The non-molluscan faunal components of the site also show no significance in terms of the relationship between the density estimates and excavation unit (Spearman's r_s = 0.144, p > 0.5, n = 16). The bone and otoliths are distributed largely between excavation units 9 and 21, with some faunal material recovered from excavation units 1, 25 and 31. Even given better preservation levels within this site, particularly compared with the other two mound sites included in this study, the density of non-molluscan material within the site is very low. This suggests that resources other than molluscs were of a minor importance within this area. In line with the fish bone identification presented for the previous mound sites, the bone and otoliths identified within this site are all of Catfish (*Arius* sp.). These remains came from excavation units 11 to 21 and 25, and were mainly highly fragmented pieces of mandible or cranium. Within this site, there are also several identifiable elements of reptile remains, including freshwater turtle carapace fragments from excavation units 13 and 19, and lizard/snake vertebrae from excavation units 11 and 15. While the distribution of charcoal within this site peaks substantially in excavation unit 13, correlation coefficients indicate that there is not a significant relationship between the density of charcoal and excavation unit (Spearman's r_s = 0.214, p > 0.2, n = 16). The relative densities of charcoal within each of the excavation units are so low, that even given the peak in higher density, there is actually very little variation in the distribution of this material throughout the site. This distribution does not conform to the expected pattern of vertical decay in organic material, largely due to the previously discussed higher preservation of organic material within the site. As with the faunal material, charcoal is a consistent, low-level component of the assemblage. The distribution of laterite/rock is almost entirely concentrated within excavation units 1, 3, 5 and 7. While there is not a significant relationship between the density of laterite/rock and excavation unit (Spearman's r_s = -0.353, p > 0.1, n = 16), the relatively low density of this material possibly relates to the position of this site on the saltflats, a location where the ground surface would not have been dominated by lateritic deposits during the formation of the site. The increased density of small lateritic pebbles in the upper excavation is likely due to pre and post-depositional flooding of the site.

Table 4.12: Quantitative data for the excavated components from BMB/045, 6mm sieve fraction.

Excavation Unit	Depth (cm)	Volume (cm³)	Laterite/Rock (g)	Vegetation (g)	Charcoal (g)	Shell (g)	Bone (g)	Otolith No/g	Crustacean (g)
1	0 to 2	5000	1.4	18.9	---	747.0	---	1/0.2	---
3	4 to 6	5000	0.4	6.0	---	1737.4	---	---	---
5	8 to 10	5000	3.5	2.6	0.5	1951.2	---	---	---
7	13 to 15	5000	2.3	2.5	0.4	1745.0	---	---	---
9	18 to 21	7500	---	1.4	1.1	2730.1	0.2	---	---
11	24 to 29	12500	---	3.2	2.6	2653.0	0.4	1/0.2	0.7
13	33 to 36	7500	---	2.8	5.8	2942.0	1.3	---	---
15	39 to 43	10000	---	0.2	3.8	2887.8	1.0	---	---
17	46 to 50	10000	---	1.1	1.4	2076.0	1.2	---	---
19	52 to 56	10000	1.0	---	1.9	2584.3	1.9	---	---
21	59 to 62	7500	---	---	---	2010.6	0.7	---	---
23	65 to 68	7500	---	1.6	1.1	1801.0	---	---	---
25	71 to 74	7500	---	<0.1	1.1	2162.0	0.5	---	---
27	79 to 82	7500	---	0.4	0.4	2665.8	---	---	---
29	85 to 88	7500	<0.1	0.1	1.1	2164.2	---	---	---
31	91 to 95	10000	2.1	---	1.4	2306.0	0.7	---	---
Totals			10.7	40.8	22.6	35163.4	7.9	0.4	0.7
% of Total Wt. (35246.5)			0.03	0.12	0.06	99.76	0.02	<0.01	<0.01

As with the previously described mounds, the formation of this site was primarily related to the exploitation and dumping of molluscan debris, albeit at a possibly more intensive level than the other mound sites investigated. The rapid rate of deposition combined with the location of the site relative to the present-day distribution of mangroves may indicate the intensive use of resources within the area relative to the final phase of progradation and the disappearance of suitable molluscan habitats.

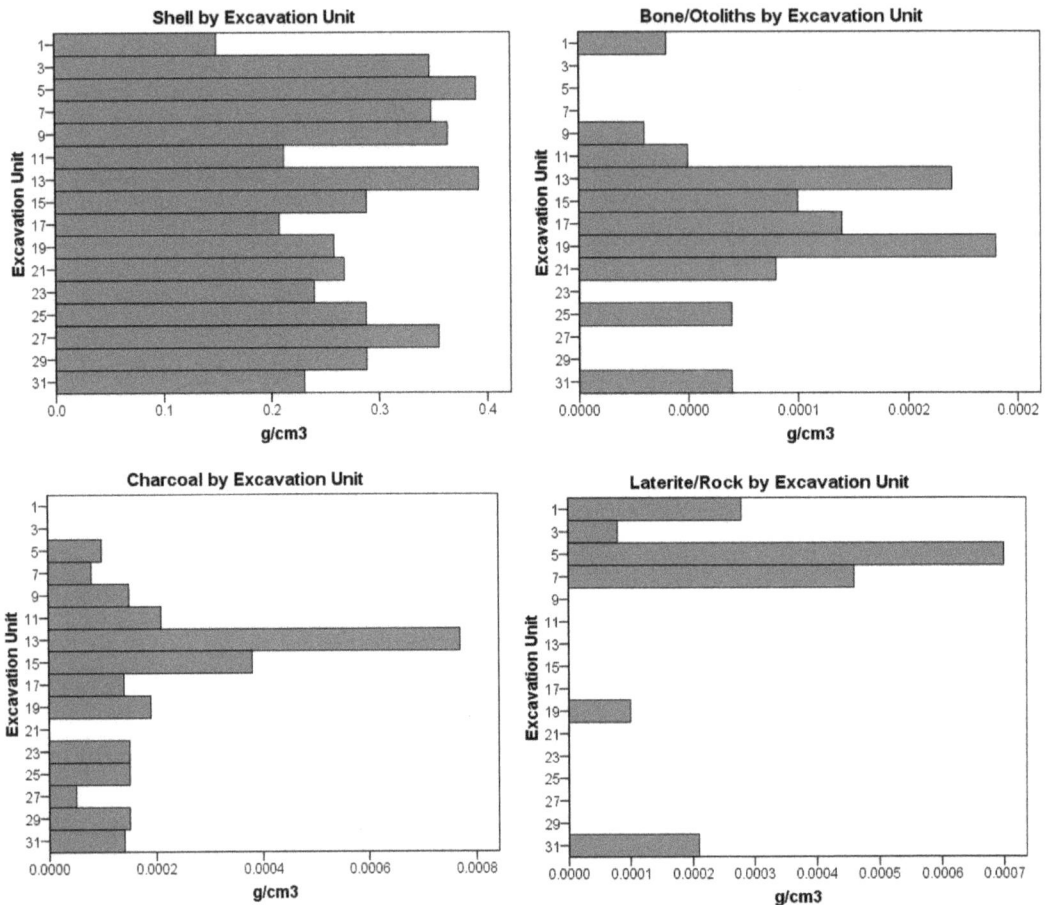

Figure 4.34: Density (g/cm³) of shell, bone/otoliths, charcoal and laterite/rock by excavation unit, BMB/045, 6mm sieve fraction.

Inter-site comparison and conclusion

There are quite distinct differences in the history of formation within and between each of the six sites described above. A comparison of the excavated components by their percentage of weight (g) for each of the six sites is presented in Table 4.13, with the contrasting patterns of total density (g/cm³) within each of the sites in Table 4.14. The rank ordering of the excavated components is based on the combined totals for all of the sites in the sample. While this does not take into account the high variability between sites, it shows that while there is some reordering in the rankings of the minor components, the two dominant excavated components (shell and laterite/rock) remain stable in terms of their rank. Other than the dominance of molluscan material, much of the variation in the abundance of the other excavated components between these sites probably relates to differences in the rate of deposition and the type of natural processes acting on the site during and after its occupation and abandonment. This particularly applies to the observable differences in the distribution and density of laterite/rock, the remains of vegetation and coral/worm shell between these deposits. Due to the ambiguous nature of charcoal within these sites, the same may be said for this material as well. An additional factor is the relative stability of the particular environmental location for each site, a point that is important for the distribution and density of laterite within these sites, given that it is the dominant land-surface within the study area.

Table 4.13: Comparison of the excavated components recovered from the six sites by percentage of weight (g), 6mm sieve fraction.

Rank		Myaoola Bay				Grindall Bay	
Order	Component	BMB/018	BMB/067b	BMB/018	BMB/067b	BMB/018	BMB/067b
1	Shell	71.58	62.3	78.13	75.17	99.3	99.76
2	Laterite/Rock	23.15	34.36	20.59	24.68	0.43	0.03
3	Coral/Worm Shell	2.4	1.81	0.06	---	---	---
4	Vegetation	1.73	0.85	0.83	0.08	0.22	0.12
5	Crustacean	1.06	0.01	0.01	0.01	<0.01	<0.01
6	Charcoal	0.03	0.01	0.38	0.03	0.02	0.06
7	Stone Artefacts	---	0.38	---	0.02	<0.01	---
8	Bone/Otolith	0.05	0.27	---	0.01	0.02	0.02

Table 4.14: Comparison of the total density of the excavated components (g/cm^3) recovered from the six sites, 6mm sieve fraction.

Rank		Myaoola Bay				Grindall Bay	
Order	Component	BMB/018	BMB/067b	BMB/084	BMB/029	BMB/071	BMB/045
1	Shell	0.06527	0.36951	1.14732	3.16258	2.64451	4.63053
2	Laterite/Rock	0.01965	0.20159	0.23043	0.81093	0.01100	0.00184
3	Vegetation	0.00131	0.00650	0.01358	0.00392	0.00632	0.00723
4	Coral/Worm Shell	0.00204	0.01030	0.00045	---	---	---
5	Charcoal	0.00002	0.00007	0.00361	0.00131	0.00053	0.00266
6	Stone Artefacts	---	0.00495	---	0.00040	0.00007	---
7	Bone/Otolith	0.00004	0.00142	---	0.00041	0.00035	0.00093
8	Crustacean	0.00100	0.00015	0.00010	0.00043	0.00012	0.00006

By far the most dominant material within all of these sites is shell. The percentage of shell by weight ranges between 62.3 and 99.8%, with variability relating to site location. For example, the average shell percentage by weight for the three sites located in Myaoola Bay is 70.8%, in comparison with an average of 91.4% for the mound sites in Grindall Bay, a pattern reflected in the density estimates for each site. There are several reasons for this apparent difference, for example, the ground surface in Grindall Bay is comparatively stable, and this area is protected to a greater degree from post-depositional disturbance, particularly from additional deposition and reworking via wind, water and storm action. Another possibility is that the rates of deposition and discard of molluscan material are higher in the mounds, resulting in a densely compact matrix of shell with very little sediment or additional material. Differences in the type of vertebrate remains identified within the sites may also relate to variations in the structure of available habitats and resource availability across the peninsula. For example, Wrasse sp. occurs in BMB/067b, a site situated close to this species' preferred habitat of near shore rocky or coral reefs. In contrast, the three mound sites all contain Catfish (*Arius* sp.), a species that inhabits estuarine to freshwater areas. This habitat zone would have been prevalent in this area during the formation of these sites. In a similar situation to the exploitation of molluscan resources within the study area, this suggests that, where available, faunal resources were exploited from within the immediate area of each site. Regardless of these differences, there is a general dearth of non-molluscan fauna within these sites, which may relate to differential preservation of this material, or alternatively, may be a reflection of a focus on molluscan resource exploitation in the area. Recovery techniques might also have a bearing on bone density as well, given that these analyses are based on the

6mm sieve residues. As a broad comparison, however, the relative densities of molluscan remains and non-molluscan faunal material in these assemblages conform to those presented for shell deposits investigated in the Darwin region that incorporated the 3mm material (Bourke 2000; Faulkner 2006). These data (Table 4.15) indicate that shell density ($t = -0.281$, $d.f. = 8$, $p > 0.5$) and non-molluscan faunal density ($t = 0.315$, $d.f. = 11$, $p > 0.5$) are not significantly different between these two regions. Further to this, Morrison (2010:216–7, 278–9, 297–309) and Veitch (1996) also present strong cases based on comparative data for the 6mm sieve material being representative of the broad range and abundance of archaeological material in mound deposits.

Table 4.15: Comparison of density estimates (g/cm^3) of shell and other faunal material from excavated sites on the Point Blane Peninsula and the Darwin region.

	Site Code	Total Excavation Volume (cm^3)	Total Shell Wt (g)	Density (g/cm^3)	Total Non-Mollusc Fauna Wt (g)	Density (g/cm^3)
Point Blane Peninsula	BMB/084	50500	4571.0	0.09051	0.8	0.00002
	BMB/018	220000	3226.8	0.01467	50.2	0.00023
	BMB/067	155000	10624.0	0.06854	48.1	0.00031
	BMB/029	105750	28329.1	0.26789	6.4	0.00006
	BMB/071	62500	28373.2	0.45397	4.9	0.00008
	BMB/045	125000	35163.4	0.28131	9.0	0.00007
Darwin Region	MA7	120000	26380.9	0.21984	29.9	0.00025
	MA1	110000	29037.3	0.26398	1.7	0.00002
	MA10	57500	6976.5	0.12133	1.5	0.00003
	HI83	980000	253288.9	0.25846	110.7	0.00011
	HI81	1600000	536695.7	0.33543	65.1	0.00004
	HI80	1190000	351541.9	0.29541	331.4	0.00028
	HI66	590000	19947.9	0.03381	18.3	0.00003

Source: Bourke 2000.

Following from this point, several researchers (e.g. Walters *et al.* 1987; McNiven 1989; Morrison 2010) have suggested that a lack of vertebrate remains in shell deposits cannot be explained by taphonomic factors alone, but probably reflects a limited range of subsistence activities at a particular site. While the bone and otolith evidence in these sites probably represents an underestimate of their importance due to poor preservation in tropical environments, the above suggestion may still hold true in this case. This is not to say that faunal resources would not have been exploited in this area, but that they may have been less significant in dietary terms, particularly in those locations of higher mollusc exploitation and discard.

As previously noted, there are a number of possible explanations for the relative paucity of stone artefacts, both in general and within the excavated contexts. Bailey (1993:9) has suggested that the rarity of artefacts in shell deposits could be misleading, possibly reflecting higher rates of accumulation in shell midden and mound sites compared with the often slower rate of sediment accumulation in other site types. While this might be the case, the scarcity of artefacts recovered from the excavations is in line with the relatively low numbers recorded during the course of the surface survey. The general pattern of low stone artefact numbers across the study area suggests that there may be another explanation. The alternative argument is that shell middens and/or mounds were used for a limited range of activities as a special-purpose location, for example as a shell-processing site (Meehan 1982; Bailey 1993:9; Cribb 1996:169), with discard of relatively few or a restricted range of artefacts. In the relative absence of other faunal and artefactual material, the focus on molluscan resources in each of the six sites suggests that, in economic terms, the function of these sites related almost exclusively to the exploitation and discard of shellfish. Therefore, in spite of the differences in formation and morphology of the shell middens and mounds in the study area, both are a manifestation of the same broad type of behaviour: the exploitation of predominantly intertidal resources and the discard of those remains.

That said, the question of explaining the distinct morphological differences between midden and mound sites remains. Following the interpretation of these sites as being primarily discard locations, one possibility is that differences in the size and shape of these sites is a reflection of the differential availability and level of exploitation of particular species. As each of these sites is dominated almost exclusively by molluscan remains, the first step is therefore to evaluate the level of variability in this resource. A close correspondence tends to exist between the species of shells present in middens and mounds, and the molluscan species that are locally available. In general, a midden or mound is indicative of shellfish gathering within the immediate vicinity. Therefore, differences in the types of species being exploited and/or changes in relative abundances through time and space may indicate an alteration in the structure of the foraging economy, particularly relative to changes in the environment.

5

Variability in Molluscan Species and Habitat Exploitation

A detailed analysis of the molluscan taxa recovered from the six excavated sites provides for an assessment of the intensity of human interaction with the environment, in this case at a finer-scale of analysis relative to broader economic patterns. As molluscan remains reflect ecological and environmental changes within the local environment, changes in the distribution and relative abundance of particular species at focal points within the landscape should be reflected in the archaeological record (Faulkner 2011:137–8). Investigating the relative proportion of mollusc species requires the consideration of a number of different economic and/or environmental processes. For example, taxonomic variability might indicate differential cultural selection and discard practices, and may also be a reflection of the environment from which resources were procured and associated differences in the availability of molluscs within and between specific localities (Bourke 2000:301). As such, an interpretation of successive short-term responses to changes in the local environment may be supported by chronological change in the relative frequencies of molluscan taxa (Bird and Frankel 1991; O'Connor and Sullivan 1994). An investigation of this issue is achieved here via species richness, relative abundance of taxa and the identification of habitats that were preferred or more intensively utilised by people in the past.

Methods for investigating molluscan diversity

Representing the number of taxa within a sample, species richness is a useful way of identifying whether these shell deposits reflect the exploitation of a wide range of edible species, or a greater focus in the exploitation of one or two particular taxa. As species richness is an effective measure of the classes represented within an assemblage, a relatively rich sample would contain a larger number of taxa in comparison with a relatively poor sample (Magurran 1988:1–7; Broughton and Grayson 1993; Broughton 1995; Nagaoka 2000:99, 2002). As an extension of this, similar patterns would be expected in assessing variability in the exploitation of those habitats from which the sample of molluscan taxa was drawn. As noted above, differences in the number of taxa and the habitats they come from may be indicative of a range of different processes, such as environmental changes affecting the distribution and density of the represented species via changes to the structure of the available habitats and/or the emphasis placed by people on particular species for exploitation (Faulkner 2011:141). The use of the number of species as a measure of assemblage richness has been criticised, the argument being that it is said to reflect average patterns in subsistence exploitation (for example Madsen 1993), and would therefore not be sensitive enough for the identification of subtle changes in economic activity over time. In fact, broad trends in the variation of species and habitat exploitation across the study area have already been established through survey data, based on differences in species richness and habitat representation (Chapter 3). The time-averaged nature of open sites lends itself to the identification of broad-scale trends, as the level of chronological resolution will often not allow subtle changes to be identified.

The mollusc species included in the following analyses are based on the edible taxa recovered from the 6mm sieve, identified primarily as those large enough to provide a reasonable amount of meat for human consumption. While Rowland (1994a:122–3) has highlighted that size on its own is not an adequate criterion for differentiating between possible non-economic and economic molluscan species, there are a number of reasons for implementing this approach here. While the identification of most taxa could be made to species level, there are several instances where the level of identification could only be made to genera or family (Faulkner 2011:141). Therefore, while the level of taxonomic identification varies, none of the taxa overlaps in terms of their identification (Nagaoka 2000:100). This means, rather than over-estimation, there is a general under-estimation of species richness within these assemblages. In addition to this, from the excavated sites in this area that form the basis for the following analyses, those species identified as non-economic form such a minor component of the shell assemblage that their exclusion does not bias the results. Non-economic shell species comprise approximately 5% by weight of the total weight of shell removed from the three midden excavations in Myaoola Bay, and less than 1% by weight from the mound sites in Grindall Bay (Faulkner 2011:141–2). In addition to their relative size, the identification of taxa as being primarily economic for these analyses is in line with previous research undertaken on coastal shell deposits in northern Australia (e.g. Meehan 1982; Clarke 1994; Mitchell 1994a; Mowat 1995; Bourke 2000). An example is the detailed research undertaken by Bourke (2000:247), who largely focussed her analyses of the molluscan fauna from shell deposits in the Darwin Harbour region on the 'macro-molluscs'. This approach has been applied consistently within and between sites in this study, and enables a more accurate analysis and interpretation of variability in subsistence and the economy.

The final factor to be considered in investigating faunal assemblage richness is that variability in species richness is often strongly related to sample size (Grayson 1984:132). The relationship between sample size and the number of taxa within an assemblage is therefore required to be taken into account whenever species richness is assessed. Table 5.1 provides the correlation coefficients for the relationship between the number of taxa identified within each site and the size of the sample. In this case, sample size is determined through MNI calculations as they may more accurately reflect the relative number of individuals in a midden sample than NISP counts (see discussion below). Only one of the six sites in this sample, the midden site BMB/018, shows a strong and significant correlation between species richness and sample size. That said, Grayson (1984:121) notes that while there may be a correlation between species richness and sample size within midden assemblages, it is possible that there is no real causal relationship. Based on previous analyses that indicate the strong effect of environmental parameters on the distribution and morphology of sites in this area, this correlation may be due to this factor acting in conjunction with the structure of the exploited mollusc populations. In most cases where a correlation is noted, the cause of this relationship is much clearer. For site BMB/018, it is more than possible that the correlation is a reflection of a situation where the small number of samples contains comparatively low relative abundance values (Grayson 1984:121; Faulkner 2011:142).

Table 5.1: Correlation coefficients for the relationship between species richness (number of taxa) and sample size (MNI) by site.

Site Type	Site Code	Pearson's r	r^2	p	No. Excavation Units
Shell Midden	BMB/018	0.937	0.8771	< 0.05	4
	BMB/067b	0.706	0.4984	> 0.2	5
	BMB/084	0.356	0.2641	> 0.2	8
Shell Mound	BMB/029	0.960	0.0091	> 0.5	11
	BMB/071	0.538	0.2893	> 0.2	6
	BMB/045	0.344	0.1184	> 0.1	16

Turning to considerations in estimating the relative abundance of molluscan species, there has been considerable debate in the archaeological literature concerning the relative merits of the number of identifiable specimens (NISP) and the minimum number of individuals (MNI) as appropriate measures of relative abundance in faunal studies. The principal identified weakness of NISP relates to the potential for variation in counts of taxa within differentially fragmented assemblages, the non-independence of specimens, and the inflation of NISP counts for those taxa with a larger number of easily identifiable elements. Increased levels of disturbance and fragmentation, in combination with differing butchery patterns (Grayson 1984:20–3) affect NISP values to a large degree. On the other hand, MNI has been criticised for its difficulty in calculation relative to NISP, problems related to the uneven distribution of animal body parts within a deposit, and its increased sensitivity to sample size (Grayson 1984:20; Marshall and Pilgram 1993:262; Giovas 2009). As a result of these criticisms of both NISP and MNI, the ability to identify all elements of a given species regardless of the level of fragmentation is important. Differential breakage is a common problem affecting shell deposits, as some mollusc species are more fragile than others. For molluscan remains, even when heavily fragmented, some species will be recognisable by their sculpture, whereas increased levels of weathering, fragmentation and degradation will render some taxa unrecognisable. Increasing fragmentation levels will therefore affect the calculated abundance of species, over-inflating the NISP values of those relatively fragile species compared to the more robust species (Marshall and Pilgram 1993:266–267; Mowat 1994, 1995:77–8, 85). Mowat's (1995:83–4) experiment assessing the effects of inter-species fragmentation goes some way to resolving this issue. As the levels of fragmentation increase within the experimental sample, the number of identifiable hinges slowly decreases, thus MNI values slowly decrease. In comparison, however, NISP values increase at a much faster rate than MNI decreases. Whereas MNI may fail to achieve one-to-one correspondence through biased under counting at levels of high fragmentation, NISP generally fails at one-to-one connection between specimens and whole individuals due to the tendency for multiple counting (Marshall and Pilgram 1993:266–267). Therefore, as fragmentation increases, NISP will over-estimate the abundance of species relative to MNI.

The effects of aggregation, however, affect MNI estimates. Where MNI values are calculated for each taxon within arbitrary excavation levels, and then calculated for the entire stratum or site, the result will be lower MNI values for the larger unit. This is because there is no guarantee that all elements from each individual will be found within any arbitrary level (Grayson 1984:67; Mowat 1995:79). The effects of aggregation are offset to a certain degree in midden analysis as molluscs have only one or two complete skeletal elements. Furthermore, the use of MNI controls the effects of aggregation in midden analysis as only the diagnostic parts of each individual are counted, and each individual is in effect only counted once (Mowat 1995:83). Molluscs also have only one or two preservable body parts, so MNI values are not calculated in the same way as for vertebrate assemblages. It is generally known prior to identification and counting of molluscan material which element will be used to define the minimum number of individuals, as diagnostic elements are often very specific to the taxon being examined (Nichol and Williams 1981:90; Mowat 1995:80; Giovas 2009). The use of MNI, rather than NISP, in midden analysis is also encouraged by the observation that with many of the molluscan taxa examined, the element used to calculate MNI, such as the hinge section of bivalves, is the most robust component of the shell. As a categorical variable, the discrete nature of MNI has also been seen to be more appropriate to research questions investigating environmental change and the nature of resource exploitation, particularly when dealing with inter-site comparisons of the relative frequency of mollusc taxa (Bourke 2000:68; Mason *et al.* 1998:309, 319; 2000:757). As a result, MNI is used here as the most appropriate measure of relative abundance for molluscan material within the Point Blane Peninsula sites.

Variability in species richness, habitat and molluscan exploitation

In total, 35 molluscan taxa have been identified for the purposes of this analysis from the six excavated sites (Table 5.2), with 21 species identified from the Grindall Bay mounds and 33 species from the Myaoola Bay middens (Faulkner 2011:142). Overall species richness follows the pattern previously identified in Chapter 3, with a higher species richness recorded for the Myaoola Bay shell deposits. This pattern suggests that variability in the distribution of species between the Grindall and Myaoola Bay sites possibly relates to the differential availability of resources across the study area, reflecting the diversity of environmental conditions and the differential distribution of molluscan habitats. Differences between the species identified on the surface of the sites compared with the excavated material possibly relate to a number of factors. It has been noted by a number of researchers in other regions of northern Australia (for example Mitchell 1993, 1994a and Hiscock 1997) that there is a certain degree of temporal and spatial intra-site variability in the distribution of species. This variability relates to the formation history of the site itself, as well as to the differential preservation of molluscan taxa. Those taxa identified for the analysis of species richness from the survey data reflect the total number of taxa identified across the surface of the site, and as such provided the basis for an analysis of species richness in very broad terms. Added to this is the generally high level of fragmentation and weathering in surface samples, making identification and quantification in these contexts difficult. As such, the excavated samples provide the opportunity to investigate possible changes in species richness and those habitats exploited with a greater degree of chronological control.

Table 5.2: The presence / absence of molluscan species of possible economic origin within the six excavated sites.

Family	Taxon	Habitat	Myaoola Bay			Grindall Bay		
			BMB/018	BMB/067b	BMB/084	BMB/029	BMB/071	BMB/045
Arcidae	*Anadara antiquata*	Littoral Sand and Mud (Intertidal/marginally subtidal)	+	+	+	+	+	+
	Anadara granosa	Littoral Sand and Mud (Intertidal/marginally subtidal)		+	+	+	+	+
	Barbatia sp.	Rock/Debris in Littoral Area, Coral Reefs	+	+	+	+		
Chitonidae	Chitonidae f.	Upper Intertidal to Shallow Sub-tidal		+	+			
Corbiculidae	*Polymesoda (Geloina) coaxans*	Coastal Rivers, Streams and Estuaries	+	+	+	+	+	+
Ellobiidea	*Cassidula angulata*	Mangroves/Mud		+		+	+	+
Fissurellidae	Fissurellidae sp.	Attached to Rocks or Debris		+	+			
Haliotidae	*Haliotis* sp.	Attached to Rocks or Debris			+			
Isognomonidae	*Isognomon isognomon*	Mangroves to Under rocks in Shallow Water	+	+	+			
Mactridae	*Mactra abbreviata*	Littoral Sand	+	+		+	+	+
Muricidae	*Chicoreus* sp.	Under Rock/Rubble in Intertidal/Sub-tidal Areas		+				
	Muricidae sp.	Under Rock/Rubble in Intertidal/Sub-tidal Areas		+				
Mytilidae	*Modiolus* sp.	Sand and Mud in Shallow Water – Estuaries	+		+	+	+	+
	Mytilidae f.	Attached to Rocks or Debris			+			
	Septifer bilocularis	Attached to Rocks or Debris	+	+			+	+
Neritidae	*Nerita* sp.	Mangrove Roots/Rocks	+	+	+	+	+	+
Ostreidae	Ostreidae f.	Mangrove Roots/Rock/Debris in Sub-tidal Areas	+	+	+	+	+	+
Pinnidae	*Pinna bicolor*	Littoral Sand/Seagrass Beds			+			
Placunidae	*Placuna placenta*	Surface of Mud/Mangroves				+	+	+
Potamididae	*Cerithidea* sp.	Shallow Mud/Mangroves Roots				+		
	Telescopium telescopium	Mangroves		+	+	+	+	+
	Terebralia sp.	Mangroves	+	+	+	+	+	+
Pteriidae	*Pinctada* sp.	Attached to Substrate in Intertidal/Sub-tidal Areas	+	+	+			
Tellinidae	*Tellina* sp.	Littoral Sand and Mud	+	+	+	+	+	+

Note: + indicates presence.

Table 5.2 (continued): The presence / absence of molluscan species of possible economic origin within the six excavated sites.

Family	Taxon	Habitat	Myaoola Bay			Grindall Bay		
			BMB/018	BMB/067b	BMB/084	BMB/029	BMB/071	BMB/045
Trochidae	*Euchelus atratus*	Shallow Water		+				
	Monodonta labio	Shallow Water	+					
	Trochus sp.	Shallow Water		+	+	+		
Turbinidae	*Turbo cinereus*	Shallow Water		+	+			
Veneridae	*Circe* sp.	Littoral Sand		+	+			
	Dosinia mira	Littoral Sand				+		
	Gafrarium sp.	Littoral Muddy Sand	+	+	+			
	Marcia hiantina	Littoral Sand	+	+	+	+	+	+
	Pitar sp.	Littoral Sand			+			
	Placamen calophyllum	Littoral Sand	+	+		+	+	+
	Tapes sp.	Littoral Sand			+			
Volutidae	*Melo amphora*	Lower Intertidal and Sub-tidal Sand/Mud		+				
Total No. Taxa			16	26	24	18	15	15

Note: + indicates presence.

Myaoola Bay Midden Sites

BMB/018: Species richness, habitat exploitation and relative abundances

Sixteen molluscan species in all were identified within the four units excavated in BMB/018. As previously noted, BMB/018 is possibly representative of short-term or ephemeral occupation, and it is not relevant to assess variation in species richness and habitat exploitation between arbitrary excavation units within approximately 10cm of cultural deposit. More importantly, within this context, it is still possible to assess the relative importance of the habitats from which the 16 species were gathered. Table 5.3 details the number and percentage of the 16 species from this site by habitat, along with the total MNI counts for each of these species, and the volume-corrected relative abundance estimates (MNI/cm^3). Species richness per habitat and the corrected relative abundance of species from each habitat are graphed in Figure 5.1. While changes in the number of taxa and the focus on habitats exploited through time cannot be assessed for BMB/018, there appears to be a more intensive focus on those species gathered from shallow areas, and those species from sand and mud flats. The site is located in an area that prior to the phases of beach-ridge development that created the present-day landscape would have resembled a headland. The area would have been predominantly a rocky coastline with some mangrove-fringed sand and mudflat areas in small, relatively protected embayments. The pattern of species and habitat richness possibly reflects the structure of the habitats within this locality at the time of site deposition approximately 3000 years ago. While richness of exploited species varies between patches, there appears to be near equal emphasis in exploitation in terms of the number of individuals gathered from within the dominant habitat areas.

Table 5.3: BMB/018, number and percentage of species, MNI values and MNI density estimates (MNI/cm³) for molluscan habitats.

Molluscan Habitats	No. of Taxa	%	Habitat MNI	% MNI	MNI/cm³
Shallow Water	4	25.00	408	51.78	0.00185
Sand/Mud Flats	7	43.75	370	46.95	0.00168
Mangroves	3	18.75	7	0.89	0.00003
Estuarine	2	12.50	3	0.38	0.00001
Totals	**16**		**788**		

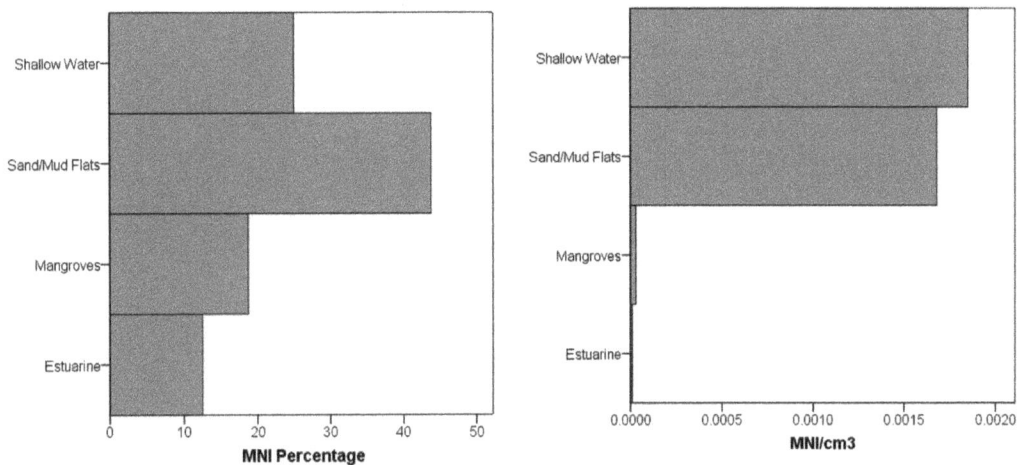

Figure 5.1: BMB/018, percentages of the number of taxa and volume-corrected MNI estimates (MNI/cm³) per habitat.

Both Grayson (1984:134) and Mowat (1995:76) have noted that the tendency in archaeological assemblages is for few species to be very abundant, while most are represented by small numbers of individuals. It is therefore appropriate to investigate the abundance of the species from the site relative to the description of species and habitat richness, as this enables the specific focus of exploitation within the site to be examined. Table 5.4 details the MNI counts and percentages for the 16 species from this site and the corrected relative abundance estimate (MNI/cm³), with the MNI percentages and abundance estimates for the three dominant species graphed in Figure 5.2. For this analysis, those species contributing greater than 5% by MNI to the overall assemblage are viewed as being dominant. Three species, at 18.8% of the total species richness, make up 91.2% by MNI of the assemblage from BMB/018. *Septifer bilocularis* is the highest-ranking species by percentage of the total MNI (48.7%) and by the corrected density estimate. *Septifer bilocularis* is found attached to hard-substrate areas within the shallow water habitat zone. In rank order, this species is followed by *Pinctada* sp. (34.8% MNI) and *Gafrarium* sp. (7.7% MNI) which collectively comprise 42.5% of the assemblage by MNI. Both of these species are found within sand and mudflat habitats. This pattern further emphasises the point made earlier, that while there is variation in species richness between exploited patches, there appears to be similar intensity of exploitation within the dominant habitat areas. It is also suggestive of the structure and distribution of molluscan resources within these habitats, which directly reflects the relative abundance of each species.

Table 5.4: BMB/018, MNI values and volume-corrected MNI estimates (MNI/cm^3) for all molluscan species (species above dashed line at > 5% MNI viewed as dominant).

Economic Molluscan Species	Habitat Category	MNI	% MNI	Density (MNI/cm^3)	Rank Order
Septifer bilocularis	Shallow Water	384	48.73	0.00175	1
Pinctada sp.	Sand/Mud Flats	274	34.77	0.00125	2
Gafrarium sp.	Sand/Mud Flats	61	7.74	0.00028	3
Marcia hiantina	Sand/Mud Flats	26	3.30	0.00012	4
Barbatia sp.	Shallow Water	17	2.16	0.00008	5
Nerita sp.	Mangroves	5	0.63	0.00002	6
Monodonta labio	Shallow Water	4	0.51	0.00002	7
Mactra abbreviata	Sand/Mud Flats	4	0.51	0.00002	7
Ostreidae f.	Shallow Water	3	0.38	0.00001	9
Tellina sp.	Sand/Mud Flats	2	0.25	0.00001	10
Placamen calophyllum	Sand/Mud Flats	2	0.25	0.00001	10
Polymesoda (Geloina) coaxans	Coastal Rivers/Estuaries	2	0.25	0.00001	10
Anadara granosa	Sand/Mud Flats	1	0.13	0.00001	13
Isognomon isognomon	Mangroves	1	0.13	0.00001	13
Terebralia sp.	Mangroves	1	0.13	0.00001	13
Modiolus sp.	Coastal Rivers/Estuaries	1	0.13	0.00001	13
Total		**788**			

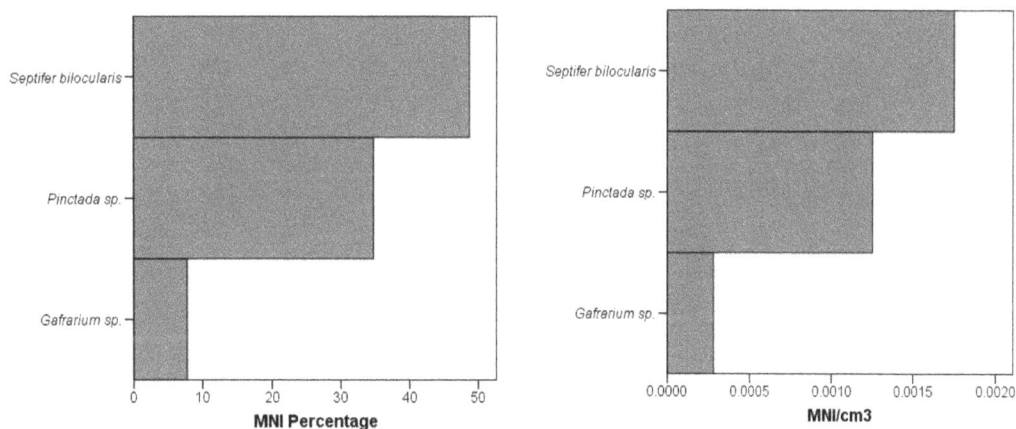

Figure 5.2: BMB/018, dominant molluscan species by MNI percentages and volume-corrected MNI (MNI/cm^3).

BMB/067b: Species richness, habitat exploitation and relative abundances

Twenty-six molluscan species were identified within the five excavation units analysed in BMB/067b. While it was not possible to isolate phases in occupation within this site based on the available radiocarbon determinations, any changes through time should be reflected by analysing variation in species richness, habitat exploitation and relative abundance estimates by excavation unit (Table 5.5). As the differences in radiocarbon dates from the surface and base of the site are significantly different, this approach enables broad scale patterns in the economy to be observed. While there is degree of variation in species richness between excavation units, with a decrease in the number of species exploited apparent in the upper units, correlation coefficients (r_s = 0.821, p > 0.05, n = 5) suggest that the relationship between species richness and excavation unit is not significant. This indicates that, given minor variation, there is a certain level of consistency in overall species richness within the site through time.

Table 5.5: BMB/067b, number of species, the percentage of the total number of species and number of species for molluscan habitats by excavation unit.

Excavation Unit	No. Species	% of Total	Shallow Water	Sand/Mud Flats	Mangroves	Estuarine
1	17	65.38	8	5	3	1
3	18	69.23	5	10	2	1
5	20	76.92	7	8	4	1
7	25	96.15	10	10	4	1
9	20	76.92	7	9	3	1
Totals	**26**		**10**	**10**	**5**	**1**

Of the 26 economic species within the site, 10 (38.5%) each come from the shallow water and sand/mud flat habitats, with five (19.2%) from the mangrove zone and only one (3.9%) gathered from coastal river/estuarine areas. This indicates that the shallow water and sand/mud flat areas were the dominant environmental zones within the area during deposition of the site. Species richness and relative abundance estimates by excavation unit are again used to determine whether there were any shifts in the focus of exploitation within and between these habitats through time. Table 5.5 details the number and percentage of species within each excavation unit by habitat. Spearman's rank correlation (r_s) is used to test the relationship between habitat species richness and excavation unit with the exception of the estuarine habitat, as there is no change in the number of species by excavation unit. Correlation coefficients calculated for these three habitats indicate that, as with overall species richness, the relationship between habitat species richness and excavation unit is not significant. In other words, there is little variation in the number of species exploited within the shallow water $(r_s = 0.103, p > 0.2, n = 5)$, sand/mud flat $(r_s = 0.410, p > 0.2, n = 5)$, or mangrove $(r_s = 0.369, p > 0.2, n = 5)$ habitat areas through time. As a contrast, Table 5.6 details the MNI of species within each excavation unit by habitat.

Table 5.6: BMB/067b, MNI values and volume-corrected MNI estimates (MNI/cm^3) for species from molluscan habitats by excavation unit.

Excavation Unit	Volume (cm³)		Shallow Water	Sand/Mud Flats	Mangroves	Estuarine
1	13000	MNI	51	140	12	4
		MNI/cm³	0.00392	0.01077	0.00092	0.00031
3	31000	MNI	99	193	2	1
		MNI/cm³	0.00319	0.00623	0.00007	0.00003
5	34000	MNI	86	237	37	1
		MNI/cm³	0.00253	0.00697	0.00109	0.00003
7	31000	MNI	90	272	26	1
		MNI/cm³	0.00290	0.00877	0.00084	0.00003
9	46000	MNI	90	256	22	2
		MNI/cm³	0.00196	0.00557	0.00048	0.00004

Testing the combined, volume-corrected species relative abundance estimates from the four habitat areas by excavation unit again suggests that there is not a strong relationship. As these results are an approximate temporal measure, they suggest that for the shallow water $(r_s = -0.900, p > 0.1, n = 5)$, sand/mud flat $(r_s = -0.600, p > 0.2, n = 5)$, mangrove $(r_s = -0.200, p > 0.2, n = 5)$ and coastal river/estuarine habitats $(r_s = -0.205, p > 0.2, n = 5)$, there is no significant change in the focus of exploitation through time. Regardless of the comparative level or intensity of use between these habitat zones, exploitation within each habitat remains consistent throughout the period of occupation. These results combined with the lack of change in species richness per habitat through time, suggests that there may have been little environmental alteration related particularly to these habitats within the immediate landscape during this period. If this interpretation of environmental stability were correct, then little to no change in the abundance of the dominant species through time would be expected. Table 5.7 details the MNI counts and percentages for the 16 species from this site, volume-corrected relative abundance estimates (MNI/cm³), and the rank order by MNI. Four species, at 15.4% of the total number in the site, make up 78.5% by MNI of the assemblage. *Anadara granosa* is the highest-ranking species by percentage of the total MNI (31.9%) and by the corrected density estimate. In rank order, this species is followed by *Marcia hiantina* (21.1% MNI), *Septifer bilocularis* (17.02% MNI) and *Gafrarium* sp. (8.5% MNI). Three of these top four ranked species, *Anadara granosa*, *Marcia hiantina* and *Gafrarium* sp., are all found in the sand and mudflats within the intertidal/subtidal zone, and collectively comprise 61.5% by MNI of the total assemblage. In contrast, *Septifer bilocularis* is found attached to hard-substrate areas within the shallow water habitat zone. In order to address possible variation in the relative abundance of the dominant molluscan species within the site over time, Table 5.8 and Figure 5.3 present the MNI values for these four taxa corrected for volume (MNI/cm³).

Table 5.7: BMB/067b, MNI values and corrected MNI estimates (MNI/cm³) for all molluscan species (species above dashed line at > 5% MNI viewed as dominant).

Economic Molluscan Species	Habitat Category	MNI	% MNI	MNI/cm³	Rank Order
Anadara granosa	Sand/Mud Flats	518	31.94	0.00334	1
Marcia hiantina	Sand/Mud Flats	342	21.09	0.00221	2
Septifer bilocularis	Shallow Water	276	17.02	0.00178	3
Gafrarium sp.	Sand/Mud Flats	137	8.45	0.00088	4
Terebralia sp.	Mangroves	78	4.81	0.00050	5
Trochus sp.	Shallow Water	57	3.51	0.00037	6
Tellina sp.	Sand/Mud Flats	44	2.71	0.00028	7
Anadara antiquata	Sand/Mud Flats	26	1.60	0.00017	8
Ostreidae f.	Shallow Water	24	1.48	0.00016	9
Muricidae sp.	Shallow Water	18	1.11	0.00012	10
Chitonidae f.	Shallow Water	17	1.05	0.00011	11
Pinctada sp.	Sand/Mud Flats	16	0.99	0.00010	12
Barbatia sp.	Shallow Water	13	0.80	0.00008	13
Nerita sp.	Mangroves	9	0.55	0.00006	14
Polymesoda (Geloina) coaxans	Coastal Rivers/Estuaries	9	0.55	0.00006	14
Telescopium telescopium	Mangroves	8	0.49	0.00005	16
Turbo cinereus	Shallow Water	5	0.31	0.00003	17
Mactra abbreviata	Sand/Mud Flats	4	0.25	0.00003	18
Melo amphora	Sand/Mud Flats	4	0.25	0.00003	18
Cassidula angulata	Mangroves	3	0.18	0.00002	20
Chicoreus sp.	Shallow Water	3	0.18	0.00002	20
Circe sp.	Sand/Mud Flats	3	0.18	0.00002	20
Placamen calophyllum	Sand/Mud Flats	3	0.18	0.00002	20
Euchelus atratus	Shallow Water	2	0.12	0.00001	24
Isognomon isognomon	Mangroves	2	0.12	0.00001	24
Fissurellidae sp.	Shallow Water	1	0.06	0.00001	26
Total		**1622**			

Table 5.8: BMB/067b, MNI and corrected MNI values for the dominant species by excavation unit.

Excavation Unit	Volume (cm³)	Anadara granosa		Marcia hiantina		Septifer bilocularis		Gafrarium sp.	
		MNI	MNI/cm³	MNI	MNI/cm³	MNI	MNI/cm³	MNI	MNI/cm³
1	13000	77	0.00592	40	0.00308	37	0.00285	18	0.00139
3	31000	89	0.00287	65	0.00210	66	0.00213	23	0.00074
5	34000	110	0.00324	84	0.00247	49	0.00144	14	0.00041
7	31000	147	0.00474	76	0.00245	53	0.00171	19	0.00061
9	46000	95	0.00207	77	0.00167	71	0.00154	63	0.00137

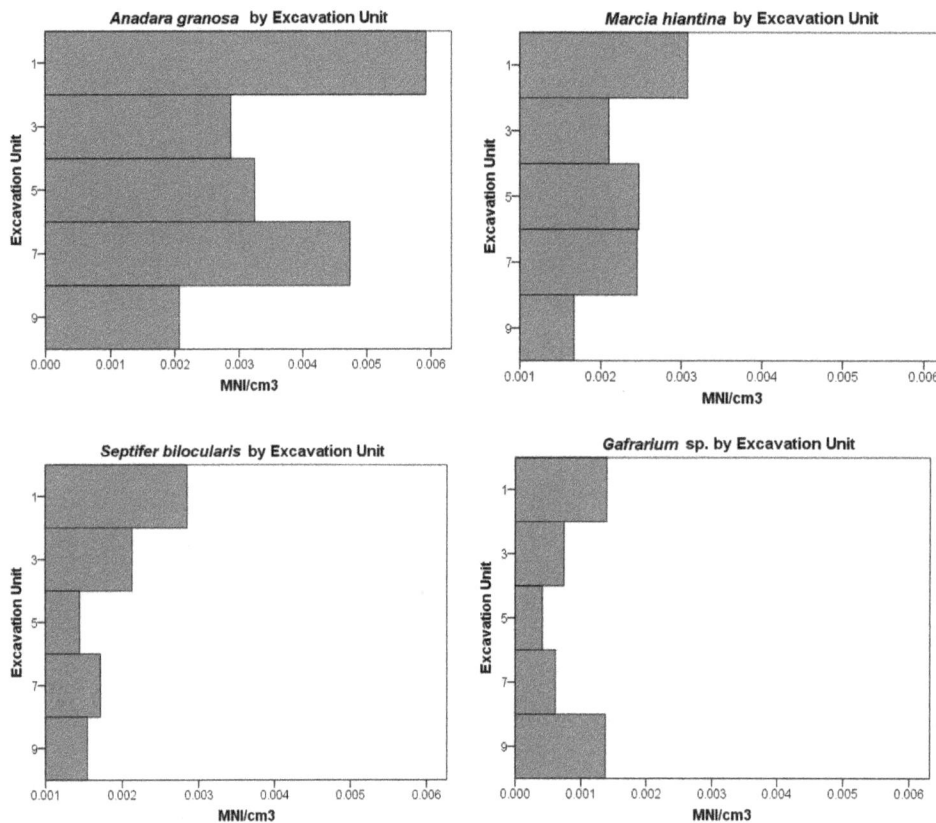

Figure 5.3: BMB/067b, corrected MNI values (MNI/cm³) for the dominant species by excavation unit.

Correlation coefficients calculated on the volume-corrected MNI counts indicate that the differences in the relative abundance of *Anadara granosa* (r_s = -0.600, p > 0.2, n = 5), *Marcia hiantina* (r_s = -0.700, p > 0.2, n = 5), *Septifer bilocularis* (r_s = -0.700, p > 0.2, n = 5) and *Gafrarium* sp. (r_s = -0.300, p > 0.2, n = 5) by excavation unit, and by extension through time, are not statistically significant. In combination with the analysis of overall species richness and species richness by habitat, the primary focus of molluscan exploitation within this site appears to remain relatively consistent throughout. This is reflected in the fact that there is no real change in the abundance of the four dominant species through time, indicating that there is no shift in those species that were the focus of exploitation.

BMB/084: Species richness, habitat exploitation and relative abundances

Twenty-four molluscan taxa in all were identified within the eight units excavated in BMB/084. In order to address the extent of possible variations through time in species and habitat richness, the data are analysed by excavation unit, with excavation units 1 and 2 combined for this analysis due to the comparatively small volumes of these units. Species richness for BMB/084 by excavation unit is detailed in Table 5.9, along with the percentages of the total number of economic species identified within the site.

Table 5.9: BMB/084, number of species, the percentage of the total number of species and number of species for molluscan habitats by excavation unit.

Excavation Unit	No. Species	% of Total	Shallow Water	Sand/Mud Flats	Mangroves	Estuarine
1 / 2	19	79.17	4	10	3	2
3	13	56.52	3	7	2	1
4	17	70.83	5	7	4	1
5	17	70.83	5	9	2	1
6	18	75.00	4	9	3	2
7	18	75.00	6	6	4	2
8	18	75.00	6	9	2	1
Total No. of Species	**24**		**8**	**10**	**4**	**2**

The number of economic species identified per excavation unit appears to remains stable. Spearman's correlation coefficient ($r_s = 0.478$, $p > 0.1$, $n = 7$) suggest that the relationship between species richness and excavation unit is neither strong nor significant. This indicates there is a high degree of consistency in the level of species richness throughout the deposit. Of the 24 economic species within the site, eight (33.3%) come from the shallow water habitat, 10 (41.7%) from the sand/mud flat habitat, with four (16.7%) from the mangrove zone and two (8.3%) gathered from coastal river/ estuarine areas. This indicates that the shallow water and sand/mud flat areas were the dominant and consistently available environmental zones within the area. This broad patterning may mask a certain level of variability within the deposit. It was noted during the course of the excavation that there was a change in the dominant taxa between the two stratigraphic units, which also relate to the variability in radiocarbon ages available from this deposit. As such, consistency in species richness may not be indicative of environmental changes within the area, or shifts in the focus of exploitation. To investigate this aspect further, species richness and relative abundance estimates by excavation unit are used to determine whether there were any shifts in the focus of exploitation between these habitats through time. Table 5.9 also details the number and percentage of species within each excavation unit by habitat. In line with overall species richness within the site, the number of economic species identified for each habitat per excavation unit remains relatively stable. Spearman correlation results for the sand and mudflats ($r_s = -0.243$, $p > 0.5$, $n = 7$), mangroves ($r_s = -0.019$, $p > 0.5$, $n = 7$) and the coastal rivers and estuaries ($r_s = 1.000$, $p > 0.5$, $n = 7$), indicate that there is not a significant relationship between species richness and excavation unit for these habitats. In comparison, there appears to be a decrease in species richness throughout the deposit for the shallow water habitat ($r_s = 0.771$, $p < 0.05$, $n = 7$). This may signify a slight restructuring of shell beds within this zone or of this habitat zone itself, affecting the diversity of available resources.

Table 5.10 presents MNI and volume-corrected MNI of species within each excavation unit by habitat. This pattern of relative abundance by habitat contrasts with that of species richness by habitat, and reinforces the point that, at least within this site, little change in the number of species exploited is not an accurate reflection of the intensity of habitat exploitation. While there appeared to be minor variability in the number of species exploited from the shallow water habitat (Figure 5.4), relative abundance estimates remain consistent throughout the deposit ($r_s = 0.036$, $p > 0.5$, $n = 7$). The relative abundance estimates from the coastal river/estuarine habitat are not presented graphically at this scale, but there is not a significant relationship with excavation unit for this habitat ($r_s = -0.468$, $p > 0.2$, $n = 7$) or for the sand/mud flat habitat ($r_s = -0.3219$, $p > 0.5$, $n = 7$). The correlation coefficients for the relationship between excavation unit and the relative abundance of mangrove species suggest that the increase in species from this habitat is significant ($r_s = -0.786$, $p < 0.05$, $n = 7$), particularly near the surface of the site (excavation units 1 and 2). There is a dramatic jump in relative abundance for this habitat area in the upper portion of the deposit, and while this may suggest a reorganisation in the structure of the mangrove zone in the area and/or an increase in the abundance of species in this zone in the recent past, this process did not apparently affect the diversity of resources within this habitat zone. Interestingly, this increase in mangrove species does not appear to have occurred at the expense of the other habitat zones, as there is no significant difference in the relative abundance estimates for the other three identified habitats.

Table 5.10: BMB/084, MNI values and volume-corrected MNI estimates (MNI/cm^3) for species from molluscan habitats by excavation unit.

Excavation Unit	Volume (cm^3)		Shallow Water	Sand/Mud Flats	Mangroves	Estuarine
1 / 2	4750	MNI	29	64	166	7
		MNI/cm^3	0.01347	0.02157	0.09153	0.00157
3	5500	MNI	17	47	16	5
		MNI/cm^3	0.00309	0.00855	0.00291	0.00091
4	8250	MNI	24	23	79	1
		MNI/cm^3	0.00291	0.00279	0.00958	0.00012
5	8500	MNI	27	99	30	13
		MNI/cm^3	0.00318	0.01165	0.00354	0.00153
6	7250	MNI	22	74	22	6
		MNI/cm^3	0.00303	0.01021	0.00303	0.00083
7	8000	MNI	44	78	12	10
		MNI/cm^3	0.00550	0.00975	0.00150	0.00125
8	8250	MNI	45	34	12	1
		MNI/cm^3	0.00546	0.00412	0.00146	0.00012

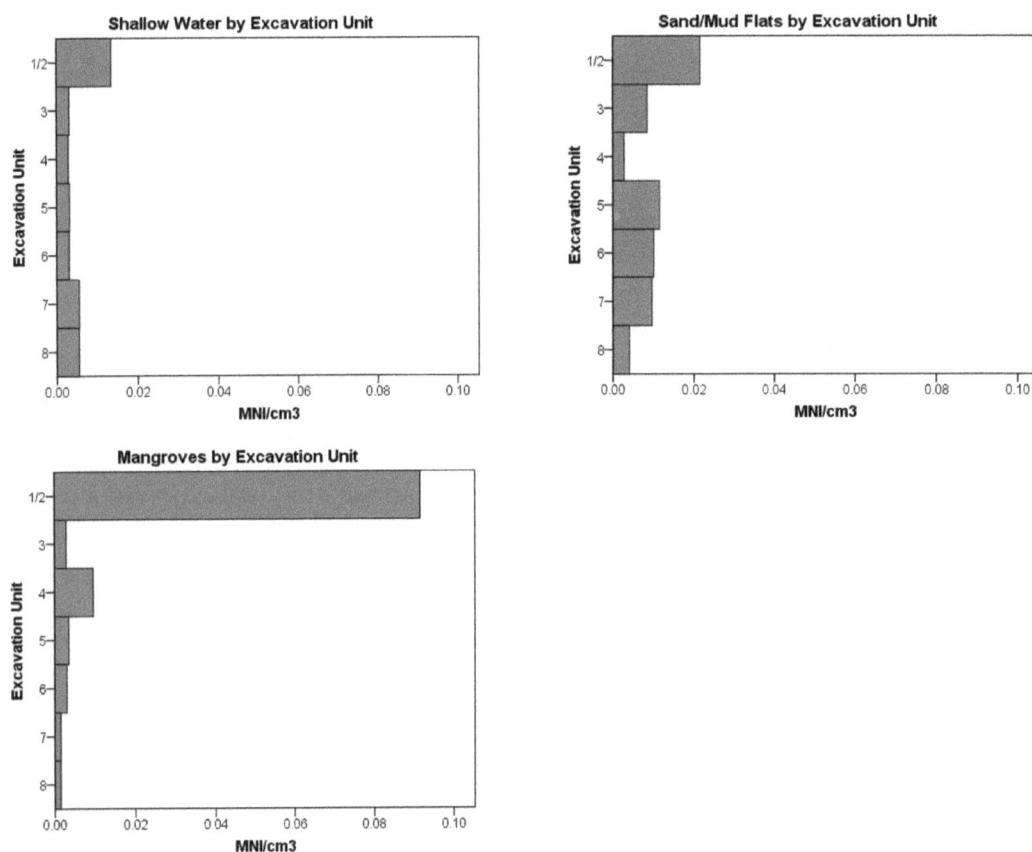

Figure 5.4: BMB/084, corrected MNI values (MNI/cm^3) for molluscan habitat by excavation unit.

Again, this type of variation in habitat exploitation throughout the site should be reflected in the relative abundance of the dominant species. Table 5.11 details the MNI counts and percentages for the 24 species from this site and a relative density estimate (MNI/cm^3). Four species, at 16.7% of the total number of species in the site, make up 76.9% by MNI of the assemblage from BMB/084. *Marcia hiantina* is the highest-ranking species by percentage of the total MNI (29.0%) and by the corrected density estimate. In rank order, this species is followed by *Isognomon isognomon* (27.8% MNI), Mytilidae f. (14.4% MNI) and *Gafrarium* sp. (5.7% MNI). Two of these top four ranked species, *Marcia hiantina* and *Gafrarium* sp., are found in the sand and mudflats within the intertidal/subtidal zone, and collectively comprise 33.5% by MNI of the total assemblage. In contrast, species from the Mytilidae family are found attached to hard-substrate areas within the shallow water habitat zone, and *Isognomon isognomon* is generally found within mangrove forests. Table 5.12 and Figure 5.5 present the MNI values for these four species corrected for volume (MNI/cm^3).

Table 5.11: BMB/084, MNI values and MNI density estimates (MNI/cm^3) for all molluscan species (species above dashed line at > 5% MNI viewed as dominant).

Economic Molluscan Species	Habitat Category	MNI	% MNI	Density (MNI/cm^3)	Rank Order
Marcia hiantina	Sand/Mud Flats	292	29.00	0.00578	1
Isognomon isognomon	Mangroves	280	27.81	0.00555	2
Mytilidae f.	Shallow Water	145	14.40	0.00287	3
Gafrarium sp.	Sand/Mud Flats	57	5.66	0.00113	4
Modiolus sp.	Coastal Rivers/Estuaries	39	3.87	0.00077	5
Trochus sp.	Shallow Water	36	3.57	0.00071	6
Terebralia sp.	Mangroves	28	2.78	0.00055	7
Nerita sp.	Mangroves	27	2.68	0.00054	8
Pinctada sp.	Sand/Mud Flats	16	1.59	0.00032	9
Anadara granosa	Sand/Mud Flats	14	1.39	0.00028	10
Circe sp.	Sand/Mud Flats	10	0.99	0.00020	11
Barbatia sp.	Shallow Water	9	0.89	0.00018	12
Ostreidae f.	Shallow Water	7	0.70	0.00014	13
Pinna bicolor	Sand/Mud Flats	7	0.70	0.00014	13
Tapes sp.	Sand/Mud Flats	7	0.70	0.00014	13
Pitar sp.	Sand/Mud Flats	6	0.60	0.00012	16
Tellina sp.	Sand/Mud Flats	6	0.60	0.00012	16
Turbo cinereus	Shallow Water	5	0.50	0.00010	18
Anadara antiquata	Sand/Mud Flats	4	0.40	0.00008	19
Polymesoda (Geloina) coaxans	Coastal Rivers/Estuaries	4	0.40	0.00008	19
Fissurellidae sp.	Shallow Water	3	0.30	0.00006	21
Haliotis sp.	Shallow Water	2	0.20	0.00004	22
Telescopium telescopium	Mangroves	2	0.20	0.00004	22
Chitonidae f.	Shallow Water	1	0.10	0.00002	24
Total		**1007**			

Table 5.12: BMB/084, MNI and corrected MNI values for the dominant species by excavation unit.

Excavation Unit	Volume (cm^3)	*Marcia hiantina*		*I. isognomon*		Mytilidae f.		*Gafrarium* sp.	
		MNI	MNI/cm^3	MNI	MNI/cm^3	MNI	MNI/cm^3	MNI	MNI/cm^3
1/2	4750	42	0.00884	161	0.03389	26	0.00547	13	0.00274
3	5500	35	0.00636	12	0.00218	10	0.00182	6	0.00109
4	8250	17	0.00206	70	0.00849	19	0.0023	0	0.00000
5	8500	78	0.00918	27	0.00318	20	0.00235	10	0.00118
6	7250	60	0.00828	9	0.00124	13	0.00179	1	0.00014
7	8000	50	0.00625	1	0.00013	35	0.00438	18	0.00225
8	8250	10	0.00121	0	0.00000	22	0.00267	9	0.00109

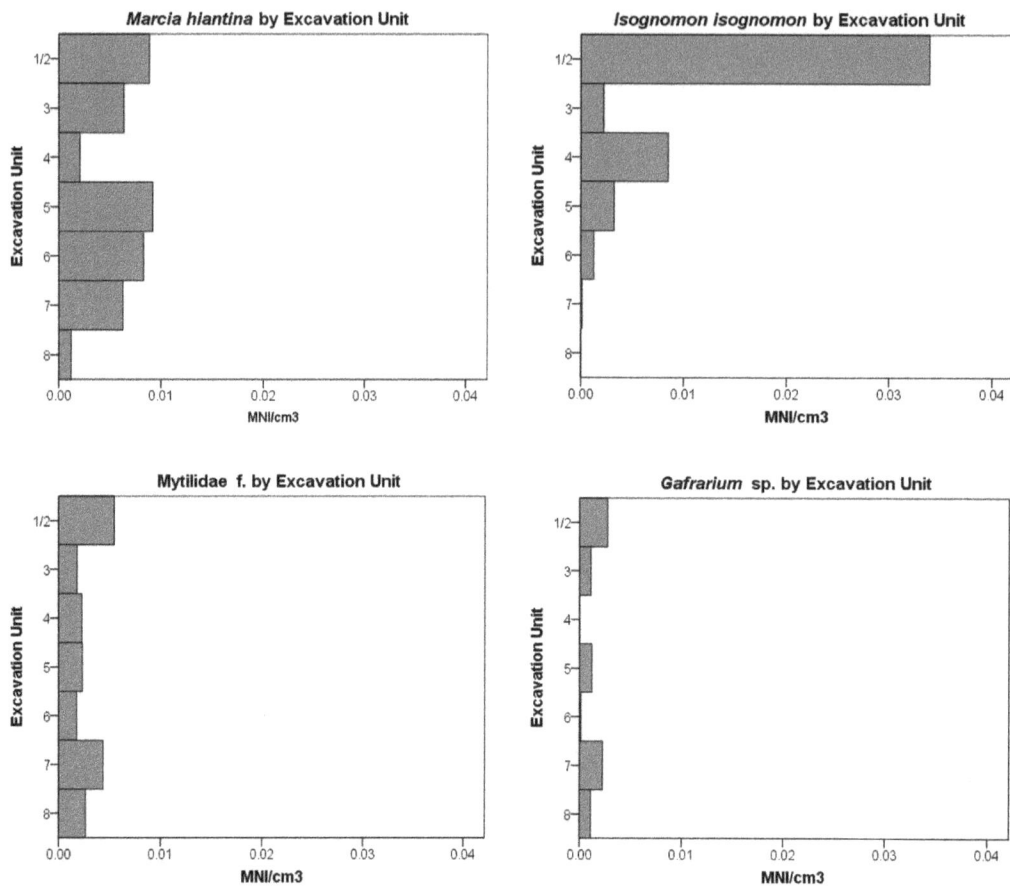

Figure 5.5: BMB/084, corrected MNI values for the dominant species by excavation unit.

In testing the relationship between relative abundance estimates of these dominant species by excavation unit, for *Marcia hiantina* (r_s = -0.500, $p > 0.2$, $n = 7$), Mytilidae f. ($r_s = 0.000$, $p > 0.5$, $n = 7$) and *Gafrarium* sp. ($r_s = -0.162$, $p > 0.5$, $n = 7$) correlation coefficients indicate that there is not a significant change through time in the level of exploitation for these species within the site. In comparison, the results of Spearman's correlations for *Isognomon isognomon* ($r_s = -0.893$, $p < 0.01$, $n = 7$) suggests that there is a significant change through time in relative abundance, supported by the observably large jump in the relative abundance estimates in the upper excavation units closer to the surface of the site. The dramatic difference in the relative abundance estimates for this species reinforces this picture of increased exploitation in the more recent past. As with the pattern of habitat relative abundance discussed previously, even with the highly increased level of *Isognomon isognomon* exploitation, there does not appear to be a corresponding decrease in the exploitation of the other three dominant species within the site. This may relate to a restructuring of habitats within the area, although the lack of a decrease in those dominant species from the sand/mud flat and shallow water habitats would suggest otherwise. Rather, the patterns of molluscan exploitation within this site are probably more indicative of a restructuring of the shell-beds within the mangrove zone itself, affecting the distribution, density and overall availability of species from this habitat.

Myaoola Bay midden site comparison

Given that the degree of variability or homogeneity in resource exploitation within the Myaoola Bay midden sites has been characterised on an individual basis, it is useful to compare these sites given that there are distinct differences in site chronologies and position within the landscape (Table 5.13). While there is a degree of variability across the Myaoola Bay sites, varying in species richness between 16 and 26, these differences are not statistically significant (χ^2 = 2.455, $d.f.$ = 3, p > 0.2). Chi-square results also indicate that species richness per habitat in the Myaoola Bay sites are not significantly different (χ^2 = 1.668, $d.f.$ = 6, p = 0.948, Cramer's V = 0.112). As species richness relates to the structure and productivity of resources within the local area, reflecting the number of species available for exploitation, little would have appeared to change through time on this exposed coastline of Myaoola Bay.

Table 5.13: Myaoola Bay sites, overall species richness and the frequency of species per habitat area.

Site	Approx.	Total Species	Shallow Water		Sand/Mud Flats		Mangroves		Estuarine	
Code	Age cal BP	Richness	No.	%	No.	%	No.	%	No.	%
BMB/018	2953	16	4	25.00	7	43.75	3	18.75	2	12.50
BMB/067	1518 - 592	26	10	38.46	10	38.46	5	19.23	1	3.85
BMB/084	424 - Modern	24	8	33.33	10	41.67	4	16.67	2	8.33

While these results may suggest a certain degree of homogeneity between these sites in terms of the number of species exploited, they are not indicative of the overall level or intensity of exploitation between environmental patches. To this end, Table 5.14 details the MNI and percentage MNI of species by each habitat zone. To investigate whether the differences in the relative abundance of species per habitat in the Myaoola Bay middens, a chi-square statistic was used, the results of which indicate that the Myaoola Bay sites are significantly different (χ^2 = 789.088, $d.f.$ = 6, p = 0.000, Cramer's V = 0.340) in terms of relative abundance per habitat.

Table 5.14: Myaoola Bay sites, MNI and percentage MNI of species per habitat area.

Site	Approx.	Shallow Water		Sand/Mud Flats		Mangroves		Estuarine	
Code	Age cal BP	MNI	%	MNI	%	MNI	%	MNI	%
BMB/018	2953	408	51.78	370	46.95	7	0.89	3	0.38
BMB/067	1518 - 592	416	25.65	1098	67.69	99	6.1	9	0.55
BMB/084	424 - Modern	208	20.66	419	41.61	337	33.47	43	4.27

Differences in the structure of the landscape between the three locations on the peninsula in which these sites are located explain the variability in the intensity of exploitation of species from these four habitat zones. When viewed in their chronological sequence, these differences may indicate larger scale processes of landscape alteration and environmental variability through time on this section of the coastline. While the sand/mud flat areas remain consistently exploited through time and by location, there is a gradual decrease in the use of species from the hard-substrate, shallow water zone. This shift in these species is also related to a corresponding increase in mangrove species exploitation, and to a lesser degree, those species inhabiting the coastal rivers and estuaries. Following the rapid phase of sea level rise, culminating and stabilising at a high-stand of approximately 2.5m above present 5000 years ago, gradual changes to the shore-line would have occurred, largely resulting from the slow sea level regression and increased sedimentation from the coastal rivers and streams. These processes would have seen a gradual restriction of the shallow water habitats, and an expansion of other habitats, particularly the mangrove forests. The shallow nature of near-shore areas around the Point Blane Peninsula may also explain the consistency of sand and mud flat species over the last 3000 years in the Myaoola Bay sites (Faulkner 2011:143–4).

Grindall Bay shell mound sites

BMB/029: Species richness, habitat exploitation and relative abundances

Eighteen molluscan taxa in all were identified from the 11 excavation units analysed for BMB/029. As this site is situated within the most northerly of the mound clusters, and possibly represents part of the earliest phase of mollusc exploitation within this area following sea level stabilisation and initial progradation, the extent of possible variations through time in species and habitat richness are important. Species richness for BMB/029 by excavation unit is detailed in Table 5.15, along with the percentages of the total number of economic species identified within the site. Spearman's correlation coefficient (r_s = -0.140, $p > 0.5$, $n = 11$) suggests that the relationship between species richness and excavation unit is neither strong nor significant. Therefore, the level of species richness appears to remain consistent throughout the occupation of the site.

Table 5.15: BMB/029, number of species, the percentage of the total number of species and number of species for molluscan habitats by excavation unit.

Excavation Unit	No. Species	% of Total	Shallow Water	Sand/Mud Flats	Mangroves	Estuarine
1	9	50.00	1	3	4	1
3	11	61.11	1	5	4	1
5	9	50.00	1	4	3	1
7	14	77.78	2	5	5	2
9	8	44.44	1	3	2	2
11	11	61.11	3	3	4	1
13	8	44.44	1	3	4	0
15	9	50.00	1	5	3	0
17	8	44.44	1	4	3	0
19	12	66.67	2	6	4	0
21	9	50.00	1	4	3	1
Total No. of Species	**18**		**3**	**7**	**6**	**2**

Of the 18 economic species within the site, three (16.7%) come from the shallow water habitat, seven (38.9%) from the sand/mud flat habitat, six (33.3%) from the mangrove zone and two (11.1%) gathered from coastal river/estuarine areas. This suggests that the mangrove fringing sand/mud flat areas and the mangroves themselves were the dominant and consistently available environmental zones within the area during the period of site deposition. Given patterns of landscape change and reorganisation following sea level rise, particularly with environmental change coinciding with progradation in these types of former shallow embayments, the emphasis on resources from these two habitat zones is not surprising. It would be expected that these habitats would dominate this type of coastline during the late Holocene. As such, the lower numbers of species exploited from hard-substrate, near shore areas and coastal rivers and estuaries reflects the differential availability and distribution of both of these habitat areas. Species richness and relative abundance estimates by excavation unit are used here to investigate possible shifts in the focus of exploitation between these habitats through time. Differences in the number of species by excavation unit are not significant for the shallow water zone (r_s = 0.116, $p > 0.5$, $n = 11$), sand and mud flats (r_s = 0.242, $p > 0.2$, $n = 11$), mangroves (r_s = -0.298, $p > 0.2$, $n = 11$) or coastal river/estuarine species (r_s = -0.544, $p > 0.05$, $n = 11$). Therefore, patterns in the number of economic species identified for each habitat through time (excavation unit) remains relatively stable.

While habitat richness appears to have remained consistent, there may well have been changes in the intensity of exploitation within these habitat zones, possibly reflecting further changes within the immediate surrounds relating to environmental processes. Therefore, the relative abundances of species per habitat need to be addressed. While there was little variation in species richness per habitat, the patterns are quite different when taking relative abundance into account (Table 5.16). There is not a significant or strong relationship between relative abundance of species from the shallow water zone and excavation unit (r_s = -0.292, p > 0.2, n = 11). On the other hand, there appears to be a significant relationship between relative abundance per habitat and excavation unit for the sand/mud flat habitat (r_s = -0.600, p < 0.05, n = 11), the mangroves (r_s = -0.620, p < 0.05, n = 11) and coastal river/estuarine habitat (r_s = -0.739, p < 0.01, n = 11). The level of significance from the estuarine habitat needs to be placed in context, as it is only a minor resource exploited within this site, and comparatively, this increase does not affect the overall economic structure.

Table 5.16: BMB/029, MNI values and volume-corrected MNI estimates (MNI/cm^3) for species from molluscan habitats by excavation unit.

Excavation Unit	Volume (cm³)		Shallow Water	Sand/Mud Flats	Mangroves	Estuarine
1	7500	MNI	1	120	19	1
		MNI/cm³	0.00013	0.01600	0.00253	0.00013
3	7500	MNI	1	164	51	1
		MNI/cm³	0.00013	0.02187	0.00680	0.00013
5	10000	MNI	7	129	67	1
		MNI/cm³	0.00070	0.01290	0.00670	0.00010
7	7500	MNI	2	302	17	2
		MNI/cm³	0.00027	0.04027	0.00227	0.00027
9	7500	MNI	3	211	4	2
		MNI/cm³	0.00040	0.02813	0.00053	0.00027
11	12500	MNI	3	291	11	1
		MNI/cm³	0.00024	0.02328	0.00088	0.00008
13	10000	MNI	2	228	9	0
		MNI/cm³	0.00020	0.02280	0.00090	0.00000
15	12500	MNI	1	102	13	0
		MNI/cm³	0.00008	0.00816	0.00104	0.00000
17	10000	MNI	1	47	9	0
		MNI/cm³	0.00010	0.00470	0.00090	0.00000
19	5000	MNI	2	29	6	0
		MNI/cm³	0.00040	0.00580	0.00120	0.00000
21	17500	MNI	2	16	13	1
		MNI/cm³	0.00011	0.00091	0.00074	0.00006

The significance for the increasing abundance of species from both the sand/mud flats and the mangroves is more indicative of economic activity. The general increase in relative abundance for these habitat zones, regardless of the level of significance attributed to these figures, relates to two main factors. There may be variations in the intensity of discard within the site through time, and/or the density of resources and general availability of species from these areas related to changes to the environment. As the Garangarri site cluster probably represents the earliest period of mound building within this system, variations in habitat exploitation may also relate to the ongoing process of progradation at the time, and the gradual establishment and proliferation of the sand/mud flat zone. As such, the dominance of mangrove species, and sand/mud flat species in particular, in terms of the number of taxa represented and relative abundance would be expected.

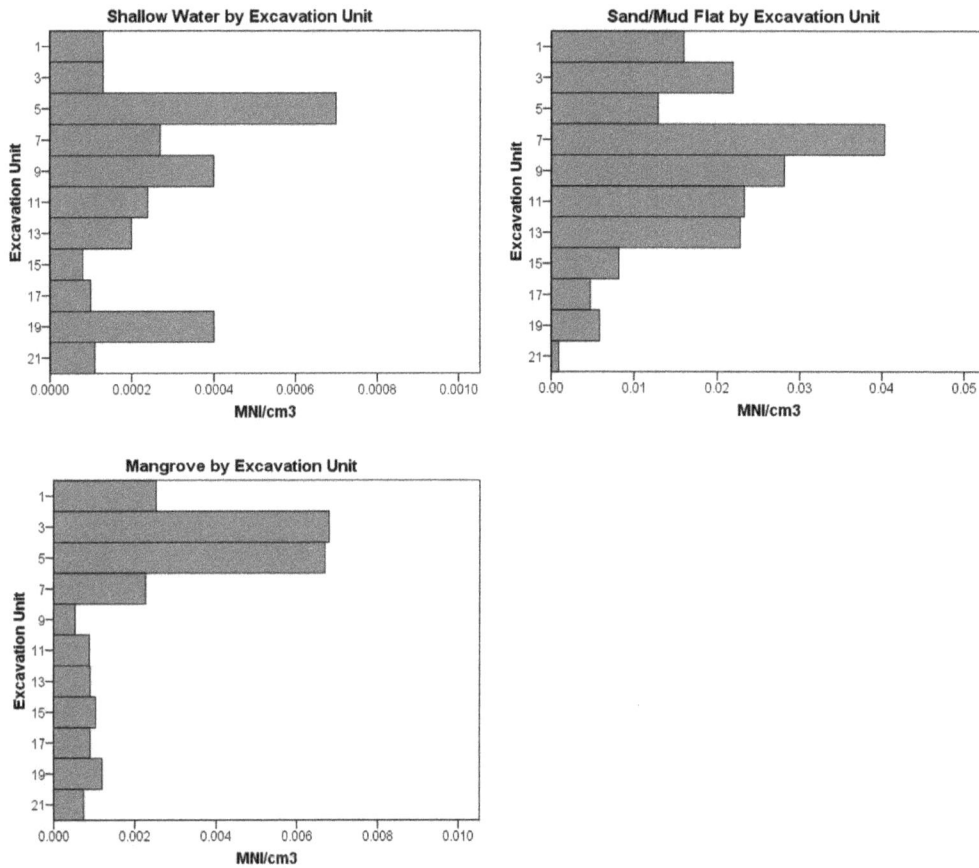

Figure 5.6: BMB/029, corrected MNI values (MNI/cm³) for molluscan habitat by excavation unit (note differences in scale).

Turning to the relative abundance of the dominant taxa within the site, Table 5.17 details the MNI counts and percentages for the 18 species from this site and a relative density estimate (MNI/cm³). Three species, at 16.7% of the total number of species in the site, make up 91.3% by MNI of the assemblage from BMB/029. By far, *Anadara granosa* is the highest-ranking species by percentage of the total MNI (68.1%) and by the corrected density estimate. In rank order, this species is followed by *Marcia hiantina* (13.48% MNI) and *Placuna placenta* (9.8% MNI). Two of these top three ranked species, *Anadara granosa* and *Marcia hiantina*, are found in the sand and mudflats within the intertidal/subtidal zone, and collectively comprise 81.6% by MNI of the total assemblage (Faulkner 2009:827). *Placuna placenta*, which occurred in dense horizontal lenses or bands throughout the deposit, is generally found within the mangroves.

Table 5.17: BMB/029, MNI values and MNI density estimates (MNI/cm³) for all molluscan species (species above dashed line at > 5% MNI viewed as dominant).

Economic Molluscan Species	Habitat Category	MNI	% MNI	Density (MNI/cm³)	Rank Order
Anadara granosa	Sand/Mud Flats	1288	68.08	0.01198	1
Marcia hiantina	Sand/Mud Flats	255	13.48	0.00237	2
Placuna placenta	Mangroves	185	9.78	0.00172	3
Anadara antiquata	Sand/Mud Flats	76	4.02	0.00071	4
Ostreidae f.	Shallow Water	21	1.11	0.00020	5
Nerita sp.	Mangroves	16	0.85	0.00015	6
Dosinia mira	Sand/Mud Flats	10	0.53	0.00009	7
Cassidula angulata	Mangroves	7	0.37	0.00007	8
Polymesoda (Geloina) coaxans	Coastal Rivers/Estuaries	6	0.32	0.00006	9
Telescopium telescopium	Mangroves	6	0.32	0.00006	9
Tellina sp.	Sand/Mud Flats	6	0.32	0.00006	9
Mactra abbreviata	Sand/Mud Flats	3	0.16	0.00003	12
Terebralia sp.	Mangroves	3	0.16	0.00003	12
Modiolus sp.	Coastal Rivers/Estuaries	3	0.16	0.00003	12
Barbatia sp.	Shallow Water	2	0.11	0.00002	15
Cerithidea sp.	Mangroves	2	0.11	0.00002	15
Trochus sp.	Shallow Water	2	0.11	0.00002	15
Placamen calophyllum	Sand/Mud Flats	1	0.05	0.00001	18
Total		**1892**			

Table 5.18 and Figure 5.7 present the MNI values for these three species corrected for volume (MNI/cm³) per excavation unit. Investigating variability in relative abundance estimates by excavation unit for *Marcia hiantina* (r_s = -0.273, $p > 0.2$, $n = 11$) indicates that the differences observed here are not significant. In other words, there is not a significant change through time in the level of exploitation for this species within the site. In comparison, the Spearman's correlation coefficients suggests that there is a highly significant change through time (excavation unit) in the relative abundance of *Anadara granosa* (r_s = -0.491, $p < 0.05$, $n = 11$) and *Placuna placenta* (r_s = -0.647, $p < 0.02$, $n = 11$) (Faulkner 2009:827).

Table 5.18: BMB/029, MNI and corrected MNI values for the dominant species by excavation unit.

Excavation Unit	Volume (cm³)	*Anadara granosa* MNI	MNI/cm³	*Marcia hiantina* MNI	MNI/cm³	*Placuna placenta* MNI	MNI/cm³
1	7500	108	0.01440	10	0.00133	16	0.00213
3	7500	119	0.01587	9	0.00120	48	0.00640
5	10000	106	0.01060	18	0.00180	62	0.00620
7	7500	256	0.03413	40	0.00533	12	0.00160
9	7500	158	0.02107	51	0.00680	3	0.00040
11	12500	231	0.01848	57	0.00456	8	0.00064
13	10000	202	0.02020	17	0.00170	4	0.00040
15	12500	60	0.00480	28	0.00224	11	0.00088
17	10000	27	0.00270	14	0.00140	7	0.00070
19	5000	13	0.00260	6	0.00120	3	0.00060
21	17500	8	0.00046	5	0.00029	11	0.00063

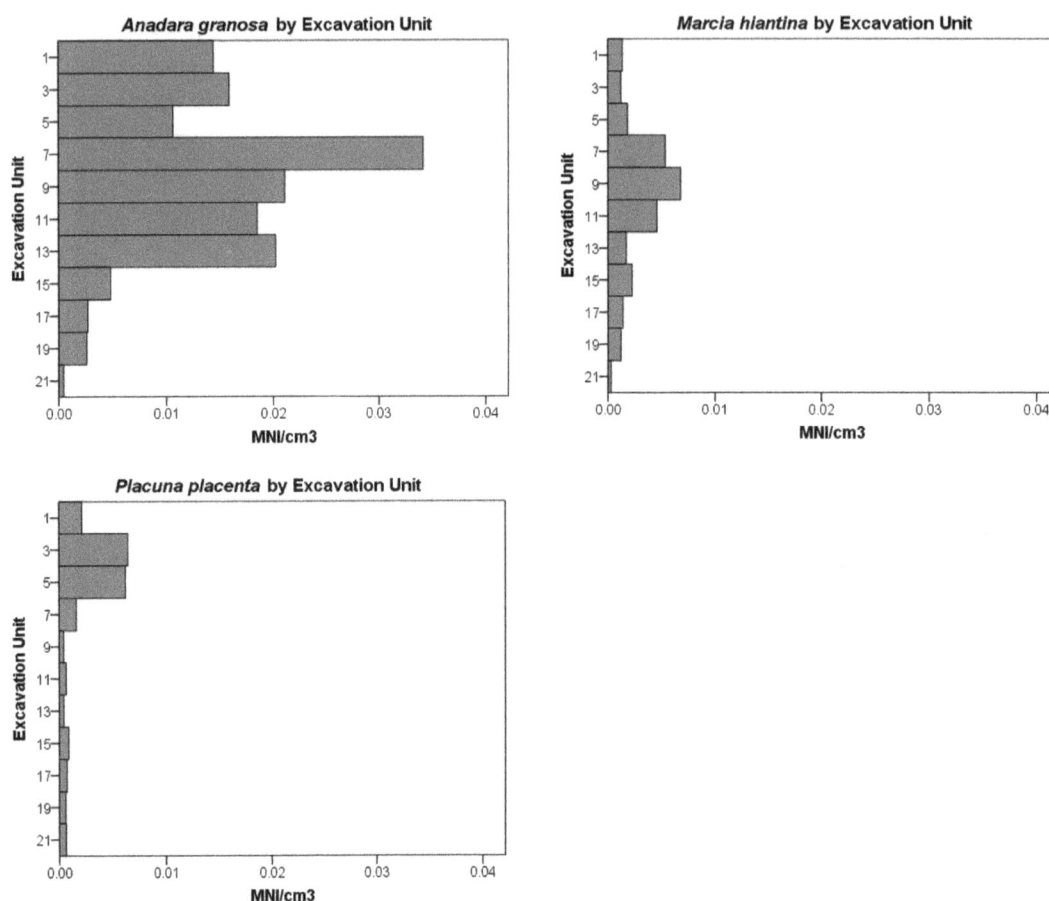

Figure 5.7: BMB/029, corrected MNI values for the dominant species by excavation unit.

It is still highly probable that this increase in *Anadara granosa* is tied strongly to those processes of landscape alteration noted earlier. The proliferation of this species probably kept pace with these changes as the sand/mud flat areas enlarged through progradation. *Anadara granosa* then became the primary focus of exploitation within this locality. While the sand/mud flats were an important resource to start with, as evidenced by the similar relative abundance estimates between *Marcia hiantina* and *Anadara granosa* for the lower portions of the deposit, it is evident that the increasing abundance of *Anadara granosa* in the environment created the stronger emphasis on this species within the area during the latter periods of occupation.

BMB/071: Species richness, habitat exploitation and relative abundances

Fifteen molluscan taxa were identified within the seven excavation units analysed for BMB/071. This site is situated within a large mound and midden cluster approximately 2km south of the Garangarri cluster. As such, it is possibly representative of ongoing use of this area following the initial phase of exploitation characterised by site BMB/029. Overall species richness within the site varies through time (Table 5.19), the Spearman's correlation coefficient (r_s = -0.880, p > 0.05, n = 6) suggests that the relationship between species richness and excavation unit is significant. While there appears to be an increase in species richness by excavation unit, between the lower and upper portions of the deposit there is an increase of only one species. It is therefore difficult to place too much emphasis on the significance of this increase in overall species richness. Turning to possible shifts in habitat exploitation, of the 15 economic species within the site, two (13.3%) come from the shallow water habitat, six (40.0%) from the sand/mud flat habitat, five (33.3%) from the mangrove zone and two (13.3%) gathered from coastal river/estuarine areas. This pattern is very similar to that found within BMB/029, and suggests that the mangrove fringing sand/mud flat areas and the mangroves themselves were the dominant habitats available during the period of occupation in the area. Again, the lower numbers of species exploited from hard-substrate, near shore areas and coastal rivers and estuaries reflects the differential distribution of these habitat areas relative to the two more dominant habitats.

Table 5.19: BMB/071, number of species, the percentage of the total number of species and number of species for molluscan habitats by excavation unit.

Excavation Unit	No. Species	% of Total	Shallow Water	Sand/Mud Flats	Mangroves	Estuarine
1	12	80.00	2	4	4	2
3	12	80.00	2	5	4	1
5	12	80.00	1	5	4	2
7	10	66.67	2	4	4	0
9	11	73.33	1	5	4	1
11	9	60.00	1	3	4	1
Total No. of Species	**15**		**2**	**6**	**5**	**2**

Comparing the number of species by excavation unit shows that there are not significant differences for the shallow water zone (r_s = -0.683, $p > 0.1$, $n = 6$), sand and mud flats (r_s = -0.309, $p > 0.5$, $n = 6$) and coastal rivers/estuaries (r_s = -0.525, $p > 0.1$, $n = 6$). As there is no change in species richness throughout the excavation for the mangrove zone, this habitat was not tested. Therefore, patterns in the number of economic species identified for each habitat through time remains relatively stable. The minor variations in habitat species richness noted between excavation units for the shallow water and coastal river/estuarine habitats, while not significant themselves, may have contributed to the significant results for overall site species richness. Figure 5.8 graphs the corrected MNI values by excavation unit and the mean MNI for each excavation unit for each habitat, and Table 5.20 details the MNI and volume-corrected MNI of species within each excavation unit by habitat. While there was little variation in species richness per habitat, the relative abundance estimates for species from these habitats again highlights greater variability in the level of exploitation.

Differences in the mean volume-corrected MNI by excavation unit are significant for the shallow water zone (r_s = -0.841, $p < 0.05$, $n = 6$) and mangroves (r_s = 1.000, $p < 0.01$, $n = 6$). In contrast, the decrease in the corrected MNI estimates by excavation unit is significant for the sand and mudflats (r_s = -0.029, $p > 0.5$, $n = 6$), as is the slight increase for the coastal rivers/estuaries zone (r_s = -0.609, $p > 0.1$, $n = 6$). As with the patterns identified for BMB/029 from the Garangarri site cluster, the decrease in the exploitation of mangrove species probably reflects variation in this particular habitat zone related to progradation and the expansion of the sand/mud flat zone. The progressive build-up of fine sediment (silt and mud) in the intertidal zone, particularly within the mangroves, encourages the establishment of beach ridges. As the ridge develops, the mangrove fringe is killed off and eventually re-establishes on the seaward edge of the new ridge (Chappell 1982:74; Woodroffe *et al.* 1985b:25). The decrease in species from the mangrove zone may relate to the process described above, while the availability of species that inhabit the other three habitats, in particular the mangrove fringing intertidal flats, remained relatively stable.

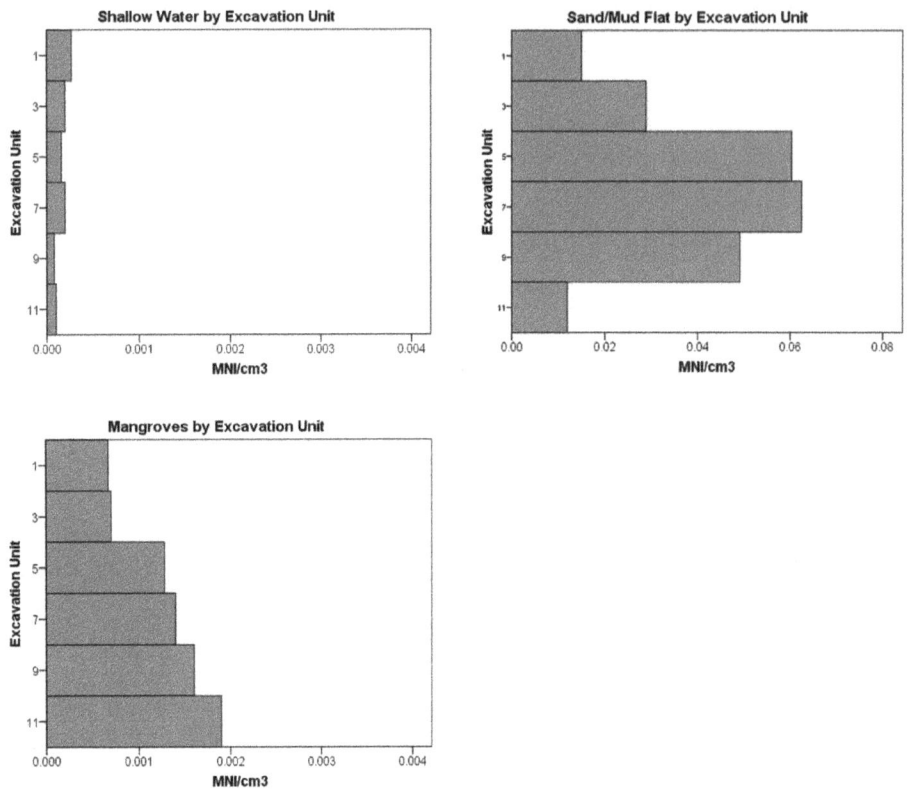

Figure 5.8: BMB/071, corrected MNI values (MNI/cm³) for molluscan habitats by excavation unit (note differences in scale).

Table 5.20: BMB/071, MNI values and volume-corrected MNI estimates (MNI/cm³) for species from molluscan habitats by excavation unit.

Excavation Unit	Volume (cm³)		Shallow Water	Sand/Mud Flats	Mangroves	Estuarine
1	7500	MNI	2	113	5	2
		MNI/cm³	0.00027	0.01507	0.00067	0.00027
3	10000	MNI	2	289	7	1
		MNI/cm³	0.00020	0.02890	0.00070	0.00010
5	12500	MNI	2	754	16	2
		MNI/cm³	0.00016	0.06032	0.00128	0.00016
7	10000	MNI	2	625	14	0
		MNI/cm³	0.00020	0.06250	0.00140	0.00000
9	12500	MNI	1	614	20	1
		MNI/cm³	0.00008	0.04912	0.00160	0.00008
11	10000	MNI	1	120	19	1
		MNI/cm³	0.00010	0.01200	0.00190	0.00010

Table 5.21 details the MNI counts and percentages for the 15 species from this site and a relative density estimate (MNI/cm³). Table 5.22 and Figure 5.9 present the MNI values for the two dominant species corrected for volume (MNI/cm³). These two species, at 13.3% of the total number of species in the site, make up 94.80% by MNI of the assemblage from BMB/071. *Anadara granosa* dominates the molluscan assemblage from this site; it is the highest-ranking species by percentage of the total MNI (87.5%) and by the corrected density estimate. The only other species to make up greater than 5% by MNI is *Mactra abbreviata* at 7.3% (both species are found in sand/mudflat areas). The Spearman's test of the relationship between the relative abundance estimates by excavation unit for *Anadara granosa* (r_s = -0.086, p > 0.5, n = 6) and *Mactra abbreviata* (r_s = -0.116, p > 0.5, n = 6) indicates that the differences observed above are not significant. In other words, there is not a significant change through time in the

level of exploitation for these species within the site (see Figure 5.9). The sheer dominance of *Anadara granosa* within this site indicates that this species was the primary focus of exploitation within this locality. This suggests that, regardless of whatever changes to the landscape were occurring within this area during the span of occupation of this site, such as the possible changes to the mangrove areas noted previously, the sand and mud flat areas remained reasonably stable (Faulkner 2009:827). By extension, the abundance and apparent reliability of *Anadara granosa* as a resource within this consistently available habitat area saw this species become the focal point within the economy.

Table 5.21: BMB/071, MNI values and MNI density estimates (MNI/cm³) for all molluscan species (species above dashed line at > 5% MNI viewed as dominant).

Economic Molluscan Species	Habitat Category	MNI	% MNI	Density (MNI/cm³)	Rank Order
Anadara granosa	Sand/Mud Flats	2286	87.49	0.03658	1
Mactra abbreviata	Sand/Mud Flats	191	7.31	0.00306	2
Placuna placenta	Mangroves	40	1.53	0.00064	3
Anadara antiquata	Sand/Mud Flats	19	0.73	0.00030	4
Nerita sp.	Mangroves	19	0.73	0.00030	4
Marcia hiantina	Sand/Mud Flats	15	0.57	0.00024	6
Cassidula angulata	Mangroves	11	0.42	0.00018	7
Telescopium telescopium	Mangroves	10	0.38	0.00016	8
Septifer bilocularis	Shallow Water	5	0.19	0.00008	9
Polymesoda (Geloina) coaxans	Coastal Rivers/Estuaries	5	0.19	0.00008	9
Ostreidae f.	Shallow Water	5	0.19	0.00008	9
Tellina sp.	Sand/Mud Flats	2	0.08	0.00003	12
Modiolus sp.	Coastal Rivers/Estuaries	2	0.08	0.00003	12
Placamen calophyllum	Sand/Mud Flats	2	0.08	0.00003	12
Terebralia sp.	Mangroves	1	0.04	0.00002	15
Total		**2613**			

Table 5.22: BMB/071, MNI and corrected MNI values for the dominant species by excavation unit.

Excavation Unit	Volume (cm³)	*Anadara granosa*		*Mactra abbreviata*	
		MNI	MNI/cm³	MNI	MNI/cm³
1	7500	105	0.01400	5	0.00067
3	10000	267	0.02670	16	0.00160
5	12500	701	0.05608	46	0.00368
7	10000	516	0.05160	104	0.01040
9	12500	589	0.04712	20	0.00160
11	10000	108	0.01080	0	0.00000

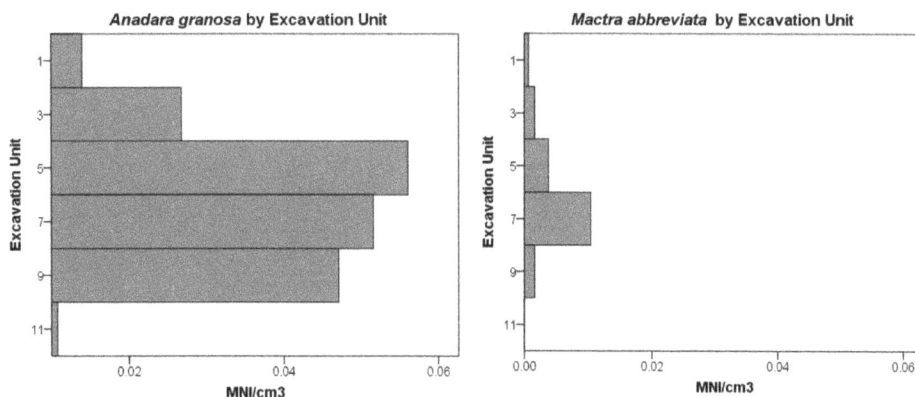

Figure 5.9: BMB/071, corrected MNI values for the dominant species by excavation unit.

BMB/045: Species richness, habitat exploitation and relative abundances

Fifteen molluscan taxa in all were identified within the 16 excavation units analysed for BMB/045. The differences in radiocarbon dates from the surface, middle and base of the site are not statistically significant, which suggests that there was extremely rapid rate of deposition, given the 1m depth of deposit within the excavated area. Any changes through time in economic activity within the site should be reflected by analysing variation in species richness, habitat exploitation and relative abundance estimates by excavation unit. Species richness for BMB/045 by excavation unit is detailed in Table 5.23, with the percentages of the total number of economic species identified within the site. While there is a certain degree of variation in species richness between excavation units, ranging between four and eleven species per unit, the Spearman's correlation coefficient (r_s = -0.074, p > 0.5, n = 16) suggest that the relationship between species richness and excavation unit is neither strong nor significant. This again indicates that there was a certain level of consistency in the number of species exploited within this site through time. Of the 15 economic species within the site, three (20.0%) come from the shallow water habitat, six (40.0%) from the sand/mud flat habitats, four (26.7%) from the mangrove zone and only two (13.3%) from coastal river/estuarine areas. In line with the other Grindall Bay sites, this suggests that the sand/mud flats were the dominant environmental zone within the area during site deposition.

Species richness and relative abundance estimates by excavation unit are again used to determine whether there were any shifts in the focus of exploitation between these habitats through time. A Spearman's rank correlation is used to test the relationship between habitat species richness and excavation unit with the exception of the estuarine habitat, as the number of species by excavation unit remains constant. These results show that there is not a significant relationship between species richness and excavation unit throughout the deposit for the shallow water zone (r_s = -0.031, p > 0.5, n = 16), mangroves (r_s = 0.428, p > 0.05, n = 16) and estuary habitat (r_s = -0.082, p > 0.5, n = 16). In contrast, there appears to be a general increase in the number of species exploited from the sand/mud flats within the site, as the relationship between species richness from this habitat area and excavation unit is significant (r_s = -0.565, p < 0.05, n = 16).

Table 5.23: BMB/045, number of species, the percentage of the total number of species and number of species for molluscan habitats by excavation unit.

Excavation Unit	No. Species	% of Total	Shallow Water	Sand/Mud Flats	Mangroves	Estuarine
1	8	53.33	1	5	2	0
3	11	73.33	2	6	2	1
5	8	53.33	1	6	1	0
7	7	46.67	0	6	1	0
9	6	40.00	0	5	1	0
11	6	40.00	0	5	1	0
13	8	53.33	1	5	2	0
15	8	53.33	1	5	2	0
17	9	60.00	1	4	3	1
19	10	66.67	2	5	3	0
21	5	33.33	1	2	2	0
23	4	26.67	1	3	0	0
25	7	46.67	1	3	2	1
27	10	66.67	1	5	3	1
29	9	60.00	1	5	3	0
31	7	46.67	0	5	2	0
Total	**15**		**3**	**6**	**4**	**2**

As a contrast, Table 5.24 details the MNI of species within each excavation unit by habitat. Testing the combined, volume-corrected species relative abundance estimates from the four habitat areas suggests that there is not a significant relationship between relative abundance and excavation unit for any of the four habitats. The Spearman's correlation coefficients indicate that for the shallow water ($r_s = 0.121$, $p > 0.5$, $n = 16$), sand/mud flat ($r_s = -0.465$, $p > 0.05$, $n = 16$), mangrove ($r_s = -0.398$, $p > 0.1$, $n = 16$) and estuarine habitats ($r_s = 0.108$, $p > 0.5$, $n = 16$), there is not a significant change in the focus of exploitation through time. Regardless of the comparative level or intensity of exploitation between these habitat zones, exploitation within each habitat remains consistent throughout the occupation of this site. While the number of species from the sand/mud flats does change significantly throughout the deposit, the relative abundance estimates of species from this habitat indicates that any change in the level of exploitation from this area is not significant. This pattern possibly indicates a slight change in the structure and density of shell-beds within this zone.

Table 5.24: BMB/045, MNI values and volume-corrected MNI estimates (MNI/cm^3) for species from molluscan habitats by excavation unit.

Excavation Unit	Volume (cm³)		Shallow Water	Sand/Mud Flats	Mangroves	Estuarine
1	5000	MNI	1	87	8	0
		MNI/cm³	0.00020	0.01740	0.00160	0.00000
3	5000	MNI	1	172	24	1
		MNI/cm³	0.00020	0.03440	0.00480	0.00020
5	5000	MNI	0	200	25	0
		MNI/cm³	0.00000	0.04000	0.00500	0.00000
7	5000	MNI	0	213	2	0
		MNI/cm³	0.00000	0.04260	0.00040	0.00000
9	7500	MNI	0	251	8	0
		MNI/cm³	0.00000	0.03347	0.00107	0.00000
11	12500	MNI	0	176	6	0
		MNI/cm³	0.00000	0.01408	0.00048	0.00000
13	7500	MNI	1	231	11	0
		MNI/cm³	0.00013	0.03080	0.00147	0.00000
15	10000	MNI	0	223	14	0
		MNI/cm³	0.00000	0.02230	0.00140	0.00000
17	10000	MNI	2	180	2	0
		MNI/cm³	0.00020	0.01800	0.00020	0.00000
19	10000	MNI	1	218	2	1
		MNI/cm³	0.00010	0.02180	0.00020	0.00010
21	7500	MNI	2	121	1	0
		MNI/cm³	0.00027	0.01613	0.00013	0.00000
23	7500	MNI	0	110	2	0
		MNI/cm³	0.00000	0.01467	0.00027	0.00000
25	7500	MNI	1	128	3	1
		MNI/cm³	0.00013	0.01707	0.00040	0.00013
27	7500	MNI	1	236	5	1
		MNI/cm³	0.00013	0.03147	0.00067	0.00013
29	7500	MNI	2	166	31	0
		MNI/cm³	0.00027	0.02213	0.00413	0.00000
31	10000	MNI	0	156	7	0
		MNI/cm³	0.00000	0.01560	0.00070	0.00000

Table 5.25 details the MNI counts and percentages for the 16 species from this site, volume-corrected relative abundance estimates (MNI/cm^3), and the rank order by MNI. Only two species, at 13.3% of the total number of species in the site, make up 91.4% by MNI of the assemblage from BMB/045. *Anadara granosa* is by far the highest-ranking species by percentage of the total MNI (74.2%) and by the corrected density estimate. In rank order, this species is followed by *Mactra abbreviata* at 17.2% by MNI (Faulkner 2009:827). These two top ranked species are found in the sand and mudflats within the intertidal/subtidal zone.

Table 5.25: BMB/045, MNI values and MNI density estimates (MNI/cm^3) for all molluscan species (species above dashed line at > 5% MNI viewed as dominant).

Economic Molluscan Species	Habitat Category	MNI	% MNI	Density (MNI/cm³)	Rank Order
Anadara granosa	Sand/Mud Flats	2253	74.21	0.01802	1
Mactra abbreviata	Sand/Mud Flats	523	17.23	0.00418	2
Cassidula angulata	Mangroves	116	3.82	0.00093	3
Pitar sp.	Sand/Mud Flats	32	1.05	0.00026	4
Tellina sp.	Sand/Mud Flats	32	1.05	0.00026	4
Placuna placenta	Mangroves	22	0.72	0.00018	6
Placamen calophyllum	Sand/Mud Flats	16	0.53	0.00013	7
Telescopium telescopium	Mangroves	13	0.43	0.00010	8
Anadara antiquata	Sand/Mud Flats	12	0.40	0.00010	9
Ostreidae f.	Shallow Water	10	0.33	0.00008	10
Modiolus sp.	Estuarine	3	0.10	0.00002	11
Barbatia sp.	Shallow Water	1	0.03	0.00001	12
Chicoreus sp.	Shallow Water	1	0.03	0.00001	12
Nerita sp.	Mangroves	1	0.03	0.00001	12
Polymesoda (Geloina) coaxans	Estuarine	1	0.03	0.00001	12
Total		**3036**			

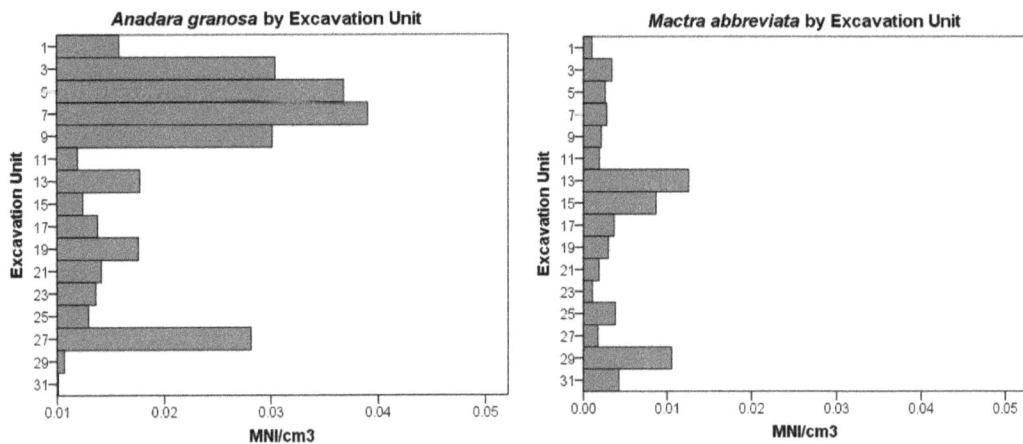

Figure 5.10: BMB/045, volume-corrected MNI values for the dominant species by excavation unit.

Figure 5.10 and Table 5.26 present the MNI values for these two species corrected for volume (MNI/cm^3) by excavation unit. Spearman's correlation coefficients indicate that the differences in the relative abundance of *Anadara granosa* ($r_s = -0.635$, $p < 0.01$, $n = 16$) and *Mactra abbreviata* ($r_s = 0.265$, $p > 0.2$, $n = 16$) by excavation unit, and by extension through time, are not statistically significant (Faulkner 2009:827). In combination with the analysis of overall species richness and species richness by habitat, the primary foci of molluscan exploitation within this site appears to remain relatively consistent throughout the period of occupation.

Table 5.26: BMB/045, MNI and corrected MNI values for the dominant species by excavation unit.

Excavation Unit	Volume (cm³)	*Anadara granosa*		*Mactra abbreviata*	
		MNI	MNI/cm³	MNI	MNI/cm³
1	5000	79	0.01580	5	0.00100
3	5000	152	0.03040	17	0.00340
5	5000	184	0.03680	13	0.00260
7	5000	195	0.03900	14	0.00280
9	7500	226	0.03013	16	0.00213
11	12500	149	0.01192	24	0.00192
13	7500	133	0.01773	94	0.01253
15	10000	124	0.01240	87	0.00870
17	10000	138	0.01380	37	0.00370
19	10000	176	0.01760	30	0.00300
21	7500	106	0.01413	14	0.00187
23	7500	102	0.01360	8	0.00107
25	7500	97	0.01293	29	0.00387
27	7500	211	0.02813	13	0.00173
29	7500	80	0.01067	79	0.01053
31	10000	101	0.01010	43	0.00430

Grindall Bay mound site comparison

The analysis of the three Grindall Bay shell mounds suggests a certain level of homogeneity in resource exploitation through time and space, particularly when the emphasis on *A. granosa* in Grindall Bay is considered relative to the increased level of molluscan diversity noted in the three Myaoola Bay middens. That said, the degree of difference or similarity in resource and habitat exploitation in these sites needs to be established. Table 5.27 presents overall species richness and habitat species richness per site. As total species richness varies between 15 and 18 across the three sites, it is apparent that there is only a very low level of species richness variability, which is not statistically significant ($\chi^2 = 0.189$, *d.f.* = 4, $p > 0.5$). Species richness by habitat for the Grindall Bay mounds follows this overall pattern, with chi-square results indicating that in the Grindall Bay mound sites the number of species exploited per habitat do not differ significantly ($\chi^2 = 0.395$, *d.f.* = 6, $p = 0.999$, Cramer's V = 0.064).

Table 5.27: Grindall Bay sites, overall species richness and the frequency of species per habitat area.

Site Code	Approx. Age cal BP	Total Species Richness	Shallow Water		Sand/Mud Flats		Mangroves		Estuarine	
			No.	%	No.	%	No.	%	No.	%
BMB/029	2287 – 1912	18	3	16.67	7	38.89	6	33.33	2	11.11
BMB/071	1483 – 1192	15	2	13.33	6	40.00	5	33.33	2	13.33
BMB/045	584 – 539	15	3	20.00	6	40.00	4	26.67	2	13.33

Analysis of the three individual sites suggests that while this level of homogeneity may accurately reflect the availability of economic species within each habitat zone, there are quite strong differences in the level of habitat exploitation. To assess these differences between the sites, Table 5.28 details the MNI and percentage MNI of species by each habitat zone. In investigating differences in the relative abundance of species per habitat by site, chi-square results indicate that there is a high level of significance in the level of exploitation per habitat across the Grindall Bay sites ($\chi^2 = 177.251$, *d.f.* = 6, $p = 0.000$, Cramer's V = 0.108).

Table 5.28: Grindall Bay sites, MNI and percentage MNI of species per habitat area.

Site Code	Approx. Age cal BP	Shallow Water		Sand/Mud Flats		Mangroves		Estuarine	
		MNI	%	MNI	%	MNI	%	MNI	%
BMB/029	2287 – 1912	25	1.32	1639	86.63	219	11.58	9	0.48
BMB/071	1483 – 1192	10	0.38	2515	96.25	81	3.10	7	0.27
BMB/045	584 – 539	12	0.40	2868	94.50	151	4.98	4	0.13

The main differences between the sites in Grindall Bay lie in comparing the two dominantly exploited habitats. There is a general increase in the exploitation of the sand and mud flat habitats in this area, whereas the shallow water and estuarine habitats remain consistently low between sites and throughout time. Although the level of exploitation within the sand and mud flats is at a high level throughout the period of occupation in Grindall Bay, the increase in taxa exploited from this habitat zone through time corresponds with a decrease in mangrove species. Therefore, while there is a degree of variability within and between the Grindall Bay shell mounds, in line with the patterns identified for the Myaoola Bay middens, changes through time are a reflection of broader environmental processes acting within this former shallow embayment. Variations in habitat exploitation relate to the ongoing process of progradation within the area through time, and the gradual establishment and proliferation of the sand/mud flat zone, generally at the expense of exploitation within the mangroves. As the process of progradation reached its limit within the area close to 500 years ago this pattern slowly changed, with a slight increase in mangrove species corresponding with slight decrease in sand/mud flat species. This final shift might reflect the relative stabilisation of sedimentary infilling within this area, and the stabilisation of mangrove distribution close to its present extent at the mouth of Grindall Bay (Faulkner 2011:144–5).

Differences in the dominant exploited species

Variations in the pattern of habitat exploitation relate primarily to micro- and macro-environmental changes through time, reflected within both the specific site locality and broader Myaoola and Grindall Bay areas. The composition of the dominant molluscan taxa by site and area (Table 5.29) is also a reflection of the effects of these processes. Species composition by rank varies markedly between the Myaoola Bay midden sites (BMB/018, BMB/067 and BMB/084). While several species occur consistently within these deposits, such as *Marcia hiantina*, *Septifer bilocularis* and *Gafrarium* sp., as previously discussed for each site, differences in species ranking relates specific habitat distribution and dominance within a given location. Variations in species composition within this area reflect broader environmental change, with changing conditions affecting the range of species available for human exploitation. In contrast, the mound sites in Grindall Bay exhibit much less variability in both the most highly ranked species and the sub-dominant species components. *Anadara granosa* is the most highly ranked species in all three sites, followed by *Mactra abbreviata* and *Marcia hiantina*, all three of which inhabit sand and mud flat areas. The only other species present, *Placuna placenta*, is found within the mangroves, and in terms of ranking, is found only within BMB/029 near the top of the system. In comparing the two areas, it appears that there was a more widespread use of species in Myaoola Bay as opposed to Grindall Bay (Faulkner 2011:146). The species composition from the Grindall Bay sites indicates a possibly more intensive focus on the sand and mud flats, as well as particular species. These interpretations of the overall molluscan composition and ranking of the dominant species are supported when comparing the percentage of the total MNI for each ranking category (Table 5.30).

Table 5.29: Dominant species ranking per site.

	Site Code	Rank 1 Species	Rank 2 Species	Rank 3 Species	Rank 4 Species
Myaoola Bay	BMB/018	*Septifer bilocularis*	*Pinctada sp.*	*Gafrarium sp.*	---
	BMB/067	*Anadara granosa*	*Marcia hiantina*	*Septifer bilocularis*	*Gafrarium sp.*
	BMB/084	*Marcia hiantina*	*Isognomon isognomon*	Mytilidae f.	*Gafrarium sp.*
Grindall Bay	BMB/029	*Anadara granosa*	*Marcia hiantina*	*Placuna placenta*	---
	BMB/071	*Anadara granosa*	*Mactra abbreviata*	---	---
	BMB/045	*Anadara granosa*	*Mactra abbreviata*	---	---

Table 5.30: MNI and percentage MNI by species ranking per site and locality.

	Site Code	Rank 1 Species		Rank 2 Species		Rank 3 Species		Rank 4 Species		Total
		MNI	%	MNI	%	MNI	%	MNI	%	MNI
Myaoola Bay	BMB/018	384	48.73	274	34.77	61	7.74	---	---	788
	BMB/067	518	31.94	342	21.09	276	17.02	137	8.45	1622
	BMB/084	292	29.00	280	27.81	145	14.40	57	5.66	1007
Grindall Bay	BMB/029	1288	68.08	255	13.48	185	9.78	---	---	1892
	BMB/071	2286	87.49	191	7.31	---	---	---	---	2613
	BMB/045	2253	74.21	523	17.23	---	---	---	---	3035

For the Myaoola Bay midden sites, while there is a decline in the relative abundance of species from rank one through to four, this general decline is gradual, particularly for sites BMB/067 and BMB/084. While the pattern for BMB/018 shows a slightly steeper decline in MNI percentages from ranks one to three, with no fourth species occurring at greater than five percent by MNI, this still follows the general trend for the Myaoola Bay area. For these midden sites, there was a relatively more evenly spread use of the available species within the area, with no one species being exploited at a level greater than 50% for the site as a whole. A comparison with the three Grindall Bay mound sites shows a distinctly different pattern of resource exploitation. These three sites are clearly dominated by *Anadara granosa*, occurring between 68 and 88% of the total molluscan assemblages recovered from these deposits. While the second ranked species in the Myaoola Bay sites vary between approximately 21 and 35% of the assemblages, within Grindall Bay sites they comprise a comparatively low 7 to 17%. While other species were exploited in the latter area, as reflected within the composition of the assemblages recovered from the Grindall Bay mound deposits, there was an overwhelming focus on one particular taxon (Faulkner 2011:146). This contrasting pattern of exploitation across the Point Blane Peninsula possibly reflects the relative stability of habitats and, by extension resource availability, throughout the period of landscape development within Grindall Bay, compared with the dynamic and changing nature of the coastline on the more exposed, eastern margin of the peninsula.

Conclusion

The composition of the molluscan assemblages from all of these sites represents the long-term, average structure of mollusc communities in each locality distributed around the Point Blane Peninsula during the period of site formation (Claassen 1998:134). In addition, the analysis of habitat exploitation and species variability detailed here provides further support for the conclusions drawn from a number of previous northern Australia coastal studies (Mowat 1995:153; Hiscock 1999:96; Bourke 2000:146). Species richness is highly variable within and between coastal sites distributed across northern Australia, but as noted by Mowat (1995:148), while there is no single explanation for this variation, there are a number of strongly contributing factors that require consideration. It is suggested here that changes in environmental conditions over time would have affected the species of shellfish available for exploitation. Further to this point, it is apparent that the differing proportions of species within these sites indicate that environmental changes operating within this region were gradual in nature. Changes in the proportion of species from the different habitat areas identified in this analysis relates to spatial and temporal variation in the availability of molluscan taxa within and between the Myaoola and Grindall Bay areas (Bailey 1994:9; Bourke 2000:143). Following from this point, molluscan procurement strategies within this area are generally characterised by a focus on any profusely available resource, with the subsequent addition of secondary, less abundant resources (Bourke 2000:312). Therefore, any changes in the species exploited can be seen to be a direct reflection of environmental changes. In line with the interpretations presented by Mowat (1995:163) for shell deposits in Western Arnhem Land, foraging behaviour on the coastal margins of the Point Blane Peninsula was highly flexible, with people actively altering their foraging strategies to incorporate increasingly abundant or newly available species (Faulkner 2011:147).

It has been argued by Hiscock and Mowat (1993) that understanding the degree of diversity in shell deposits provides an opportunity for the re-evaluation of models developed to explain the past use of coastal landscapes. While variability in species richness, habitat use and the exploitation of certain species has been tied here to the environment, there is also a cultural or behavioural component that needs to be considered (Faulkner 2011:147–8). It has further been suggested that the relative proportion of mollusc species may be related to differing site functions and the intensity of site use, and as such a reflection of cultural selection and discard practices, rather than being solely representative of the environment from which these resources were procured (Jerardino 1998; Bourke 2000:301; Morrison 2000, 2003). As a result, variations in the intensity of site deposition and resource exploitation, as well as the overall chronological patterns of occupation across the study area, need to be taken into account to assess any changes in the foraging economy and potential differences in site function.

6

Investigating Variability in the Intensity of Occupation and Resource Use

The previously highlighted analyses of the spatial and temporal patterning in the archaeological record across the Point Blane Peninsula have demonstrated a close relationship between the structure of the economy and those environmental changes noted more broadly across northern Australia and the Indo-Pacific region. Variation in the exploitation of specific resources and habitats indicates that resources were targeted in a highly localised pattern across time and space. Following from this, the question of whether the archaeological record reflects differing site functions and changes in the intensity of both site and resource use requires attention. As such, the following analyses assess whether the available archaeological evidence is best characterised as reflecting cultural selection and discard practices, or as a representation of the environmental and ecological parameters in place during the late Holocene. To achieve this, site densities, site morphology and intensity of resource exploitation, as well as the overall chronological patterns of occupation for the study area, must be addressed in order to assess possible changes in the foraging economy and differences in site function.

Temporal and spatial evidence

The available sample of radiocarbon age determinations from sites on the Point Blane Peninsula is relatively large, with 39 dates having been obtained from 20 sites. In order to produce a broadly representative chronology for the study area, the distribution of these sites across the peninsula reflects a range of site types in varying environmental contexts (Faulkner 2008:81–84). These ages are listed in chronological order according to their broad location on the Point Blane Peninsula, with the calibrated ages for Myaoola Bay in Table 6.1 and Grindall Bay in Table 6.2. Taking these ages together, these dates again demonstrate a late Holocene sequence of occupation within the area, ranging from 2953 cal BP to the present, with the majority of the radiocarbon dates clustered between approximately 2500 BP and the present. Although this grouping lends itself to a certain degree of time and space averaging (see Lyman 2003), coarse patterning in the distribution of dates in this way is still evident. In line with suggestions by Bailey (1983, 1999) for the time lag in the appearance of coastal sites in the Weipa area, it is suggested here that the general chronological pattern from the Point Blane Peninsula relates to occupation following sea level rise and a time lag in the establishment of habitats suitable for the proliferation of resources in this particular area. In reviewing all of the radiocarbon dates available, however, while being characterised as relatively long-term, occupation on the Point Blane Peninsula does not appear to have been continuous in all areas.

Several key elements that can create uncertainty in the interpretation of chronological patterns of shorter durations need to be acknowledged in the interpretation of the radiocarbon ages from the Point Blane Peninsula. These aspects include regional and localised differences in the marine reservoir effect and ΔR correction values, as well as isotopic fractionation and the determination of $\delta^{13}C$ values (e.g. Mangerud 1972; Olsson 1974; Spennemann and Head 1996; Ingram 1998; Ulm 2002, 2006a, 2006b; Deo *et al.* 2004; Douka *et al.* 2010; England *et al.* 2012). 17 of the 39 radiocarbon dates obtained for this study do not have determined $\delta^{13}C$ values, with estimates of 0.0±0.0 to 0.0±2.0 used to arrive at conventional radiocarbon ages for these samples. This can be problematic, as a deviation of $1^o/_{oo}$ will produce an error of approximately 16 years in determining the radiocarbon age (Mangerud 1972:147–8). While these differences are minor when investigating the broader chronological trends from both Myaoola and Grindall Bays, this does add a slight degree of uncertainty, as estuarine shell taxa are known to exhibit highly variable $\delta^{13}C$ values. Further to this, Ulm (2002, 2006b) has demonstrated a lack of consistency in ΔR values within and between regions. This is relevant here, as Myaoola Bay is characterised by terrestrial river input into open and shallow water, contrasting with the predominantly estuarine and mangrove fringed Grindall Bay. Therefore, there may well be a degree of variability in ΔR values between these areas given the differences apparent in processes of landscape formation and environmental conditions (Faulkner 2008:86). Given these factors, a more extensive and high-resolution dating program in combination with the determination of estuarine specific ΔR values for the Point Blane Peninsula would strengthen the interpretation of these radiocarbon sequences. That said, based on the chronological patterns presented here relative to variations in use of the landscape and resources through time, it is still possible to draw tentative conclusions regarding human behaviour and use of the area.

Previous analyses of the available radiocarbon dates from the Point Blane Peninsula (Faulkner 2008, 2009, 2011, in press) identified a number of chronological phases based on statistically significant differences in calibrated age ranges in Myaoola and Grindall Bays. While the recalibration of these dates using the ΔR correction value of 55±98 recommended for the Gulf of Carpentaria (Ulm 2006b) removes or closes the gaps between these phases, those previously identified trends are still apparent in the calibrated radiocarbon age distributions within and between these areas. Within Myaoola Bay, the radiocarbon estimates cluster predominantly between 683 cal BP and the present (Figure 6.1), preceded by two dates at 1115 and 1518 cal BP. There is one date at 2953 cal BP that is significantly different, and clearly separate to the dominant clustering of radiocarbon dates for this area. This grouping of dates may be explained as resulting from behavioural and/or taphonomic issues. This pattern may relate to sporadic or low intensity occupation of this margin of the peninsula prior to approximately 1000 BP (e.g. Rowland 1983:73; Hall and Hiscock 1988:11), or alternatively might reflect gaps in the visibility of older sites in the area due to the dynamic nature of beach ridge development along this area of coastline. While it is true that the absence of sites does not indicate the absence of people, and by extension, ephemeral evidence for occupation may not indicate ephemeral occupation (Cribb 1986; Bourke 2000:354), the latter argument is more convincing when this chronological patterning is considered relative to the sites located within the Grindall Bay area. The radiocarbon ages available for sites located in Grindall Bay suggests that occupation in this area spans an approximate 1800 year period, with initial occupation at 2287 cal BP, and use of the area phasing out around 526 cal BP (Figure 6.2). In comparison with the chronological pattern from Myaoola Bay, there is a concentration in site deposition between approximately 2287 and 1009 cal BP, with another grouping of radiocarbon determinations occurring between 584 and 526 cal BP. The peaks and troughs in the Grindall Bay chronological sequence may relate to localised variability in the intensity of occupation and use of resources within this area. While the archaeological record across the Point Blane Peninsula has undoubtedly been affected by post-depositional disturbance and destruction, as noted above, it is still possible to cautiously draw conclusions from these chronological patterns relative to variations in the structure of the economy and the nature of the landscape itself.

In comparing the radiocarbon ages from the two bay areas, there appear to have been two main phases of occupation on the Point Blane Peninsula: an initial phase between approximately 3000 and 1000 BP, and a second phase between approximately 1000 BP and the present. Use of the more exposed coastal areas of Myaoola Bay may have been more sporadic between 2953 and 1115 cal BP, contrasting with a pattern of more intensive use of Grindall Bay during this time. In the second phase, the patterning of ages in Myaoola Bay suggests a period of comparatively more intensive use throughout the last 1000 years. During this second phase, there was one relatively short and intense period of site deposition between approximately 584 and 526 cal BP in Grindall Bay. The trough observable in the summed probability distribution preceding this second phase of occupation and site deposition in Grindall Bay was previously interpreted as reflecting a hiatus in use of the area (Faulkner 2008, 2009, in press), but perhaps relates more to a change in the intensity of resource exploitation and/or site deposition. To some degree, the clustered patterns of age determinations reflects the age of the surfaces onto which these sites were deposited (Holdaway *et al.* 2002:358, 2005:45). For example, the relative dearth of radiocarbon dates prior to approximately 1000 BP in Myaoola Bay conceivably relates to ongoing processes of beach ridge development that have the potential to distort and/or disturb the archaeological record of this area. While it is possible that the relative discontinuities in the chronological pattern for this area may in part reflect preservation and sampling issues, use of Myaoola Bay prior to 1000 BP appears to have been more sporadic and of lower intensity compared with the second occupation phase identified between 1000 BP and the present (as also evidenced by site morphology and deposition).

Table 6.1: Radiocarbon age estimate ranges for sites in Myaoola Bay.

Site Code	Site Type	Square	Excavation Unit	Depth (cm)	Lab Code	Sample	δ¹³C (*estimate)	¹⁴C Age (years BP)	1σ cal Age BP (68.3% probability)	2σ cal Age BP (95.4% probability)	Cal Age BP Median
BMB/084	Midden Complex	Test Pit 1	1	0 - 1	ANU-11911	*M. hiantina*	0.0 ± 2.0*	122.3%±1.0%	Modern	Modern	--
BMB/084	Midden Complex	Test Pit 1	4	4 - 7	ANU-11914	*M. hiantina*	0.0 ± 2.0*	360 ± 60	Modern	Modern	--
BMB/084	Midden Complex	Test Pit 1	5	7 - 11	ANU-11912	*M. hiantina*	0.0 ± 2.0*	460 ± 70	Modern	Modern	--
BMB/084	Midden Complex	Test Pit 3	5	12 - 15	ANU-12093	*M. hiantina*	0.0 ± 2.0*	470 ± 60	Modern	Modern	--
BMB/016	Midden	Test Pit 1	3	6 - 10	ANU-11497	*M. hiantina*	0.0 ± 2.0*	580 ± 60	1#–257	1#–374	168
BMB/022	Midden	Test Pit 1	4	9 - 14	ANU-11716	*S. bilocularis*	0.2 ± 0.2	630 ± 70	1#–306	1#–418	207
BMB/015	Midden	Test Pit 1	5	10 - 13	ANU-11498	*M. hiantina*	0.4 ± 0.1	640 ± 50	68–315	1#–414	213
BMB/116	Mound	Test Pit 1	1	0 - 1	ANU-12019	*A. antiquata*	0.0 ± 2.0*	650 ± 60	77–333	1#–426	225
BMB/084	Midden Complex	Test Pit 1	7	14 - 17	ANU-11913	*M. hiantina*	0.0 ± 2.0*	860 ± 70	309–516	149–643	424
BMB/003	Midden	Test Pit 1	1	0 - 5	ANU-11501	*M. hiantina*	0.2 ± 0.1	900 ± 50	336–549	274–640	461
BMB/067b	Midden	Test Pit 1	1	0 - 2	Wk-17745	*A. granosa*	2.2 ± 0.2	1063 ± 35	511–661	433–773	592
BMB/116	Mound	Test Pit 1	11	32 - 36	ANU-12020	*A. antiquata*	0.0 ± 2.0*	1120 ± 60	531–719	473–869	638
BMB/017	Midden	Test Pit 1	3	5 - 8	ANU-11500	*G. tumidum*	0.0 ± 2.0*	1160 ± 80	547–771	485–911	676
BMB/084	Midden Complex	Test Pit 3	10	29 - 34	ANU-12094	*M. hiantina*	0.0 ± 2.0*	1170 ± 60	561–770	505–897	683
BMB/067a	Midden	Test Pit 1	1	1 - 5	ANU-11715	*A. granosa*	3.0 ± 0.2	1620 ± 80	992–1247	856–1367	1115
BMB/067b	Midden	Test Pit 1	9	27 - 31	ANU-11714	*A. granosa*	2.0 ± 0.2	2010 ± 80	1369–1657	1269–1809	1518
BMB/018	Midden	Test Pit 1	3	11 - 17	ANU-11503	*S. bilocularis*	0.0 ± 0.0	3200 ± 70	2779–3080	2700–3263	2953

Note: # are suspect due to impingement on the end of the calibration data set.

Source: Calibration data from CALIB 6.1.1, marine04.14c (Hughen *et al.* 2004), ΔR = 55±98 (Ulm 2006b).

Table 6.2: Radiocarbon age estimate ranges for sites in Grindall Bay.

Site Code	Site Type	Square	Excavation Unit	Depth (cm)	Lab Code	Sample	δ¹³C (*estimate)	¹⁴C Age (years BP)	1σ cal Age BP (68.3% probability)	2σ cal Age BP (95.4% probability)	Cal Age BP Median
BMB/036	Mound	N/A	N/A	Surface	ANU-12018	A. granosa	0.0 ± 2.0*	980 ± 130	389–667	239–847	526
BMB/045	Mound	Test Pit 1	1	0 - 2	ANU-11717	A. granosa	3.5 ± 0.2	990 ± 60	461–637	314–708	539
BMB/045	Mound	Test Pit 1	16	43 - 46	ANU-11718	A. granosa	-3.7 ± 0.2	1040 ± 60	492–659	375–781	577
BMB/045	Mound	Test Pit 1	31	91 - 95	ANU-11719	A. granosa	3.1 ± 0.2	1050 ± 60	49–664	387–791	584
BMB/061	Midden	Test Pit 1	1	0 - 4	ANU-11720	A. granosa	4.6 ± 0.2	1510 ± 50	900–1137	776–1243	1009
BMB/061	Midden	Test Pit 1	4	9 - 12	Wk-25466	A. granosa	-3.8 ± 0.2	1684 ± 35	1071–1280	951–1373	1178
BMB/071	Mound	Test Pit 1	1	0 - 3	ANU-11722	A. granosa	2.9 ± 0.2	1700 ± 60	1067–1299	936–1412	1192
BMB/061	Midden	Test Pit 1	7	17 - 22	ANU-11721	A. granosa	4.1 ± 0.2	1720 ± 50	1095–1320	962–1433	1213
BMB/052	Mound	N/A	N/A	Surface	Wk-17744	A. granosa	-3.3 ± 0.2	1763 ± 37	1152–1367	1039–1496	1258
BMB/071	Mound	Test Pit 1	6	19 - 24	ANU-11723	A. granosa	-2.5 ± 0.2	1810 ± 60	1176–1419	1053–1551	1310
BMB/071	Mound	Test Pit 1	11	42 - 46	ANU-11724	A. granosa	3.1 ± 0.2	1980 ± 60	1343–1599	1259–1753	1483
BMB/101	Mound	N/A	N/A	Surface	ANU-11894	A. granosa	0.0 ± 2.0*	2010 ± 80	1369–1657	1269–1809	1518
BMB/093	Mound	N/A	N/A	Surface	ANU-11893	A. granosa	0.0 ± 2.0*	2240 ± 80	1617–1924	1485–2101	1779
BMB/082	Mound	N/A	N/A	Surface	ANU-11892	A. granosa	0.0 ± 2.0*	2340 ± 70	1747–2047	1591–2210	1900
BMB/029	Mound	Test Pit 1	4	8 - 11	ANU-11499	A. granosa	-4.0 ± 0.1	2350 ± 60	1771–2058	1613–2207	1912
BMB/029	Mound	Test Pit 1	8	23 - 28	ANU-11502	A. granosa	0.0 ± 2.0*	2360 ± 60	1788–2074	1646–2242	1925
BMB/029	Mound	Test Pit 1	1	0 - 3	ANU-11496	A. granosa	-3.4 ± 0.1	2410 ± 50	1850–2120	1728–2279	1985
BMB/029	Mound	Test Pit 1	12	41 - 45	ANU-11505	A. granosa	-2.8 ± 0.1	2420 ± 50	1858–2129	1742–2287	1997
BMB/029	Mound	Test Pit 1	14	49 - 53	ANU-11494	A. granosa	-2.6 ± 0.1	2460 ± 50	1892–2171	1795–2314	2045
BMB/033	Mound	N/A	N/A	Surface	ANU-12017	A. granosa	0.0 ± 2.0*	2540 ± 60	2010–2290	1853–2420	2140
BMB/029	Mound	Test Pit 1	16	58 - 62	ANU-11504	A. granosa	-3.1 ± 0.2	2630 ± 60	2085–2380	1952–2595	2245
BMB/029	Mound	Test Pit 1	20	75 - 81	ANU-11495	A. granosa	0.0 ± 2.0*	2660 ± 60	2122–2435	1995–2648	2287

Source: Calibration data from CALIB 6.1.1, marine04.14c (Hughen *et al.* 2004), ΔR = 55±98 (Ulm 2006b).

In contrast, the absence of sites in Grindall Bay dating prior to approximately 2287 cal BP likely relates to processes of landscape and habitat formation in the area via sedimentary infilling and progradation (Woodroffe *et al.* 1985a, 1985b; Clark and Guppy 1988), and the effects these processes had on the availability and proliferation of molluscan resources. Rather than reflecting post-depositional or sampling issues, the clustering of radiocarbon determinations into two main phases in this Grindall Bay (based on the summed probability distribution), particularly in comparison with the patterns identified in Myaoola Bay, may be more firmly related to occupation and resource exploitation. The present day Grindall Bay landscape has formed as a result of Holocene sea level rise and subsequent progradation, however the sites are relatively well protected from extreme environmental conditions, particularly in the form of strong wind and wave action. All of the sites that fall between 2287 and 1009 cal BP are located on the laterite ridge bordering this area that forms a comparatively stable surface. The two sites that provide the radiocarbon dates falling between 584 and 526 cal BP, however, are both located on the surface of the saltflats away from the laterite ridge. Rather than a period of local abandonment (as presented in Faulkner 2008, 2009), the clustering of radiocarbon dates in combination with differences in the location of sites between these two phases indicates a shift in the intensity of landscape and resource utilisation. This pattern has implications for human behaviour linked to the formation of the peninsula following sea level rise, and the subsequent differential patterning of resource distribution and exploitation. As has been noted by Holdaway *et al.* (2002:362), variability in the record of radiocarbon determinations at different times may reflect a situation where long-term human adaptation involved a discontinuous use of space, indicating relatively different or changing patterns of human-environment interactions. If variability in the radiocarbon record does represent discontinuous occupation, then the late Holocene may well be characterised by differences in the distribution and intensity of foraging behaviour through time and space, and not represent a period of stable, long-term adaptation to the environment (see Fanning and Holdaway 2001; Attenbrow 2004; Holdaway *et al.* 2005; Faulkner 2006, 2008, in press; Ulm 2006a for similar arguments).

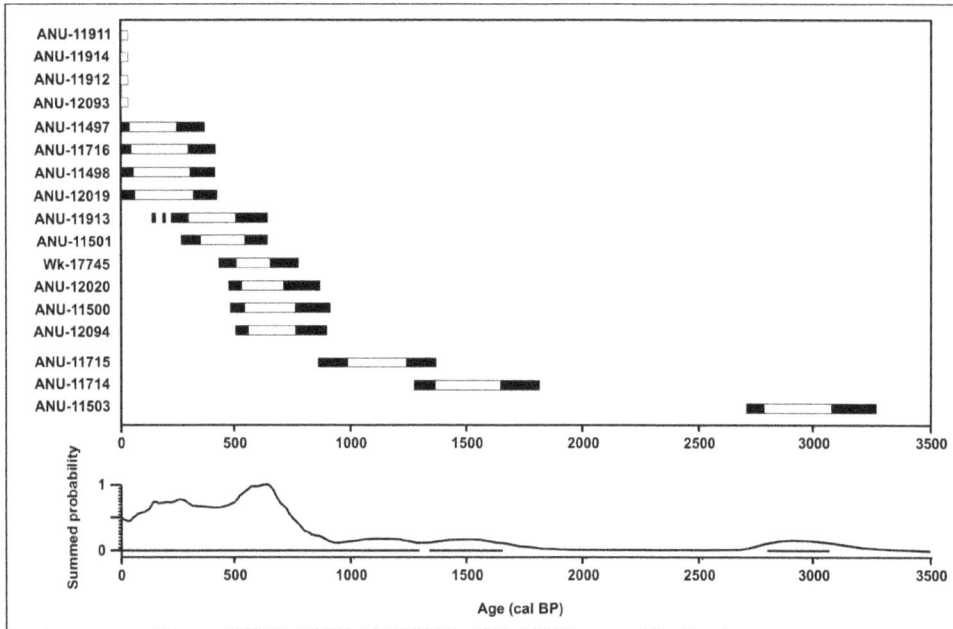

Figure 6.1: Comparison of the 1 and 2σ calibrated radiocarbon ages for sites on Myaoola Bay (above), and the calibrated radiocarbon age summed probability plot (below).

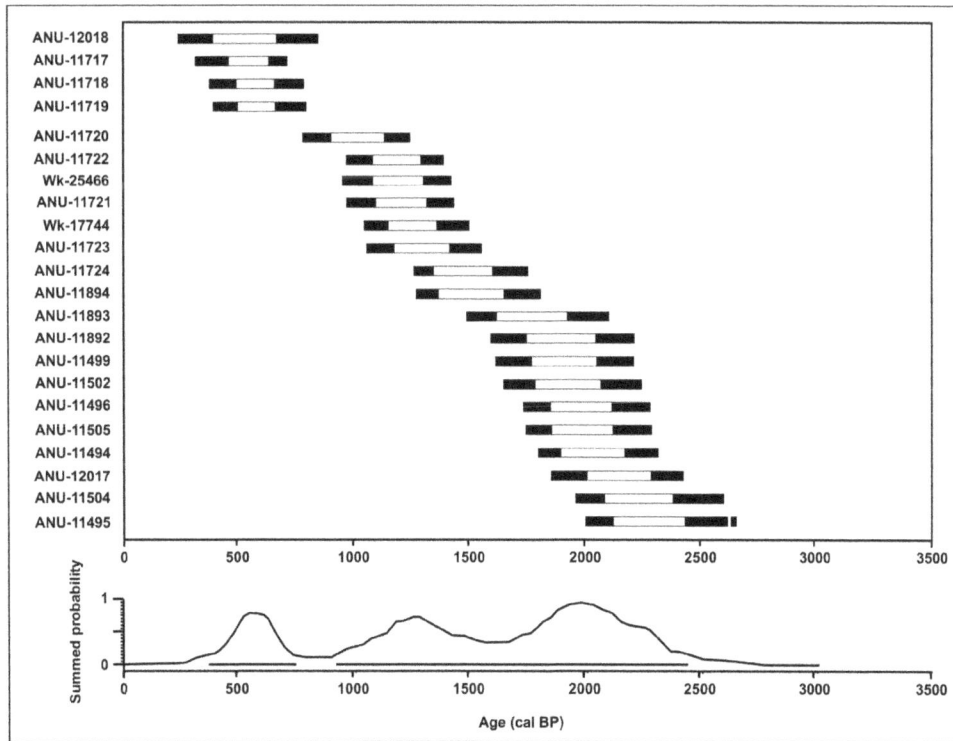

Figure 6.2: Comparison of the 1 and 2σ calibrated radiocarbon ages for sites on Grindall Bay (above), and the calibrated radiocarbon age summed probability plot (below).

Variation in occupation intensity: Shell middens and mounds

In analysing variations in the spatial and temporal intensity of occupation within a given region, rates of site accumulation based on the number of sites per unit of time have often been used (Attenbrow 2004:1). Added to this, referred to as changes in 'the intensity of site use', quantitative differences in the discard of cultural material in individual sites, such as stone artefacts or faunal remains, have also been used as providing evidence for assessing the extent to which the use of specific locations varies over time (Morwood 1981; Attenbrow 2004:1; also Ulm 2006a). While viewing the archaeological record from the Point Blane Peninsula in this way would be useful, there are a number of obstacles in using these methods.

Given the issues noted above relating to the available radiocarbon dates, the level of chronological resolution is limited within each of the sites, and has therefore enabled only a basic understanding of variations in site formation across the study area. Although trends in molluscan exploitation have still been identified within and between each site, analysis in terms of differences in rates of accumulation and the degree of occupation intensity is limited. While there are observable differences between the excavated sites across the Point Blane Peninsula, the number and weight of shell per unit volume are a measure of geometric density, and do not necessarily accurately reflect rates of accumulation per unit time within these deposits (Bailey and Craighead 2003:182). As noted by Stein *et al.* (2003:309–10), the period of time over which site accumulation occurred will also have an effect on the level of detail obtained in determining accumulation rates. This is particularly relevant when examining sites with rapid formation indicated via radiocarbon dating, as is the case with several of the sites analysed here, where potentially variable rates of accumulation relative to shorter-term phases of occupation may not be distinguishable. In addition to this, the number of radiocarbon dating samples employed in calculating accumulation rates affects their accuracy, and ultimately the interpretation of human behaviour based on these data. Those rates based on only two or three samples, which is the number generally available within the sample of the six excavated sites detailed in Chapters 4 and 5 (and often in other north Australian shell mound studies, e.g. Bourke 2000, Morrison 2010), will not provide the level of detail required for an accurate evaluation (Stein *et al.* 2003:310). For this reason, therefore, the density of shell mound and midden sites on the margins of the peninsula per kilometre of coastline, combined with an examination of site area and volume, are used here in place of accumulation and/or discard rates to investigate possible differences in resource use and the intensity of occupation (Faulkner 2006, in press). There are also limitations in the application of this type of analysis, largely due to potential variability in patterns of site establishment, use and reuse through time, and particularly in combination with post-depositional processes that can limit site visibility or alter site morphology, however, this approach is well suited to identifying broad-scale trends in human behaviour. Relative to the chronological patterns identified above, and as occupation of the peninsula has been characterised as being localised and temporally discrete, it is argued here that variations in the density and size of the shell deposits across the Point Blane Peninsula provides a reasonable measure of the distribution and intensity of human behaviour (for similar arguments see Jerardino *et al.* 2008; Jerardino 2010). Bailey (1994:108), for example, has also argued that with a larger resident population, the resulting shell debris on a given stretch of coastline will be larger and more numerous, based on the reasonable assumption that the quantity of shell discarded and site size can be correlated with the intensity of human activity.

Thirty-four sites were recorded along approximately 22km of coastline in Myaoola Bay, with 1.54 sites/km. In contrast, 85 sites were recorded along the approximately 13km surveyed in Grindall Bay, with 6.54 sites/km (Table 6.3). There are therefore approximately four times more sites per kilometre of coastline (or former coastline) surveyed in Grindall Bay than recorded in Myaoola Bay, indicating the possibility of a higher level of occupation intensity and resource exploitation in the former location. The number of sites per cluster is also compared here between these two areas (Table 6.3). This is a useful measure, as resources are generally not distributed in a homogeneous way in coastal areas, with variability in the abundance of resources evident relative to the length of available shoreline (Waselkov 1987:133; Rowland 1994b:155). There are implications for human behaviour and population density relative to these kinds of environmental or ecological patterns, and by extension may be used as further evidence in investigating the intensity of occupation (e.g. Lourandos and Ross 1994; Bourke 2000:107). Regarding this issue, Bailey (1975a:VII:42–4, 1983:567) has argued that the clustering of shell mounds at Weipa has resulted from people operating within a non-linear landscape placing themselves in the optimal position to exploit both marine and terrestrial resources. Therefore, the clustering of sites is another feature of the site distribution pattern, a phenomenon that has implications for human population density, and by extension, may be used as evidence for more intensive occupation (e.g. Lourandos and Ross 1994; Bourke 2000:107; Morrison 2010:318–324; Faulkner in press). The clustering of sites in both Myaoola and Grindall Bays is highlighted in Figure 6.3. The divisions between the site clusters are defined primarily by the distribution or positioning of sites relative to surrounding environmental or geographic features. Sites concentrated around headlands are separated from those dispersed along open beaches in a linear fashion, or where significant natural features like watercourses separate sites. Six site clusters have been determined for both Myaoola and Grindall Bays, and the density of sites per cluster corresponds reasonably well with the number of sites per kilometre of coastline surveyed. There is an average of 5.67 sites per cluster in Myaoola Bay, two and a half times less than that found in Grindall Bay, where there is an average of 14.17 sites per cluster. As the number of sites per cluster potentially reflects the density of occupation relative to the focal points of resource exploitation within each area, there would appear to have been a greater intensity of occupation and use of resources in Grindall Bay.

Table 6.3: Site density estimates for Myaoola and Grindall Bays, Point Blane Peninsula.

	Myaoola Bay	Grindall Bay
Approx. Length of Coastline Surveyed (km)	22	13
Number of Sites Recorded	34	85
Number of Sites per Kilometre Surveyed	1.54	6.54
Number of Site Clusters	6	6
Average Number of Sites per Cluster	5.67	14.17

Table 6.4: Descriptive statistics for site areas in Myaoola and Grindall Bays.

	Myaoola Bay	Grindall Bay
Descriptive Statistics – Site Area (m^2)		
Mean	1085.02	490.46
Median	79.39	238.35
Standard Deviation	3282.40	1179.77
Minimum	0.50	22.44
Maximum	16000	10620
Descriptive Statistics – Site Volume (m^3)		
Mean	111.76	461.26
Median	7.94	113.72
Standard Deviation	328.04	1023.02
Minimum	0.05	2.24
Maximum	1600	7327.80
Number of Sites	**34**	**85**

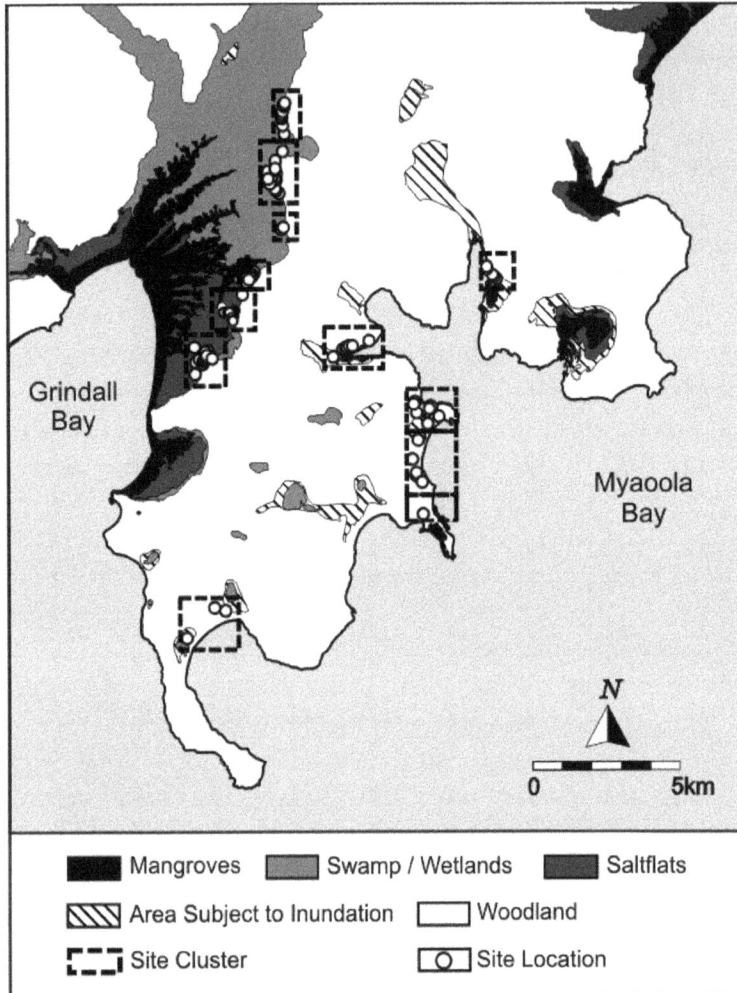

Figure 6.3: The distribution of site clusters (shell deposits only) on the margins of the Point Blane peninsula.

Source: Based on Baniyala 1:50 000 Topographic Map.

This interpretation is further supported by comparing mean site area and volume between the two margins of the peninsula (Table 6.4). Comparing site morphology between these two areas, the Myaoola Bay shell deposits generally conform to a pattern of low, horizontally spread middens, with larger mounded shell deposits dominating the margins of Grindall Bay. Mann-Whitney U tests indicate that there are significant differences in both site area ($U = 998.5$, $z = -2.867$, $p = 0.004$, $r = 0.26$) and site volume ($U = 646.5$, $z = -4.903$, $p = 0.000$, $r = 0.45$) between Myaoola and Grindall Bays. While site area is generally larger within Myaoola Bay, reflecting the greater horizontal spread of the sites in this area, in assessing variation in the potential intensity of resource use and site formation, the fact that a far greater volume of material was deposited within the sites in Grindall Bay is of more importance. Individually, the chronological patterns for the two sides of the Point Blane Peninsula, and variations in site density and site morphology are only suggestive of differences in occupation intensity. When viewed in combination, however, the interpretations presented here are strengthened. Based on the density of sites and volume of material deposited within the Grindall Bay sites, combined with the available radiocarbon ages, there appears to have been a greater intensity of occupation and exploitation of resources relative to the Myaoola Bay area (Faulkner in press). If this is indeed the case, then there should also be an observable effect on the primarily exploited resource within the Grindall Bay sites. That is, with a higher level of human predation, the size and structure of the *Anadara granosa* population in the area may have been affected.

Anadara granosa: Biology and ecology

As noted by Catterall and Poiner (1987:119) many previous attempts at investigating the effects of exploitation through midden analysis have been hampered by a lack of information on the biology and ecology of the exploited species (although see Jerardino *et al.* 1992; Bourke 2000, 2002; Campbell 2008; Faulkner 2009, in press; Giovas *et al.* 2010). Fortunately, these parameters can be addressed for *Anadara granosa*, the dominant species within the mounded shell deposits in this area and across much of northern Australia. Presently, marine bivalve molluscs of the family Arcidae (subfamily Anadarinae) are an important source of protein for coastal populations in many tropical, subtropical and warm temperate areas (Broom 1985:1). The molluscan bivalve genus *Anadara* is distributed worldwide, and in the Indo-Pacific region is economically important in the Philippines, Thailand, Malaysia and Borneo (Pathansali and Soong 1958:26). Along the north Australian coastline at present *A. granosa* has disappeared entirely from natural coastal habitats, is confined to specific regions, or exists in very low densities (e.g. Morrison 2003, 2010). Reasons provided for the disappearance of *Pinctada nigra* within the Transkei region of South Africa may equally apply to the relative absence of *A. granosa* across northern Australia: a combination of relatively high exploitation pressure, together with the low occurrence or disappearance of suitable habitat (de Boer *et al.* 2000:295).

A. granosa are essentially soft substrate dwellers, occurring naturally in large estuarine mudflats bordered on the landward margin by mangrove forests. This species thrives under comparatively calm conditions especially in shallow inlets or bays, with a sub-stratum of fine, soft, flocculent mud (Pathansali and Soong 1958:27). Although *Anadara* are found in sandy-mud areas, they have not been observed to settle or establish colonies in these areas comparable in size and number to those in fine, soft brackish mud, particularly off mangrove forests (Pathansali 1966:90; Broom 1985:4). In terms of the establishment and proliferation of shell beds, the three most important factors are the nature of the substrate, salinity levels, and the slope of bed. Most species of *Anadara* are intertidal or marginally subtidal in their distribution. They usually settle on muddy shores between mean high water of neap tides (MHWN) and mean low water of neap tides (MLWN). Neap tide refers to either of the two tides that occur at the first or last quarter of the moon when the tide-generating forces of the sun and moon oppose each, producing the smallest rise and fall in tidal level. *A. granosa* usually do not extend into the area above MHWN, which is usually dominated by mangrove swamp forests. Peak densities are usually encountered around mid-tide level, although in some regions they are dense subtidally, and this degree of variation likely relates to different salinity regimes (Broom 1985:4). This species is able to function relatively efficiently at salinities above 23 parts per thousand, although young individuals can continue normal feeding activity at a lower salinity than older specimens, down to 18 parts per thousand. This species has the ability to cope with short-term salinity fluctuations, but are characteristically stenohaline (Bayne 1973:804; Broom 1985:6; Peterson and Wells 1998). Therefore, the known distribution of *A. granosa* coincides with a salinity range of around 26 to 31 parts per thousand, with short-term fluctuations (Broom 1985:6). The optimal habitats are therefore protected from strong wave action, and situated outside the mouth of estuaries and tidal creeks, with a salinity range between 18 to 30 parts per thousand (Pathansali 1966:91).

Temperatures to which this species are exposed vary according to their geographical range. For example, the average water temperature throughout the year experienced by *A. granosa* in Malaysia is generally around 29° to 32° C, though sub-populations on higher shore areas may be subjected to a temperature range of 25° to 40° C, coinciding with minimal water movement (Broom 1985:7). Other ecological criteria for *A. granosa* shell bed establishment and proliferation include a moderate seaward slope between 5-15°. If the gradient is too small, the culture will be exposed for too long between tides, and where the gradient is too great, growth can be inhibited. The shell bed should also not be near a strong current, but currents should be strong enough to transport natural food (Broom 1985:47; Tiensongrusmee and Pontjoprawiro 1988: section 3). From spatfall observations, it has been demonstrated that *A. granosa* displays a definite seasonality in its breeding cycle, though some spawning probably takes place throughout the year (Broom 1985:24). Seasonal salinity fluctuations are thought to play a major part in the seasonality of this species. There are two possible spawning cues, almost certainly linked in some way to the seasonal salinity depression, and periods of high rainfall may depress temperatures on the intertidal mudflat (Pathansali and Soong 1958:26; Pathansali 1966:85, 90; Broom 1985:24).

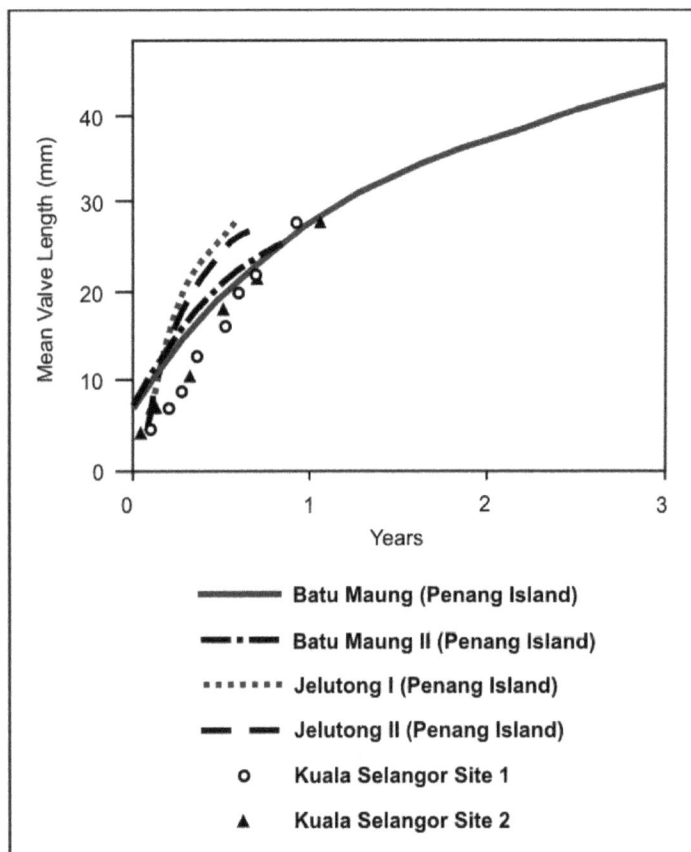

Figure 6.4: Growth rates for *Anadara granosa* from commercial culture beds in Malaysia.

Source: After Faulkner 2009; data from Broom 1982a:73 and Pathansali 1966:98.

Growth rates are known to be affected by environmental conditions and population density (Tiensongrusmee and Pontjoprawiro 1988: section 4.5-4.6). It was found in two natural populations that growth rates could vary enormously between subpopulations subject to different environmental conditions (Broom 1985:16). At higher shore levels, compensatory feeding or metabolic activity would be likely to help maintain growth in the face of increasing exposure, although there is also probably a level above which growth rates decline rapidly with increasing exposure unless preceded by death of the organism due to the increasing effects of other factors, such as thermal stress (Broom 1985:17). On natural beds where density was less than 11 per square metre, *A. granosa* grows from a range of 4-10mm diameter to 18-32 mm in 8 months, whilst on commercial beds where the density was 500-1000/square metre, 10-12 months elapsed before harvest size of 24-30 mm was attained (Pathansali and Soong 1958:28; Broom 1985:14). It is expected that *A. granosa* would attain sexual maturity at about 25mm in shell length in northern Australia, when they are approximately 6 months old (Pathansali and Soong 1958:27; Pathansali 1966:85; Broom 1983b:215, 1985:23). In general, *A. granosa* is characterised by rapid growth rates, early maturity and a short lifespan. High fecundity and rapid growth rates of *A. granosa* results in biomass dominance, often comprising from 33% up to 97% of the standing biomass in sand/mudflat habitats (Broom 1982b:138; 1983a:395; 1985:10–11). Data from commercially cultured populations in Malaysia (Figure 6.4) demonstrates rapid growth: approximately 50% of the population reaches a size of 25.4mm within 6 months (Pathansali 1966:89), and between 30-32mm in 8 to 12 months (Pathansali and Soong 1958:28; Broom 1985:14). Extrapolating from the data presented in Figure 6.4 suggests a short lifespan of approximately 5-6 years as there is a progressive decrease in growth rate as size increases (Broom 1982a:74). Mortality rates are relatively high, particularly in the younger smaller age/size classes (Broom 1982b:142), with overall mortality in some commercial plots over one year amounting to 80% (Pathansali and Soong 1958). Mortality rates of 20-50% have been recorded in other populations, much of which can be attributed to natural predation or environmental fluctuations (e.g. salinity) (Broom 1983a:395; Broom 1985:19). In terms of maximum size, Broom (1985:15) has suggested that individuals larger than 53.5mm would rarely occur in natural populations, and Pathansali (1966) has proposed a theoretical maximum size of 63mm. Valve lengths of 58-69mm have been recorded from live-collected specimens housed in the Queensland Museum collection (Faulkner 2010:1944), and Lamprell and Healy (1998:54) recorded a maximum shell length of 76mm.

Morrison (2003, 2010), Clune and Harrison (2009) and Harrison (2009) have recently emphasised that *A. granosa* is an extremely "fragile" species, sensitive to minor environmental alterations and mass mortality rates. While some of the *A. granosa* biological and ecological literature is reviewed by these authors (particularly by Morrison 2003:2, 2010:299), this argument appears to hinge more on an understanding of contemporary habitat structure and recent observations of prevalence in modern coastal environments. As such, it has been suggested that it is unlikely that *A. granosa* would have been seasonally available in large quantities, as it is prone to dramatic population reductions due to environmental shifts. *A. granosa* will, however, successfully cope with short-term environmental fluctuations that would adversely affect other species, although populations are not as resilient to sustained environmental changes beyond tolerable limits (e.g. tidal cover, temperature, salinity levels) (Davenport and Wong 1986; Nakamura and Shinotsuka 2007). As a species, *A. granosa* have been seen to be characteristically successful in exploiting a niche typified by fluctuating physical variables (tidal cover, salinity, temperature) as well as difficult trophic conditions (high suspended solids loads) for suspension feeders. As a broad generalisation, this species is likely to dominate intertidal and marginally subtidal muddy substrates in areas where there is an estuarine influence (Broom 1985:10, 32). While the natural conclusion would be that this species would not experience devastating mortalities via natural levels of predation (Broom 1985:10, 33), intensive exploitation combined with size selection may have an effect. For example, it was observed that within commercial culture plots, problems in maintaining viable populations occurred largely because of the rapid growth of *Anadara granosa*, where the removal of larger individuals occurred before the onset of the major breeding season (Pathansali 1966:88, 92).

Investigating the intensity of resource exploitation

Methods for testing the level of exploitation

There are increasing numbers of archaeological studies conducted worldwide investigating the potential effects of human exploitation on various marine and freshwater molluscan taxa, essentially aimed at measuring potential resource depletion (e.g. Swadling 1976, 1977; Botkin 1980; Spennemann 1987; Yesner 1988; Jerardino 1997; Lightfoot and Cerrato 1998; Bourke 2000, 2002; Peacock 2000; Mannino and Thomas 2001, 2002; Bailey and Craighead 2003; Masse *et al.* 2006; Braje *et al.* 2007; Milner *et al.* 2007; Antczak *et al.* 2008; Baez and Jackson 2008; Bailey *et al.* 2008; Bailey and Milner 2008; Erlandson *et al.* 2008; Jerardino *et al.* 2008; Morrison and Cochrane 2008; Nielsen 2008; Parkington 2008; Peacock and Mistak 2008; Rick *et al.* 2008; Whitaker 2008; Faulkner 2009; Yamazaki and Oda 2009; Giovas *et al.* 2010; Thangavelu *et al.* 2011). In many of these studies, a reduction in average shell size and changes in the relative abundance of higher-ranked resources in the archaeological record are viewed as indicating increased pressure via human or environmental factors (e.g. Botkin 1980:135; Koike 1986; Spennemann 1989; Mannino and Thomas 2001; de Boer and Prins 2002; although see Giovas *et al.* 2010 for size increase through time). In terms of human induced resource depression, interpretations are often linked to economic intensification stemming from increased population size and/or density, as well as changes in residential mobility (e.g. Beaton 1991; Lupo, 2007:160– 1). The effectiveness of these studies are often borne out by considering that, with continued or intensive human exploitation of a given resource, the population structure of the resource is often altered (Hockey and Bosman 1986; de Boer *et al.* 2000:287; de Boer *et al.* 2002:250), an effect that can often be discerned in the archaeological record. The general archaeological criteria proposed by a number of researchers (e.g. Claassen 1998:45; Mason *et al.* 1998:317; Mason *et al.* 2000:757, 759; Mannino and Thomas 2002:458) to examine the potential of intensive human exploitation or over-exploitation are as follows:

1. The relative abundance of preferred species will decrease through a midden deposit;

2. Mean shell length will decrease from the bottom of the deposit to the top. A general decrease in the age-size structure of the population would have to be shown, reflected by a decrease in the average size of individuals collected and/or an increase in the number of juveniles;

3. The mean or modal size of the archaeologically derived populations of a species, when examined against figures for an unexploited population of the same species, will be significantly smaller;

4. Less easily procured species will increase in number through a midden deposit;

5. Less easily processed species will increase in number.

Based on this, criteria for investigating the effects of intensive exploitation should include a reduction in the mean age of individuals through a sequence of deposits (Claassen 1986:130), possibly in conjunction with changes in mean shell size, and the ratio of adults to juveniles. High levels of human predation will potentially not only reduce the range and number of resources available for exploitation, but the size of the individuals comprising the exploited population may also decrease (Botkin 1980:125). It can therefore be hypothesised that different levels of exploitation intensity will have a direct effect on the composition of the population. If the intensity of exploitation changes, the size and age structure of the population will be altered, and therefore, increased intensity will correspond with a decrease in the size and age structure. This type of pattern may indicate that more of the prey population was being removed than could be replaced by natural increase or yearly growth rates of surviving individuals (Botkin 1980:126, 135; Faulkner 2009). While Whitaker (2008:1121) states that continued harvesting would not result in decreased productivity within the shell beds as sexually immature individuals are too small to be economically feasible and the removal of larger individuals relieves competitive pressure, if the size at maturity exceeds the rejection size then there is a risk that all or most reproductively active individuals will be removed from the population, potentially reducing the recruitment rate (Catterall and Poiner 1987:120). The predator-prey balance, which may be stable at lower exploitation levels, will become inherently unstable as the intensity of exploitation increases. In some respects, species-specific spawning and growth rates can counter these processes. For example, it has been suggested that species characterised as having high fecundity, such as *A. granosa*, may be able to withstand high predatory pressure (Catterall and Poiner 1987:120; Hockey *et al* 1988:361; de Boer *et al.* 2000:288; Faulkner 2009, in press). The impact of exploitation, however, will also depend on the vulnerability of the given species over time regardless of fecundity. A decrease in the mean size of certain species can negatively affect fertility, due to the relatively greater contribution of larger individuals to the reproductive output of the species. Therefore, consistent removal of the larger, more mature individuals may result in a decrease in the population size (Waselkov 1987:134; de Boer *et al.* 2000:288; de Boer *et al.* 2002: 250; Faulkner 2009, in press), leaving it susceptible to the effects of intensive exploitation.

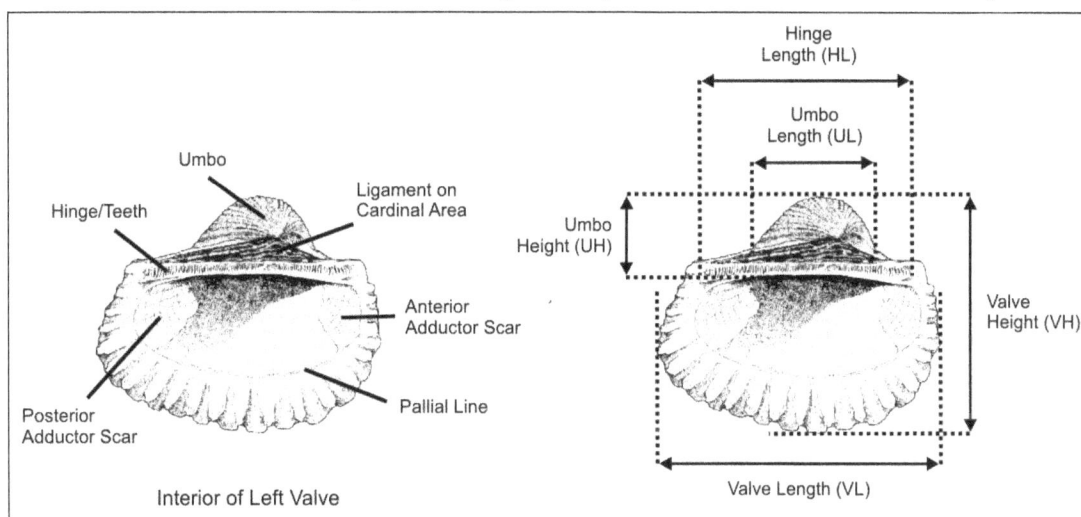

Figure 6.5: *Anadara granosa* valve terminology and measured attributes for predicting maximum valve length from morphometric equations.

Source: After Faulkner 2010:1944, valve redrawn from Poutiers 1998:147.

In bivalves, changes in shell size have frequently been investigated by measuring the greatest valve length, also referred to as the maximum anterior-posterior measurement of complete shells (e.g. Spennemann 1987:85, 89; Claassen 1998:108; Bailey and Craighead 2003:187). The use of only complete shells for metrical analyses has the potential to introduce bias into the sample via differential patterns of fragmentation relative to size (Jerardino and Navarro 2008; Thangavelu *et al.* 2011). In order to investigate changes in size throughout the *A. granosa* dominated deposits, therefore, complete and fragmented valves were measured and reconstructive morphometric equations (as outlined in Faulkner 2010) applied to the fragmentary valves for the establishment of full lengths (Figure 6.5).

The analysis of size frequency distributions and size variability of mollusc species, regardless of whether they are natural and/or cultural in origin, requires the expected size distribution or demographic curve to be established (Claassen 1998:111). While recruitment rates and levels of juvenile survivorship (Claassen 1998:108) can influence mean and/or modal size of a population, mean shell size can also vary depending on whether a population has been subjected to human exploitation. Using data published by Pathansali (1966) on Malaysian *A. granosa* commercial populations, where larger individuals had been removed via continuous harvesting, Broom (1985:15) established mean asymptotic valve lengths of between 29.6 and 35.9mm. Broom (1985:15) also presents data from two other Malaysian study sites not subjected to continued exploitation (Pathansali 1966; Broom 1982a, 1983) where mean asymptotic shell lengths of 44.4 to 49.6mm were recorded. Mollusc species like *A. granosa* that are referred to as being r-selecting (Bailey 1999; Veitch 1999a) occur in variable and/or unpredictable environments, are small bodied, generally have a single phase of reproduction with rapid growth rates, and typically a short lifespan with high mortality often occurring in the younger age/size classes (Pianka 1970:593; Claassen 1998:29). In unexploited communities with normal recruitment of young, size frequency distributions should be more negatively skewed towards the larger size classes, with low proportion of small individuals due to very rapid growth, and higher mortality rates early in the life-cycle creating a grading pattern into a higher number of larger individuals (Deevey 1947:285-286; Claassen 1998:108; Peacock 2000:189; Randklev *et al.* 2009:205–206). In populations where recruitment is seasonal, lifespan is short and there is little individual variability in growth rates, a bimodal or polymodal size distribution should be expected, with each peak or distinct mode representing a spawning event (Claassen 1998:109; Gosling 2003:169–170; Campbell 2008:113). This pattern of bimodality indicates that any organism with generation times greater than a year must be adapted to cope with a range of conditions (Pianka 1970:596). With rapid growth in the early stages and a constant rate of recruitment, however, the distinctiveness of these modal peaks may lessen to a degree, and each year class or cohort will effectively merge into the older/larger size classes (Gosling 2003:169–170). Within archaeological assemblages, a polymodal frequency distribution may relate to seasonal recruitment, but could also reflect averaged phases in site deposition given the time-averaged nature of the archaeological record.

Establishing these parameters is difficult due to a lack of comparative size frequency data from modern natural *A. granosa* shell beds; however, they are supported to a certain degree by the data presented in Figure 6.6. Size frequency data from five commercial culture plot samples in Malaysia (adapted from Ng 1986) demonstrates these general patterns while still highlighting the degree of variability in growth and size frequencies between different populations of the same species. For this study, measurements were based on monthly random samples of approximately 500 individual molluscs taken from each of the culture plots, and valve length measurements were obtained with vernier callipers to the nearest 0.1mm. Plots B and C were measured over 12 months, representing a single period of recruitment in each population; as such these show a distinctly unimodal pattern. These plots have a comparatively normal distribution (with only a slight positive skew), without a clear or distinct peak near the mean, and the size frequency distributions are more clustered with minimal tails into the smaller and/or larger size classes. This is not unexpected, as Claassen (1998:108) has suggested that when an age cohort (individuals who were recruited during the same period) is plotted as a size frequency histogram, it will generally appear as a normal or slightly positively skewed distribution. As a contrast, Plots A, D and E were measured over 17 months, and these distributions display the bimodal pattern associated with successive recruitment phases. The variability in the peak of each distribution probably relates to variations in growth rates within and between recruitment phases, as well as environmental conditions specific to each plot location. The commercial culture plot data also suggests that there would be a grading into the larger age classes through time with a relatively negative skew.

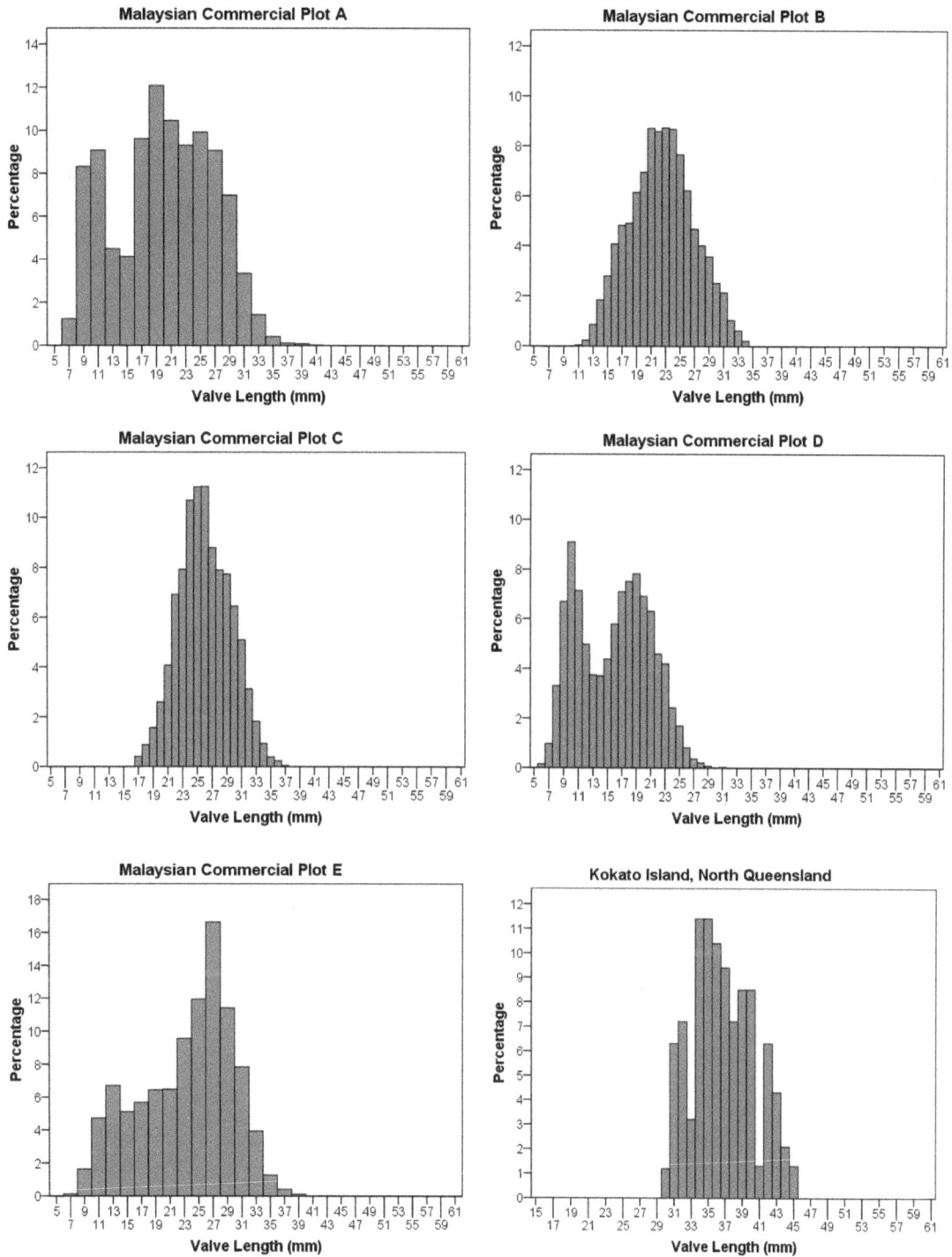

Figure 6.6: Size frequency distributions drawn from Malaysian commercial plots A, B, C, D and E; live collected sample from natural shell bed near Kokato Island, north Queensland. Note variation in percentage scales and size classes, with data from plots A and E only available in 2mm size classes.

Source: Malaysian commercial data from Ng 1986; Kokato Island data redrawn from Bailey 1993:10.

As a further comparison, a size frequency plot is presented of data obtained from the measurement of 97 *A. granosa* valves (obtained from 50 individuals) collected in 1972 from a location near Kokato Island, within the Embley River feeding into Albatross Bay in the Weipa area (Bailey 1977:138, 1993:7, 9–10). This sample was originally collected to examine the condition of the shell and patterns of valve breakage relative to recently observed methods of processing (Bailey 1977:137–138). The Kokato Island sample also displays a negative skew, and the shape of the size frequency distribution is similar to those of Plots B and C, but it is missing the minor peak in the smaller size classes that might be expected of an established population with constant rates of recruitment. There are a number of possible reasons for this difference, such as small sample size, bias in size selection, method of collection, or a lack of natural recruitment in this population (see for example discussion by Morrison 2003 specific to the Weipa area). It does, however, display modal values highlighted by Broom (1985) and Pathansali (1966) as being consistent with a natural population, and as such, is a useful comparison with archaeological data.

Finally, it is important to acknowledge that there are several inter-related factors that can create similar patterns. It has been noted that environmental change, habitat-specific parameters, human exploitation, and temporal variation in the size of accessible shell species can all contribute to variability or a mean decrease in shell size (Hockey and Bosman 1986:12; Hockey *et al.* 1988:353–4, Lasiak 1991a, 1991b; Jerardino 1997; Claassen 1998; de Boer *et al.* 2000:294; Campbell 2008; Faulkner 2009, in press; Randklev *et al.* 2009). Factors such as mean annual sea surface temperatures, increases or decreases in salinity levels, increased exposure of the shell beds, and the density of the shell bed itself are all known to affect the productivity and growth rates of molluscan species, and have been noted above in the previous section for *A. granosa*. Communities can also be characterised by short-term fluctuations in taxonomic composition and number of individuals (Claassen 1998:49; Bourke 2000:190). As an example, Lasiak's (1991a, 1991b) modern ecological studies on the South African coast have indicated that interannual environmental and ecological fluctuations, such as mortality and recruitment rates, could account for differences observed between exploited and non-exploited populations. While these are important considerations, the nature of the archaeological record must also be kept in mind. Mannino and Thomas (2001:1110), have suggested that the time-averaged nature of archaeological deposits means that these kind of short-term events are effectively masked by longer-term trends in exploitation and occupation (see also Braje *et al.* 2007; Erlandson *et al.* 2008; Faulkner 2009).

Size frequency distributions and valve size variability

Based on the discussion presented above, comparisons of size frequency distributions in molluscan assemblages need to be interpreted with caution. Regardless of whether a shell deposit originates from natural or cultural processes, the shape of the size frequency distribution can reflect:

1. The nature or structure of the source population as well as the depositional environment;

2. The nature of the transport agent (i.e. water movement, predatory harvesting - including humans); and

3. Any post-depositional processes in operation (Claassen 1998:113–114; Ford 1989:164).

There are, however, a number of patterns in size frequency distributions that could be expected in cultural shell deposits. It has been suggested that size distributions that conform to a normal curve should be a rare occurrence in middens or mounds, and where they do occur, may reflect size sorting via taphonomic processes rather than cultural processes of size-selection (Claassen 1998:113–114). While there will be a degree of size-selection in operation during human harvesting of mollusc species (e.g. Meehan 1982; Bailey 1993; Bourke 2000, 2002; Faulkner

2006, 2009), the sizes of the molluscs collected will, to a certain degree, reflect those that are available for exploitation from within the population (see discussion by Meehan 1982:133,135). Given the biological and ecological characteristics of *A. granosa*, a size frequency distribution conforming to a normal curve would not be expected. Additionally, while year-round harvesting can potentially produce both positively and negatively skewed distributions (Lasiak 1993); long-term and/or consistent harvesting would be expected to produce a positively skewed size distribution (Bailey 1993:10; Claassen 1998:113–114). With more intensive harvesting, these patterns would be expected in combination with lower mean and/or modal size.

Size frequency data and descriptive statistics are presented here from five of the sites excavated on the Point Blane Peninsula (Figure 6.7 and Table 6.5). As previously noted, three of the five sites (BMB/029, BMB/071 and BMB/045) are characteristic of the *A. granosa* dominated shell mounds prevalent across much of the tropical north Australian coast, being mounded deposits of dense, tightly packed shell. Although not incorporated into the previous analyses of Chapters 4 and 5, the *A. granosa* size data from the Grindall Bay midden BMB/061 (located in the Dilmitjpi cluster with BMB/071) are included here to extend the chronological sequence for the exploitation of this species in the area (see Faulkner 2009, in press). This site is positioned approximately 200m to the east of BMB/071, bordering a lower lying swamp and *Eucalypt* woodland. Measuring 13.0 by 10.9m, excavation of this site reached a depth of approximately 22cm, with no observable stratigraphic changes within the densely packed shell deposit. The age estimates available for this site (Table 6.2) indicates rapid accumulation, with occupation of approximately 204 years between 1213 and 1009 cal BP. In line with the chronological patterns from three Grindall Bay shell mounds, the 'test sample significance' function of the CALIB v6.1.1 program indicates that the 2σ calibrated ages for the three radiocarbon samples from BMB/061 are statistically indistinguishable at the 95% confidence level (t = 2.10, *d.f.* = 2). As a potential contrast, the Myaoola Bay site BMB/067b is also presented here, as it is a dispersed, horizontally spread midden containing large amounts of shell within dark humic sediments, and may represent different patterns of occupation and resource exploitation.

Table 6.5: Descriptive statistics for Grindall Bay mounds (BMB/029, BMB/071, BMB/045) and midden (BMB/061); and Myaoola Bay shell midden BMB/067b.

	BMB/029	BMB/071	BMB/061	BMB/045	BMB/067[b]
Mean	35.73	31.93	33.31	33.39	32.02
Median	36.35	31.98	33.23	33.62	32.11
Mode	35.01[a]	31.17[a]	31.93[a]	30.96[a]	30.31[a]
Std. Dev.	6.48	6.34	6.11	5.99	5.53
Maximum	58.08	53.62	54.39	51.90	55.56
Minimum	15.54	13.38	17.18	10.72	14.61
Skewness[b]	-0.074	0.128	0.255	0.006	-0.005
Kurtosis[b]	-0.041	-0.453	0.157	-0.272	0.208
No.	2309	4300	1551	4041	1378
No. (%) Juvenile (<25mm)	129 (5.59)	725 (16.86)	151 (9.74)	384 (9.50)	156 (11.32)

a. Multiple modes exist, the smallest value is presented; b. In an ideal normal distribution skewness and kurtosis values are 0

All five sites present mean valve lengths ranging between 32 and 36mm, and modal values between 30 and 35mm. These values fall within the range of average asymptotic shell lengths of 29.6 to 35.9mm for continuously harvested populations derived by Broom (1985:15). Broom (1985:16–7) also notes that these values are based on an artificially seeded population and may not reflect the mean size of a continuously exploited natural population, however, they provide a baseline comparison for size relative to exploitation. Similar values for *A. granosa* valve length have been reported from shell mound deposits in other regions of northern Australia. For example, the work of Bourke (2000, 2002:40) at Hope Inlet (in the Darwin region) demonstrates mean valve lengths of between 28 and 35mm from three excavated shell mounds (HI80, HI81 and HI83), and Bailey (1993:10) presents modal values in the 25 to 35mm range for the Kwamter Mound in Weipa, north Queensland. Those data suggests continuous harvesting, with the range of size classes present in the sites being indicative of those present within the population, with some potential size-selective focus on the larger individuals available.

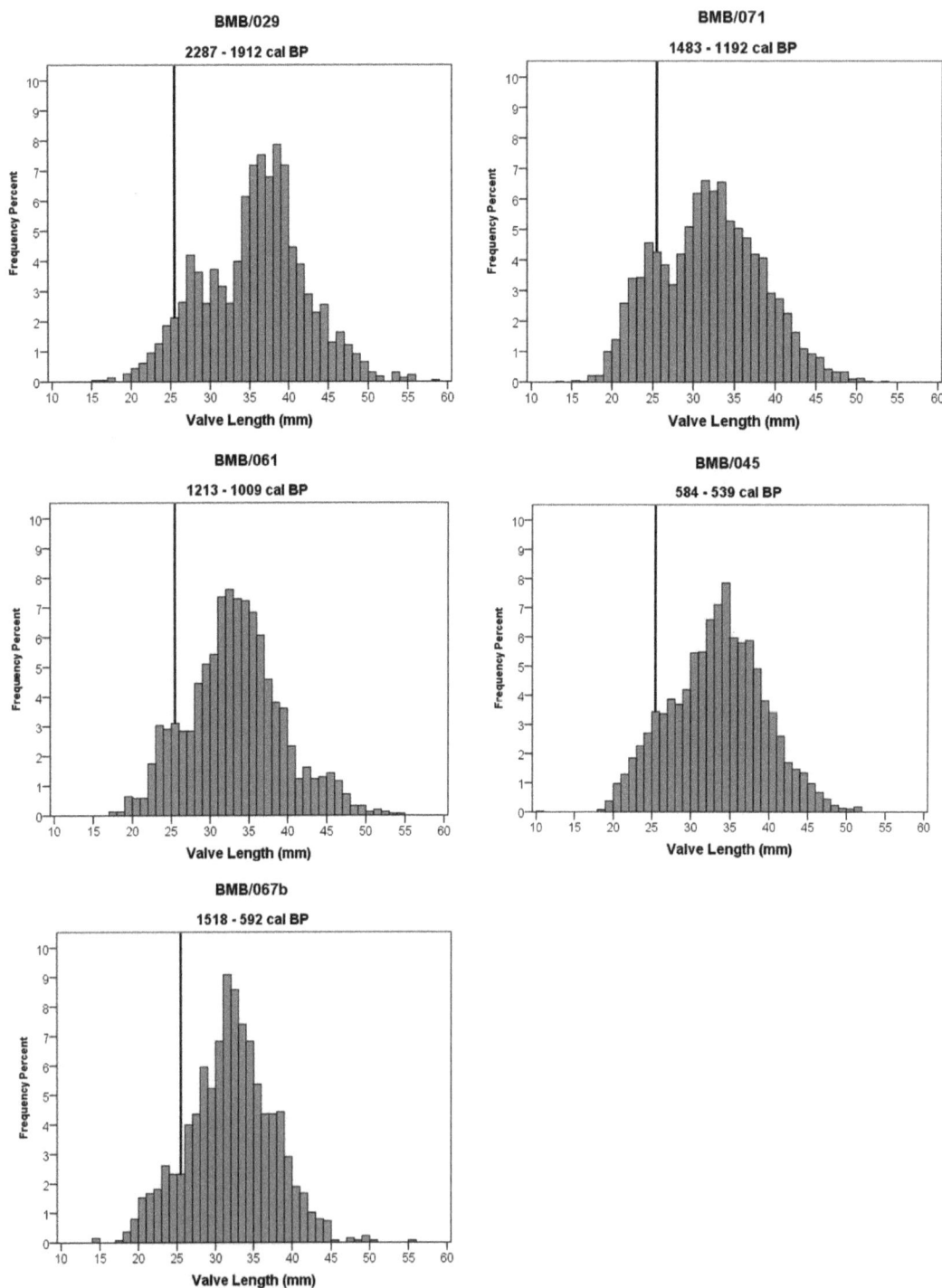

Figure 6.7: *Anadara granosa* size frequency distributions from the Grindall Bay mounds (BMB/029, BMB/071, BMB/045) and midden (BMB/061); and from the Myaoola Bay midden BMB/067b. Black line indicates expected valve size at which sexual maturity is reached (25mm).

A Kruskal-Wallis test confirms that the trends observed in the central tendency for valve length across these five sites are significant (χ^2 = 593.93, *d.f.* = 4, *p* < 0.001), and post-hoc pairwise comparisons employing Mann-Whitney *U* tests (Table 6.6) indicate that, with the exceptions of BMB/071 and BMB/067b, and BMB/061 and BMB/045, *A. granosa* valve size for these deposits as a whole are significantly different. All of the distributions are bimodal, all present non-normal distributions (Kolmogorov-Smirnov test results: BMB/029 D = 0.055, *d.f.* = 2309, *p* = 0.000; BMB/071 *D* = 0.39, *d.f.* = 4300, *p* = 0.000; BMB/061 *D* = 0.34, *d.f.* = 1551, *p* = 0.000; BMB/045 *D* = 0.023, *d.f.* = 4041, *p* = 0.000; BMB/067b *D* = 0.033, *d.f.* = 1378, *p* = 0.001), with the degree of variability in skewness and kurtosis values between sites possibly relating to the intensity of harvesting and duration of site formation.

Table 6.6: Results of Mann-Whitney *U*-tests comparing *Anadara granosa* valve size from the Grindall Bay mounds (BMB/029, BMB/071, BMB/045) and midden (BMB/061); and from the Myaoola Bay midden BMB/067b.

Site pair	No.	Mean Rank	Sum of Ranks	U	Z	p
BMB/029	2309	4018.88	9279597.5	3315997.5	-22.289	0.000
BMB/071	4300	2921.66	12563147.5			
BMB/029	2309	2116.73	4887521.0	1360633.0	-12.667	0.000
BMB/061	1551	1653.26	2564209.0			
BMB/029	2309	3621.10	8361125.5	3636438.5	-14.641	0.000
BMB/045	4041	2920.89	11803299.5			
BMB/029	2309	2083.43	4810648.0	1038049.0	-17.679	0.000
BMB/067b	1378	1442.80	1988180.0			
BMB/071	4300	2833.50	12184041.0	2936891.0	-6.975	0.000
BMB/061	1551	3182.45	4935985.0			
BMB/071	4300	3894.05	16747037.5	7499887.5	-10.812	0.000
BMB/045	4041	4465.05	18043273.5			
BMB/071	4300	2829.12	12165220.0	2918070.0	-0.843	0.399
BMB/067b	1378	2871.89	3957461.0			
BMB/061	1551	2752.31	4268830.5	3065254.5	-1.268	0.205
BMB/045	4041	2813.46	11369197.5			
BMB/061	1551	1543.67	2394231.0	946623.0	-5.341	0.000
BMB/067b	1378	1376.45	1896754.0			
BMB/045	4041	2802.95	11326715.0	2408644.0	-7.490	0.000
BMB/067b	1378	2437.43	3358775.0			

Both BMB/071 and BMB/045 display positive skew and negative kurtosis values, without comparatively sharp peaks or long tails to the distribution. These kinds of patterns would be indicative of populations subjected to continuous and relatively intensive harvesting. A similar interpretation can be offered for BMB/061, although this site displays a greater degree of positive skew and positive kurtosis, indicating a higher central peak and a long tail into the larger valve size classes. This site is more similar to the distribution from BMB/045, as also indicated by the lack of a significant difference in *A. granosa* valve size between these deposits as a whole. BMB/029 displays a slight negative skew, but as this site was formed during the earlier phase of mound formation in Grindall Bay, it would be expected that the distribution would lean towards the larger size classes. In contrast, the shell midden BMB/067b, while still displaying a slight bimodal distribution, is negatively skewed with a positive kurtosis value. This site was formed over a longer period with a lower level of exploitation intensity. Thus harvesting within this particular area of the peninsula may have been more seasonally restricted and less intensive, and while continuous was possibly punctuated through time to a greater degree than would have occurred in the shell mounds. It is also possible that this pattern represents a combination of human harvesting with location specific environmental differences, with BMB/067b located in a more exposed, smaller embayment in Myaoola Bay. The fact that there is not a significant difference between this site and BMB/071 in *A. granosa* size when comparing the overall deposit requires further investigation, as the depositional histories and specific locations are very different. In general, these distributions highlight the expected combination of human size-selectivity and *A. granosa* population structures.

There is also some variability in the proportion of juveniles represented in these deposits through time and space. Within BMB/029, there are proportionally fewer juveniles within this site (5.6%). As *A. granosa* is known to have a high reproductive and growth rates, this percentage is suggestive of a stable, well-established population. While the small number of juveniles could be a result of the exploitation of sexually immature individuals, the representation of so many large individuals in fact suggests that this population may not have previously been exploited, or more likely regularly exploited at a low level. As noted previously, this pattern may relate to the earliest phase of occupation within the overall system and the structure of the environment within this specific locality. The considerable size overlap with the Kokato Island sample also suggests that this mound may document the initial exploitation of *A. granosa* within this area, or a minimal exploitation of *A. granosa*, phasing into possibly longer-term, more intensive utilisation. In contrast, the BMB/071 pattern is consistent with continuous exploitation of *A. granosa* and/or the use of a population already reduced by higher levels of exploitation. There is an apparent reduction in the availability of *A. granosa* within the upper size ranges compared with BMB/029, particularly given the higher percentage of juveniles (16.9%). This indicates that as people are exploiting this resource to a greater degree, a reduction in mollusc size within the natural population means there is a gradual shift towards smaller sizes. For both BMB/061 and BMB/045, while still present, the reduction in the size of the bimodal peaks may mean either that these sites accumulated before further recruitment within the natural population, or that the time-averaged nature of the deposits has smoothed-out this type of patterning. While being more restricted in the overall size range compared with the other Grindall Bay mound sites, both BMB/061 and BMB/045 show a shift away from the type of pattern demonstrated for BMB/071, back towards that shown in BMB/029 relative to mean size and the percentage of juveniles (each at 9.5%).

As these size frequency distributions present a fairly coarse-grained pattern of potential exploitation from time-averaged contexts, the next step is to investigate any potential size variability throughout each of the deposits in more detail. To this end, boxplots of *A. granosa* valve length by excavation unit for each of the five sites are presented in Figure 6.8, and descriptive statistics for *Anadara granosa* length by excavation unit (including the percentage of juveniles) are presented in Table 6.7 for BMB/029, BMB/071, BMB/061, BMB/045 and BMB/067b.

Table 6.7: Descriptive statistics for *Anadara granosa* valve size from the Grindall Bay mounds (BMB/029, BMB/071, BMB/045) and midden (BMB/061); and from the Myaoola Bay midden BMB/067b.

Site	Excavation Unit	Mean	Median	Std. Dev.	Min	Max	No.	No./(%) Juvenile (<25mm)
BMB/029	1	35.86	36.51	7.11	20.43	58.08	185	11 (5.95)
	3	34.62	35.23	7.77	16.71	55.91	229	28 (12.23)
	5	35.09	34.89	6.94	22.34	50.48	188	11 (5.85)
	7	34.04	34.11	6.60	19.42	55.20	493	39 (7.91)
	9	36.90	37.31	6.02	15.54	54.94	301	18 (5.98)
	11	37.36	37.78	4.53	19.44	51.61	382	4 (1.05)
	13	35.11	35.70	6.12	21.30	53.98	340	15 (4.41)
	15	38.21	38.94	7.18	23.02	55.22	102	2 (1.96)
	17	38.66	38.80	5.42	26.35	51.42	36	0 (0.00)
	19	36.44	36.64	5.04	25.75	47.01	43	0 (0.00)
	21	38.74	39.55	5.58	24.71	44.13	10	1 (10.00)
BMB/071	1	29.68	30.09	5.58	17.19	46.26	181	40 (22.10)
	3	30.38	30.31	6.27	15.64	51.76	442	103 (23.30)
	5	31.78	31.82	6.52	13.38	53.62	1408	275 (19.53)
	7	30.96	31.31	5.37	19.17	48.66	952	110 (11.55)
	9	31.66	31.47	5.97	17.30	49.24	1073	158 (14.73)
	11	33.86	34.06	6.40	16.51	50.75	244	39 (15.98)
BMB/061	1	31.18	31.03	6.41	19.06	51.74	35	8 (22.86)
	2	33.07	32.77	6.20	18.12	52.57	244	26 (10.66)
	3	33.95	33.93	6.64	18.50	53.48	356	33 (9.27)
	4	33.40	33.22	5.90	17.18	54.39	600	51 (8.50)
	5	33.20	33.20	5.10	21.13	49.39	164	12 (7.32)
	6	32.51	32.91	5.96	21.57	47.89	75	9 (12.00)
	7	32.48	32.51	6.52	20.27	52.54	77	12 (15.58)
BMB/045	1	31.65	32.16	5.40	18.02	44.88	122	15 (12.30)
	3	33.40	33.56	4.36	20.66	45.39	283	13 (4.59)
	5	33.58	33.37	4.45	18.45	50.15	335	9 (2.69)
	7	31.34	31.28	5.42	20.86	47.55	355	46 (12.96)
	9	32.27	32.05	5.39	21.09	47.26	404	30 (7.43)
	11	33.08	33.31	5.52	20.47	48.00	272	21 (7.72)
	13	32.99	33.65	5.64	20.36	45.42	232	26 (11.21)
	15	34.27	35.38	5.60	19.75	48.53	200	12 (6.00)
	17	32.18	32.38	6.61	19.51	47.67	234	38 (16.24)
	19	30.98	31.28	7.58	18.60	51.23	306	95 (31.05)
	21	34.50	34.28	4.65	23.93	51.76	210	5 (2.38)
	23	33.69	33.61	4.43	10.72	48.30	176	5 (2.84)
	25	35.40	34.65	5.64	20.02	50.73	179	7 (3.91)
	27	35.84	36.89	6.81	19.58	51.90	410	35 (8.54)
	29	34.15	34.06	7.76	19.16	51.58	150	24 (16.00)
	31	36.66	36.82	6.06	22.82	47.61	173	3 (1.73)
BMB/067b	1	33.54	32.77	5.32	23.14	49.12	50	2 (4.00)
	2	32.44	33.04	5.20	20.07	47.35	117	10 (8.55)
	3	31.68	32.05	5.48	20.07	44.80	193	27 (13.99)
	4	31.67	31.64	5.54	14.61	44.83	267	27 (10.11)
	5	32.15	32.38	5.12	18.80	44.45	174	17 (9.77)
	6	32.02	31.82	5.59	18.53	49.57	310	37 (11.94)
	7	31.99	32.28	6.01	18.76	55.56	170	21 (12.35)
	8	32.24	32.03	5.72	17.90	50.65	97	11 (11.34)

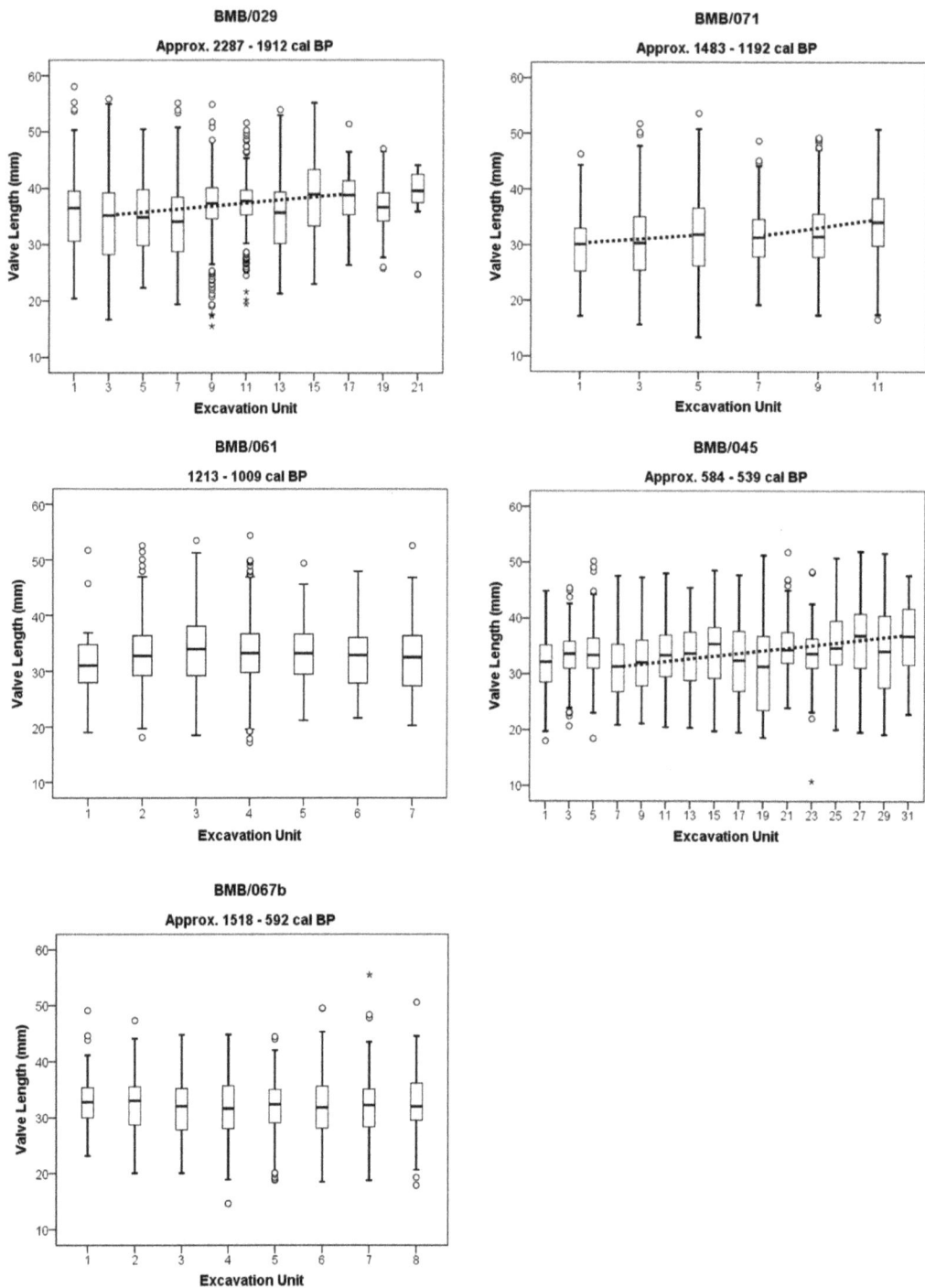

Figure 6.8: Boxplots of *Anadara granosa* valve size from the Grindall Bay mounds (BMB/029, BMB/071, BMB/045) and midden (BMB/061); and from the Myaoola Bay midden BMB/067b (dashed line indicates significant difference at 0.05 level).

While the samples from each excavation unit do not conform to a normal distribution, similar to the size frequency distribution for the sites as a whole, ANOVA tests have been conducted for each site. ANOVA is not as sensitive to violations of the assumption of normality given good sample size (Pallant 2007:110, 204), and has been proven to be an effective statistical test in other archaeological mollusc studies (Jerardino and Navarro 2008; Jerardino *et al.* 2008; Faulkner 2010; Jerardino 2010), particularly in investigating similar questions of potential resource depression. For the three shell mound sites, ANOVA tests indicate that there is a high degree of variability in mean valve size (BMB/029: $F = 10.863$, $d.f. = 10$, $p = 0.000$; BMB/071: $F = 27.996$, $d.f. = 5$, $p = 0.000$; BMB/045: $F = 20.108$, $d.f. = 15$, $p = 0.000$). Post-hoc comparisons using the Dunnett's C test indicates significant differences at the 0.05 level in mean valve size within each of these three sites, indicating an overall trend for size decrease throughout a significant portion of these deposits (Figure 6.8). In contrast, within both BMB/061 (ANOVA: $F = 1.903$, $d.f. = 6$, $p = 0.077$) and BMB/067b (ANOVA: $F = 0.931$, $d.f. = 7$, $p = 0.481$) the degree of variability is not significant, nor is there a significant trend of size decrease through time. Therefore, the previously identified similarity in size frequency distribution between these sites and shell mounds BMB/071 and BMB/045 respectively are not supported with a finer-grained analysis of valve size variability throughout the deposits.

There are also general trends within BMB/029 and BMB/071 for increasing numbers of juveniles, which again may reflect higher intensity exploitation as available sizes decrease within the shellbed. In comparison, the percentage of juveniles in BMB/061 does not demonstrate a clear trend, decreasing from the base of the deposit to stabilisation, with an increase in excavation unit 1. While BMB/045 demonstrates a high degree of variability in the percentage of juveniles, this site represents shorter-term deposition, and this pattern may represent time-averaged variability in population structure. A more significant contrast is found within BMB/067b, where the proportions of juveniles are relatively stable throughout the excavation units, proportionally decreasing in the upper portion of the deposit. This would suggest more ephemeral exploitation of the resource over the approximate 900 years of site formation, whereby natural recruitment rates can keep pace with the level of exploitation intensity. While there a few studies available for comparison, detailed metrical analyses have been undertaken on mounded shell deposits in north Queensland and in the Darwin region of the Northern Territory. For the Kwamter mound site in Weipa, north Queensland, Bailey (1993:10) interprets the size frequency pattern as showing no evidence of sustained size decrease typical of over-exploitation, and therefore concludes that the archaeological samples are reflective of a mollusc population subjected to continuous, but not overly excessive, levels of human predation (see Faulkner 2009). A similar interpretation has been proposed by Bourke (2000:318–20) for patterns of *A. granosa* exploitation within the Darwin Harbour mounds. Individually, the Blue Mud Bay sites could be interpreted in a similar way (particularly for BMB/061 and BMB/067b), even given the significant decrease in *A. granosa* size throughout each of the three Grindall Bay mounds. When the five sites are compared, however, the patterns of exploitation appear to be quite different, with the three Grindall Bay shell mounds demonstrating a significant decline in valve size, compared with the comparatively stable pattern exhibited within both BMB/061 and BMB/067b. Given that *A. granosa* is able to cope with short-term fluctuating environmental variables and to be biomass dominant in mudflat environments (due predominantly to its breeding and growth rates), the data presented here are more significant when viewed in terms of the overall pattern within Grindall Bay (Faulkner 2009, in press).

Chronological trends in Anadara granosa exploitation within Grindall Bay

The general archaeological criteria used for assessing the degree of molluscan exploitation suggests that the relative abundance of preferred species should decrease throughout a midden or mound deposit, coupled with an increase in the number of less easily procured and/or processed species. As discussed in Chapter 5, relative abundance patterns for *A. granosa*, as the preferred species within the three Grindall Bay shell mound sites analysed here, demonstrates that this species represents between approximately 68 and 88% of the molluscan assemblages. Based on the criteria outlined above, if human predation had adversely affected this species, it should decline in relative abundance within and between these deposits. In fact, even in excluding BMB/061 from this discussion, relative abundance estimates for *A. granosa* increase significantly throughout the deposit in BMB/029, and remain at a relatively high, stable level in BMB/071 and BMB/045. Added to this, less easily procured and/or processed species do not appear to have been generally utilised within these sites, let alone increase in number (Faulkner 2009). The analysis of valve size by excavation unit does indicate, however, that mean shell length has decreased significantly throughout the deposits of the three mound sites, and the decrease in mean size is generally accompanied by a general decrease in the age-size structure of the populations. *A. granosa* valve size and proportion of juveniles from the midden BMB/061 presents an anomalous pattern in comparison with the mounds. As such, it is important to determine how these four sites relate to each other within the longer-term sequence of occupation and *A. granosa* exploitation within this area. To investigate this issue, mean valve length within each excavation unit from the four Grindall Bay sites is plotted by approximate age (Figure 6.9). Previous analyses of several of these sites have been based on broad analytical units according to chronological phases identified by statistically significant differences in calibrated age ranges (e.g. Faulkner 2006, 2009:840). Recalibration of the radiocarbon dates has effectively removed these differences, however, and the principal means of investigating longer-term trends in Grindall Bay is achieved here by focusing on the excavation unit as the main unit of analysis. To construct a chronological sequence from the Grindall Bay mounds and midden, each un-dated excavation unit has been assigned an approximate age based on age depth curves. While the inherent assumption of this approach is that the excavation units were deposited at regular intervals relative to the dated portions of the deposit, given the general rapid nature of formation in these sites this approach enables the exploration of potentially finer-grained variability in valve size across the Grindall Bay sequence as a whole.

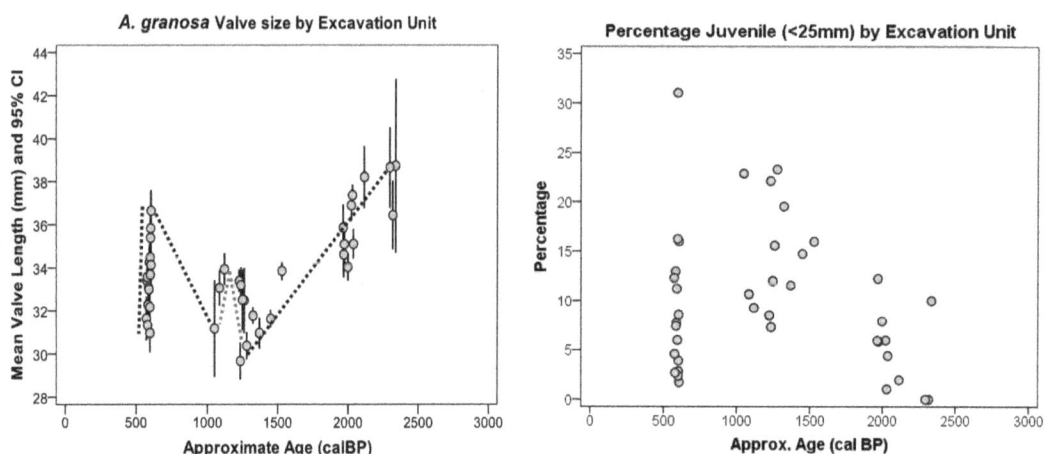

Figure 6.9: *Anadara granosa* mean valve size / 95% confidence interval (dashed black line indicates significant difference at 0.05 level, with dashed grey line indicating possible recovery and subsequent decline); and % of juveniles (<25mm) by excavation unit / age cal BP.

As with the analyses conducted for the individual shell mounds, across the whole sequence there is a high degree of variability in mean *A. granosa* valve size (ANOVA: $F = 27.396$, $d.f. = 10656$, $p = 0.000$), however several trends in the intensity of exploitation can be identified. These patterns in mean *A. granosa* valve size are also relatively reflected in the percentages of juveniles plotted by approximate age (Figure 6.9), indicating a relationship across the whole Grindall Bay sequence between valve size variability and the structure of the exploited population. As *A. granosa* is a rapidly reproducing and fast growing species, a low intensity of human exploitation would be likely to result in the size of collected molluscs remaining relatively stable throughout a sequence of occupation. Comparative stability in the size of this species is seen between 2287 and 2140 cal BP, and arguably between 1310 and 1009 cal BP. If collection practices were intensified while the species' reproduction and growth rates remained relatively constant, however, then it would be expected that the average size of the remaining shellfish within the population would decrease significantly over time (Waselkov 1987:134). Between 2140 and 1310 cal BP, as well as 584 and 526 cal BP, there are significant reductions in the size of *A. granosa*, which may indicate increasing human exploitation during these periods. Within the overall sequence, there is one phase of significant size increase. This occurs between 1009 and 584 cal BP, which appears to reflect a decrease in the intensity of exploitation during this particular period, and potentially a decrease in the level of occupation and site formation within this part of the study area, allowing the shell beds to recover and stabilise. As noted above, variation in mean valve size between 1310 and 1009 cal BP are not statistically significant, and one interpretation may be of relative stability during this period; however, this could also reflect a period of rebound or recovery and subsequent decline (Rick *et al.* 2008). This pattern may relate to variability or lowering of the intensity of harvesting during this period, changes in environmental processes such as sedimentation, or a combination of the two. The finer scale pattern presented in ordering the excavation units chronologically demonstrates that there was also a significant decrease between 584 and 526 cal BP. After this period it appears that shell mounds ceased to be formed within Blue Mud Bay, and *Anadara granosa* is largely absent from the archaeological record of the area. This would suggest that BMB/045 represents rapid and intensive exploitation of *A. granosa* before its ultimate decline and/or disappearance from this area.

While it is more likely that hunter-gatherers would have collected shellfish based on their size rather than age, size is not independent of age in these populations. Consequently, larger and older shells would be expected to dominate the midden samples as hunter-gatherers would preferentially select the larger, higher meat-yielding individuals (Mannino and Thomas 2002:459–60). However, smaller size classes have to be collected if the size ranges represented within a population are significantly reduced (Tonner 2005:1403; Faulkner 2009:831). As indicated by the percentage of juveniles by excavation unit and approximate age (although the degree of variability is higher in this case), there is a relationship between decreasing valve size and an increase in younger/smaller individuals within these sites. This strengthens the previous interpretation relative to mean size, that an increase in the younger age classes within the sequence prior to, and following, the period spanning 1009 to 584 cal BP reflects intensive exploitation and resource depression. It also suggests that the decrease in occupation and resource exploitation intensity within the area enabled the natural population of *A. granosa* to recover from the effects of predation. The patterns of site formation and rapid deposition with this analysis of *A. granosa* size and age structure within these deposits, combined with the structure of the environment and patterns of progradation, suggests that this resource was subject to long-term intensive exploitation rising to a final peak before the species' ultimate decline and/or disappearance.

While not included in this final analytical stage given its different site morphology and location, the Myaoola Bay midden site of BMB/067b is nevertheless important within the context of *A. granosa* exploitation in Blue Mud Bay. This site demonstrates differences in valve size throughout the sequence of occupation that reflect both lower intensity collecting relative to the three mound sites in particular, as well as location-specific environmental structure. With stability in shell size throughout the approximately 930 years of deposition within this site, human exploitation of the shellbeds in this area was less focussed and less intense over the long-term (and *A. granosa* was only marginally the dominant species). This pattern may also relate to the site location, in a more exposed section of the coast potentially subjected to higher wave action and turbidity levels. This area is also more constrained in size, which would have limited the expansion of shell beds in a location with comparatively limited mudflat development through time. As such, the conditions for *A. granosa* shell bed establishment and proliferation were less optimal in comparison with the more sheltered, extensive areas of Grindall Bay, and as such, the pattern of mollusc exploitation was different.

In line with the interpretations of Bailey (1993:10) and Bourke (2000:318–20), the individual patterns identified for each of the shell deposits in Grindall Bay could be viewed as indicating that exploitation of *A. granosa* was long-term if not continuous, but not overly intensive. Viewing these sites as part of a longer-term trend changes this interpretation, suggesting that the patterns of exploitation were intensive, albeit with some discontinuity based on the available chronologies for the area. Therefore, intensified human predation pressure will not only result in a decrease in average shell size, but also in a lower average age among collected specimens (Faulkner 2009). Additionally, patterns of size variability can be produced by shifts in environmental and climatic conditions. Productivity and growth rates of molluscan species are known to be affected by variations in mean annual sea surface temperatures, salinity levels and increased shell bed exposure, and these factors have all been noted specifically for *A. granosa* (Broom, 1985:4–7; Pathansali, 1966:90–91). While there are a number of significant palaeoenvironmental changes that occurred throughout the mid-to-late Holocene, however, this level of variability appears to fall within the environmental and climatic ranges tolerated by *A. granosa*. While there were changes in sea surface temperature during the mid-to-late Holocene of 1.5°C to 2.0°C relative to present conditions (Gagan *et al.* 2004:131–2), based on presently available data, this does not appear to have been on a scale that would have had an adverse affect on *A. granosa* populations. Salinity levels appear to have peaked between approximately 500 and 200 BP, but this occurs at the end of the period of shell mound formation in Blue Mud Bay. While variation in salinity levels within Grindall Bay, either representing depressed salinity via freshwater influx or heightened levels due to restricted circulation within the area, might explain some of the variability seen in the *A. granosa* size through time, this would not explain the broader patterns noted here. When viewing the longer-term pattern of mean *A. granosa* valve size, the larger scale peaks and troughs in this sequence also do not appear to correlate with any of the currently known climatic changes for the broader region. It must also be acknowledged, however, that ongoing processes of progradation, combined with increasing aridity during the mid-to-late Holocene, may have played a part in creating these patterns to a certain degree. For example, continuing processes of sedimentation would have gradually changed the gradient or slope of the coastal plain, eventually reducing freshwater input and tidal inundation in these areas (Woodroffe *et al.* 1986), a process that would have led to the gradual isolation of the shell beds (Macintosh 1982:13). Combined with variations in the intensity of human exploitation, as well as possible changes in salinity levels noted above within the localised area, this may explain the degree of variability observed in mean valve size within Grindall Bay. That said, the available data does not explain the longer trends in size decrease, nor the period of *A. granosa* size recovery prior to cessation in mound formation around 500 years ago. Due to the range of possible environmental causes for size change in molluscs, particularly those that may adversely affect *A. granosa* populations operating at scales that may not be currently observable, the longer-term trends identified in the archaeological sample suggests the patterns presented here can be cautiously attributed to human predation (e.g. Mannino and Thomas 2002; Braje *et al.* 2007; Erlandson *et al.* 2008; Faulkner 2009, in press). This interpretation is strengthened when this detailed examination of *A. granosa* size variability is viewed in combination with the broader archaeological evidence for site chronology, distribution and morphology.

The archaeological criteria outlined above for investigating potential anthropogenically induced resource depression must be assessed on a species-specific basis, as each species will respond differently to exploitation. Over-exploitation, or more accurately in this case, long-term intensive exploitation, may represent a range of possibilities for a molluscan population. There may be a reduction in the average size and age of the exploited species, below those that would be found in natural populations not exposed to human predation. There may also be a reduction in the age structure of the population that might reduce breeding capacity and recruitment, and hence population levels of molluscs on the shore (Mannino and Thomas 2001:1112–3, 2002:464). The data also suggests that the exploitation of *A. granosa* within the area was both long-term and intensive. While not conforming to the generally expected patterns for over-exploitation of a resource, the biological and ecological characteristics of *A. granosa* mean that, as a species, it effectively resists the effects of human predation (see for example Catterall and Poiner 1987:120; Hockey *et al.* 1988:361; de Boer *et al.* 2000:288). When viewed as a long-term pattern, however, it is apparent that human predation did have an effect on the structure of the population (Faulkner 2009:831, in press), particularly when viewed in combination with longer-term environmental processes.

Conclusion

The interpretations of the archaeological evidence presented here strongly indicate that there were several phases of economic reorganisation throughout the discernible 3000 years of occupation for the Point Blane Peninsula. The radiocarbon determinations indicate that there was an initial phase of occupation between 3000 and 1000 BP, with a second phase occurring between approximately 1000 BP and the present. Within this broad phasing, variability in the occupation and exploitation of resources within both Myaoola and Grindall Bays are evident. Between 3000 and 1000 BP there was sporadic or low level use of Myaoola Bay, contrasting with more focussed and intensive use of Grindall Bay. During the second phase, the radiocarbon evidence suggests that there was a change to a comparatively more intensive use of Myaoola Bay throughout the last 1000 BP. During this second phase of occupation, there was a relatively short, intense period of site deposition between approximately 584 and 526 cal BP in Grindall Bay. Discontinuities in radiocarbon dates in Grindall Bay preceding 584 cal BP suggests that there was a shift in the use of this particular area, an interpretation that is supported by the analysis of *A. granosa* size variation through time. These chronological differences are complemented by evidence of variations in the intensity of occupation and resource exploitation as assessed by variations in site size and content.

Based on differences in the density and morphology of sites, there was a greater intensity of occupation and resource exploitation correlated with mound building in Grindall Bay compared with the midden sites in Myaoola Bay. This evidence is further supported by the analysis of *A. granosa* exploitation from the four mound and midden sites. A consistent reduction in the size and age structure of *A. granosa* through time is viewed here as a reflection of intensive, long-term exploitation. Further to this point, the cessation of mound formation in the area appears to coincide with a period of economic reorganisation leading into the kind of patterns noted by Mitchell (1994a) for the pre-Macassan contact period. The interpretation of shell mound construction on the Point Blane Peninsula suggests that molluscan exploitation, particularly between 2287 and 1009 cal BP, was much more intense and focussed, and as such is distinct from those exploitation patterns observed during the historic period. The primary difference between shell middens and shell mounds is in fact one of degree, rather than kind, with morphological differences stemming from variations in the intensity of discard at particular locations through time. In a broad sense, these sites reflect more constant, intensive harvesting of *A. granosa* (see also Clune 2002; Faulkner 2006; Morrison 2010). Rather than being viewed in isolation as an anomaly, mounds are considered here as forming one aspect of the overall spectrum of the economic structure of the area, which also included smaller sites and surface scatters (Cribb

1996:169; Bailey 1999:105). As such, the mounds on the Point Blane Peninsula suggest neither low level harvesting, such as seasonal exploitation by small foraging groups (Bailey 1975a; Bourke 2000), nor occasional high intensity harvesting by larger groups for ceremonial purposes (e.g. Bourke 2000, 2005; Morrison 2003; Clune and Harrison 2009).

There are also a number of broader implications based on the patterns described here for shifts in economic activity through time, particularly related to the interpretation of the shell mounds outlined above. Given the extent of variability in the late Holocene archaeological record of the Point Blane Peninsula identified here, it follows that phases of reorganisation in the foraging economy may well have been accompanied by alterations in the importance of molluscs in the economy, population size and levels of mobility on the coast.

7

Reaching the Potential: The Archaeological Evidence for Late Holocene Change and Variability

The primary objective here has been to examine and explain the occurrence of coastal shell middens and mounds on the Point Blane Peninsula within a context of significant, broader environmental change and re-structuring of the regional resource base. Following from this, and given the archaeological evidence for economic reorganisation on the Point Blane Peninsula, this research has also aimed to characterise the nature and variability of this regional coastal economy. In fact, spatial and temporal variability defines human economic activity in this area during the late Holocene. Research conducted in other areas also provides an indication that this level of inter and intra-regional variation is a common feature of the archaeological record of coastal northern Australia. That said, the degree or extent of change and variability in human economic behaviour has often been underestimated in northern coastal Australia, particularly given the use of ethnographic data to interpret archaeological material. In comparison, here the interpretive framework for the variability observed in the coastal foraging economies of northern Australia is provided via the nature and timing of broader environmental, climatic and ecological changes. Within this framework, the archaeological evidence indicates that human/environmental interactions during this period were fluid in nature and complex, and in some respects of a magnitude greater than has previously been interpreted for other coastal regions.

Characterising late Holocene economic activity on the Point Blane Peninsula

The archaeological record of the Point Blane Peninsula is characterised by a high level of variability through space and time, particularly in the intensity of resource exploitation, and in the use of a range of molluscan resources and habitat areas. Through time, much of this variability appears to relate to changes in the structure of the coastal environment, tied strongly to long-term processes of climatic and environmental alterations that were in operation throughout the Holocene (Faulkner 2011). As the study area is a peninsula, the dominant resources, particularly prior to the formation of the wetland areas via ongoing progradation and sedimentary infilling, were located within the coastal zone. Shell mounds and middens are located in the landscape in those areas where there would have been easy access to abundant and varied resources, often differentially available along the coastline (Bailey 1975a, 1983; McNiven 1992:498–9). Variability in the distribution of shell mounds and middens are apparent, mainly the contrast between the lower, horizontally spread midden sites found in Myaoola Bay, and the mounded shell deposits that dominate the Grindall Bay landscape. This pattern relates to a number of factors. Firstly, it is a function of sea level regression and differential landscape changes in these areas, with processes of successive beach-ridge development and seaward sedimentation on the largely unprotected coast of Myaoola Bay, and the gradual progradation of the large sheltered embayment in Grindall Bay and subsequent wetland formation. Secondly, this pattern reflects behavioural factors relating to the density of resources within different localities, the intensity of resource use, and the pattern of refuse discard.

The distribution of sites combined with the available radiocarbon age determinations across the peninsula indicates that the sites documented in the area fall broadly within an age range between 2953 cal BP and the present. Within this age range, there appears to have been limited or low level use of this area prior to approximately 2500 BP, although this may relate to factors of site visibility and/or post-depositional destruction of archaeological material. Between 2287 and 526 cal BP, there was a phase of intensive occupation on the margin of Grindall Bay corresponding with a large number of mounded shell deposits. Within this period, there appears to be a decrease in the intensity of exploitation of *A. granosa*, and potentially a decrease in the level of occupation and site formation between 1009 to 584 cal BP. In addition to this, between 1310 and 1009 cal BP there appears to be a period of rebound or recovery in *A. granosa* populations with a subsequent decline. Evidence for occupation Myaoola Bay during this period is relatively limited until approximately 1115 cal BP. With the cessation of mound accumulation occurring around 526 cal BP, there was an increase in the evidence for occupation and resource use on the more exposed coastal margin of the peninsula (see also discussions in Bourke *et al.* 2007; Faulkner 2008, 2011, in press). Due to the abundance of surface and sub-surface water on the Point Blane Peninsula, at least on a seasonal basis, approximately 80% of sites in the area are located within 200m of freshwater, and all sites on the peninsula are located within a maximum 2km of water. Given that water was apparently readily accessible across the study area, therefore, other factors are more influential in determining site location and morphology, such as changes in the structure of the shoreline from maximum sea level highstand to the present, and the effect of this process on the dispersal of suitable habitats containing exploitable food resources. It is possible, however, that some of the variability in the use of the peninsula may relate to the differential availability of water through time (e.g. during drought conditions), in combination with other resources. Overall, the archaeological data from this area, particularly in combination with the environmental and climatic processes acting on the northern Australian coastline more broadly during the mid-to-late Holocene, suggests that there was an ongoing process of economic reorganisation relative to the abundance and availability of resources.

Chronological variation in mollusc and habitat exploitation

Interpretations of coastal environmental or cultural change have been successfully derived from midden analysis, particularly relating to their influence on strategies of resource procurement, social organisation and population demography. These interpretations have been primarily based on perceptible changes in the relative frequency of molluscan taxa or rates of shell discard through time (e.g. Schrire 1982:233–4; O'Connor and Sullivan 1994:24; Allen and Barton n.d.:88, 104–6). Across the Point Blane Peninsula, the exploitation of molluscan resources varies both spatially and temporally to a considerable degree (Faulkner 2011). Variations in the pattern of molluscan species and habitat exploitation here relate to micro- and macro-environmental changes, with a definite contrast in the use of specific resources and habitats through time. This is evident in the high degree of species composition variability within the Myaoola Bay midden sites. Although a number of taxa were consistently exploited through time, such as *Marcia hiantina, Septifer bilocularis* and *Gafrarium* sp., differences in the relative abundance of these species within and between the sites on this margin of the peninsula appear to relate to the variable distribution and dominance of near-shore shallow water and mangrove habitats. Changes to the environment are reflected in both species composition and the intensity of species exploitation, due to the fact that changing environmental conditions would undoubtedly have affected the range and density of species available for exploitation.

There was a relatively consistent use of the taxa recovered from the midden sites located in Myaoola Bay, with no one species being exploited at a level greater than 50% within these sites. In turn, chronological variations in the intensity of exploitation of taxa from different habitat zones are also explained by contrasting landscape structures. These differences reflect larger-scale environmental changes and landscape alteration on the exposed coastal margin of Myaoola Bay through time. For example, while there is only a minor decrease in the exploitation of species from the sand and mud flat areas, there is a marked overall decrease in the use of species from the hard-substrate, shallow water zone. The decline in species abundance from these habitats corresponds with an increase in mangrove species, particularly the exploitation of *Isognomon isognomon* in the more recent past. In contrast, the shell mound sites located on the margin of Grindall Bay exhibit much less variability in the relative abundance of both the dominant and sub-dominant species. The taxonomic composition from the mounds indicates a more intensive focus on one habitat zone and one particular species. While other species were exploited to varying degrees during the overall period of site formation in Grindall Bay, *Anadara granosa* is the most abundant species in all three of the shell mound sites investigated in detail, followed by *Mactra abbreviata* and *Marcia hiantina*, all three of which inhabit sand and mud flat areas. The other sub-dominant species present, the mangrove bivalve *Placuna placenta*, is found only within BMB/029 near the top of the sequence.

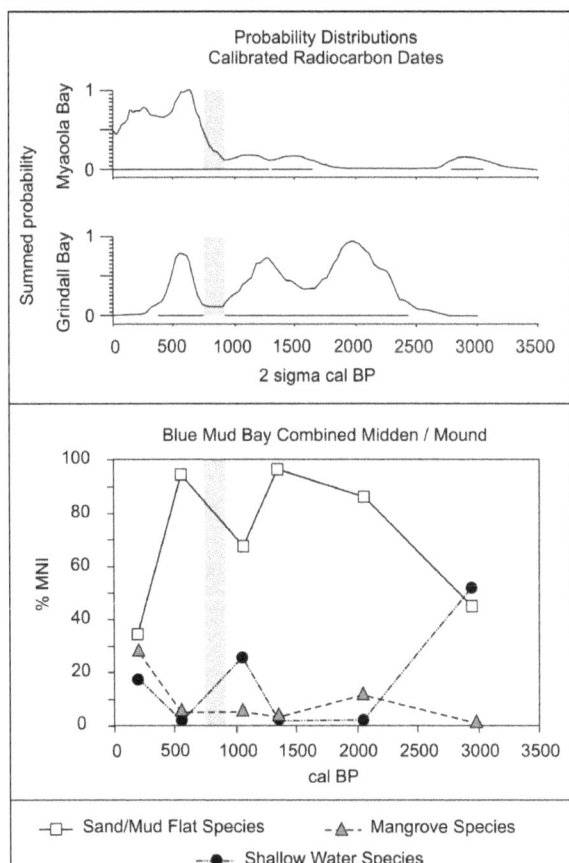

Figure 7.1: Chronological variation in the exploitation of mollusc species by habitat, with calibrated radiocarbon age summed probability plots for Myaoola and Grindall Bays (grey shading indicates phase of significant *A. granosa* size recovery in the Grindall Bay sites).

Source: Redrawn from Bourke *et al.* 2007; Faulkner 2011, in press.

The overall pattern of molluscan resource and habitat use on the Point Blane peninsula is as follows (Bourke *et al.* 2007:96; Faulkner 2011:147): prior to approximately 2500 BP there was a greater focus on the shallow water, near shore zone in conjunction with the sand and mud flats (Figure 7.1). Between approximately 2500 and 500 BP, and associated with the period of mound formation in the study area, there was an increasingly heavy reliance on species from the sand and mud flats relative to a decline in the relative abundance of species from the harder substrate, near shore areas. Depending on site location during this period there was a degree of variability in the use of species from the mangroves through time. Around 1000 BP there is a decline in sand/mudflat species with an associated increase in shallow water molluscs; however, this is more a reflection of the Myaoola Bay sites than the shell mounds of Grindall Bay. There was an increase in the use of mangrove species after approximately 500 BP, corresponding with a slight decline in exploitation of the sand and mud flats. In the Grindall Bay area in particular, these variations in habitat exploitation relate to the ongoing process of progradation, and the gradual establishment and proliferation of the sand/mud flat zone, often at the expense of exploitation within the mangroves. This pattern slowly changed as the process of progradation reached its limit within the area close to 500 years ago, with a slight decrease in sand/mud flat species corresponding with a slight increase in mangrove species. This final phase is likely to represent the relative stabilisation of the mangrove distribution close to its present extent at the mouth of Grindall Bay following long-term sedimentary infilling within the area. As such, the composition of the molluscan assemblages within the sites on the Point Blane Peninsula represents the long-term, average structure of mollusc communities in the area during the known period of occupation (see also Mowat 1995:153; Claassen 1998:134; Hiscock 1999:96; Bourke 2000:146).

Related to environmental changes linked to stabilisation and establishment of the coast following sea level rise, and patterns of progradation and sedimentary infill of shallow embayments across the Point Blane Peninsula, variability in molluscan exploitation through time is a reflection of the dynamic and changing nature of this coastline throughout the late Holocene (Bourke *et al.* 2007:96; Faulkner 2011:147). This illustrates the flexible nature of foraging behaviour on the coastal margins of this area, providing further support for the interpretation that people actively changed their foraging strategies to incorporate increasingly abundant or newly available species (Mowat 1995:163; Bourke *et al.* 2007). Similar patterns of shifting resource and habitat use relative to environmental changes have been observed between 1000 and 700 BP in other areas of northern Australia. In the Darwin region between approximately 2000 to 500 BP, midden and mound composition indicates that coastal foraging was focussed primarily on sand and mud flat habitats, with only minor exploitation of the mangroves. One hypothesis proposed for the cessation of mound formation in the area around 700 to 500 years ago is that it is associated with environmental change in shoreline characteristics at that time (Hiscock 1997, 1999). Hiscock (1997:447–9) has suggested that this particular economic system ceased approximately 700 years ago due to rapid environmental change, where mangroves expanded at the expense of other habitats, eventually leading to the disappearance of the productive *A. granosa* shell beds (Hiscock 1997:447–8, 1999:99). Further detailed research in the area by Bourke (2000, 2005) has reinforced this interpretation. Similar evidence for economic shifts relative to environmental change is also provided from the Blyth River region of northern central Arnhem Land via analysis of material excavated from the Ji-bena earth mound. Based on the available radiocarbon estimates, the period of deposition for this site spans the period between approximately 1000 and 500 BP (Brockwell *et al.* 2005:86). This site presently borders the large freshwater swamp of Balpilja near the mouth of the Blyth River, and based on geomorphological research undertaken in the area, this site is located on a prograded landscape that is no older than 2000 BP (Brockwell *et al.* 2005). Analysis of the Ji-bena earth mound material indicates that the dominant molluscan taxa exploited within the earlier phases of occupation within the Ji-bena earth mound were *Dosinia* sp. and *Mactra* sp., both of which inhabit sand and mud flats. During the last 1000 years, the relative abundance estimates of these species are greatly reduced, a decline that corresponds with the appearance and increasing abundance of freshwater turtle. In contrast with the patterns outlined for both Blue Mud Bay and Darwin Harbour, mangrove species were continually exploited throughout the history of the site, albeit to a reduced level within the upper excavation units. These changes have been related to the transition from estuarine to freshwater conditions in the area, marked by a possible reorganisation in foraging behaviour relative to the structure of the resource base (Brockwell *et al.* 2005).

Mounding behaviour: social and environmental interpretations

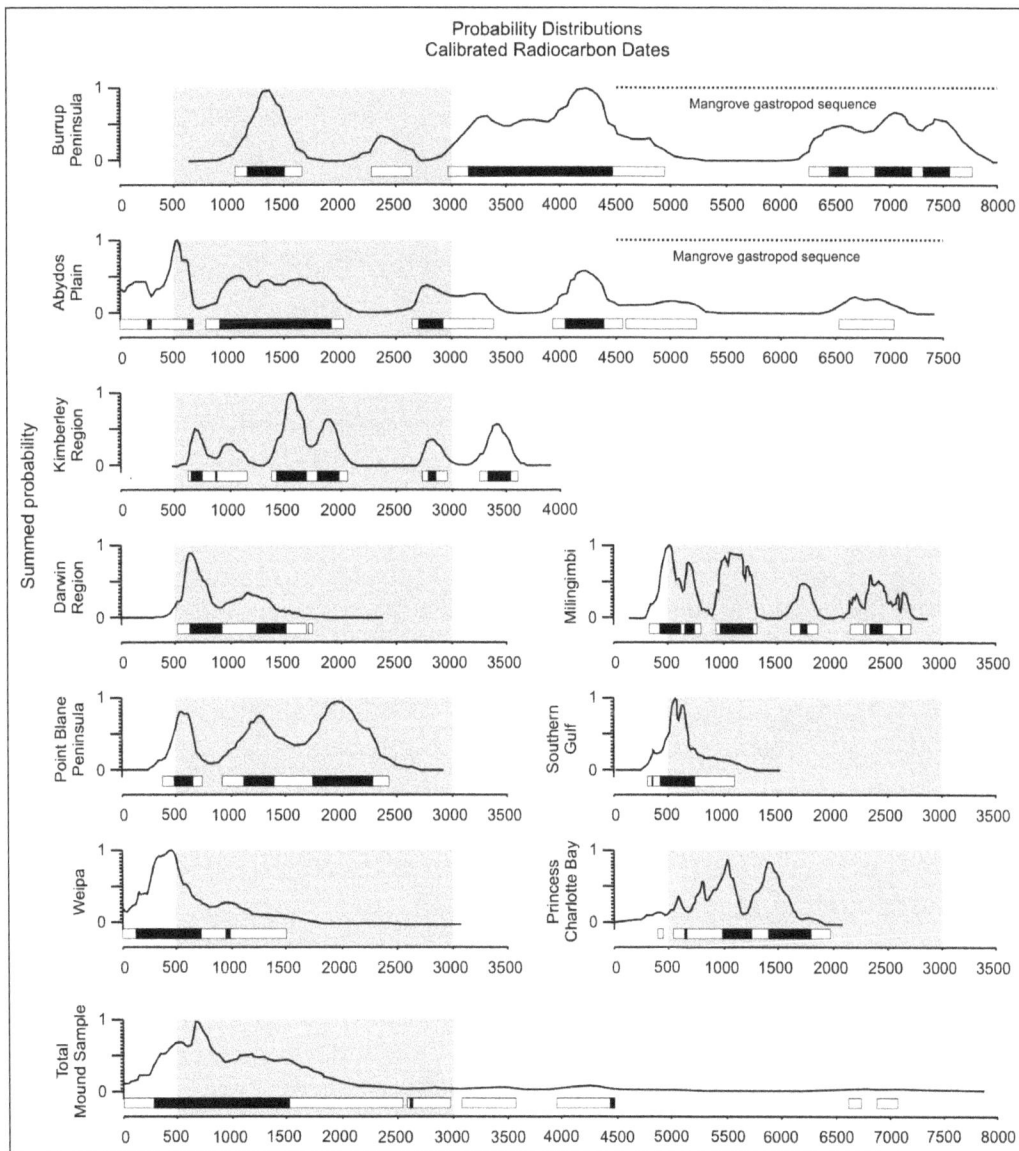

Figure 7.2: Comparison of the calibrated radiocarbon summed probability distributions (BP) from *Anadara granosa* dominated mound deposits in coastal regions across northern Australia (grey shading indicates principal phase of mound formation).

In explaining long-term economic change, and particularly where the aim is to gain an insight into *A. granosa* mound formation, the focus of research needs to be placed on the analysis of trends in prehistoric resource exploitation through time. What is required in an archaeological study of this type, therefore, is the analysis of relative changes in patterns of resource exploitation and their relationship to environmental factors (Bailey 1981a:13). While ideally this should be based on localised changes in the environment, in the absence of detailed local palaeoenvironmental data, information from the broader north Australian and Indo-Pacific region is used to contextualise regional variation in the nature and timing of resource exploitation. It has been suggested that the main period of *A. granosa* dominated shell mound formation across northern Australia is chronologically confined to the period between approximately 3000–2000 BP and 800–500 BP (Hiscock and Faulkner 2006; Hiscock 2008; Brockwell *et al.* 2009; Faulkner 2009). A sample of 223 radiocarbon determinations from 121 shell mound sites situated in various locations across northern Australia (see Figure 7.2) are presented here to further investigate this chronological patterning, particularly relative to broadly known environmental changes during the mid-to-late Holocene. All the radiocarbon determinations are from *A. granosa* dominated shell mounds, and have been calibrated using CALIB 6.1.1 in order to ensure a robust comparison across broad regions. The currently available subregional ΔR values for these north Australian areas have been applied in calibration, with a value of 12±7 for Princess Charlotte Bay (Ulm 2006b), 74±78 for Weipa and the Southern Gulf (Ulm *et al.* 2010a), 55±98 for Blue Mud Bay (Ulm 2006b), 65±24 for Milingimbi and the Darwin Region (Brockwell *et al.* 2009), 58±17 for the Kimberley (O'Connor *et al.* 2010), and 70±70 for the Pilbara (Ulm 2006b). The probabilities for each location have been ranked and summed to find the 1σ (68.3%) and 2σ (95.4%) confidence intervals and the relative areas under the probability curve, with the total area under the probability curve normalised to one (e.g. Brockwell *et al.* 2009).

The patterns presented here, with regional chronological variability, confirm that the dominant phase of *A. granosa* shell mound formation across much of northern Australia occurs largely within the 3000 to 500 cal BP period. The chronological patterns currently available from the Darwin region, Milingimbi and Blue Mud Bay all fall neatly within this time period. From the southern coast of the Gulf of Carpentaria, specifically the Barbara Cove Mound on the Edward Pellew Islands and Bayley Point Mound on the mainland near Doomadgee (Robins *et al.* 1998; Sim and Wallis 2008), and Princess Charlotte Bay in north Queensland (Beaton 1985; Ulm and Reid 2000) there is some evidence from age determinations for mound formation after approximately 500 cal BP, although this is minor in terms of the overall distribution from both areas in addition to inherent error ranges in radiocarbon calibration. The sequences from Western Australia (the Burrup, Abydos Plain and Kimberley regions) demonstrate longer sequences, although the greater antiquity in these sites generally reflects the transition within the same sites from the mangrove gastropod *Terebralia* or *Telescopium* spp. dominated assemblages of the early Holocene (8000 to 6000 cal BP) to overlying *A. granosa* mounded deposits of the mid-to-late Holocene (after 4500 cal BP) (Clune and Harrison 2009). For Western Australia, O'Connor (1999) has highlighted a shifting chronological pattern, whereby a gradation in dates for the *A. granosa* dominated portions of the deposits move north along the coast, with a decline in mound formation around 1000 cal BP (O'Connor 1999; Clune 2002). Recently, Harrison (2009) has argued that mounds on the Abydos Plain near Port Hedland continued to be formed into the more recent past; however the anthropogenic origin of these deposits is ambiguous (see Sullivan *et al.* 2011). As noted above, the appearance of *A. granosa* mounds in the mid-to-late Holocene appears to relate to environmental change, with a shift in diet relative to habitat formation and/or replacement from mangrove-dominated shorelines (Burns 1994:10; O'Connor 1999; although see Veitch 1999a for a contrasting social argument). The Weipa area presents a markedly different chronological pattern in comparison with the other north Australian coastal regions (Morrison 2010). There is a major peak centred on 500 cal BP, with a significant proportion of the calibrated age ranges extending into the last 500 years. It has previously been argued that the cessation of shell mound formation across the north of Australia occurred between 800 and 500 years ago due to changing environmental and ecological conditions becoming less favourable for *A. granosa* (Hiscock and Faulkner 2006; Hiscock 2008; Brockwell *et al.* 2009; Faulkner 2009). In response, it has been suggested that this generalised explanation is less applicable when focussing on specific regions across north Australia, with particular reference to the patterns seen within the Weipa area (Shiner and Morrison 2009:53–54; Morrison 2010; Ulm 2011). This is undoubtedly the case given the recent chronological evidence provided by Morrison's (2010) research. The localised persistence of habitats suitable for *A. granosa* within the Weipa area may go some way to explaining this distinct chronological pattern.

Even given the variability in regional chronologies exhibited in the Western Australian and Weipa sites, the major period of mound formation across the northern coast occurs between 3000 and 500 years ago. With broadly similar patterns of foraging reorganisation occurring in widely separated geographic areas, it would appear that broader scale processes of environmental change were indeed one of the primary causes behind economic change on the coast of northern Australia during the late Holocene (see Figure 7.3). While there are regional differences in the timing and nature of late Holocene changes in the coastal foraging economy, this almost certainly relates to localised environmental conditions occurring within broader patterns of climatic and environmental change. In general, however, there appears to be a strong correlation between shifting patterns in human economic activity relative to overall Holocene climatic and environmental parameters across northern Australia (O'Connor 1999; Faulkner 2006; Bourke *et al.* 2007; Morrison 2010). The timing of mound deposition across much of northern Australia, with those exceptions noted here, varies to only a minor degree. This suggests that the timing and nature of sand and mud flat development, creating suitable habitats for the proliferation of molluscan species, in particular *A. granosa*, occurred in broadly similar ways. There are a number of optimal environmental conditions required for the establishment and proliferation of *Anadara granosa* shell beds (see also discussion in Bourke *et al.* 2007). This species naturally occurs in large estuarine mudflats that are bordered on the landward margin by mangrove forests. It thrives within the comparatively calm conditions afforded by shallow inlets or bays, particularly with a sub-stratum of fine, soft, flocculent mud (Pathansali and Soong 1958:27). The three most important factors for shell bed establishment are the nature of the substrate, salinity levels, and slope of bed. The optimal habitat for *A. granosa* needs to be protected from strong wave action, and situated outside the mouth of estuaries and tidal creeks, with a salinity range between 18 to 30 parts per thousand (Pathansali 1966:91). Following the marine transgression, more extensive mangrove forests developed on low relief shorelines bordering estuaries and tidal flats within broad shallow embayments (Woodroffe *et al.* 1986, 1988). Regardless of the timing and extent of this phase across northern Australia, the structure of environments within these embayments was broadly similar. While sedimentation continued throughout this phase, with the cessation of the large mangrove swamps and the transition into the sinuous phase of progradation along the river systems, the level of coastal progradation appears to have accelerated markedly between approximately 4000 and 2000 BP (Woodroffe *et al.* 1986). In combination with the slow pattern of sea level recession, continued fluvial and marine sedimentation within these former shallow embayments provided the intertidal mudflats suitable for *A. granosa* shell beds. On the Point Blane Peninsula, based on the radiocarbon estimates from the two sites located within the most northerly cluster of mounds closest to the mouth of the Dhuruputjpi River in Grindall Bay, the establishment of the appropriate habitats and of the *A. granosa* shell beds likely occurred at approximately 2500 BP. Significantly, this approximate age is the same as that proposed for the Darwin Region by Bourke (2000:325).

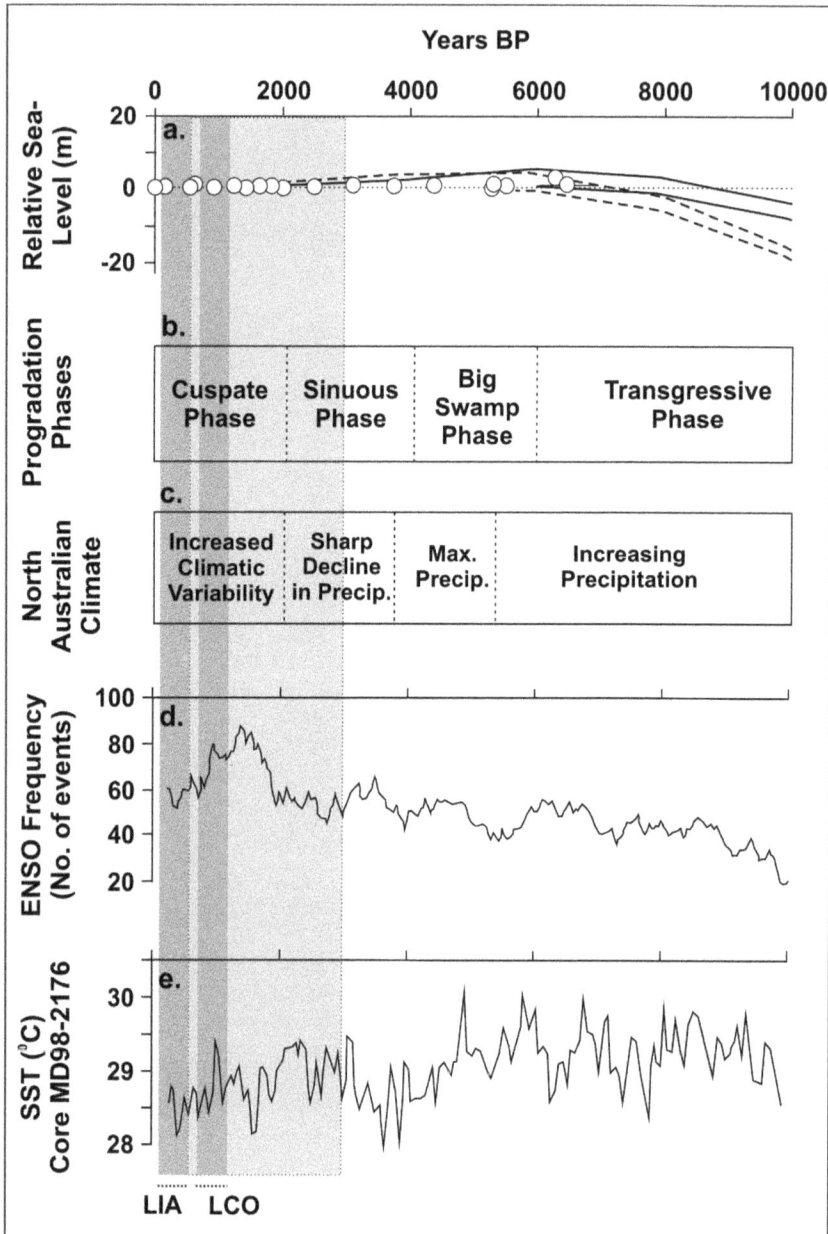

Figure 7.3: Holocene palaeoenvironmental patterns for Australasia and the Indo-Pacific contrasted with the major period of mound formation (3000 to 500 BP) across northern Australia; darker grey shading indicates Little Ice Age and Little Climatic Optimum.

Source: Data derived from: (a) Nakiboglu *et al.* 1983; (b) Woodroffe *et al.* 1986; (c) Shulmeister 1992, 1999; (d) Gagan *et al.* 2004; (e) Brijker *et al.* 2007.

These broad environmental patterns help to define the reasons for the appearance of *A. granosa*, and by extension the appearance of mounds, across northern Australia. A similar line of evidence can be used to explain the variations in the use of the Point Blane Peninsula highlighted by the radiocarbon estimates, site morphology and distribution, and differential use of resources through time. The general climatic pattern suggests that following the period of maximum effective precipitation between approximately 5000 and 3500 BP, often referred to as the Holocene environmental optimum (Kershaw 1983, 1995; Gagan *et al.* 1994; Shulmeister 1999:83; Gagan and Chappell 2000:44), there was a period of reduced interannual variability and a sharp decline in effective precipitation, beginning around 3500 BP and ending somewhere between 2500 and 2000 BP (Chappell 2001:177). There is also a body of evidence in support of high variability in late Holocene precipitation across north Australia (Clarke *et al.* 1979; Lees *et al.* 1990; Shulmeister 1992; Shulmeister and Lees 1992). Interestingly, the major period of mound building on the Point Blane Peninsula falls within the period of increased climatic variability between 2500 BP and the present, following the sharp reduction in effective precipitation. While perhaps not being a major reason for the intensive use of *A. granosa*, the mass collection of this resource may have helped to buffer coastal populations against climatic instability during this time. Within this late Holocene period of climatic variability, spanning the period from 2500–2000 BP to the present, there appear to be several punctuated phases of rapid climatic change, as well as higher levels of aridity in tropical areas (between approximately 1200 and 1000 BP, and 600 to 150 BP). This period of higher aridity is supported by a peak in ENSO activity between 1500 and 1000 BP (Gagan *et al.* 2004:135; Jones and Mann 2004). These two late Holocene phases of climate change correspond with several possible phases of behavioural change noted in the archaeological record on the Point Blane Peninsula (Bourke *et al.* 2007; Faulkner in press). There is evidence for a warm dry (relative to today) period about 1200 to 700 BP in low latitudes named the Little Climatic Optimum (or Medieval Warm Period), followed by a period of anomalously cold, dry conditions referred to as the Little Ice Age between approximately 600 to 100 BP (Nunn 2000:716). Following a phase of a higher climatic instability and aridity between 1200 and 1000 BP, the transition between the Little Climatic Optimum and the Little Ice Age was marked by rapid cooling and two stages of sea level fall throughout the Pacific Basin at approximately 650 BP and 500 BP (Nunn 1998, 2000). The changes noted in resource use and the potential decrease in occupation intensity in Grindall Bay occurs between approximately 1009 and 584 cal BP. Importantly, Hendy *et al.* (2002) have also suggested that conditions in the tropical southwest Pacific during the Little Ice Age were consistently more saline than present, largely between approximately 500 and 200 BP. There are a number of implications for this pattern relative to the evidence of *A. granosa* valve size and possible decrease in economic activity in Grindall Bay. Rapid climate change may well have adversely affected the *A. granosa* shell beds by altering the environmental parameters for optimal habitat conditions, which at best would have decreased their productivity and viability in conjunction with the patterns of long-term intensive exploitation previously outlined, and at worst destroyed the shell beds entirely. In addition, an increase in aridity may have affected the distribution and availability of freshwater within the study area, which may have contributed to the need for economic reorganisation during this phase.

Between 584 and 526 cal BP, there is a clear period of *A. granosa* population rebound/recovery and proliferation in the area, corresponding with a final phase of intensive exploitation and mound building. A similar argument to that presented above for the commencement of mound building across northern Australia is suggested here for the cessation of mound building on the Point Blane Peninsula. Changes in environmental and climatic conditions approximately 800 to 500 years ago, depending on regional variation in the timing of these changes, correlates with the cessation of mound building across several north Australian coastal areas. The termination of mounding on the Point Blane Peninsula relates to the effective removal of suitable habitats for *A. granosa*, a change that resulted in this species either disappearing entirely, or occurring in very low densities in northern Australia as seen at present (Bourke *et al.* 2007). There are a number of interrelated environmental and climatic factors that contributed to the disappearance of the habitats and conditions suitable for the *A. granosa* biomass at this time. As noted by Bourke *et al.* (2007:97) continuing processes of sedimentation would have gradually changed the gradient of the coastal plain, eventually reducing tidal inundation and freshwater input (Woodroffe *et al.* 1986), leading to changing conditions for *A. granosa* (see also Chappell and Grindrod 1984; Beaton 1985 and Bailey 1999 for similar arguments). A further factor that may explain the decline of *A. granosa* is the sustained accretion of the mudflats and subsequent colonisation by mangroves, increasing the elevation of the substratum and gradually isolating the shell beds from tidal movement (Macintosh 1982:13). There also appear to have been changes in sea levels and salinity levels at this time that would have had a significant impact on the large *A. granosa* beds. The effects of these climatic changes do not appear to have been geographically limited, as distinct cultural changes have been observed across a number of other areas worldwide. These changes include variability in population growth, population dislocations and changes in settlement patterns, urban abandonment, state collapse, increasing conflict and the cessation of long-distance trade (e.g. Larson and Michaelsen 1990; Raab and Larson 1997; Jones *et al.* 1999; Nunn 2000, 2003; de Menocal 2001; Field 2004; Bourke *et al.* 2007). This evidence contradicts the idea that there is little significant correlation between environmental change and changes in the Holocene archaeological record (e.g. Barker 1999:120), and these examples reinforce the notion that there are significant implications of environmental and climatic change for human behaviour, particularly when viewed as an interactive process. These patterns of change through time also have implications for previous interpretations of the role of mounds in the structure of coastal economies, the intensity of molluscan resource exploitation, and potential variability in population size and levels of mobility.

While a number of hypotheses have been suggested to explain the construction of shell mounds across northern Australia, particularly contrasting arguments over low-level economic (Jones 1975:25; Bailey 1975a, 1983, 1994, 1999; Cribb 1996; Bourke 2000) or higher-intensity ceremonial causes for this behaviour (Bourke 2000, 2002, 2005; Morrison 2003; Clune and Harrison 2009), these explanations have largely been based on directly interpreting these sites with the use of ethnographies. Much of this work has used data on human behaviour derived from the ethnoarchaeological research of Meehan (1982) in northern-central Arnhem Land. This direct application of more recent observations of foraging behaviour can be problematic in this context, as *A. granosa*-dominated shell mounds do not correspond with any one of the midden types defined by Meehan (1982:168), a factor she herself noted in her discussion of the shell mounds in the Blyth River region. In addition, the interpretation of mound sites as reflecting ceremonial activity relies heavily on the ethnographic data for large-scale social gatherings in northern Australia drawn from a relatively wide area, as well as perceived differences in the cultural rules of discard (see for example Frazer 1937; Thomson 1949; Warner 1969; Elkin 1978). These arguments have drawn on historical and anthropological descriptions of Aboriginal peoples' perception of place and their connection to religious and political beliefs (Hiscock and Faulkner 2006). The analogous use of post-contact ethnographic records in this way heavily implies that there were several thousand years of cultural continuity across much of northern Australia, although it should be noted that based on Morrison's (2010) research, the Weipa patterns may suggest otherwise for that region. If this were true, then why is it that very few of the explanations offered by Indigenous people for these sites relate to ceremonial activity? Furthermore, if the construction of these sites was the result of widespread large-scale ceremonial activity, how can we account for the high degree of variability in the explanations that have been provided? In fact, the structure of the environment and differences in the availability and abundance of resources prior to this time may preclude the direct use of ethnographic analogy, particularly in many of the regions in which shell mounds occur. This is largely due to the fact that economic behaviours, as observed ethnographically, are based on the contemporary structure of the environment and climate, and particularly on recent patterns of seasonal resource density and availability.

Further to the issue regarding ceremonial arguments for shell mound formation, these kinds of interpretations often refer to the observations of Meehan (1982:66) and Warner (1969:463) regarding a relationship between intensified periods of mollusc harvesting and ceremonial activities. These observations have been cited by Bourke (2005), Clune and Harrison (2009). Morrison (2003) and Harrison (2009) in support of the interpretation of large, single species shell mounds as sites associated with ceremonial gatherings. The lack of species diversity in the *A. granosa* mounds is used as evidence to support the suggestion that shell mound composition should be more variable, incorporating a wider range of marine and terrestrial resources, if occupation was longer-term in nature. This argument essentially hinges predominantly on the position that *A. granosa* was not seasonally available in large numbers. Therefore if mound formation occurred over longer periods of time, then taxonomic composition would be more variable due to seasonal changes in *A. granosa* availability in the local environment, in combination with associated shifts in exploitation strategies (Morrison 2003:2; Harrison 2009:73). It is important to note that while Meehan (1982) does indicate an increase in mollusc harvesting during ceremonial gatherings, she also makes the point that, even in the recent past in the Blyth River area, *A. granosa* continued to be collected throughout the year and served as a staple resource (Meehan 1982:77). With reference to the relative proportion of mollusc species and morphological differences between the more recent horizontally spread middens and prehistoric mounded deposits, Meehan (1982:117, 168) also suggests that the mounds actually reflect different foraging behaviours to those seen ethnographically. In some respects, these differences have also been highlighted by Bourke (2000:282) in noting that the absence of specific resources from mound sites, such as dugong, turtle and magpie geese, may be due to the unsuitability of local environmental conditions for these animals at the time that the mound deposits were formed.

Importantly, Todd (1991:232) has noted that differences in seasonal resource structures in the past may well have permitted systems of use by humans that were very different from those employed later and documented ethnographically. This also relates to changing environmental conditions, particularly long-term patterns of change. Based on the archaeological data obtained from the shell mounds on the Point Blane Peninsula, an alternative hypothesis can therefore be proposed, whereby coastal foragers operated within a distinctly different economic pattern during the period of *A. granosa* mound accumulation to that seen historically, with medium-sized groups of people regularly and intensively exploiting shell beds. This model is based on the inter- and intra-site chronological patterns, the observed differences in site density and morphology, and the focussed and intensive exploitation of *A. granosa* over a long period of time (e.g. Hiscock 2008; Faulkner 2009, in press). An alternative suggestion, therefore, is that the observable differences between shell mounds and ethnographically observed foraging behaviour, patterns of discard and site function, and the resultant patterning of cultural midden material within the landscape relates to variability in settlement strategies and resource exploitation, patterns of mobility and population size between the pre-contact and historic periods. These differences are masked to a certain degree where the ethnographies are relied upon to interpret mound deposits, and where it is assumed that patterns of settlement, resource exploitation, levels of mobility and population size have been constant through time. The archaeological evidence from the Point Blane Peninsula suggests that the shell mounds within the study area are not consistent with either continuous low-level harvesting or sporadic high intensity harvesting of *A. granosa*, but in drawing in the evidence from non-mounded shell deposits, are instead more indicative of long-term, focussed and intensive resource exploitation and occupation. More broadly, the variability across the peninsula suggests that the identified occupation phases may relate to the differential and localised availability of other resources in the area through time, particularly water and vegetable foods. This is particularly relevant given the increase in ENSO activity and associated variability in precipitation within the last 3000 years. These interpretations potentially indicate a more constant, intensive exploitation of this resource than observed in the recent past (as also suggested by Clune 2002 and more recently Morrison 2010).

The various suggestions relating to mounding behaviour, particularly the contrasting interpretations of ceremonial activity, low-level economic or the suggestion made here of focussed and intensive exploitation, can be assessed relative to the intensity of foraging and shell size variability. Unfortunately, other than research undertaken in the Darwin and Weipa regions, few detailed metrical studies on *A. granosa* from shell mound deposits are available to form a comparison with the data outlined here. Seasonal, low-intensity economic exploitation by small mobile groups and relatively sporadic, higher-intensity foraging by large groups for ceremonial purposes (although Harrison and Clune 2009 suggest annual harvesting) would place a certain amount of pressure on the natural *A. granosa* populations. The expectation would be that we would see indications of resource depression within single deposits, but not over the longer-term pattern as populations would be able to recover due to the high fecundity and recruitment rates characteristic of *A. granosa*. Patterns of intra-site valve size decrease in the Darwin region mounds have been interpreted by Bourke (2000, 2002) as reflecting predation pressure during individual site formation, although not to the point where there was a long-term impact on the shell beds. For the Kwamter mound site in Weipa, north Queensland, Bailey (1993:10) interprets the size frequency pattern as showing no evidence of sustained size decrease typical of over-exploitation, and therefore concludes that the archaeological samples are reflective of a mollusc population subjected to continuous, but not overly excessive, levels of human predation. The Kwamter data is based on a total site pattern, and while it indicates a population subject to human harvesting, size-frequency data presented at such a coarse scale does not allow for detailed evaluation of variability in valve size through time. For this particular species, the longer-term patterns are essential for assessing potential resource depression given high fecundity (see Faulkner 2009 and in press for this argument regarding longer-term analysis of *A. granosa* human predation). Data obtained from the base, middle and surface of the Hope Inlet mound deposits provides more information on valve size variability (Bourke 2000, 2002). When ordered chronologically, these data indicate a significant decline in mean valve length from 35 to 30mm during the earlier phase ($t = 780.71$, $d.f. = 2519$, $p < 0.001$), followed by a period of relative stability with mean lengths of approximately 30mm. Following a period of possible population recovery, there is a subsequent significant decline in size to approximately 500 BP ($t = -312.19$, $d.f. = 1413$, $p < 0.001$), when mounding appears to cease in the region. These patterns are similar in many respects to that seen on the Point Blane Peninsula, and would appear to indicate significant predation pressure throughout these sequences. The suggestion here is not that all regions containing *A. granosa*-dominated mounds will demonstrate the same patterns as presented in these analyses, but rather that metrical analyses need to be considered in detail as a possible way to disentangle aspects of human behaviour that may be related to variability in exploitation intensity.

The role of molluscs in coastal economies

Following from the final point made above, one issue that has divided most researchers investigating coastal hunter-gatherer economies is the value of coastal resources and habitats to human populations, particularly the importance of molluscan resources in the diet. The vast quantities of shell that are sometimes found in archaeological deposits, in addition to apparent abundance and ease of collection of marine molluscs, have stimulated interest in the place of these resources in human economies. For example, in interpreting shell deposits in the archaeological record, some researchers proposed that coastal habitats were only rich on a seasonal basis, and that despite representing large volumes of material archaeologically, molluscan resources may only represent a minor, if regular and seasonally reliable, portion of the diet (Bailey 1975a, 1975b; Cohen 1977; Meehan 1977, 1982; Osborn 1977; Parkington 1981; Beaton 1985). Following this position, others (most notably Perlman 1980; Yesner 1980; Rowly-Conwy 1983; Erlandson

1988, 1994) have suggested that coastal resources, and particularly molluscs, played a highly significant dietary role, and may have been 'protein staples' when other meat was unavailable, predominantly in areas with carbohydrate-rich plant food.

There are a number of difficulties involved in assessing the role of molluscan resources in human diets. As noted by Newsome *et al.* (2004:1102), inherent sampling and preservational biases make it difficult to quantify past human diets, especially in coastal areas where people had access to a wide range of marine and terrestrial food sources. In many cases, only a small sample of the site is excavated, providing a relatively limited representation of the range and/or quantity of faunal material (Mannino and Thomas 2002:465). Based on preservational factors, it is also often assumed that the dominance of molluscs in midden deposits signifies a gross over-representation of their dietary importance, with other non-molluscan faunal material being substantially under-represented (Hobson and Collier 1984; Bourke 2000:256; and discussions in Collier and Hobson 1987). While it is difficult to estimate from the archaeological data the relative contribution of molluscan and non-molluscan resources, it is still possible to investigate patterns of resource use and suggest possible interpretations based on the data at hand. The relative absence of non-molluscan fauna recovered from the excavated sites on the Point Blane Peninsula has been interpreted in economic terms here as reflecting a foraging pattern focussed on the exploitation and discard of molluscs. While this pattern may be a product of differential preservation or issues of sample recovery, the comparative lack of fauna, particularly terrestrial fauna (other than reptile), on the Point Blane Peninsula, can also be explained as a product of differential landscape and resource structure. As the study area is a peninsula, the dominant resources, particularly prior to the formation of the wetland areas, were located within the coastal zone. Interpretations presented for the Darwin region contrast with this idea (Bourke 2000:251), however it must be noted that this region would have contained a greater variety of habitats, and by extension a greater variety of available faunal resources. Bourke (2000:256–7) also suggests that the presence and range of non-molluscan faunal remains in the Darwin region sites indicates that a wide range of resources were clearly exploited, albeit resources that are much less visible archaeologically. Further to this point, given the probable level of preservation and bone decay, she proposed that these data approximate the ethnographically recorded economies of northern Australia. Bourke suggested that the data does not support the notion that the function of these deposits solely reflects the gathering and cooking of molluscs, and that the range of faunal remains in each site suggests a home-base aspect, similar to that proposed by Meehan (1982, 1988a). While the range of non-molluscan fauna present in the Darwin Harbour mound sites are consistent with the type of resources exploited ethnographically, the relative quantities, or proportions, are not. The values reported for that region are similar to those reported for the sites on the Point Blane Peninsula (see Chapter 4).

Even given that vertebrate fauna may well be under-represented in midden and mound deposits, they do appear to form a particularly minor component of the excavated assemblages from the Point Blane Peninsula. As has been posited by a number of other researchers for Australian contexts (e.g. Walters *et al.* 1987:92; McNiven 1989:46; Morrison 2010:308–9) it is suggested here that the paucity of vertebrate remains in the shell deposits from the Point Blane Peninsula cannot be explained by taphonomic factors or recovery processes alone (see Chapters 3 and 4), but is more likely to be a reflection of a limited range of subsistence activities. This interpretation, principally regarding the *A. granosa* shell mounds and as discussed in Chapter 4, is also supported by similar observations from mounds noted in other regions, particularly with the work of Morrison (2010) and Veitch (1996). While differential preservation is undoubtedly a contributing factor in combination with the analysis of only the 6mm residue in this study, the comparative lack of hard skeletal elements, such as teeth or otoliths, suggests that vertebrate fauna may not have been as an important part of coastal economies compared with the more recent past. This is particularly relevant for the period of mound formation in northern Australia, and has implications for the use of ethnographic data to infer dietary contributions. One of the main discrepancies between the ethnographic and archaeological records is the change in shell discard patterns over time. The ethnographies suggest a change in practices of shell discard from mollusc consumption, resulting in low, horizontally spread out middens rather than the large shell mounds that accumulated before living memory (Bourke 2000:280, 2005:40). Similar differences between the ethnographic and archaeological records have been reported from the Pacific Coast of North America. Based on these data, it has been suggested that it is not appropriate to use ethnographic models to uncritically interpret data from prehistoric sites, and that the differences observed between the ethnographic and archaeological datasets have implications for models of subsistence practice, settlement patterns and seasonal rounds (Moss and Erlandson 1995:29).

Based on this and previous discussions relating to environmental change and variability in the use of resources and habitats, it is highly likely that the contribution of molluscs to the economy follows no single pattern. In fact, the emphasis on molluscan resources probably varied considerably through time and space, and at inter- and intra-regional levels (see for example Erlandson 1988:107; Jones 1991:429, 436; Yesner *et al.* 2003:289; Jerardino 2010). In general terms, the archaeological data from the Point Blane Peninsula suggest that there were quite dramatic differences in the use of resources through time. The period between 2287 and 526 cal BP appears to have been one of quite intensive molluscan exploitation, as evidenced by the spatial and chronological density of shell mounds in the area. After 526 cal BP, with the disappearance of suitable habitats for *A. granosa* in the area, the structure of the economy appears to more closely approximate that of the pre-contact period directly preceding the period during which the historic evidence and ethnographic records were derived, with a decreased use of molluscs evidenced by changes in shell discard practices and habitat use. As observed by Bailey (1975b:45), it is quite clear that the occurrence of large shell mounds alone cannot be taken as sufficient evidence either of prolonged occupation, or an annual economy primarily dependent on molluscs. On the other hand, ecological data suggest that molluscs, and particularly bivalves, are capable of yielding very high output under specific conditions. The possibility that molluscan resources were a dominant component of the diet during the mound period cannot be excluded, as there were some environments dominated by molluscs and largely devoid of other resources, such as islands or peninsulas (Bailey 1975b:58). While this statement correlates well with the data from the study area, it may be possible to extend the premise to other areas containing mounded shell deposits, as these sites are often located in areas that would also have been characterised by high resource biomass (Perlman 1980:272; Rowland 1994b:155; Mannino and Thomas 2002:465). More importantly, molluscan resources may have become more significant where larger-bodied faunal resources were not in abundant enough supply, a situation not uncommon to coastal regions (Glassow and Wilcoxon 1988:47; Erlandson 2001:294; Mannino and Thomas 2002). Provided that adequate water and plant resources were available in the area to offset the effects of protein poisoning (see discussions by Speth and Spielmann 1983; Speth 1987; Noli and Avery 1988), the proliferation of *A. granosa* in the late Holocene may well have enabled hunter-gatherers in coastal areas to refocus their subsistence activities to take advantage of an abundant and seemingly reliable resource.

Implications for population size and mobility

Using archaeological data to assess changes in population size and levels of mobility in hunter-gatherer groups is extremely difficult. Frequently used markers of cultural and demographic change include deviations through time in the rate of site accumulation, both in numbers of sites and deposition of stone artefacts. Interpretations of regional cultural change in population demography or social organisation have also been derived in similar ways through midden analyses, with emphasis on discard rates of shell and/or the relative frequency of molluscan taxa through time (e.g. Allen and Barton n.d.:88, 104–6; Schrire 1982:233–4). These archaeological indicators are often interpreted at a regional, or local, scale as evidence of changing land- and resource-use patterns, including population increase or redistribution (Kelly 1992:56; Attenbrow 2004:1). As a complicating factor, there are a range of other behaviours that may just as easily account for these kinds of changes in sites and artefacts. For example, they could be the result of the re-organisation of habitation patterns and subsistence strategies, including the adoption of different mobility patterns in the face of environmental change (Attenbrow 2004:1–2), as well as simply reflecting changes in the frequency of re-occupation in a specific locality (Davidson 1990:44; Kelly 1992:56).

The use of accumulation rates to infer changes in population size and mobility is problematic for a number of reasons (as also discussed in Chapter 6). Using only two or three radiocarbon estimates to calculate the rate of site accumulation, as is often the case for shell deposits in northern Australia, is not an accurate measure as it does not take into account variations in the history of site formation (Stein *et al.* 2003:310). In addition, the established convention of small area excavation in Australia for these sites, generally between 1m^2 and 0.5m^2, while providing a decent sample to evaluate the relative densities of material from the sites, does not enable interpretation of overall site formation. In effect, this method may only represent the rate of accumulation for the excavated area, due to both horizontal and vertical variations in deposition within the site (see for example Mitchell 1993; Hiscock 1997, 2005). Further problems can occur where accumulation rates are used in conjunction with the ethnographic data to model changes in population size. Importantly, different combinations of behavioural elements can be consistent with statistically indistinguishable radiocarbon estimates and rapid accumulation of these deposits, particularly when extrapolating population size and levels of mobility (largely seasonal) from a combination of archaeological and ethnographic data (Bailey 1975b:57; Meehan 1982a:166; Bourke 2000:346). Following this point, it is becoming more widely accepted that ethnographic observations of population density and mobility are poor indicators of pre-contact patterns. As noted by both Beaton (1990:28, 33) and Peterson (1971:241), population limiting factors may occur at intervals beyond the observational period of the ethnographer, and even where there are detailed ethnographic indications of population size relative to the subsistence base (e.g. Meehan 1982; Bird *et al.* 2004), our perception of population trajectory leading into that ethnographic pattern is often inadequate. Essentially, the scales of observation between archaeological data and ethnographic observation do not correspond, and therefore sample points of short duration cannot be used to make inferences regarding the causes or properties of longer-term processes (Winterhalder *et al.* 1988:320–2; Erlandson 2001:295). One way forward is to contextualise those models of varying population size and patterns of mobility suggested for late Holocene northern Australia within the established interpretations of foraging behaviour and the potential economic productivity within a given area, in addition to observing established environmental and climatic patterns. Changes in climate, resources and habitats are not simply background information of little relevance when examining potential changes in population size and patterns of settlement, but must be considered as a constantly shifting set of problems and opportunities, altering the framework for human behaviour (Koike 1986:27; Haberle and David 2004:177). For example, climatic changes on decadal to century time scales can have devastating consequences on human populations by disrupting both resource exploitation and settlement patterns. In effect, these climatic forces call for an ongoing process that probably involves demographic expansion, or contraction, at various scales (Haberle and David 2004:177).

In many respects, this kind of approach is entirely dependent on the scale of analysis; decadal scale patterns are almost impossible to discern from the archaeological record given the error margins in dating methods (although see Morrison 2010 for a different perspective). A sample of archaeological sites containing any type of subsistence data, large enough for reliable interpretation, often represents a palimpsest of activities ranging over a substantial period of time, and as such, is representative of average trends in human behaviour (Bailey 1981b:109). The long time scales of archaeological inquiry result in a situation where small-scale fluctuations are smoothed out. For example, aspects such as oscillating patterns of population pressure become a constant. Therefore, issues of scale affect research questions, particularly those directed at linear or uni-directional interpretations of behaviour (Bailey 1981b:108). This issue is particularly relevant for the work of Haberle and David (2004) in correlating the long-term climatic and archaeological data for the Cape York Peninsula. In acknowledging the generally accepted pattern of long-term increase in population size (for example Beaton 1985, 1990; Davidson 1990; White *et al.* 1990), it was suggested that increased social regionalism and socio-structural transformation followed a major and sustained population increase during the early-to-mid Holocene climatic optimum, with increases in human population tied to high biomass productivity in north Queensland by approximately 6000 BP. When natural levels of bio-production decreased and climatic variability increased during the late Holocene, larger regional populations began to fission into new and distinctively smaller land-owning and land-using groups around 3700 BP. Following this there was a broad-spectrum revolution on mainland Australia, with the use of smaller, intensive resources (such as seeds, molluscs and toxic plants). It was argued that this process of socio-structural and dietary innovation enabled an increase in human population to be sustained over the short- and long-term (Haberle and David 2004:172–7). This argument is similar in many respects to the 'broad-spectrum revolution' hypothesis proposed for Australia and other areas of the world (Flannery 1969; Cohen 1977; Lourandos 1980, 1983; Hayden 1981; Veitch 1996:85–6 1999b:60). In this case, it is argued that the archaeological record reflects a coherent pattern of more or less continuous population expansion, accommodated by progressive environmental and economic adaptations, such as a broadening diet and intensive exploitation of secondary resources, in conjunction with distinct cultural changes.

The main problem with this argument is that it can be interpreted in a way that glosses over the particular challenges posed to coastal groups during the mid-to-late Holocene resulting from those environmental and climatic changes previously outlined. The effects of changes to the environment following the marine transgression, possibly affecting the type, distribution and density of resources, may well have had dramatic effects on human population structures. As these processes would have continued for some time after sea level stabilisation, it is possible that population sizes may actually have been reduced as a result. The ongoing development of coastal habitats leading into the late Holocene created a situation where the establishment and relatively long-term proliferation of resources, such as *A. granosa*, may have enabled an increase in population size. This was possibly only a moderate increase as the available data are more suggestive of an increase in the intensity of resource exploitation and site deposition. This ties into the notion whereby any factor that reduces the environmental challenges that hunter-gatherers must face may lead to substantial population increases (Stiner and Munro 2002:206). While the intensive use of these resources may well signify a 'new, specialised and focussed subsistence strategy' (Haberle and David 2004:172) between approximately 3000 and 500 BP on the north Australian coast, it was not a pattern that continued into the present in most areas, and as such it was not a unidirectional or linear progression in human behaviour. The subsequent restructuring of the economy on the Point Blane Peninsula, and in other areas of coastal northern Australia, relates to a general decrease in biomass of coastal resources around 500 BP and extending into the more recent past. This pattern may well correspond with a decrease in population size (Hiscock 1986) or patterns of demographic reorganisation (Hiscock 1999:99–100).

Added to this, several researchers (e.g. Winterhalder *et al.* 1988:323; Stiner *et al.* 1999; Stiner *et al.* 2000; Boone 2002:12–5; Stiner and Munro 2002; Lupo and Schmitt 2005:347) have suggested that hunter-gatherer populations are liable to have characteristically fluctuating population sizes through time, largely based on the availability, density and distribution of resources. This argument relies on a strong relationship between overall carrying capacity, prey density and population density. People may well have responded to opportunities afforded by a productive marine coastal environment, rather than being forced to do so as a consequence of population pressure. It has also been argued that, instead of being a mere response to population growth occurring elsewhere, the adoption of coastal subsistence strategies can be a substantial causal factor behind population growth (Yesner 1987; Erlandson 2001:289; Mannino and Thomas 2002). Rather than population pressure, an alternative argument is that the increasing abundance of smaller bodied resources, such as molluscs, may have lead to a restructuring of foraging practices to focus on these resources. Related to the regional population density of the resource, and compared with larger bodied animals, the abundance and relative proximity of these resources would have increased the return rates from mass collecting relative to handling and processing (Madsen and Schmitt 1998:451–2; Lupo and Schmitt 2005:336).

Related to these possible variations in population size and foraging reorganisation, there are direct implications for patterns of settlement and levels of mobility, particularly given environmental changes and resource availability during the mid-to-late Holocene. Increasing population sizes may eventually lead to lower levels of mobility, or alternatively, as mobile populations become increasingly sedentary, their populations grow (Kelly 1992:58–9, 1998:19). As with evaluating variation in population size, assessing changes in mobility depends on the scale of analysis in conjunction with the use of ethnographic analogy. Long-term regional views of increasing sedentism throughout the Holocene do not take into account shorter-term fluctuations, and create an averaged, unidirectional pattern (Perlman 1985:48). The use of ethnographic data feeds into this model, particularly for the interpretation of the late Holocene archaeological record, where there has been an assumed, if not explicitly acknowledged, level of cultural continuity in patterns of settlement and seasonal mobility. This situation has arisen largely as a result of many archaeologists' tendency to think of mobility in terms of a continuum of residential mobility, from highly mobile to completely sedentary, but also possibly as a point of no return, a behavioural threshold from which more sedentary populations cannot return to a mobile lifestyle (Kelly 1992:50). In defining differing levels of mobility, Binford (1980) distinguished between residential mobility, the movement of the entire band or local group from one camp to another, and logistical mobility, foraging movements of individuals or small task groups out from, and back to, the residential camp (see also Kelly 1992). Added to this is the concept of territorial or long-term mobility, encompassing cyclical movements of a group of people among a set of territories, largely as a conservation measure, or as a response to subsistence stress. These differences are strongly linked to the subsistence base and related variations in demography, with low growth rates among groups with higher levels of long-term mobility.

The argument proposed here is similar for that previously outlined for possible changes in population size, largely due to the fact that, although many variables affect mobility, subsistence and foraging strategies are likely to be the primary ones (Perlman 1985; Kelly 1992:46). It is not possible to assess changes in population size and levels of mobility prior to 3000 BP on the Point Blane Peninsula due to the lack of archaeological evidence, based on the climatic and environmental data available for the region, however, it is possible that regional populations were smaller and more mobile, largely as a result of rising sea levels. These patterns may well have been maintained following sea level stabilisation, due to patchily distributed resources along the coastline, relative to ongoing processes of coastal habitat reorganisation. In line with changes to the organisation of the foraging economy and already hypothesised changes to the size of populations in the area following 3000 BP, the establishment of expansive sand and mud flats through progradation and sedimentary infill, and the proliferation of a reasonably stable and dependable resource, could very well have created a situation that enabled people to lower their levels of mobility. The fact that *A. granosa* is not as seasonally constrained as other resources is likely to have been a contributing factor to this pattern. The spatial and chronological density of shell mounds in Grindall Bay, in combination with the contemporary occurrence of lower-lying shell middens in Myaoola Bay, indicates that there were changes to both residential and logistical mobility. The suggestion made here is that these factors provided people with the opportunity to become semi-sedentary, rather than fully sedentary, during this time.

While the abundance of *A. granosa* may have permitted semi-sedentary occupation of some coastal areas during a period of relative climatic instability, other resources would also have been necessary to fulfil dietary requirements. Support for this hypothesis, while limited to a certain degree by the very small sample size, comes from the stone artefacts. All of the artefacts in the study area are predominantly of locally available raw materials, indicating a localised use of resources, a pattern that goes some way towards reinforcing the interpretation of semi-sedentary occupation for the area. Bourke (2000:140, 262–3) has noted a similar pattern in Darwin Harbour, where local stone dominates the assemblages during the period of mound formation, with an increase in exotic stone procurement after approximately 500 BP. This pattern suggests lower levels of mobility preceding 500 BP, corresponding with a reduction in trade and exchange of stone raw material. The important archaeological problem of distinguishing more permanently settled from seasonally settled occupations, as well as assessing the pressure, or intensity, of predation, may ultimately only be resolved with quantifiable measures that can determine seasonal and annual periods of occupation (Russo 1998:159). Russo (1998:148–9; see also Koike 1986:28) suggests that the use of modal size classes in archaeological shell analyses, and therefore an investigation of the population age structure, may be a useful measure of seasonal resource exploitation. This does not appear to be the case here, although this may relate to a combination of rapid site formation, chronological resolution, and the particular nature of *A. granosa* itself (e.g. rapid growth). This hypothesis could be resolved by examining incremental growth structures in combination with stable isotopic analyses as measures of seasonality (see for example Luebbers 1978; Lightfoot and Cerrato 1988; Milner 2001; Mannino *et al.* 2003; Jones *et al.* 2005; Stephens *et al.* 2008).

After approximately 526 cal BP, the dramatic change to the structure of the resource base on the Point Blane Peninsula may have been accompanied by a corresponding increase in levels of mobility and a decrease in population size. Evidence for this type of change has been noted in the archaeological records of other areas, particularly through the stone artefact assemblages (e.g. Hiscock 1986, 1999; Bourke 2000). With a reduction in the available resource biomass on the Point Blane Peninsula, the potential for the over-exploitation of intertidal resources may well have necessitated regular mobility for these resources to be sustainable. During this period, foraging behaviour and seasonal mobility began to more closely approximate the ethnographically observed patterns of high seasonal resource availability, which was possibly linked to the continuing development of wetland areas and shifting economic focus by people on the resources in these locations. In this case, the highly seasonal nature of resource availability would have required cyclical or episodic patterns of movement within broad coastal areas, or further afield into non-coastal areas (Yesner 1987:293; Mannino and Thomas 2002:467). While these are the general patterns for the study area, in effect, resource density and availability will exhibit a logistic population response, with human populations expanding and contracting accordingly. The relationship between forager and prey biomass is time dependent; it is consistent but it is not proportional, linear, or direct. Therefore, it is unlikely that a stable equilibrium and fixed relationship exists between forager and prey biomass (Winterhalder *et al.* 1988:320). For example, variations in the spatial distribution of both midden and mound sites between 2287 and 526 cal BP, in conjunction with the level of chronological variability observed within and between the mound sites, suggest that population size and levels of mobility would not have been stable within this period.

Concluding remarks: The ebb and flow of human behaviour

The issue of how much change and variability in economic and social systems occurred during the late Holocene in Blue Mud Bay is addressed here with a particular focus on the nature and structure of the archaeological record. In combination with data on environmental and climatic processes acting on the northern Australian coastline during the mid-to-late Holocene, these data have enabled a number of phases of economic reorganisation to be identified relative to the abundance and availability of specific resources. These phases also indicate that economic and social change during this period was multi-directional, rather than following a linear or progressive developmental model.

The suggestion here is that the *A. granosa*-dominated shell mounds on the Point Blane Peninsula are not consistent with either continuous low level harvesting or sporadic high intensity harvesting, but are consistent with a more focussed level of activity within the landscape. As such, this interpretation relates to coastal foragers operating within a distinctly different economic pattern during the period of *A. granosa* mound formation to that seen historically, with people regularly and intensively exploiting shell beds. Therefore, the observable differences between shell mounds and ethnographically observed foraging behaviour, patterns of discard and site function, and the resultant patterning of cultural midden material within the landscape relates to variability in settlement strategies and resource exploitation, patterns of mobility and population size between the pre-contact and historic periods. The ongoing development of coastal habitats leading into the late Holocene created a situation where the establishment and relatively long-term proliferation of resources, such as *A. granosa*, may have enabled a lowering of mobility levels and an increase in population size. This was possibly only a moderate increase, as the data are more suggestive of an increase in the intensity of resource exploitation and site deposition. The spatial and chronological density of shell mounds on the Point Blane Peninsula, in combination with the contemporary occurrence of lower lying shell middens on the opposite coastline, suggests that there were changes to both residential and logistical mobility. The suggestion is that these factors provided people with the opportunity to become semi-sedentary, rather than fully sedentary, during this time. The restructuring of the economy on the Point Blane Peninsula after approximately 526 cal BP relates to a general decrease in biomass of coastal resources extending into the more recent past. This pattern is interpreted here as corresponding with an increase in levels of mobility and a decrease in population size. With a reduction in the available resource biomass on the Point Blane Peninsula, the potential for the over-exploitation of intertidal resources may well have necessitated regular mobility for these resources to be sustainable. During this period, particularly following the cessation of mound formation, patterns of foraging and seasonal mobility began to more closely approximate the ethnographically observed type of organisation noted for the pre-Macassan contact period.

In interpreting the archaeological record from the Point Blane Peninsula in this way, it is also important to recognise the limitations of archaeological data, particularly in relation to economic and social systems. Due to processes of differential preservation of material, such as the breakdown of organic material or the post-depositional destruction or disturbance of sites, a complete record of past human behaviour is rarely, if ever, presented within the archaeological record. Archaeological data are therefore drawn, not from a complete body of information, but from the evidence that has survived. For example, the shell midden and mound sites recorded in the study area may represent a smaller proportion of the overall possible economy of people inhabiting this area throughout the late Holocene. For these reasons, interpretations of archaeological material are made carefully and objectively, based on the observable evidence. In recognising these restrictions, archaeological material of the kind found on the Point Blane Peninsula can still tell us a great deal about human behaviour. The diversity of the archaeological record indicates the range of activities carried out in the past, the intensity of occupation within an area, and the relative time span for occupation and use of the landscape. Archaeological research on the Point Blane Peninsula has identified significant patterns of economic and social change during the late Holocene, patterns that are often not recognised for other areas of coastal northern Australia. The most likely reason for this is the direct reliance on the ethnographies as an interpretive tool, and the scales of analysis between archaeology and ethnography simply do not match. Using ethnographies to directly interpret the archaeological record can lead to the depiction of prehistory as a generalised representation of the kind of behaviour recorded during the historic period. The process of analogical reasoning in this way leads to an interpretive model that relies more heavily on generalised ethnographic patterns than it does on archaeological evidence (Moss and Erlandson 1995:29). As a result, regional patterns of change and variability through time are often obscured, preventing the development of alternative or multiple versions of the past. By viewing the archaeological record as reflecting human-environmental interactive processes, an opportunity is provided in which change can be recognised in a number of ways. For example, differential focus on resources, variations in group size and levels of mobility can all be identified. It has also been shown that human-environment interactions are non-linear or progressive. The use of ethnographies does not often allow for this, as it assumes a continuum of behaviour from when the ethnographies were recorded into the more distant past. When it is acknowledged that the interaction of people with their environment is not a passive process, because neither human behaviour nor the environments that people inhabit are static, then the potential arises for multi-directional phases of human behaviour and change to be recognised.

Within the Blue Mud Bay region, shell mounds represent a broad phase of economic restructuring, one that was characterised by an intensive focus on specific resources and landscapes. These mounds represent variability in the intensity of molluscan exploitation and discard, rather than reflecting a continuation of the kind of foraging behaviour observed during the historic period. It would appear that it is only when these sites are placed within a strict ethnographic framework, and analysed in isolation from other archaeological evidence, that the interpretation of these sites becomes problematic. Interpretations often conform to the types of economic and social systems recorded during the historic period, regardless of the fact that shell mounds do not conform to any ethnographic pattern. As has been noted by Rowland (1999a:34), complex, non-linear relationships frequently occur between humans and their environments. As such, environmental explanations of cultural change need not be considered more, or less, deterministic than those that consider the role of social factors. In effect, the impacts of environmental variability will depend as much on the previous history, size and density, and adaptive strategies of a population as on the scale and duration of the environmental change itself (Rowland 1999a:34). The archaeological evidence presented here indicates that foraging behaviour on the coastal margins of the Point Blane Peninsula was indeed flexible and dynamic. Through time, people actively changed their foraging strategies to incorporate newly available or increasingly abundant species. Rather than being forced into molluscan exploitation through increasing population pressure (Veitch 1996:85-6, 1999b:60; Haberle and David 2004:177), the abundance of *A. granosa* between approximately

2287 and 526 cal BP may have enabled people to moderately increase population size while decreasing levels of mobility. During this period, the exploitation of molluscan resources was far more focussed and intensive than was observed during the historic period, contrary to the interpretations of a number of other researchers who have relied on the ethnographies to explain the role of molluscs within the diet (e.g. Bailey 1975a; Bourke 2000). Within this general pattern, variability in mound size and patterns of occupation are seen to reflect the differential variability in the availability of other resources in the area through time, inclusive of non-molluscan resources such as water and vegetable foods. Following the cessation of mound formation, there appears to have been a broadening or diversification of the diet. This increase in diet breadth appears to have been related to the disappearance of the reliable, productive molluscan resources, combined with the development of extensive wetland systems. A greater focus on a diversity of seasonally available resources from different terrestrial and aquatic habitats after 526 cal BP, the majority of which were seasonally constrained in their abundance and distribution, indicates that the nature of foraging and land-use were beginning to approximate the seasonal round of more recent observations. Tied to these changing patterns of resource exploitation are increased levels of mobility and a decrease in group size.

The arguments presented above are also relevant for countering the large-scale, continent-wide models of human behaviour, such as the 'Intensification' model. Lourandos and Ross (1994:59) have criticised the use of small-scale regional studies for identifying patterns of human behaviour, stating that challenging small components of the model ignores the general patterns that it explains. It has been shown by a number of other researchers (e.g. Hiscock 1986; Holdaway et al. 2002, 2005; Attenbrow 2004; Asmussen 2005; Ulm 2006a), however, that the only way to evaluate a model of this scope is an assessment on a regional basis. Regardless of the region in focus, all of these studies have demonstrated that the archaeological record of the late Holocene was a period of greater variability than had previously been thought. In addition, while there is a high degree of regional variability in the timing and nature of change, these studies have shown that many of these changes are neither linear, nor progressive. There was no clear trajectory in human behaviour from simple to complex, nor was there a unidirectional pattern of decreasing mobility or population growth. This suggests that the uncritical application of broad, low-resolution models to different regional contexts does not take into account the degree of variability in human behaviour that existed, an approach that is simplistic and essentially flawed. Following this point, it is suggested that the variability in resource exploitation, economic reorganisation and changes in population size and levels of mobility through time identified here may broadly apply to other coastal regions of northern Australia as a result of similar environmental and climatic changes. Given that the findings of this research are based on one area of eastern Arnhem Land, the potential for regional variability, and the possibility of comparable archaeological manifestations of different behaviours should not be ignored. This is particularly the case when this research is viewed in combination with the detailed archaeological studies undertaken by both Bourke (2000) and Morrison (2010). By the same token, given similar coastal environments and similar processes of Holocene environmental and climatic change along the north Australian coast, the possibility undoubtedly exists that, at a broad scale, shell mounds reflect similar processes in other areas. This is not to suggest that these patterns and interpretations can be extrapolated and simply applied to other regions across the north, particularly given the evidence for inter- and intra-regional variability in the archaeological record, but undoubtedly, the potential is there for re-evaluation of existing interpretations.

Based on the results presented here, what has been made abundantly clear is that there has been a greater degree of economic and social reorganisation during the late Holocene in coastal northern Australia than may have been previously been accepted. In acknowledging the complexity of human behaviour apparent within the Holocene archaeological record, as has also been seen in the chronological and spatial diversity from a number of other regional studies scattered across the continent, it is evident that local or regionally focussed studies must be conducted to provide the context for the 'bigger picture', not the other way around. Only in this way can the extent of human behavioural variability through time and space be adequately investigated.

References

Alexander, V.M. 2009. *One archaeologist's midden is another's shell mound: Defining the criteria for describing and classifying shell mounds.* Unpublished BA (Honours) Thesis. The University of Sydney, Sydney.

Allan, R., J. Lindesay and D. Parker 1996. *El Niño, Southern Oscillation and climatic variability.* CSIRO Australia, Collingwood.

Allen, H. and G. Barton n.d. *Ngarradj Warde Djobkeng: White Cockatoo Dreaming and the prehistory of Kakadu.* Oceania Monograph 37. University of Sydney, Sydney.

Allen, M.S. 2006. New ideas about Late Holocene climate variability in the Central Pacific. *Current Anthropology* 47: 521–535.

Ambrose, W. 1967. Archaeology and shell middens. *Archaeology and Physical Anthropology in Oceania* 2: 169–187.

Andrefsky, W. 1994a. Raw-material availability and the organization of technology. *American Antiquity* 59(1): 21–34.

_____. 1994b. The geological occurrence of lithic material and stone tool production strategies. *Geoarchaeology* 9(5): 375–391.

_____. 1998. *Lithics: Macroscopic approaches to analysis.* Cambridge Manuals in Archaeology. Cambridge University Press, Melbourne.

Andrus, C.F.T., D.E. Crowe, D.H. Sandweiss, E.J. Reitz and C.S. Romanek 2002. Otolith $\delta^{18}O$ record of mid-Holocene sea surface temperature in Peru. *Science* 295: 1508–1512.

Antczak, A., J.M. Posada, D. Schapira, M.M. Antczak, R. Cipriani, and I. Montano 2008. A history of human impact on the Queen Conch (*Strombus gigas*) in Venezuela. In A. Antczak and R. Cipriani (eds) *Early human impact on megamolluscs*, pp. 49–64. BAR International Series 1865. Archaeopress, Oxford.

Asmussen, B. 2005. *Dangerous harvest revisited: Taphonomy, methodology and intensification in the Central Queensland Highlands*, Australia. Unpublished PhD Thesis. The Australian National University, Canberra.

Attenbrow, V. 2004. *What's changing: Population size or land-use patterns? The archaeology of Upper Mangrove Creek, Sydney Basin.* Terra Australis 21. ANU E Press, Canberra.

Baez, P.R. and D.S. Jackson 2008. Exploitation of *loco, Concholepas concholepas* (Gastropoda: Muricidae), during the Holocene of Norte Semiarido, Chile. In A. Antczak and R. Cipriani (eds) *Early human impact on megamolluscs*, pp. 79–94. BAR International Series 1865. Archaeopress, Oxford.

Bailey, G.N. 1975a. *The role of shell middens in prehistoric economies.* Unpublished PhD Thesis. University of Cambridge, Cambridge.

_____. 1975b. The role of molluscs in coastal economies: The results of midden analysis in Australia. *Journal of Archaeological Science* 2: 45–62.

_____. 1977. Shell mounds, shell middens, and raised beaches in the Cape York Peninsula. *Mankind* 11(2): 132–143.

_____.1981a. Concepts of resource exploitation: Continuity and discontinuity in palaeoeconomy. *World Archaeology* 13(1): 1–15.

Bailey, G.N. 1981b. Concepts, time-scales and explanations of economic prehistory. In A. Sheridan and G.N. Bailey (eds) *Economic archaeology: Towards an integration of ecological and social approaches* pp. 97–117. BAR International Series 96. Archaeopress, Oxford.

_____. 1983. Problems of site formation and the interpretation of spatial and temporal discontinuities in the distribution of coastal middens. In P.M. Masters and N.C. Flemming (eds) *Quaternary coastlines and marine archaeology: Towards the prehistory of land bridges and continental shelves*, pp. 559–582. Academic Press, London.

_____. 1993. Shell mounds in 1972 and 1992: Reflections on recent controversies at Ballina and Weipa. *Australian Archaeology* 37: 1–18.

_____. 1994. The Weipa shell mounds: Natural or cultural? In M. Sullivan, S. Brockwell and A. Webb (eds) *Archaeology in the North: Proceedings of the 1993 Australian Archaeological Association Conference*, pp. 107–129. The North Australian Research Unit, The Australian National University, Darwin.

_____. 1999. Shell mounds and coastal archaeology in northern Queensland. In J. Hall and I.J. McNiven (eds) *Australian coastal archaeology*, pp. 105–112. ANH Publications. Department of Archaeology and Natural History, The Australian National University, Canberra.

Bailey, G.J, J. Chappell and R. Cribb 1994. The origin of *Anadara* shell mounds at Weipa, North Queensland, Australia. *Archaeology in Oceania* 29: 69–80.

Bailey, G.N. and A.S. Craighead 2003. Late Pleistocene and Holocene coastal palaeoeconomies: A reconsideration of the molluscan evidence from northern Spain. *Geoarchaeology: An International Journal* 18(2): 175–204.

Bailey, G., J. Barrett, O. Craig, and N. Milner 2008. Historical ecology of the North Sea Basin: An archaeological perspective and some problems of methodology. In T.C. Rick and J.M. Erlandson (eds) *Human impacts on ancient marine ecosystems: A global perspective*, pp. 215–242. University of California Press, Berkeley.

Bailey, G.N. and N. Milner 2008. Molluscan archives from European Prehistory. In A. Antczak and R. Cipriani (eds) *Early human impact on megamolluscs*, pp. 111–134. BAR International Series 1865. Archaeopress, Oxford.

Bamforth, D. 1986. Technological efficiency and tool curation. *American Antiquity* 51: 38–50.

Banning, E.B. 2002. *Archaeological survey*. Manuals in Archaeological Method, Theory and Technique. Springer, New York.

Barber, M. 2002. *Blue Mud Bay Project final report: Resource use and ecological knowledge at Yilpara (Bäniyala) Outstation. November 2002*. Unpublished report to the Northern Land Council.

_____. 2005. *Where the clouds stand: Australian Aboriginal relationships to water, place, and the marine environment in Blue Mud Bay, Northern Territory*. Unpublished PhD Thesis. The Australian National University, Canberra.

Barker, B. 1996. Maritime Hunter-Gatherers on the tropical coast: A social model for change. In S. Ulm, I. Lilley and A. Ross (eds) *Australian Archaeology '95: Proceedings of the 1995 Australian Archaeological Association Annual Conference*, pp. 31–43. Tempus 6. Anthropology Museum, University of Queensland, St Lucia.

_____. 1999. Coastal occupation in the Holocene: Environment, resource use and resource continuity. In J. Hall and I.J. McNiven (eds) *Australian coastal archaeology*, pp. 119–127. ANH Publications. Department of Archaeology and Natural History, Australian National University, Canberra.

_____. 2004. *The sea people: Late Holocene maritime specialisation in the Whitsunday Islands, Central Queensland*. Terra Australis 20. Pandanus Books, Research School of Pacific and Asian Studies, The Australian National University, Canberra.

Barz, R.K. 1977. *Some theoretical and practical aspects of midden sampling as applied to a site at St George's Basin, Jervis Bay, A.C.T.* Unpublished BA (Honours) Thesis. The Australian National University, Canberra.

Bayne, B. 1973. The responses of three species of bivalve mollusc to declining oxygen tension at reduced salinity. *Comparative Biochemistry and Physiology Part A: Physiology* 45: 793–806.

Beaton, J. 1985. Evidence for a coastal occupation time-lag at Princess Charlotte Bay (North Queensland) and implications for coastal colonisation and population growth theories for Aboriginal Australia. *Archaeology in Oceania* 20: 1–20.

_____. 1990. The importance of past population for prehistory. In B. Meehan and N. White (eds) *Hunter-Gatherer demography: Past and present*, pp. 23–40. Oceania Monograph 39. University of Sydney, Sydney.

Beaton, J. 1991. Extensification and intensification in central California prehistory. *Antiquity* 65: 946–952.

Berndt, R.M. 1951. Ceremonial exchange in western Arnhem Land. *Southwestern Journal of Anthropology* 7(2): 156–176.

_____. 1965. External influences on the Aboriginal. *Hemisphere* 9(3): 2–9.

Binford, L.R. 1980. Willow smoke and dog's tails: Hunter-Gatherer settlement systems and archaeological site formation. *American Antiquity* 45: 4–20.

_____. 1982. The archaeology of place. *Journal of Anthropological Archaeology* 1: 5–31.

Bird, C.F.M. and D. Frankel 1991. Chronology and explanation in western Victoria and south-east South Australia. *Archaeology in Oceania* 26: 1–16.

Bird, D.W., J.L. Richardson, P.M. Veth and A.J. Barham 2002. Explaining shellfish variability in middens on the Meriam Islands, Torres Strait, Australia. *Journal of Archaeological Science* 29: 457–469.

Birdsell, J.B. 1953. Some environmental and cultural factors influencing the structuring of Australian Aboriginal populations. *American Naturalist* 87(834): 171–207.

Blackburn, H. 1980. *Marine shells of the Darwin area*. Museum and Art Gallery of the Northern Territory, Darwin.

Bleed, P. 1986. The optimal design of hunting weapons: maintainability or reliability. *American Antiquity* 51: 737–747.

Boone, J.L. 2002. Subsistence strategies and early human population history: An evolutionary ecological perspective. *World Archaeology* 34(1): 6–25.

Botkin, S. 1980. Effects of human predation on shellfish populations at Malibu Creek, California. In T.K. Earle and A.L. Christenson (eds) *Modelling change in prehistoric subsistence economies*, pp. 121–139. Academic Press, New York.

Bourke, P. 2000. *Late Holocene Indigenous economies of the tropical Australian coast: An archaeological study of the Darwin region*. Unpublished PhD Thesis. Northern Territory University, Darwin.

_____. 2002. Shell mounds and stone axes: Prehistoric resource procurement strategies at Hope Inlet, northern Australia. *Bulletin of the Indo-Pacific Prehistory Association* 22: 35–44.

_____. 2003. Advent of *Anadara* mounds and theories on Mid-Late Holocene changes in forager economic strategies – a comment. *Australian Archaeology* 56: 42–44.

_____. 2005. Archaeology of shell mounds of the Darwin coast: Totems of an ancestral landscape. In P. Bourke, S. Brockwell and C. Fredericksen (eds) *Darwin archaeology: Aboriginal, Asian and European heritage of Australia's top end*, pp. 29–49. Charles Darwin University Press, Darwin.

Bourke, P., S. Brockwell, P. Faulkner, and B. Meehan 2007. Climate variability in the mid to late Holocene Arnhem Land Region, North Australia: Archaeological archives of environmental and cultural change. *Archaeology in Oceania* 42: 91–101.

Bousman, C.B. 2005. Coping with risk: Later stone age technological strategies at Blydefontein Rock Shelter, South Africa. *Journal of Anthropological Archaeology* 24: 193–226.

Bowdler, S. 1983. Sieving seashells: Midden analysis in Australian archaeology. In G. Connah (ed.) *Australian field archaeology: A guide to techniques*, pp. 135–144. Australian Institute of Aboriginal Studies, Canberra.

Braje, T.J., D.J. Kennett, J.M. Erlandson and B.J. Culleton 2007. Human impacts on nearshore shellfish taxa: A 7,000 year record from Santa Rosa Island, California. *American Antiquity* 72: 735–756.

Brantingham, P.J., J.W. Olsen, J.A. Rech and A.I. Krivoshapkin 2000. Raw material quality and prepared core technologies in northeast Asia. *Journal of Archaeological Science* 27: 255–271.

Braun, D.R., J.C. Tactikos, J.V. Ferraro and J.W.K. Harris 2005. Flake recovery rates and inferences of Oldowan hominin behaviour: A response to Kimura 1999, 2002. *Journal of Human Evolution* 48(5): 525–531.

Brijker, J.M., S.J.A. Jung, G.M. Ganssen, T. Bickert and D. Kroon 2007. ENSO related decadal scale climate variability from the Indo-Pacific Warm Pool. *Earth and Planetary Science Letters* 253: 67–82.

Brock, J. 2001. *Native plants of northern Australia*. Reed New Holland, Sydney.

Brockwell, S., P. Faulkner, P. Bourke, A. Clarke, C. Crassweller, D. Guse, B. Meehan, and R. Sim 2009. Radiocarbon dates from the Top End: A cultural chronology for the Northern Territory coastal plains. *Australian Aboriginal Studies* 2: 54–76.

Brockwell, S., B. Meehan and B. Ngurrabangurraba 2005. An-barra archaeological project: A progress report. *Australian Aboriginal Studies* 1: 84–89.

Brookfield, H. and B. Allan 1989. High-altitude occupation and environment. *Mountain Research and Development* 9: 201–209.

Broom, M.J. 1982a. Analysis of the growth of *Anadara granosa* (Bivalvia: Arcidae) in natural, artificially seeded and experimental populations. *Marine Ecology - Progress Series* 9: 69–79.

_____. 1982b. Structure and seasonality in a Malaysian mudflat community. *Estuarine, Coastal and Shelf Science* 15(2): 135–150.

_____. 1983a. Mortality and production in natural, artificially-seeded and experimental populations of *Anadara granosa* (Bivalvia: Arcidae). *Oecologia* 58: 389–397.

_____. 1983b. Gonad development and spawning in *Anadara granosa* (L.) (Bivalvia: Arcidae). *Aquaculture* 30: 211–219.

_____. 1985. *The biology and culture of marine bivalve molluscs of the genus Anadara*. ICLARM Studies and Reviews 12. International Centre for Living Aquatic Resources Management, Manila.

Broughton, J.M. 1995. *Resource depression and intensification during the Late Holocene, San Francisco Bay: Evidence from the Emeryville Shellmound vertebrate fauna*. Unpublished PhD Thesis. University of Washington, Seattle.

Broughton, J.M. and D.K. Grayson 1993. Diet breadth, Numic expansion, and White Mountain faunas. *Journal of Archaeological Science* 20: 331–336.

Bureau of Meteorology, Department of Science 1986. *District rainfall deciles – Australia*. Australian Government Publishing Service, Canberra.

Bureau of Meteorology, Department of Administrative Services 1988. *Climatic averages: Australia*. Australian Government Publishing Service, Canberra.

_____. 1989. *Selected rainfall statistics: Australia*. Australian Government Publishing Service, Canberra.

Bureau of Meteorology, Department of the Environment 1998. *Climate of the Northern Territory*. National Capital Printing, Canberra.

Burns, T. 1994. *Mound over matter. Origins of shell and earth mounds of Northern Australia: An evaluation of mounds on Channel Island and Middle Arm mainland, Darwin Harbour.* Unpublished BA (Honours) Thesis. Northern Territory University, Darwin.

_____. 1999. Subsistence and settlement patterns in the Darwin coastal region during the Late Holocene period: A preliminary report of archaeological research. *Australian Aboriginal Studies* 1: 59–69.

Bush, A.B.G. 2001. Pacific sea surface temperature dominates orbital forcing of the Early Holocene monsoon. *Quaternary Research* 55: 25–32.

Byrne, D. 1980. Dynamics of dispersion: The place of silcrete in archaeological assemblages from the Lower Murchison, Western Australia. *Archaeology and Physical Anthropology in Oceania* 15: 110–119.

Campbell, G. 2008. Beyond means to meaning: Using distributions of shell shapes to reconstruct past collecting strategies. *Environmental Archaeology* 13: 111–121.

Casteel, R.W. 1970. Core and column samples. *American Antiquity* 35(4): 465–467.

Catterall, C.P. and I.R. Poiner 1987. The potential impact of human gathering on shellfish populations, with reference to some NE Australian intertidal flats. *OIKOS* 50: 114–122.

Chappell, J. 1982. Sea levels and sediments: Some features of the context of coastal Archaeological sites in the tropics. *Archaeology in Oceania* 17: 69–78.

_____. 1983. Sea level changes, 0 to 40 KA. In A. Grindrod (ed.) *CLIMANZ: A symposium of results and discussions concerned with Late Quaternary climatic history of Australia, New Zealand and surrounding seas.* Department of Biogeography and Geomorphology, Research School of Pacific Studies, The Australian National University, Canberra.

_____. 1990. The effects of sea level rise on tropical riverine lowlands. In J.C. Pernetta and P.J. Hughes (eds) *Implications of expected climate changes in the South Pacific region: An overview,* pp. 68–75. UNEP regional Seas Reports and Studies No. 128.

_____. 1993. Late Pleistocene coasts and human migrations in the Austral region. In A. Andrews (ed.) *A community of culture: The people and prehistory of the Pacific,* pp. 43–48. Department of Prehistory, School of Pacific Studies, The Australian National University, Canberra.

_____. 2001. Climate before agriculture. In S. O'Connor (ed.) *Histories of old ages: Essays in honour of Rhys Jones,* pp. 171–183. Pandanus Books, Research School of Pacific and Asian Studies, The Australian National University, Canberra.

Chappell, J. and J. Grindrod 1984. Chenier plain formation in northern Australia. In B.G. Thom (ed.) *Coastal geomorphology in Australia,* pp. 197–231. Academic Press, Sydney.

Chappell, J., A. Omura, T. Esat, M. McCulloch, J. Pandolfi, Y. Ota and B. Pillans 1996. Reconciliation of Late Quaternary sea levels derived from coral terraces at Huon Peninsula with deep sea oxygen isotope records. *Earth and Planetary Science Letters* 141(1): 227–236.

Chappell, J., E.G. Rhodes, B.G. Thom and E. Wallensky 1982. Hydro-isostasy and the sea level isobase of 5500BP in north Queensland, Australia. *Marine Geology* 49: 81–90.

Chappell, J. and B.G. Thom 1977. Sea levels and coasts. In J. Allen, J. Golson and R. Jones (eds) *Sunda and Sahul: Prehistoric studies in Southeast Asia, Melanesia and Australia*, pp. 275–291. Academic Press, London.

Chivas, A.R., A. Garcia, S. van der Kaars, M.J.J. Couapel, S. Holt, J.M. Reeves, D.J. Wheeler, A.D. Switzer, C.V. Murray-Wallace, D. Banerjee, D.M. Price, S.X. Wang, G. Pearson, N.T. Edgar, L. Beaufort, P. De Deckker, E. Lawson and C.B. Cecil 2001. Sea-level and environmental changes since the last Interglacial in the Gulf of Carpentaria, Australia: An overview. *Quaternary International* 83–85: 19–46.

Claassen, C.L. 1986. Shellfishing seasons in the prehistoric southeastern United States. *American Antiquity* 51(1): 21–37.

_____. 1991. Normative thinking and shell-bearing sites. *Archaeological Method and Theory* 3: 249–298.

_____. 1998. *Shells*. Cambridge University Press, Cambridge.

Clark, R.L. and J.C. Guppy 1988. A transition from mangrove forest to freshwater wetland in the monsoon tropics of Australia. *Journal of Biogeography* 15: 665–684.

Clarke, A. 1994. *The winds of change: An archaeology of contact in the Groote Eylandt Archipelago, Northern Australia*. Unpublished PhD Thesis. The Australian National University, Canberra.

_____. 2000a. Time, tradition and transformation: The archaeology of intercultural encounters on Groote Eylandt, Northern Australia. In R. Torrence and A. Clarke (eds) *The archaeology of difference: Negotiating cross-cultural engagements in Oceania*, pp. 142–181. One World Archaeology 38. Routledge, London.

_____. 2000b. 'The Moormans Trowsers': Aboriginal and Macassan interactions and the changing fabric of Indigenous social life. In S. O'Connor and P. Veth (eds), *East of Wallace's Line. Modern Quaternary research in South-East Asia*, pp. 315–335. A.A. Balkema, Rotterdam.

_____. 2002. The ideal and the real: cultural and personal transformations of archaeological research on Groote Eylandt, northern Australia. *World Archaeology* 34(2): 249–264.

Clarke, M.F., R.J. Wasson and M.A.J. Williams 1979. Point Stuart chenier and Holocene sea levels in northern Australia. *Search* 10(3): 90–92.

Clarkson, C.J. 2004. *Technological provisioning and assemblage variation in the eastern Victoria River Region, Northern Australia: A Darwinian approach*. Unpublished PhD Thesis. The Australian National University, Canberra.

Clune, G. 2002. Abydos: An archaeological investigation of Holocene adaptations on the Pilbara Coast, northwestern Australia. Unpublished PhD Thesis. The University of Western Australia, Perth.

Clune, G. and R. Harrison 2009. Coastal shell middens of the Abydos coastal plain, Western Australia. *Archaeology in Oceania* 44(Supplement 1): 70–80.

Cohen, M.N. 1977. *The food crisis in prehistory*. Yale University Press, New Haven.

Collier, S. and K.A. Hobson 1987. The importance of marine protein in the diet of coastal Australian Aborigines. *Current Anthropology* 28(4): 559–564.

Coombs, H.C., B. Dexter and L.R. Hiatt 1980. The outstation movement in Aboriginal Australia. *Australian Institute of Aboriginal Studies Newsletter, New Series* 14: 1–23.

Cosgrove, R.F. 1991. *The illusion of riches: Issues of scale, resolution and explanation of Pleistocene human behaviour.* Unpublished PhD Thesis. La Trobe University, Bundoora.

Cotter, M 1996. Holocene environmental change in Deception Bay, Southeast Queensland: A palaeogeographical contribution to MRAP Stage II. In S. Ulm, I. Lilley and A. Ross (eds) *Australian Archaeology '95: Proceedings of the 1995 Australian Archaeological Association Annual Conference,* pp. 193–205. *Tempus* 6. Anthropology Museum, The University of Queensland, St Lucia.

Cotterell, B. and J. Kamminga 1987. The formation of flakes. *American Antiquity* 52(4): 675–708.

Cribb, R. 1986. A preliminary report on archaeological findings in Aurukun Shire, western Cape York. *Queensland Archaeological Research* 3: 133–158.

Cribb, R. 1996. Shell mounds, domiculture and ecosystem manipulation on western Cape York Peninsula. In P. Hiscock and P. Veth (eds) *Archaeology of northern Australia: Regional perspectives,* pp. 150–174. *Tempus* 4. Anthropology Museum, The University of Queensland, St Lucia.

Davenport, J. and T.M. Wong 1986. Responses of the blood cockle *Anadara granosa* (L.) (Bivalvia: Arcidae) to salinity, hypoxia and aerial exposure. *Aquaculture* 56: 151–162.

David, B. and H. Lourandos 1997. 37,000 years and more in tropical Australia: Investigating long-term archaeological trends in Cape York Peninsula. *Proceedings of the Prehistoric Society* 63: 1–23.

Davidson, D.S. 1935. Archaeological problems of northern Australia. *Journal of the Royal Anthropological Institute of Great Britain and Ireland* 65: 145–183.

Davidson, I. 1990. Prehistoric Australian demography. In B. Meehan and N. White (eds) *Hunter-gatherer demography: Past and present,* pp. 41–58. Oceania Monograph 39. University of Sydney, Sydney.

Davis, S. 1984. Aboriginal claims to coastal waters in northeastern Arnhem Land, Northern Australia. *Senri Ethnological Studies* 17: 231–251.

de Boer, W.F., A.F. Blijdenstein and F. Longamane 2002. Prey choice and habitat use of people exploiting intertidal resources. *Environmental Conservation* 29(2): 238–252.

de Boer, W.F., T. Pereira and A. Guissamulo 2000. Comparing recent and abandoned shell middens to detect the impact of human exploitation on the intertidal system. *Aquatic Ecology* 34: 287–297.

de Boer, W.F. and H.H.T. Prins 2002. The community structure of a tropical intertidal mudflat under human exploitation. *ICES Journal of Marine Science* 59: 1237–1247.

Deevey, E.S. 1947. Life tables for natural populations of animals. *The Quarterly Review of Biology* 22: 283–314.

deMenocal, P.B. 2001. Cultural responses to climate change during the Late Holocene. *Science* 292: 667–673.

Deo, J.N., J.O. Stone and J.K. Stein 2004. Building confidence in shell: Variations in the marine radiocarbon reservoir correction for the Northwest Coast over the past 3,000 years. *American Antiquity* 69(4): 771–786.

Diaz, H.F. and V. Markgraf 1992. Introduction. In V. Markgraf (ed.) *El Niño: Historical and Paleoclimatic Aspects of the Southern Oscillation,* pp. 1–16. Cambridge University Press, Cambridge.

Dibble, H.L. 1985. Raw material variation in Levallois flake manufacture. *Current Anthropology* 26(3): 391–393.

Dixon, J.M. and L. Huxley 1985. *Donald Thomson's mammals and fishes of northern Australia*. Thomas Nelson Australia, Melbourne.

Douka, K., T.F.G. Higham and R.E.M. Hedges 2010. Radiocarbon dating of shell carbonates: Old problems and new solutions. *Munibe Supplemento* 31: 18–27.

Dunlop, C.R. and L.J. Webb 1991. Flora and vegetation. In C.D. Haynes, M.G. Ridpath and M.A.J. Williams (eds) *Monsoonal Australia: Landscape, ecology and man in the northern lowlands*, pp. 41–60. A.A. Balkema, Rotterdam.

Dunnell, R.C. and W.S. Dancey 1983. The siteless survey: A regional scale data collection strategy. In M.B. Schiffer (ed.) *Advances in Archaeological Method and Theory 6*, pp. 267–287. Academic Press, New York.

Elkin, A.P. 1978. *Studies in Australian totemism*. AMS Press, New York.

Ellison, J.C. 1993. Mangrove retreat with rising sea-level, Bermuda. *Estuarine, Coastal and Shelf Science* 37: 75–87.

Enfield, D.B. 1989. El Niño, past and present. *Review of Geophysics* 27: 159–187.

_____. 1992. Historical and prehistorical overview of El Niño/Southern Oscillation. In V. Markgraf (ed.) *El Niño: Historical and paleoclimatic aspects of the Southern Oscillation*, pp. 96–118. Cambridge University Press, Cambridge.

England, J., A.S. Dyke, R.D. Coulthard, R. McNeely and A. Aitken 2012. The exaggerated radiocarbon age of deposit-feeding molluscs in calcareous environments. *Boreas* 10: 1–12.

Erlandson, J.M. 1988. The role of shellfish in prehistoric economies: A protein perspective. *American Antiquity* 53(1): 102–109.

_____. 1994. *Early hunter-gatherers of the California coast*. Plenum Press, New York.

_____. 2001. The archaeology of aquatic adaptations: Paradigms for a new millennium. *Journal of Archaeological Research* 9(4): 287–350.

Erlandson, J.M., T.C. Rick, T.J. Braje, A. Steinberg and R.L. Vellanoweth 2008. Human impacts on ancient shellfish: A 10,000 year record from San Miguel Island, California. *Journal of Archaeological Science* 35: 2144–2152.

Esposito, V. 2005. *Sorting shells: An examination of archaeological criteria used to identify cultural shell material*. Unpublished BA (Honours) Thesis. The Australian National University, Canberra.

Evans, N. 1992. Macassan loanwords in top end languages. *Australian Journal of Linguistics* 12: 45–91.

Evans, N. and R. Jones 1997. The cradle of the Pama-Nyungans: Linguistic and archaeological speculations. In P. McConvell and N. Evans (eds) *Archaeology and linguistics : Aboriginal Australia in global perspective*, pp. 385–415. Oxford University Press, Melbourne.

Fanning, P. and S. Holdaway 2001. Stone artefact scatters in western NSW, Australia: Geomorphic controls on artefact size and distribution. *Geoarchaeology: An International Journal* 16(6): 667–686.

Faulkner, P. 2006. *The ebb and flow: An archaeological investigation of Late Holocene economic variability on the coastal margin of Blue Mud Bay, Northeast Australia*. Unpublished PhD Thesis. Australian National University, Canberra. _____. 2008. Patterns of chronological variability in occupation on the coastal margin of Blue Mud Bay. *Archaeology in Oceania* 43: 81–88.

_____. 2009. Focused, intense and long-term: Evidence for granular ark (*Anadara granosa*) exploitation from late Holocene shell mounds of Blue Mud Bay, northern Australia. *Journal of Archaeological Science* 36: 821–834.

_____. 2010. Morphometric and taphonomic analysis of granular ark (*Anadara granosa*) dominated shell deposits of Blue Mud Bay, northern Australia. *Journal of Archaeological Science* 37: 1942–1952.

_____. 2011. Late Holocene mollusc exploitation and changing near-shore environments: a case study from the coastal margin of Blue Mud Bay, northern Australia. *Environmental Archaeology* 16(2): 137–150.

_____. in press. Late Holocene coastal economies and the *Anadara granosa* dominated shell mounds of northern Australia: Evidence from Blue Mud Bay, northeast Arnhem Land. In M. Roksandic, S. Mendonça, S. Eggers, M. Burchell and D. Klokler (eds) *The cultural dynamics of shell middens and shell mounds: A worldwide perspective*, University of New Mexico Press, Albuquerque.

Faulkner, P. and A. Clarke 2009. Artefact assemblage characteristics and distribution on the Point Blane Peninsula, Blue Mud Bay, Arnhem Land. *Australian Archaeology* 69: 21–28.

Field, J.S. 2004. Environmental and climatic considerations: A hypothesis for conflict and the emergence of social complexity in Fijian prehistory. *Journal of Anthropological Archaeology* 23: 79–99.

Flannery, K.V. 1969. Origins and ecological effects of early domestication in Iran and the Near East. In P.J. Ucko and G.W. Dimbleby (eds) *The domestication and exploitation of plants and animals*, pp. 73–100. Aldine Publishing Company, Chicago.

Fleming, K., P. Johnston, D. Zwartz, Y. Yokoyama, K. Lambeck and J. Chappell 1998. Refining the eustatic sea-level curve since the Last Glacial Maximum using far-field and intermediate sites. *Earth and Planetary Science Letters* 163: 327–342.

Foley, R. 1977. Space and energy: A method for analysing habitat value and utilisation in relation to archaeological sites. In D.L. Clarke (ed.) *Spatial archaeology*, pp. 163–187. Academic Press, London.

_____. 1981a. *Off-site archaeology and human adaptation in eastern Africa: An analysis of regional artefact density in the Amboseli, southern Kenya.* Cambridge Monographs in African Archaeology 3, BAR International Series 97. Archaeopress, Oxford.

_____. 1981b. Off-site archaeology: An alternative approach for the short-sited. In I. Hodder, G. Isaac and N. Hammond (eds) Pattern of the past: Essays in honour of David Clarke, pp. 152–184. Cambridge University Press, Cambridge.

Ford, P.J. 1989. Molluscan assemblages from archaeological deposits. *Geoarchaeology: An International Journal* 4: 157–173.

Frakes, L.A., B. McGowan and J.M. Bowler 1987. Evolution of Australian environments. In D.W. Walton (ed.) *Fauna of Australia*, pp. 1–16. Australian Government Publishing Service, Canberra.

Frazer, J.G. 1910. *Totemism and exogamy: A treatise on certain early forms of superstition and society.* MacMillan, London.

Gagan, M.K., L.K. Ayliffe, D. Hopley, J.A. Cali, G.E. Mortimer, J. Chappell, M.T. McCulloch and M.J. Head 1998. Temperature and surface-ocean water balance of the Mid-Holocene tropical western Pacific. *Science* 279: 1014–1018.

Gagan, M.K. and J. Chappell 2000. Massive corals: Grand archives of ENSO. In R.H. Grove and J. Chappell (eds) *El Niño – history and crisis: Studies from the Asia-Pacific region*, pp. 35–50. The White Horse Press, Cambridge.

Gagan, M.K., A.R. Chivas and P.J. Isdale 1994. High-resolution isotopic records of the Mid-Holocene tropical western Pacific. *Earth and Planetary Sciences* 121: 549–558.

Gagan, M.K., E.J. Hendy, S.G. Haberle and W.S. Hantoro 2004. Post-glacial evolution of the Indo-Pacific warm pool and El Niño-Southern Oscillation. *Quaternary International* 118-119: 127–143.

Gaughwin, D. and R. Fullagar 1995. Victorian offshore islands in a mainland coastal economy. *Australian Archaeology* 40: 38–50.

Giovas, C. M. 2009. The shell game: Analytic problems in archaeological mollusc quantification. *Journal of Archaeological Science* 36: 1557–1564.

Giovas, C. M., S.M. Fitzpatrick, M. Clark and M. Abed 2010. Evidence for size increase in an exploited mollusc: Humped conch (*Strombus gibberulus*) at Chelechol ra Orrak, Palau from ca. 3000-0 BP. *Journal of Archaeological Science* 37: 2788–2798.

Glantz, M.H. 1991. Introduction. In N. Nicholls (ed.) *Teleconnections linking world-wide climate anomalies: Scientific basis and societal impact*, pp. 1–11. Cambridge University Press, Cambridge.

Glantz, M.H., R.W. Katz and N. Nicholls 1991. *Teleconnections linking world-wide climate anomalies: Scientific basis and societal impact.* Cambridge University Press, Cambridge.

Glassow, M.A. and L.R. Wilcoxon 1988. Coastal adaptations near Point Conception, California, with particular regard to shellfish exploitation. *American Antiquity* 53(1): 36–51.

Godfrey, M.C.S. 1989. Shell midden chronology in southwestern Victoria: Reflections of change in prehistoric population and subsistence? *Archaeology in Oceania* 24: 65–69.

Gosling, E. 2003. *Bivalve molluscs: Biology, ecology and culture.* Blackwell Publishing, Oxford.

Graumlich, L.J. 1993. A 1000-year record of temperature and precipitation in the Sierra Nevada. *Quaternary Research* 39: 248–255.

Grayson, D.K. 1984. *Quantitative zooarchaeology: Topics in the analysis of archaeological fauna.* Orlando Academic Press, Orlando.

Grayson, D.K. and S.C. Cole 1998. Stone tool assemblage richness during the Middle and Early Upper Palaeolithic in France. *Journal of Archaeological Science* 25: 927–938.

Grindrod, J., P. Moss and S. van der Kaars 1999. Late Quaternary cycles of mangrove development and decline on the north Australian continental shelf. *Journal of Quaternary Science* 14(5): 465–470.

Haberle, S. 2000. Vegetation response to climate variability: A palaeoecological perspective on the ENSO phenomenon. In R.H. Grove and J. Chappell (eds) *El Niño – history and crisis: Studies from the Asia-Pacific region*, pp. 66–78. The White Horse Press, Cambridge.

Haberle, S. and B. David 2004. Climates of change: Human dimensions of Holocene environmental change in low latitudes of the PEPII transect. *Quaternary International* 118–119: 165–179.

Haines, P.W., D.J. Rawlings, I.P. Sweet, B.A. Pietsch, K.A. Plumb, T.L. Madigan and A.A. Krassay 1999. *1:250000 geological map series, explanatory notes: Blue Mud Bay SD53-7.* Department of Mines and Energy, Northern Territory Geological Survey, Australian Geological Survey Organisation, Northern Territory Geological Survey, Darwin.

Hall, H.J. and P. Hiscock 1988. Platypus Rockshelter (KB:A70), Southeast Queensland: Chronological changes in site use. *Queensland Archaeological Research* 5: 42–62.

Harrison, R. 2009. The archaeology of the Port Hedland coastal plain and implications for understanding the prehistory of shell mounds and middens in northwestern Australia. *Archaeology in Oceania* 44(Supplement 1): 81–98.

Hayden, B. 1981. Research and development in the stone age: Technological transitions among hunter-gatherers. *Current Anthropology* 22(5): 519–531.

Head, L. 1983. Environment as artefact: A geographic perspective on the Holocene occupation of southwestern Victoria. *Archaeology in Oceania* 18: 73–80.

_____. 1986. Palaeoecological contributions to Australian prehistory. *Archaeology in Oceania* 21: 121–129.

Hendy, E.J., M.K. Gagan, C.A. Alibert, M.T. McCulloch, J.M. Lough and P.J. Isdale 2002. Abrupt decrease in tropical Pacific sea surface salinity at end of Little Ice Age. *Science* 295: 1511–1514.

Hinton, A. 1978. *Guide to Australian shells*. Robert Brown and Associates, Port Moresby.

_____. 1979. *Shells of New Guinea and the central Indo-Pacific*. Jacaranda Press, Hong Kong.

Hiscock, P. 1984. Raw material rationing as an explanation of assemblage differences: A case study of Lawn Hill, northwest Queensland. In G.K. Ward (ed.) *Archaeology at ANZAAS, Canberra 1984*, pp. 178–190. Department of Prehistory and Anthropology, Faculty of Arts, The Australian National University, Canberra.

_____. 1985. The need for a taphonomic perspective in stone artefact analysis. *Queensland Archaeological Research* 2: 82–97.

_____. 1986. Technological change in the Hunter River Valley and the interpretation of Late-Holocene change in Australia. *Archaeology in Oceania* 21(1): 40–50.

_____. 1988. *Prehistoric settlement patterns and artefact manufacture at Lawn Hill, north-west Queensland*. Unpublished PhD Thesis. The University of Queensland, St Lucia.

_____. 1989. Artefact recording in the field. In J. Flood, I. Johnson and S. Sullivan (eds) *Sites and bytes: Recording Aboriginal places in Australia*, pp. 20–38. Special Australian Heritage Publication Series No. 8. Australian Heritage Commission, Australian Government Publishing Service, Canberra.

_____. 1994. Technological responses to risk in Holocene Australia. *Journal of World Prehistory* 8: 267–292.

_____. 1996. Mobility and technology in the Kakadu coastal wetlands. *Indo-Pacific Prehistory Association Bulletin* 15: 151–157.

_____. 1997. Archaeological evidence for environmental change in Darwin Harbour. In J.R. Hanley, G. Caswell, D. Megirian and H.K. Larson (eds) *The marine flora and fauna of Darwin Harbour, Northern Territory, Australia. Proceedings of the Sixth International Marine Biological Workshop*, pp. 445–449. Museum and Art Galleries of the Northern Territory and the Marine Sciences Association, Darwin.

_____. 1999. Holocene coastal occupation of Western Arnhem Land. In J. Hall and I.J. McNiven (eds) *Australian coastal archaeology*, pp. 91–103. ANH Publications. Department of Archaeology and Natural History, Australian National University, Canberra.

_____. 2001. Sizing up prehistory: Sample size and composition of artefact assemblages. *Australian Aboriginal Studies* 1: 48–62.

_____. 2002. Quantifying the size of artefact assemblages. *Journal of Archaeological Science* 29: 251–258.

_____. 2005. Coastal cowboys: The development of speculative models of molluscan midden matter in the Darwin region. In P. Bourke, S. Brockwell and C. Fredericksen (eds) *Darwin archaeology: Aboriginal, Asian and European heritage of Australia's top end*, pp. 19–28. Charles Darwin University Press, Darwin.

_____. 2008. Archaeology of ancient Australia. Routledge, London.

Hiscock, P. and P. Faulkner 2006. Dating the dreaming? Creation of myths and rituals for mounds along the northern Australian coastline. *Cambridge Archaeological Journal* 16: 209–222.

Hiscock, P. and P.J. Hughes 1983. One method of recording scatters of stone artefacts during site surveys. *Australian Archaeology* 17: 87–98.

Hiscock, P. and P.J. Hughes 2001. Prehistoric and World War II use of shell mounds in Darwin Harbour, Northern Territory, Australia. *Australian Archaeology* 52: 41–45.

Hiscock, P. and S. Mitchell 1993. *Stone artefact quarries and reduction sites in Australia: Towards a type profile.* Australian Heritage Commission, Technical Publications Series No. 4. Australian Government Printing Service, Canberra.

Hiscock, P. and F. Mowat 1993. Midden variability in the coastal portion of the Kakadu region. *Australian Archaeology* 37: 18–24.

Hobbs, D. 1984. Surveying techniques useful in Archaeology. In G. Connah (ed.) *Australian field archaeology: A guide to techniques*, pp. 43–63. Australian Institute of Aboriginal Studies, Canberra.

Hobson, K.A. and S. Collier 1984. Marine and terrestrial protein in Australian Aboriginal diets. *Current Anthropology* 25: 238–240.

Hockey, P.A.R. and A.L. Bosman 1986. Man as an intertidal predator in Transkei: Disturbance, community convergence and management of a natural food resource. *OIKOS* 46: 3–14.

Hockey, P.A.R., A.L. Bosman and W.R. Siegfried 1988. Patterns and correlates of shellfish exploitation by coastal people in Transkei: An enigma of protein production. *Journal of Applied Ecology* 25: 353–363.

Holdaway, S.J., P.C. Fanning, M. Jones, J. Shiner, D.C. Witter and G. Nicholls 2002. Variability in the chronology of Late Holocene Aboriginal occupation on the arid margin of southeastern Australia. *Journal of Archaeological Science* 29: 351–363.

Holdaway, S., P. Fanning and J. Shiner 2005. Absence of evidence or evidence of absence? Understanding the chronology of Indigenous occupation of western New South Wales, Australia. *Archaeology in Oceania* 40: 33–49.

Holdaway, S.J., J. Shiner and P. Fanning 2004. Hunter-gatherers and the archaeology of discard behavior: An analysis of surface stone artefacts from Sturt National Park, western New South Wales, Australia. *Asian Perspectives* 43: 34–72.

Holdaway, S., D. Witter, P. Fanning, R. Musgrave, G. Cochrane, T. Doelman, S. Greenwood, D. Pigdon and J. Reeves 1998. New approaches to open site spatial archaeology in Sturt National Park, New South Wales, Australia. *Archaeology in Oceania* 33: 1–19.

Holdaway, S. and L. Wandsnider 2006. Temporal scales and archaeological landscapes from the eastern desert of Australia and intermontane North America. In G. Lock and B.L. Molyneaux (eds) *Confronting scale in archaeology: Issues of theory and practice*, pp. 183–202. Springer, New York.

Holmgren, M., M. Scheffer, E. Ezcurra, J.R. Gutiérrez and G.M.J. Mohren 2001. El Niño effects on the dynamics of terrestrial ecosystems. *Trends in Ecology and Evolution* 16(2): 89–94.

Hope, G. and J. Golson 1995. Late Quaternary change in the mountains of New Guinea. *Antiquity* 69: 818–830.

Hopley, D. and B.G. Thom 1983. Australian sea levels in the last 15,000 years: A review. In D. Hopley (ed.) *Australian sea levels in the last 15,000 years: A review*, pp. 3–26. Australian Report for IGCP 61, Monograph Series – Occasional Paper No. 3. Department of Geography, James Cook University of North Queensland, Townsville.

Hubble, G.D., R.F. Isbell and K.H. Northcote 1983. In *Soils: An Australian viewpoint*, pp. 17–47. Academic Press, Melbourne.

Hughen, K.A., M.G.L. Baillie, E. Bard, A. Bayliss, J.W. Beck, C.J.H. Bertrand, P.G. Blackwell, C.E. Buck, G.S. Burr, K.B. Cutler, P.E. Damon, R.L. Edwards, R.G. Fairbanks, M. Friedrich, T.P. Guilderson, B. Kromer, F.G. McCormac, S.W. Manning, C. Bronk Ramsey, P.J. Reimer, R.W. Reimer, S. Remmele, J.R. Southon, M. Stuiver, S. Talamo, F.W. Taylor, J. van der Plicht and C.E. Weyhenmeyer 2004. Marine04 marine radiocarbon age calibration, 26–0 ka BP. *Radiocarbon* 46: 1059–86.

Hughes, M.K. and P.A. Brown 1992. Drought frequency in central California since 101 B.C. recorded in giant Sequoia tree rings. *Climate Dynamics* 6: 161–167.

Ingram, B.L. 1998. Differences in radiocarbon age between shell and charcoal from a Holocene shellmound in Northern California. *Quaternary Research* 49(1): 102–110.

Isaac, G.L. 1981. Stone age visiting cards: Approaches to the study of early land-use patterns. In I. Hodder, G.L. Isaac and N. Hammond (eds) *Patterns in the past: Studies in honour of David Clarke*, pp. 131–156. Cambridge University Press, Cambridge.

Isbell, R.F. 1983. Kimberley – Arnhem – Cape York (III). In *Soils: An Australian viewpoint*, pp. 189–199. Academic Press, London.

Jerardino, A. 1997. Changes in shellfish species composition and mean shell size from a Late-Holocene record of the west coast of southern Africa. *Journal of Archaeological Science* 24: 1031–1044.

Jerardino, A. 1998. Excavations at Poncho's Kitchen Midden, Western Cape Coast, South Africa: Further observations from the megamidden period. *South African Archaeologist Bulletin* 53: 16–25.

Jerardino, A. 2010. Large shell middens in Lamberts Bay, South Africa: A case of hunter-gatherer resource intensification. *Journal of Archaeological Science* 37: 2291–2302.

Jerardino, A., G.M. Branch and R. Navarro 2008. Human impact on precolonial west coast marine environments of South Africa. In T.C. Rick and J.M. Erlandson (eds) *Human impacts on ancient marine ecosystems: A global perspective*, pp. 279–296. University of California Press, Berkeley.

Jerardino, A., J.C. Castilla, J.M. Ramirez and N. Hermosilla 1992. Early coastal subsistence patterns in central Chile: A systematic study of the marine-invertebrate fauna from the site of Curaumilla-1. *Latin American Antiquity* 3: 43–62.

Jerardino, A. and R. Navarro 2008. Shell morphometry of seven limpet species from coastal shell middens in southern Africa. *Journal of Archaeological Science* 35: 1023–1029.

Jochim, M.A. 1981. *Strategies for survival: Cultural behaviour in an ecological context.* Academic Press, New York.

Johnson, I. 1980. Bytes from sites: The design of an excavation data recording system. In I. Johnson (ed.) *Holier than thou: Proceedings of the 1978 Kioloa Conference on Australian Prehistory*, pp. 91–118. Department of Prehistory, Research School of Pacific Studies, The Australian National University, Canberra.

Jones, D.S., I.R. Quitmyer and C.F.T. Andrus. 2005. Oxygen isotopic evidence for greater seasonality in Holocene shells of *Donax variabilis* from Florida. *Palaeogeography, Palaeoclimatology, Palaeoecology* 228: 96–108.

Jones, P.D. and M.E. Mann 2004. Climate over past millennia. *Reviews of Geophysics* 42: 1–42.

Jones, R. 1975. The Neolithic, Palaeolithic and the hunting gardeners: Man and land in the Antipodes. In R.P. Suggate and M.M. Cresswell (eds) *Quaternary studies*, pp. 21–34. Bulletin No. 13. Royal Society of New Zealand, Wellington.

_____. 1985. Archaeological conclusions. In R. Jones (ed.) *Archaeological research in Kakadu National Park*, pp. 291–298. ANPWS Special Publication 13. Australian National Parks and Wildlife Service, Canberra.

Jones, R. and N. White 1988. Point blank: Stone tool manufacture at the Ngilipitji quarry, Arnhem Land, 1981. In B. Meehan and R. Jones (eds) *Archaeology with ethnography: An Australian perspective*, pp. 51–87. Department of Prehistory, Research School of Pacific Studies, The Australian National University, Canberra.

Jones, T.L. 1991. Marine-resource value and the priority of coastal settlement: A California perspective. *American Antiquity* 56(3): 419–443.

Jones, T.L., G.M. Brown, L.M. Raab, J.L. McVickar, W.G. Spaulding, D.J. Kennett, A. York and P.L. Walker 1999. Environmental imperatives reconsidered: Demographic crises in western North America during the Medieval Climatic Anomaly. *Current Anthropology* 40(3): 137–170.

Judge. W.J., J.I. Ebert and R.K. Hitchcock 1975. Sampling in regional archaeological surveys. In J.W. Mueller (ed.) *Sampling in archaeology*, pp. 82–123. The University of Arizona Press, Tucson.

Keen, I. 1997. A continent of foragers: Aboriginal Australia as a 'regional system'. In P. McConvell and N. Evans (eds) *Archaeology and linguistics: Aboriginal Australia in global perspective*, pp. 261–273. Oxford University Press, Melbourne.

———. 2003. *Aboriginal economy and society: Australia at the threshold of colonisation*. Oxford University Press, Melbourne.

Kelly, R.L. 1992. Mobility/sedentism: Concepts, archaeological measures, and effects. *Annual Review of Anthropology* 21: 43–66.

———. 1998. Foraging and sedentism In T.R. Rocek and O. Bar-Yosef *Seasonality and sedentism: Archaeological perspectives from Old and New World sites*, pp. 9–23. Peabody Museum of Archaeology and Ethnology, Harvard University, Cambridge.

Kershaw, A.P. 1983. The vegetation record from Northeastern Australia 7±2ka. In J.M.A. Chappell and A. Grindrod (eds) *CLIMANZ 1*, pp. 100–101. The Australian National University, Canberra.

———. 1995. Environmental change in greater Australia. *Antiquity* 69: 656–675.

Kershaw, A.P. and H.A. Nix 1989. The use of bioclimatic envelopes for estimation of quantitative palaeoclimatic values. In T.H. Donnelly and R.J. Wasson (eds) *CLIMANZ 3, Proceedings of the Symposium*, pp. 78–85. Division of Water Resources, CSIRO, Canberra.

Kim, J.H., R.R. Schneider, D. Hebbeln, P.J. Müller and G. Wefer 2002. Last deglacial sea-surface temperature evolution in the southeast Pacific compared to climate changes on the South American continent. *Quaternary Science Reviews* 21: 2085–2097.

Knox, J.C. 1993. Large increases in flood magnitude in response to modest changes in climate. *Nature* 361: 430–432.

Koike, H. 1986. Prehistoric hunting pressure and paleobiomass: An environmental reconstruction and archaeological analysis of a Jomon Shellmound area. In T. Akazawa and C.M. Aikens (eds) *Prehistoric hunter-gatherers in Japan: New research methods*, pp. 27–53. The University Museum Bulletin No. 27, Tokyo.

Koutavas, A., J. Lynch-Steiglitz, T.M.J. Marchitto and J.P. Sachs 2002. El Niño-like pattern in Ice Age tropical Pacific sea surface temperature. *Science* 297: 226–231.

Kress, J.H. 2000. The malacoarchaeology of Palawan Island. *Journal of East Asian Archaeology* 2(1–2): 285–328.

Kuhn, S.L. 1991. "Unpacking" reduction: Lithic raw material economy in the Mousterian of west-central Italy. *Journal of Anthropological Archaeology* 10: 76–106.

———. 1992. On planning and curated technologies in the Middle Paleolithic. *Journal of Anthropological Research* 48: 185–214.

———. 1995. *Mousterian lithic technology: An ecological perspective*. Princeton University Press, New Jersey.

Lambeck, K. 2002. Sea level change from mid Holocene to Recent time: An Australian example with global implications. *Geodynamics Series* 29: 33–50.

Lambeck, K. and J. Chappell 2001. Sea level change through the last glacial cycle. *Science* 292: 679–686.

Lambeck, K. and M. Nakada 1990. Late Pleistocene and Holocene sea-level change along the Australian coast. *Palaeogeography, Palaeoclimatology, Palaeoecology* 89: 143–176.

Lambeck, K., Y. Yokoyama and T. Purcell 2002. Into and out of the Last Glacial Maximum: Sea-level change during Oxygen Isotope Stages 3 and 2. *Quaternary Science Reviews* 21: 343–360.

Lamprell, K. and J. Healy 1998. *Bivalves of Australia, Volume 2.* Backhuys Publishers, Leiden.

Lamprell, K. and T. Whitehead 1992. *Bivalves of Australia, Volume 1.* Crawford House Press, Bathhurst.

Larson, D.O. and J. Michaelsen 1990. Impacts of climatic variability and population growth on Virgin branch Anasazi cultural developments. *American Antiquity* 55(2): 227–249.

Lasiak, T. 1991a. The susceptibility and/or resilience of rocky littoral molluscs to stock depletion by the Indigenous coastal people of Transkei, southern Africa. *Biological Conservation* 56: 245–264.

_____. 1991b. Is there evidence of over-exploitation of mussel stocks on the Transkei coast? *South African Journal of Marine Science* 10: 299–302.

_____. 1993. Temporal and spatial variations in exploited and non-exploited populations of the inter-tidal limpet *Cellana capensis. Journal of Molluscan Studies* 59: 295–307.

Lees, B. 1992a. The development of chenier sequence on the Victoria Delta, Joseph Bonaparte Gulf, northern Australia. *Marine Geology* 103: 214–224.

Lees, B.G. 1992b. Geomorphological evidence for Late Holocene climatic change in northern Australia. *Australian Geographer* 23(1): 1–10.

Lees, B.G., Y. Lu and J. Head 1990. Reconnaissance thermoluminescence dating of northern Australian coastal dunefields. *Quaternary Research* 34: 169–185.

Lees, B., Y. Lu and D.M. Price 1992. Thermoluminescence dating of dunes at Cape Lampert, east Kimberleys, northwestern Australia. *Marine Geology* 106: 131–139.

Lightfoot, K.G. and R.M. Cerrato 1988. Prehistoric shellfish exploitation in coastal New York. *Journal of Field Archaeology* 15: 141–149.

Lourandos, H. 1980. Change or stability?: Hydraulic hunter-gatherers and population in temperate Australia. *World Archaeology* 11: 245–266.

_____. 1983. Intensification: A Late Pleistocene–Holocene archaeological sequence from southwestern Victoria. *Archaeology in Oceania* 18: 81–94.

_____. 1985. Intensification and Australian prehistory. In T.D. Price and J.A. Brown (eds) *Prehistoric hunter-gatherers: The emergence of cultural complexity*, pp. 385–423. Academic Press, Orlando.

_____. 1997. *Continent of hunter-gatherers: New perspectives in Australian prehistory.* Cambridge University Press, Cambridge.

Lourandos, H. and B. David 1998. Comparing long-term archaeological and environmental trends: North Queensland, arid and semi-arid Australia. *The Artefact* 21: 104–114.

Lourandos, H. and A. Ross 1994. The great 'Intensification Debate': Its history and place in Australian archaeology. *Australian Archaeology* 39: 54–63.

Luebbers, R.A. 1978. *Meals and menus: A study of change in prehistoric coastal settlements in South Australia.* Unpublished PhD Thesis. The Australian National University, Canberra.

Lupo, K.D. 2007. Evolutionary foraging models in zooarchaeological analysis: Recent applications and future challenges. *Journal of Archaeological Research* 15: 143–189.

Lupo, K.D. and D.N. Schmitt 2005. Small prey hunting technology and zooarchaeological measures of taxonomic diversity and abundance: Ethnoarchaeological evidence from central African forest foragers. *Journal of Anthropological Archaeology* 24: 335–353.

Lyman, R.L. 2003. The influence of time averaging and space averaging on the application of foraging theory in zooarchaeology. *Journal of Archaeological Science* 30(5): 595–610.

Macintosh, D.J. 1982. Fisheries and aquaculture significance of mangrove swamps, with special reference to the Indo-West Pacific region. In J.F. Muir and R.J. Roberts (eds) *Recent advances in aquaculture*, pp. 5–85. Croom and Helm, Sydney.

Macknight, C.C. 1970. Archaeological discoveries in northern Australia and their protection. In F.D. McCarthy (ed.) *Aboriginal antiquities in Australia: Their nature and preservation*, pp. 95–98. Prehistory and Material Culture Series 3. Australian Institute of Aboriginal Studies, Canberra.

Macknight, C.C. 1976. *The voyage to Marege*. Melbourne University Press, Melbourne.

Macknight, C.C. and W.J. Gray 1970. *Aboriginal stone pictures in eastern Arnhem Land*. Australian Institute of Aboriginal Studies, Canberra.

Madsen, D.B. 1993. Testing diet breadth models: Examining adaptive change in the Late Prehistoric Great Basin. *Journal of Archaeological Science* 25: 321–329.

Madsen, D.B. and D.N. Schmitt 1998. Mass collecting and the diet breadth model: A Great Basin example. *Journal of Archaeological Science* 25: 445–455.

Magurran, A.E. 1988. *Ecological diversity and its measurement*. Croom Helm, London.

Mangerud, J. 1972. Radiocarbon dating of marine shells, including a discussion of apparent age of recent shells from Norway. *Boreas* 1: 143–172.

Mannino, M.A. and K.D. Thomas 2001. Intensive Mesolithic exploitation of coastal resources? Evidence from a shell deposit on the Isle of Portland (southern England) for the impact of human foraging on populations of intertidal rocky shore molluscs. *Journal of Archaeological Science* 28: 1101–1114.

————. 2002. Depletion of a resource? The impact of prehistoric human foraging on intertidal mollusc communities and its significance for human settlement, mobility and dispersal. *World Archaeology* 33(3): 452–474.

Mannino, M.A., B.F. Spiro and K.D. Thomas. 2003. Sampling shells for seasonality: Oxygen isotope analysis on shell carbonates of the inter-tidal gastropod *Monodonta lineata* (da Costa) from populations across its modern range and from a Mesolithic site in southern Britain. *Journal of Archaeological Science* 30(6): 667–679.

Markgraf, V., J.R. Dodson, A.P. Kershaw, M.S. McGlone and N. Nicholls 1992. Evolution of Late Pleistocene and Holocene climates in the circum-south Pacific land areas. *Climate Dynamics* 6: 193–211.

Marks, A., H. J. Hietala and J.K. Williams 2001. Tool standardization in the Middle and Upper Palaeolithic: A closer look. *Cambridge Archaeological Journal* 11: 17–44.

Marshall, F. and T. Pilgram 1993. NISP vs MNI in quantification of body-part representation. *American Antiquity* 58(2): 261–269.

Mason, R.D., M.L. Peterson and J.A. Tiffany 1998. Weighing vs counting: Measurement reliability and the California School of midden analysis. *American Antiquity* 63(2): 303–324.

Mason, R.D., M.L. Peterson and J.A. Tiffany 2000. Weighing and counting shell: A response to Glassow and Claassen. *American Antiquity* 65(4): 303–324.

Masse, W. B., J. Liston, J. Carucci and J.S. Athens 2006. Evaluating the effects of climate change on environment, resource depletion, and culture in the Palau Islands between AD 1200 and 1600. *Quaternary International* 151: 106–132.

May, S.K., P.S.C. Taçon, D. Wesley and M. Travers 2010. Painting history: Indigenous observations and depictions of the 'other' in northwestern Arnhem Land, Australia. *Australian Archaeology* 71: 57–65.

McArthur, M. 1960. Food consumption and dietary levels of groups of Aborigines living on naturally occurring foods. In C.P. Mountford (ed.) *Records of the American-Australian Scientific Expedition to Arnhem Land (Volume 2): Anthropology and Nutrition*, pp. 90–135. Melbourne University Press, Melbourne.

McCarthy, F.D. and M. McArthur 1960. The food quest and the time factor in Aboriginal economic life. In C.P. Mountford (ed.) *Records of the American-Australian Scientific Expedition to Arnhem Land (Volume 2): Anthropology and Nutrition*, pp. 145–194. Melbourne University Press, Melbourne.

McCarthy, F.D. and F.M. Setzler 1960. The archaeology of Arnhem Land. In C.P. Mountford (ed.) *Records of the American-Australian Scientific Expedition to Arnhem Land (Volume 2): Anthropology and Nutrition*, pp. 215–295. Melbourne University Press, Melbourne.

McCarthy, L. and L. Head 2001. Holocene variability in semi-arid vegetation: New evidence from *Leporillus* middens from the Flinders Ranges, South Australia. *The Holocene* 11: 681–689.

McConvell, P. 1990. The linguistic prehistory of Australia: Opportunities for dialogue with archaeology. *Australian Archaeology* 31: 3–27.

McDonald, N.S. and J. McAlpine 1991. Floods and draughts: The northern climate. In C.D. Haynes, M.G. Ridpath and M.A.J. Williams (eds) *Monsoonal Australia: Landscape, ecology and man in the northern lowlands*, pp. 19–29. A.A. Balkemam, Rotterdam.

McGlone, M.S., A.P. Kershaw and V. Markgraf 1992. El Niño/Southern Oscillation climatic variability in Australasian and South American paleoenvironmental records. In V. Markgraf (ed.) *El Niño: Historical and paleoclimatic aspects of the Southern Oscillation*, pp. 435–462. Cambridge University Press, Cambridge.

McNiven, I. 1989. Aboriginal shell middens at the mouth of the Maroochy River, Southeast Queensland. *Queensland Archaeological Research* 6: 28–52.

_____. 1992. Shell middens and mobility: The use of off-site faunal remains, Queensland, Australia. *Journal of Field Archaeology* 19: 495–508.

_____. 1999. Fissioning and regionalisation: The social dimensions of changes in Aboriginal use of the Great Sandy Region, southeast Queensland. In J. Hall and I.J. McNiven (eds) *Australian coastal archaeology*, pp. 157–168. ANH Publications. Department of Archaeology and Natural History, Australian National University, Canberra.

McPhail, M.K. and G.S. Hope 1985. Late Holocene mire development in montane southeastern Australia: A sensitive climatic indicator. *Search* 15: 344–349.

Meehan, B. 1977. Man does not live by calories alone: The role of shellfish in a coastal cuisine. In J. Allen, J. Golson and R. Jones (eds) *Sunda and Sahul: Prehistoric studies in South-East Asia, Melanesia and Australia*, pp. 493–531. Academic Press, London.

_____. 1982. *Shell bed to shell midden*. Australian Institute of Aboriginal Studies, Canberra.

_____. 1983. A matter of choice? Some thoughts on shell gathering strategies in northern Australia. In C. Grigson and J. Clutton-Brock (eds) *Animals in Archaeology 2: Shell Middens, Fishes and Birds*, pp. 3–17. BAR International Series 183. Archaeopress, Oxford.

_____. 1988a. The 'Dinnertime Camp'. In B. Meehan and R. Jones (eds) *Archaeology with ethnography: An Australian perspective*, pp. 171–188. Department of Prehistory, Research School of Pacific Studies, The Australian National University, Canberra.

_____. 1988b. Changes in Aboriginal exploitation of wetlands in northern Australia (Appendix 2). In D. Wade-Marshall and P. Loveday (eds) *Floodplains research. Northern Australia: Progress and prospects Volume 2*, pp. 1–23. North Australian Research Unit, The Australian National University, Darwin.

_____. 1991. Wetland hunters: Some reflections. In C.D. Haynes, M.G. Ridpath and M.A.J. Williams (eds) *Monsoonal Australia: Landscape, ecology and man in the northern lowlands*, pp. 197–206. A.A. Balkema, Rotterdam.

Meehan, B., S. Brockwell, J. Allen and R. Jones 1985. The wetland sites. In R. Jones (ed.) *Archaeological research in Kakadu National Park*, pp. 103–153. ANPWS Special Publication 13. Australian National Parks and Wildlife Service, Canberra.

Milner, N. 2001. At the cutting edge: Using thin sectioning to determine season of death of the European Oyster, *Ostrea edulis*. *Journal of Archaeological Science* 28(8): 861–873.

Milner, N., J. Barrett and J. Welsh 2007. Marine resource intensification in Viking Age Europe: The molluscan evidence from Quoygrew, Orkney. *Journal of Archaeological Science* 34: 1461–1472.

Mitchell, S. 1993. Shell mound formation in northern Australia: A case study from Croker Island, northwestern Arnhem Land. *The Beagle* 10(1): 179–192.

_____. 1994a. *Foreign contact and Indigenous economies on the Cobourg Peninsula, north-western Arnhem Land*. Unpublished PhD Thesis. Northern Territory University, Darwin.

_____. 1994b. Stone exchange network in north-western Arnhem Land: Evidence for recent chronological change. In M. Sullivan, S. Brockwell and A. Webb (eds) *Archaeology in the North: Proceedings of the 1993 Australian Archaeological Association Conference*, pp. 188–200. The North Australian Research Unit, The Australian National University, Darwin.

_____. 1995. Foreign contact and Indigenous exchange networks on the Cobourg Peninsula, north-western Arnhem Land. *Australian Aboriginal Studies* 2: 44–48.

_____. 1996. Dugongs and dugouts, sharptacks and shellbacks: Macassan contact and Aboriginal marine hunting on the Cobourg Peninsula, north western Arnhem Land. *Bulletin of the Indo-Pacific Prehistory Association* 15: 181–191.

Morphy, F. 2004. *A linguistic report on the Yolngu people of Blue Mud Bay, in relation to their claim to Native Title in the land and sea*. Unpublished Report, Prepared at the Instruction of the Northern Land Council.

Morphy, H. 2004. *An anthropological report on the Yolngu people of Blue Mud Bay, in relation to their claim to Native Title in the land and sea*. Unpublished Report, Prepared at the Instruction of the Northern Land Council.

Morrison, A.E. and E.E. Cochrane 2008. Investigating shellfish deposition and landscape history at the Natia Beach site, Fiji. *Journal of Archaeological Science* 35: 2387–2399.

Morrison, M. 2000. *Sea change? Marxism, ecological theory, and the Weipa shell mounds*. Unpublished BA Honours Thesis. James Cook University, Townsville.

_____. 2003. Old boundaries and new horizons: The Weipa shell mounds reconsidered. *Archaeology in Oceania* 38(1): 1–8.

_____. 2010. *The shell mounds of Albatross Bay: An archaeological investigation of Late Holocene production strategies near Weipa, north eastern Australia*. Unpublished PhD Thesis. Flinders University, Adelaide.

Morton, B. 1983. Mangrove bivalves. In W.D. Russell-Hunter (ed.) *The Mollusca*, Vol. 6, pp. 77–139. Academic Press, New York.

Morwood, M.J. 1981. Archaeology of the Central Queensland Highlands: The stone component. *Archaeology in Oceania* 16: 1–52.

Moss, M.L. and J.M. Erlandson 1995. Reflections on North American Pacific coast prehistory. *Journal of World Prehistory* 9(1): 1–45.

Mowat, F.M. 1994. Size really does matter: factors affecting shell fragmentation. In M. Sullivan, S. Brockwell and A. Webb (eds) *Archaeology in the North: Proceedings of the 1993 Australian Archaeological Association Conference*, pp. 201–210. The North Australian Research Unit, The Australian National University, Darwin.

_____. 1995. *Variability in Western Arnhem Land shell midden deposits*. Unpublished MA Thesis. Northern Territory University, Darwin.

Muckle, R.J. 1985. *Archaeological considerations of bivalve shell taphonomy*. Unpublished MA Thesis. Simon Fraser University.

Nagaoka, L.A. 2000. *Resource depression, extinction, and subsistence change in prehistoric southern New Zealand*. Unpublished PhD Thesis. University of Washington, Seattle.

_____. 2002. The effects of resource depression on foraging efficiency, diet breadth, and patch use in southern New Zealand. *Journal of Anthropological Archaeology* 21: 419–422.

Nakamura, Y. and Y. Shinotsuka 2007. Suspension feeding and growth of ark shell *Anadara granosa*: Comparison with ubiquitous species *Scapharca subcrenata*. *Fisheries Science* 73: 889–986.

Nakiboglu, S.M., K. Lambeck and P. Aharon 1983. Postglacial sea-levels in the Pacific: Implications with respect to deglaciation regime and local tectonics. *Tectonophysics* 91: 335–358.

Newsome, S.D., D.L. Phillips, B.C. Culleton, T.P. Guilderson and P.L. Koch 2004. Dietary reconstruction of an Early to Middle Holocene human population from the Central California coast: Insights from advanced stable isotope mixing models. *Journal of Archaeological Science* 31: 1101–1115.

Ng F.O. 1986. *Growth and mortality of the Malaysian cockle (Anadara granosa L.) under commercial culture: Analysis through length-frequency data*. Bay of Bengal Programme: Development of Small-Scale Fisheries, Swedish International Development Authority, Food and Agriculture Organisation of the United Nations.

Nichol, R. and L. Williams 1981. Quantifying shell midden: Weights or numbers? *New Zealand Archaeological Association Newsletter* 24(2): 87–91.

Nielsen, N. 2008. Marine molluscs in Danish Stone Age Middens: A case study on Krabbesholm II. In A. Antczak and R. Cipriani (eds) *Early human impact on megamolluscs*, pp. 157–167. BAR International Series 1865. Archaeopress, Oxford.

Nix, H.A. and J.D. Kalma 1972. Climate as a dominant control in the bio-geography of northern Australia and New Guinea. In D.L. Walker (ed.) *Bridge and barrier: The natural and cultural history of Torres Strait*, pp. 61–92. The Australian National University Press, Canberra.

Noli, D. and G. Avery 1988. Protein poisoning and coastal subsistence. *Journal of Archaeological Science* 15: 395–401.

Nott, J., E. Bryant and D. Price 1999. Early-Holocene aridity in tropical northern Australia. *The Holocene* 9(2): 231–236.

Nunn, P.D. 1998. Sea-level changes over the past 1000 years in the Pacific. *Journal of Coastal Research* 14(1): 23–30.

_____. 2000. Environmental catastrophe in the Pacific Islands around A.D. 1300. *Geoarchaeology: An International Journal* 15(7): 715–740.

_____. 2003. Revising ideas about environmental determinism: Human-environmental relations in the Pacific Islands. *Asia Pacific Viewpoint* 44(1): 63–72.

O'Connor, S. 1996. Where are the middens? An overview of the archaeological evidence for shellfish exploitation along the northwestern Australian coastline. *Bulletin of the Indo-Pacific Prehistory Association* 15: 165–180.

_____. 1999. A diversity of coastal economies: Shell mounds in the Kimberley region in the Holocene. In J. Hall and I.J. McNiven (eds) *Australian coastal archaeology*, pp. 37–50. ANH Publications. Department of Archaeology and Natural History, Australian National University, Canberra.

O'Connor, S. and M. Sullivan 1994. Distinguishing middens and cheniers: A case study from the southern Kimberley, Western Australia. *Archaeology in Oceania* 29: 16–28.

O'Connor, S. and P. Veth 1993. Where the desert meets the sea: A preliminary report of the archaeology of the Kimberley coast. *Australian Archaeology* 37: 25–34.

O'Connor, S., S. Ulm, S.J. Fallon, A. Barham and I. Loch 2010. Pre-bomb marine reservoir variability in the Kimberley region, Western Australia. *Radiocarbon* 52 (2–3): 1158–1165.

Odell, G.H. 1996. Economizing behaviour and the concept of "curation". In G.H. Odell (ed.) *Stone tools: Theoretical insights into human prehistory*. Plenum Press, New York.

Olsson, I.U. 1974. Some problems in connection with the evaluation of C14 dates. *Geologiska Foreningens i Stockholm Forhandlingar* 96: 311–320.

O'Neil, D.H. 1993. Excavation sample size: A cautionary tale. *American Antiquity* 53(3): 523–529.

Orton, J. 2008. A useful measure of the desirability of different raw materials for retouch within and between assemblages: The raw material retouch index (RMRI). *Journal of Archaeological Science* 35(4): 1090–1094.

Osborn, A.J. 1977. Strandloopers, mermaids, and other fairytales: Ecological determinants of marine resource utilization – the Peruvian case. In L.R. Binford (ed.) *For theory building in archaeology*, pp. 157–205. Academic Press, New York.

Pallant, J. 2007. *SPSS survival manual: A step by step guide to data analysis using SPSS for Windows*. Allen and Unwin, Crows Nest.

Parkington, J.E. 1981. The effects of environmental change on the scheduling of visits to Elands Bay Cave, Cape Province, South Africa. In I. Hodder, G. Isaac and N. Hammond (eds) *Pattern of the past: Studies in honour of David Clarke*, pp. 341–362. Cambridge University Press, Canberra.

_____. 2008. Limpet sizes in Stone Age archaeological contexts at the Cape, South Africa: Changing environment or human impact? In A. Antczak and R. Cipriani (eds) *Early human impact on megamolluscs*, pp. 169–178. BAR International Series 1865. Archaeopress, Oxford.

Pathansali, D. 1966. Notes on the biology of the cockle, *Anadara granosa* L. *Proceedings of the Indo-Pacific Fisheries Council* 11(2): 84–98.

Pathansali, D. and M.K. Soong 1958. Some aspects of cockle (*Anadara granosa*L.) culture in Malaya. *Proceedings of the Indo-Pacific Fisheries Council* 8(2): 26–31.

Paton, R. 1994. Speaking through stones: A study from northern Australia. *World Archaeology* 26(2):172–184.

Paton, T.R. and M.A.J. Williams 1972. The concept of laterite. *Annals of the Association of American Geographers* 62(1): 42–56.

Peacock, E. 2000. Assessing bias in archaeological shell assemblages. *Journal of Field Archaeology* 27: 183–196.

Peacock, E. and S. Mistak 2008. Freshwater mussel (*Unionidae*) remains from the Bilbo Basin Site, Mississippi, U.S.A.: Archaeological considerations and resource management implications. *Archaeofauna: International Journal of Zooarchaeology* 17: 9–20.

Perlman, S.M. 1980. An optimum diet model, coastal variability, and hunter-gatherer behaviour. In M.B. Schiffer (ed.) *Advances in archaeological method and theory3*, pp. 257–310. Academic Press, New York.

————. 1985. Group size and mobility costs. In S.W. Green and S.M. Perlman (eds) *The archaeology of frontiers and boundaries*, pp. 33–50. Academic Press, New York.

Peterson, N. 1971. Open sites and the ethnographic approach to the archaeology of hunter-gatherers. In D.J. Mulvaney and J. Golson (eds) *Aboriginal man and environment in Australia*, pp. 239–248. The Australian National University Press, Canberra.

————. 1973. Camp site location amongst Australian hunter-gatherers: Archaeological and ethnographic evidence for a key determinant. *Archaeology and Physical Anthropology in Oceania* 8(3): 173–193.

Peterson, C.H. and F.E. Wells 1998. Molluscs in marine and estuarine sediments. In P.L. Beesley, G.J.B. Ross and A. Wells (eds) *Mollusca: The southern synthesis*, pp. 36–46. Fauna of Australia, Vol.5. Part A. CSIRO, Melbourne.

Pianka, E.R. 1970. On r- and K-selection. *The American Naturalist* 104(940): 592–597.

Pickering, M.P. 1997. *Wangala time, Wangala law: Hunter-gatherer settlement patterns in a sub-humid to semi-arid environment*. Unpublished PhD Thesis. La Trobe University, Bundoona.

Plog. S., F. Plog and W. Wait 1978. Decision making in modern surveys. In M.B. Schiffer (ed.) *Advances in archaeological method and theory 1*, pp. 383–421. Academic Press, New York.

Poutiers, J.M. 1998. Bivalves (Acephala, Lamellibranchia, Pelecypoda). In K.E. Carpenter and V.H. Niem (eds) *The living marine resources of the western central Pacific: Volume 1. Seaweeds, corals, bivalves and gastropods*, pp. 124–362. FAO Species Identification Guide for Fishery Purposes. Food and Agriculture Organization of the United Nations, Rome.

Prebble, M., R. Sim, J. Finn and D. Fink 2005. A Holocene pollen and diatom record from Vanderlin Island, Gulf of Carpentaria, lowland tropical Australia. *Quaternary Research* 64: 357–371.

Raab, L.M. and D.O. Larson 1997. Medieval Climatic Anomaly and punctuated cultural evolution in coastal southern California. *American Antiquity* 62: 319–336.

Randklev, C.R., S. Wolverton and J.H. Kennedy 2009. A biometric technique for assessing prehistoric freshwater mussel population dynamics (family: Unionidae) in north Texas. *Journal of Archaeological Science* 36: 205–213.

Redman, C.L. 1987. Surface collection, sampling and research design: A retrospective. *American Antiquity* 52(2): 249–256.

Rhoads, J.W. 1980. But how did you know where to look? Ethnographic facts and archaeological strategies. In I. Johnson (ed.) *Holier than thou: Proceedings of the 1978 Kioloa Conference on Australian Prehistory*, pp. 147–150. Department of Prehistory, Research School of Pacific Studies, The Australian National University, Canberra.

Rhodes, E.G. 1980. *Models of Holocene coastal progradation, Gulf of Carpentaria*. Unpublished PhD Thesis. The Australian National University, Canberra.

_____. 1982. Depositional model for a chenier plain, Gulf of Carpentaria, Australia. *Sedimentology* 29: 201–221.

Rick, T.C., J.M. Erlandson, T.J. Braje, J.A. Estes, M.H. Graham and R.L. Vellanoweth 2008. Historical ecology and human impacts on coastal ecosystems of the Santa Barbara Channel region, California. In T.C. Rick and J.M. Erlandson (eds) *Human impacts on ancient marine ecosystems: A global perspective*, pp. 77–101. University of California Press, Berkeley.

Roberts, A. 1991. *An analysis of mound formation at Milingimbi, N.T.* Unpublished M.Litt. Thesis. University of New England, Armidale.

_____. 1994. Cultural landmarks: The Milingimbi mounds. In M. Sullivan, S. Brockwell and A. Webb (eds) *Archaeology in the North: Proceedings of the 1993 Australian Archaeological Association Conference*, pp. 176–187. The North Australian Research Unit, The Australian National University, Darwin.

Robins, R.P., E.C. Stock and D.S. Trigger 1998. Saltwater people, saltwater country: Geomorphological, anthropological and archaeological investigations of the coastal lands in the southern Gulf Country of Queensland. *Memoirs of the Queensland Museum, Cultural Heritage Series* 1(1): 75–126.

Rodbell, D.T., G.O. Seltzer, D.M. Anderson, M.B. Abbott, D.B. Enfield and J.H. Newman 1999. A ~15,000-year record of El Niño-driven alluviation in southwestern Ecuador. *Science* 283: 516–521.

Ross, A., B. Anderson and C. Campbell 2003. Gunumbah: Archaeological and Aboriginal meanings at a quarry site on Moreton Island, southeast Queensland. *Australian Archaeology* 57: 75–81.

Roth, B. and H. Dibble 1998. Production and transport of blanks and tools at the French Middle Paleolithic site of Combe-Capelle Bas. *American Antiquity* 63: 47–62.

Rowland, M.J. 1983. Aborigines and environment in Holocene Australia: Changing paradigms. *Australian Aboriginal Studies* 2: 62–77.

_____. 1994a. Size isn't everything: Shells in mounds, middens and natural deposits. *Australian Archaeology* 39: 118–124.

_____. 1994b. Mounds around the world: A contribution to understanding Australian shell middens and mounds. In M. Sullivan, S. Brockwell and A. Webb (eds) *Archaeology in the North: Proceedings of the 1993 Australian Archaeological Association Conference*, pp. 142–161. The North Australian Research Unit, The Australian National University, Darwin.

_____. 1999a. Holocene environmental variability: Have its impacts been underestimated in Australian pre history? *The Artefact* 22: 11–40.

_____. 1999b. The Keppel Islands - A '3000 year' event revisited. In J. Hall and I.J. McNiven (eds) *Australian coastal archaeology*, pp. 141–156. ANH Publications. Department of Archaeology and Natural History, Australian National University, Canberra.

Rowly-Conwy, P. 1983. Sedentary hunters: The Ertebølle example. In G.N. Bailey (ed.) *Hunter-gatherer economy in prehistory*, pp. 111–126. Cambridge University Press, Cambridge.

Russo, M. 1998. Measuring sedentism with fauna: Archaic cultures along the southwest Florida coast. In T.R. Rocek and O. Bar-Yosef (eds) *Seasonality and sedentism: Archaeological perspectives from Old and New World sites*, pp. 143–164. Peabody Museum of Archaeology and Ethnology, Harvard University, Cambridge.

Schiffer, M.B., A.P. Sullivan and T.C. Klinger 1978. The design of archaeological surveys. *World Archaeology* 10: 1–28.

Schrire, C. 1972. Ethno-archaeological models and subsistence behaviour in Arnhem Land. In D.L. Clarke (ed.) *Models in archaeology*, pp. 653–670. Methuen, London.

_____. 1982. *The Alligator Rivers: Prehistory and ecology in western Arnhem Land*. Terra Australis 7. Department of Prehistory, Research School of Pacific Studies, The Australian National University, Canberra.

Shackleton, J.C. 1988. Reconstructing past shorelines as an approach to determining factors affecting shellfish collecting in the prehistoric past. In G. Bailey and J. Parkington (eds) *The archaeology of prehistoric coastlines*, pp. 11–21. Cambridge University Press, Cambridge.

Shackleton, J.C. and T.H. Van Andel 1986. Prehistoric shore environments, shellfish availability, and shellfish gathering at Franchthi, Greece. *Geoarchaeology: An International Journal* 1: 127–143.

Shiner, J. 2004. *Place as occupational histories: Towards an understanding of deflated surface artefact distributions in the West Darling, New South Wales, Australia*. Unpublished PhD Thesis. The University of Auckland, Auckland.

Shiner, J. and M. Morrison 2009. The contribution of heritage surveys towards understanding the cultural landscape of the Weipa bauxite plateau. *Australian Archaeology* 68: 52–55.

Short, J.W. and D.G. Potter 1987. *Shells of Queensland and the Great Barrier Reef: Marine gastropods*. Golden Press, Drummoyne.

Shulmeister, J. 1992. A Holocene pollen record from lowland tropical Australia. *The Holocene* 2: 107–116.

_____. 1999. Australasian evidence for Mid-Holocene climate change implies precessional control of Walker Circulation in the Pacific. *Quaternary International* 57/58: 81–91.

Shulmeister, J. and B. Lees 1992. Morphology and chronostratigraphy of a coastal dunefield: Groote Eylandt, northern Australia. *Geomorphology* 5: 521–534.

Shulmeister, J. and B.G. Lees 1995. Pollen evidence from tropical Australia for the onset of an ENSO-dominated climate at c.4000 BP. *The Holocene* 5: 10–18.

Sim, R. 2002. *Preliminary results from the Sir Edward Pellew Islands Archaeological Project, Gulf of Carpentaria, 2000–2001*. Unpublished Report to the Australian Institute of Aboriginal and Torres Strait Islander Studies, Canberra.

Sim, R. and L.A. Wallis 2008. Northern Australian offshore island use during the Holocene: The archaeology of Vanderlin Island, Sir Edward Pellew Group, Gulf of Carpentaria. *Australian Archaeology* 67: 95–106.

Singh, G. and J. Luly 1991. Changes in vegetation and seasonal climates since the last full glacial at Lake Frome, South Australia. *Palaeogeography, Palaeoclimatology, Palaeoecology* 84: 75–86.

Sloss, C.R., C.V. Murray-Wallace and B.G. Jones 2007. Holocene sea-level change on the southeast coast of Australia: A review. *The Holocene* 17(7): 999–1014.

Specht, R.L. 1958. The climate, geology, soils and plant ecology of the northern portion of Arnhem Land. In R.L. Specht and C.P. Mountford (eds) *Records of the American-Australian Scientific Expedition to Arnhem Land Volume 3: Botany and plant ecology*, pp. 327–414. Melbourne University Press, Melbourne.

_____. (ed.) 1964. *Records of the American-Australian Scientific Expedition to Arnhem Land Volume 4: Zoology*. Melbourne University Press, Melbourne.

Spenneman, D.H.R. 1987. Availability of shellfish resources on prehistoric Tongatapu, Tonga: Effects of human predation and changing environment. *Archaeology in Oceania* 22(3): 81–96.

_____. 1989. Effects of human predation and changing environment on some mollusc species on Tongatapu, Tonga. In J. Clutton-Brock (ed.) *The walking larder: Patterns of domestication, pastoralism and predation*, pp. 326–335. Unwin Hyman, London.

Spennemann, D.H.R. and M.J. Head 1996. Reservoir modification of radiocarbon signatures in coastal and nearshore waters of eastern Australia: The state of play. *Quaternary Australasia* 14(1): 32–39.

Speth, J.D. 1987. Early Hominid subsistence strategies in seasonal habitats. *Journal of Archaeological Science* 14: 13–29.

Speth, J.D. and K.A. Spielmann 1983. Energy source, protein metabolism, and hunter-gatherer subsistence strategies. *Journal of Anthropological Archaeology* 2: 1–31.

Stein, J.K., J.N. Deo and L.S. Phillips 2003. Big sites - short time: Accumulation rates in archaeological sites. *Journal of Archaeological Science* 30: 297–316.

Stephens, M., D. Mattey, D.D. Gilbertson and C.V. Murray-Wallace. 2008. Shell-gathering from mangroves and the seasonality of the Southeast Asian Monsoon using high-resolution stable isotopic analysis of the tropical estuarine bivalve (*Geloina erosa*) from the Great Cave of Niah, Sarawak: Methods and reconnaissance of molluscs of early Holocene and modern times. *Journal of Archaeological Science* 35(10): 2686–2697.

Stiner, M.C. and N.D. Munro 2002. Approaches to prehistoric diet breadth, demography, and prey ranking systems in time and space. *Journal of Archaeological Method and Theory* 9(2): 181–214.

Stiner, M.C., N.D. Munro and T.A. Surovell 2000. The tortoise and the hare: Small game use, the broad-spectrum revolution, and Palaeolithic demography. *Current Anthropology* 41(1): 39–73.

Stiner, M.C., N.D. Munro, T.A. Surovell, E. Tchernov and O. Bar-Yosef 1999. Paleolithic population growth pulses evidenced by small animal exploitation. *Science* 283: 190–194.

Stuiver, M. and P.J. Reimer 1993. Extended 14C database and revised CALIB radiocarbon calibration program. *Radiocarbon* 35: 215-230.

Sullivan, M.E. 1989. Recording shell midden sites. In J. Flood, I. Johnson and S. Sullivan (eds) *Sites and bytes: Recording Aboriginal places in Australia*, pp. 49–53. Special Australian Heritage Publication Series no. 8. Australian Government Publishing Service, Canberra.

Sullivan, M. 1996. Northern Australian landscapes. In P. Hiscock and P. Veth (eds) *Archaeology of northern Australia: Regional perspectives*, pp. 1–8. *Tempus* 4. Anthropology Museum, The University of Queensland, St Lucia.

Sullivan, M. and S. O'Connor 1993. Middens and cheniers: Implications of Australian research. *Antiquity* 67: 776–788.

Sullivan, M., P. Hughes and A. Barham 2011. Abydos Plain - equivocal archaeology. *Technical Reports of the Australian Museum* 23(2): 7–29.

Sullivan, S. 1984. Making a discovery: The finding and reporting of Aboriginal sites. In G. Connah (ed.) *Australian field archaeology: A guide to techniques*, pp. 1–9. Australian Institute of Aboriginal Studies, Canberra.

Sundstrom, L. 1993. A simple mathematical procedure for estimating the adequacy of site survey strategies. *Journal of Field Archaeology* 20: 91–96.

Swadling, P. 1976. Changes induced by human exploitation in prehistoric shellfish populations. *Mankind* 10: 156–162.

_____. 1977. Central Province shellfish resources and their utilisation in the prehistoric past of Papua New Guinea. *The Veliger* 19: 293–302.

Taçon, P.S.C., S.K. May, S.J. Fallon, M. Travers, D. Wesley and R. Lamilami 2010. A minimum age for early depictions of southeast Asian praus in the rock art of Arnhem Land, Northern Territory. *Australian Archaeology* 71: 1–10.

Telford, R.J., E. Heegaard and H.J.B. Birks 2004. The intercept is a poor estimate of a calibrated radiocarbon age. *The Holocene* 14(2): 296–298.

Thangavelu, A., B. David, B. Barker, J-M. Geneste, J-J. Delannoy, L. Lamb, N. Araho and R. Skelly 2011. Morphometric analyses of *Batissa violacea* shells from Emo (OAC), Gulf Province, Papua New Guinea. *Archaeology in Oceania* 46: 67–75.

Thomas, D.H. 1975. Non-site sampling in archaeology: Up the creek without a site? In J.W. Mueller (ed.) *Sampling in archaeology*, pp. 61–81. The University of Arizona Press, Tucson.

Thomson, D.F. 1939. The seasonal factor in human culture: Illustrated from the life of a contemporary nomadic group. *Proceedings of the Prehistoric Society* 5(2): 209–221.

_____. 1949. *Economic structure and the ceremonial exchange cycle in Arnhem Land*. Macmillan, Melbourne.

_____. 1957. Early Macassar visitors to Arnhem Land and their influence on its people. *Walkabout* 23(7): 29–31.

_____. 1983. *Donald Thomson in Arnhem Land: Compiled and introduced by Nicolas Peterson*. Currey O'Neil, South Yarra.

Thunell, R., D. Anderson, D. Gellar and Q. Miao 1994. Sea-surface temperature estimates for the tropical western Pacific during the Last Glaciation and their implications for the Pacific Warm Pool. *Quaternary Research* 41: 255–264.

Tiensongrusmee, B. and S. Pontjoprawiro 1988. *Cockle Culture*. INS/81/008/Manual 12.

Tindale, N.B. 1925–1926. Natives of Groote Eylandt and of the west coast of the Gulf of Carpentaria. *Records of the South Australian Museum* 3(1): 61–102; (2): 103–134.

Todd, L.C. 1991. Seasonality studies and Paleoindian subsistence strategies. In M.C. Stiner (ed.) *Human predators and prey mortality*, pp. 217–238. Westview Special Studies in Archaeological Research. Westview Press, Boulder.

Tonner, T.W.W. 2005. Later Stone Age shellfishing behaviour at Dunefield Midden (Western Cape, South Africa). *Journal of Archaeological Science* 32: 1390–1407.

Torgersen, T., M.F. Hutchison, D.E. Searle and H.A. Nix 1983. General bathymetry of the Gulf of Carpentaria and the Quaternary physiology of Lake Carpentaria. P*alaeogeography, Palaeoclimatology, Palaeoecology* 41: 207–225.

Tudhope, A.W., C.P. Chilcott, M.T. McCulloch, E.R. Cook, J. Chappell, R.M. Ellam, D.W. Lea, J.M. Lough and G.B. Shimmield 2001. Variability in the El Niño-Southern Oscillation through a glacial-interglacial cycle. *Science* 291: 1511–1517.

Turner, D.H. 1974. *Tradition and transformation: A study of Aborigines in the Groote Eylandt area, northern Australia*. Australian Aboriginal Studies No. 53. Australian Institute of Aboriginal Studies, Canberra.

Ugan, A., J. Bright and A. Rogers 2003. When is technology worth the trouble? *Journal of Archaeological Science* 30: 1315–1329.

Ulm, S. 2002. Marine and estuarine reservoir effects in Central Queensland, Australia: Determination of ΔR values. *Geoarchaeology: An International Journal* 17(4): 319–348.

_____. 2006a. *Coastal themes: An archaeology of the Southern Curtis Coast, Queensland*. Terra Australis 24. ANU E Press, Canberra.

_____. 2006b. Australian marine reservoir effects: A guide to ΔR Values. *Australian Archaeology* 63: 57–60.

_____. 2011. Coastal foragers on southern shores: Marine resource use in northeast Australia since the late Pleistocene. In N.F. Bicho, J.A. Haws and L.G. Davis (eds) *Trekking the shore: Changing coastlines and the antiquity of coastal settlement*, pp. 441–461. Interdisciplinary Contributions to Archaeology. Springer, New York.

Ulm, S. and J. Reid 2000. Index of dates from archaeological sites in Queensland. *Queensland Archaeological Research* 12: 1–129.

Ulm, S., G. Jacobsen, P. Memmott, R. Robins, I. Lilley, D. Rosendahl and C. Dalley 2010a. *Marine carbon reservoir variability in the Southern Gulf of Carpentaria*. Progress Report for AINGRA09025. Unpublished Report to Australian Institute Nuclear Science and Engineering.

Ulm, S., N. Evans, D. Rosendahl, P. Memmott and F. Petchey 2010b. Radiocarbon and linguistic dates for occupation of the South Wellesley Islands, northern Australia. *Archaeology in Oceania* 45(1):39–43.

Veitch, B. 1996. Evidence for Mid-Holocene change in the Mitchell Plateau, Northwest Kimberley, Western Australia. In P. Hiscock and P. Veth (eds) *Archaeology of northern Australia: Regional perspectives*, pp. 66–89. *Tempus* 4. Anthropology Museum, The University of Queensland, St Lucia.

_____. 1999a. *What happened in the Mid-Holocene? Archaeological evidence for change from the Mitchell Plateau, northwest Kimberley, Western Australia*. Unpublished PhD Thesis. The University of Western Australia, Perth.

_____. 1999b. Shell middens on the Mitchell Plateau: A reflection of a wider phenomenon? In J. Hall and I.J. McNiven (eds) *Australian coastal archaeology*, pp. 51–64. ANH Publications. Department of Archaeology and Natural History, Australian National University, Canberra.

Veth, P., S. O'Connor and L.A. Wallis 2000. Perspectives on ecological approaches in Australian Archaeology. *Australian Archaeology* 50: 54–66.

Vita-Finzi, C. and E.S. Higgs 1970. Prehistoric economy in the Mount Carmel area of Palestine: Site catchment analysis. *Proceedings of the Prehistoric Society* 36: 1–37.

Walker, P.H. and B.E. Butler 1983. Fluvial processes. In *Soils: An Australian Viewpoint*, pp. 83–90. Academic Press.

Walker, A. and R.D.P. Zorc 1981. Austronesian loanwords in Yolngu-Matha of northeast Arnhem Land. *Aboriginal History* 5(2): 109–134.

Walters, I., P. Lauer, A. Nolan, G. Dillon and M. Aird 1987. Hope Island: Salvage excavations of a Kombumerri site. *Queensland Archaeological Research* 4: 80–95.

Warner, W.L. 1969. *A Black civilization: A social study of an Australian tribe*. Peter Smith, Gloucester.

Waselkov, G.A. 1987. Shellfish gathering and shell midden archaeology. In M.B. Schiffer (ed.) *Advances in archaeological method and theory10*, pp. 93–210. Academic Press, New York.

Wasson, R.J. 1986. Geomorphology and Quaternary history of the Australian continental dunefields. *Geographical Review of Japan* 59B: 55–67.

Wasson, R.J. and M. Claussen 2002. Earth system models: A test using the Mid-Holocene in the Southern Hemisphere. *Quaternary Science Reviews* 21: 819–824.

Webb, J.A. and M. Domanski 2007. The relationship between lithology, flaking properties and artefact manufacture for Australian silcretes. *Archaeometry* 50(4): 555–575.

Webster, P.J. and T.N. Palmer 1997. The past and the future of El Niño. *Nature* 390: 562–564.

Wells, F.E. and C.W. Bryce 1988. *Seashells of Western Australia*. Western Australian Museum, Perth.

Wells, L.E. and J.S. Noller 1999. Holocene coevolution of the physical landscape and human settlement in northern coastal Peru. *Geoarchaeology: An International Journal* 14(8): 755–789.

Whitaker, A.R. 2008. Incipient aquaculture in prehistoric California? Long-term productivity and sustainability vs immediate returns for the harvest of marine invertebrates. *Journal of Archaeological Science* 35: 1114–1123.

White, C. 1969. *Report on field trip to Caledon Bay, Northern Territory Dec./Jan 1968–9*. Document No. 69/816. Unpublished Report to the Australian Institute of Aboriginal Studies, Canberra.

_____. 1970. *Report on field trip to Yirrkala and Port Bradshaw, Northern Territory, August–September, 1969*. Unpublished Report to the Australian Institute of Aboriginal Studies, Canberra.

White, N., B. Meehan, L. Hiatt and R. Jones 1990. Demography of contemporary hunter-gatherers: Lessons from Arnhem Land. In B. Meehan and N. White (eds) *Hunter-gatherer demography: Past and present*, pp. 171–185. Oceania Monograph 39. University of Sydney, Sydney.

Wilson, B.A., P.S. Brocklehurst, M.J. Clark and K.J.M. Dickinson 1990. *Vegetation survey of the Northern Territory: Explanatory notes to accompany 1:1000 000 map sheets*. Technical Report Number 49. Conservation Commission of the Northern Territory, Palmerston.

Winterhalder, B., W. Baillargeon, F. Capalletto, R. Daniel and C. Prescott 1988. The population ecology of hunter-gatherers and their prey. *Journal of Anthropological Archaeology* 7: 289–328.

Woodroffe, C.D. 1981. Mangrove swamp stratigraphy and Holocene transgression, Grand Cayman Island, West Indies. *Marine Geology* 41: 271–294.

_____. 1988. Changing mangrove and wetland habitats over the last 8000 years, Northern Australia and South-East Asia. In D. Wade-Marshall and P. Loveday (eds) *Floodplains research. Northern Australia: Progress and prospects Volume 2*, pp. 1–33. North Australian Research Unit, Darwin.

_____. 1995. Response of tide-dominated mangrove shorelines in northern Australia to anticipated sea-level rise. *Earth Surface Processes and Landforms* 20: 65–85.

Woodroffe, C.D., J. Chappell, B.G. Thom and E. Wallensky 1985a. Geomorphology of the South Alligator tidal river and plains, Northern Territory. In K.N. Bardsley, J.D.S. Davie and C.D. Woodroffe (eds) *Coasts and tidal wetlands of the Australian monsoon region: A collection of papers presented at a conference held in Darwin 4–11 November, 1984*, pp. 3–16. Mangrove Monograph 1. The Australian National University, Darwin.

Woodroffe, C.D., J. Chappell, B.G. Thom and E. Wallensky 1985b. Stratigraphy of the South Alligator tidal river and plains, Northern Australia. In K.N. Bardsley, J.D.S. Davie and C.D. Woodroffe (eds) *Coasts and tidal wetlands of the Australian monsoon region: A collection of papers presented at a conference held in Darwin 4–11 November, 1984,* pp. 17–30. Mangrove Monograph 1. North Australian Research Unit, The Australian National University, Darwin.

Woodroffe, C.D., J. Chappell, B.G. Thom and E. Wallensky 1986. *Geomorphological dynamics and evolution of the South Alligator tidal river and plains, Northern Territory.* Mangrove Monograph 3. North Australian Research Unit, The Australian National University, Darwin.

Woodroffe, C.D., J. Chappell and B.G. Thom 1998. Shell middens in the context of estuarine development, South Alligator River, Northern Territory. *Archaeology in Oceania* 23: 95–103.

Woodroffe, S.A. 2009 Testing models of mid to late Holocene sea-level change, North Queensland, Australia. *Quaternary Science Reviews* 28(23–24): 2474–2488.

Woodroffe, S.A. and B.P. Horton 2005. Holocene sea-level changes in the Indo-Pacific. *Journal of Asian Earth Sciences* 25(1): 29–43.

Wright, R.V.S. 1971. Prehistory in the Cape York Peninsula. In D.J. Mulvaney and J. Golson (eds) *Aboriginal man and environment in Australia,* pp. 133–140. The Australian National University Press, Canberra.

Yamazaki, T. and S. Oda 2009. Changes in shell gathering in an early agricultural society at the head of Ise Bay, Japan. *Journal of Archaeological Science* 36: 2007–2011.

Yesner, D. R. 1980. Maritime hunter-gatherers: Ecology and prehistory. *Current Anthropology* 21(6): 727–750.

_____. 1987. Life in the 'Garden of Eden': Causes and consequences of the adoption of marine diets by human societies. In M. Harris and E.B. Ross (eds) *Food and evolution: Toward a theory of human food habits,* pp. 285–310. Temple University Press, Philadelphia.

_____. 1988. Island biogeography and prehistoric human adaptation on the southern coast of Maine (U.S.A.). In Bailey, G. and J.E. Parkinson (eds) *The archaeology of prehistoric coastlines,* pp. 53–63. Cambridge University Press, Cambridge.

Yesner, D.R., M.J. Figuerero Torres, R.A. Guichon and L.A. Borrero 2003. Stable isotope analysis of human bone and ethnohistoric subsistence patterns in Tierra del Fuego. *Journal of Anthropological Archaeology* 22: 279–291.

Yokoyama, Y., A. Purcell, K. Lambeck and P. Johnston 2001. Shore-line reconstruction around Australia during the Last Glacial Maximum and Late Glacial Stage. *Quaternary International* 83–85: 9–18.

Yunupingu, B., L. Yunupingu-Marika, D. Marika, B. Marika, B. Marika, R. Marika and G. Wightman 1995. *Rirritjingu ethnobotany: Aboriginal plant use from Yirrkala, Arnhem Land, Australia.* Northern Territory Botanical Bulletin No. 21. Parks and Wildlife Commission of the Northern Territory, Darwin.

Zaar, U., G. Prowse and I. Matthews 1999. *Water resources of east Arnhem Land.* Department of Lands, Planning and Environment, Natural Resources Division, Northern Territory, Darwin.

www.ingramcontent.com/pod-product-compliance
Lightning Source LLC
Chambersburg PA
CBHW040453290326
41929CB00059B/3463